FORECLOSURE DEFENSE SURVIVAL PLAYBOOK

AF687664

By James Young

A homeowner who took on the banks as a pro se litigant, fought for years, kept the records, learned the system, and created this book so the next homeowner can learn, stand up, and fight back.

This publication is dedicated to homeowners who were told to give up, told they could not win, and told the system was too big to challenge. It was written from lived experience, hard lessons, persistence, and the belief that knowledge in the hands of ordinary people can become a powerful defense.

Printed in the United States of America

"***But when a long train of abuses and usurpations, pursuing invariably the same Object evinces a design to reduce them under absolute Despotism, it is their right, it is their duty, to throw off such Government, and provide new Guards for their future security.***"

This book was written so that pro se homeowners can better understand what they are facing, preserve what matters, and fight back with greater clarity, preparation, and resolve.

TABLE OF CONTENTS

Click a chapter title to jump to the first page.

TABLE OF CONTENTS (Continued)

Click a chapter title to jump to the first page.

TABLE OF CONTENTS (Continued)

Click a chapter title to jump to the first page.

LEGAL DISCLAIMER

Educational Use Only — Not Legal Advice

This publication is provided solely for educational, informational, and general defense-awareness purposes. It is not legal advice, does not constitute the practice of law, and must not be relied upon as a substitute for advice, strategy, analysis, or representation from a licensed attorney familiar with the reader's specific facts, jurisdiction, and legal circumstances.

Neither the author, nor any editor, researcher, employee, contractor, agent, publisher, designer, distributor, printer, production participant, or any other person or entity involved in the creation, production, publication, distribution, marketing, transmission, or delivery of this publication makes any representation, warranty, guarantee, or promise—express or implied—regarding the accuracy, completeness, timeliness, reliability, suitability, availability, legality, or results that may be obtained from the use of this publication.

No attorney-client relationship, fiduciary relationship, advisory relationship, agency relationship, or other professional relationship is created by the purchase, possession, reading, use, or reliance upon this publication. The laws, rules, procedures, deadlines, evidentiary standards, and foreclosure practices discussed herein vary widely by state, court, judge, lender, servicer, and factual situation, and may change at any time without notice.

The author and all persons or entities associated with the creation, production, and delivery of this publication expressly disclaim all liability for any loss, damage, cost, expense, claim, sanction, judgment, penalty, missed deadline, adverse ruling, foreclosure outcome, or other consequence of any kind arising out of or related to the use, misuse, interpretation, misinterpretation, reliance upon, or inability to use this publication or any sample language, strategy, checklist, form, citation, theory, or discussion contained in it.

Readers are strongly encouraged to seek personalized advice from a qualified, licensed attorney in the appropriate jurisdiction before taking or refraining from taking any legal action. This publication is not a substitute for competent legal counsel, case-specific review, or individualized professional advice.

By using this publication, the reader acknowledges and agrees that all use is at the reader's own risk, that no particular outcome is promised or guaranteed, and that any examples, case discussions, templates, explanations, or strategies are provided for general educational purposes only and may not apply to any specific matter.

Use of this publication signifies acceptance of these terms and limitations.

Printed in the United States of America

Printed in the United States of America

AI RESOURCE

LEVEL THE PLAYING FIELD

Go to www.cetient.com

Centient is an AI legal platform connected to legal databases designed to help homeowners organize, analyze, and respond more effectively.

SIGN UP FOR THE PRO PLAN

PROMO CODE: 9OVNPVQP

- Use this AI resource as a powerful tool in your defense strategy.
- Upload your documents and let the AI help sort, organize, and draft responses.
- I have tested many AI tools, and this is the best one I found for this kind of work.
- This is a valuable resource, but it is still a tool — always review the output carefully.

Website: www.cetient.com | Promo Code: 9OVNPVQP

$40.00 Credit

Foreclosure Defense Survival Playbook

Fight Back & Win Your Home!

By a homeowner who was in your situation

Practical guidance. Real-world strategy. Stronger defense.

www.HomeOwnerForeclosureBook.com

Also find us on the Google Play Store and Apple App Store

Search for "Foreclosure Defense Pro"

Tools, guidance, and support designed to help homeowners take action.

CHAPTER 1: UNDERSTANDING FORECLOSURE

What You're Facing and Why You Can Fight Back

You're Not Alone

Every year, more than 2 million American families face foreclosure. Behind that cold statistic are people just like you—people who never thought this would happen to them. People who worked hard, paid their bills, and then something went wrong.

Maybe you lost your job. Maybe you got sick. Maybe your mortgage payment jumped when the interest rate adjusted. Or maybe you were sold a loan you never should have qualified for in the first place.

Whatever brought you here, know this: You are not the first person to face foreclosure, and you won't be the last. More importantly, foreclosure is not a done deal. Banks make mistakes. The law gives you rights. And homeowners win these fights every single day.

This chapter explains what foreclosure actually is, why it's so important to fight back, and how to use this book to save your home.

What Is Foreclosure?

In simple terms, **foreclosure is the legal process lenders use to take your home when you fall behind on mortgage payments.**

When you bought your house, you signed two important documents: - **The promissory note:** Your promise to repay the loan - **The mortgage (or deed of trust):** The lender's right to take your house if you don't pay

Think of the mortgage as a security agreement. The bank gives you money to buy the house. You agree that if you don't pay them back, they can take the house and sell it to get their money back.

The Foreclosure Process in Plain English

Here's what happens in a typical foreclosure:

1. **You miss payments** — Usually 3-4 months behind

2. **The lender sends notices** — Warning letters, "Notice of Default"
3. **The lender starts legal action** — Either files a lawsuit (judicial foreclosure) or records a notice of sale (non-judicial foreclosure)
4. **The property is sold** — At a public auction or sheriff's sale
5. **You must leave** — Eviction proceedings if you don't move out

The entire process can take anywhere from 3 months to 2+ years, depending on your state and how aggressively you defend.

Why Foreclosure Matters So Much

Losing your home isn't just about losing a building. It's about losing:

Your Financial Foundation

- **Your equity disappears** — Years of mortgage payments, down payments, and improvements: gone
- **Your credit is destroyed** — A foreclosure stays on your credit report for 7 years and can drop your score by 100-160 points
- **Future housing becomes difficult** — Renting with a foreclosure on your record is harder. Buying another home? Nearly impossible for years.

Your Family's Stability

- **Your children's school district** — Foreclosure often forces moves to different neighborhoods
- **Your community ties** — Years of relationships, neighbors, local connections: severed
- **Your sense of security** — The psychological toll of losing your home is devastating

Your Future Wealth

A foreclosure doesn't just take your home today. It makes building wealth harder for the next decade. Higher interest rates. Larger security deposits. Limited job opportunities (yes, employers sometimes check credit).

This is why fighting foreclosure matters. This is why the battle is worth it.

The Truth About Banks

Here's something the banks don't want you to know: **They don't always have their paperwork in order.**

During the 2000s housing boom, mortgages were sold and resold so many times that the paperwork became a mess. Banks used people who signed thousands of documents without reading them. Documents were backdated. Important papers were lost. The ownership trail became broken.

When the foreclosure crisis hit, courts started looking closely at these documents. And homeowners started winning.

What Homeowners Discovered

Homeowners who fought back found that banks often: - **Couldn't prove they owned the loan** — The paperwork was missing or fraudulent - **Violated federal laws** — Truth in Lending Act, RESPA, fair debt collection practices - **Made servicing errors** — Misapplied payments, charged improper fees, lost documents - **Failed to follow procedures** — Missed notices, wrong addresses, skipped steps

Every one of these is a potential defense. Every one gives you leverage to negotiate—or win.

Two Types of Foreclosure

Every state handles foreclosure differently. The first thing you need to know is which type applies to you.

Judicial Foreclosure

In a **judicial foreclosure**, the lender must sue you in court. This is required in about 22 states, including:

Connecticut, Delaware, Florida, Hawaii, Illinois, Indiana, Iowa, Kansas, Kentucky, Louisiana, Maine, Nebraska, New Jersey, New Mexico, New York, North Dakota, Ohio, Oklahoma, Pennsylvania, South Carolina, Vermont, and Wisconsin.

Why this matters: Because there's a court case, you have the right to defend yourself. You can file an answer. You can demand documents. You can force the bank to prove every single element of their case.

Non-Judicial Foreclosure

In a **non-judicial foreclosure**, the lender doesn't go to court. Instead, they follow a state-specific process of notices and recorded documents, culminating in a public auction.

This is faster and cheaper for the lender—but it doesn't mean you're defenseless. You can still file a lawsuit to challenge the foreclosure. You still have rights.

> **CRITICAL:** Find out which type of foreclosure your state uses. This determines your timeline, your defenses, and your strategy. See Appendix A for a state-by-state breakdown.

Your Rights as a Homeowner

The law gives you rights in foreclosure. Don't let anyone tell you otherwise.

Federal Protections

The 120-Day Rule (RESPA) Before filing foreclosure, most lenders must wait until you're more than 120 days behind on payments. This gives you time to ask for a loan modification or other options.

Loss Mitigation Rights If you apply for a loan modification, the lender must: - Acknowledge receipt of your application within 5 days - Notify you if your application is incomplete - Give you a decision before foreclosing

Fair Debt Collection Practices If a debt collector is involved in your foreclosure, they must follow strict rules. They cannot: - Call you at unreasonable hours - Use abusive language - Make false threats - Contact you if you've hired an attorney

State Law Protections

Every state has extra protections: - **Notice requirements** — Specific letters that must be sent, by certain dates - **Right to cure** — In some states, you can stop foreclosure by catching up on payments - **Redemption periods** — After foreclosure, some states give you time to get your home back - **Limits on deficiency judgments** — Some states limit how much the bank can chase you for after foreclosure

---

The Three Phases of Foreclosure Defense

Every foreclosure defense follows three phases. Understanding them helps you plan.

Phase 1: Pre-Foreclosure (You're Behind But No Action Yet)

What to do: - Apply for loan modification immediately - Gather all your mortgage documents - Start documenting your financial hardship - Contact a HUD-approved housing counselor (free)

Timeline: 30-120 days before formal foreclosure starts

Phase 2: Active Foreclosure (The Process Has Begun)

What to do: - Respond to all court papers (if judicial) or notices (if non-judicial) - Demand proof of the bank's right to foreclose - Explore all defenses covered in this book - Consider bankruptcy if appropriate

Timeline: 3 months to 2+ years, depending on your state and strategy

Phase 3: Post-Foreclosure (The Sale Has Happened)

What to do: - Check for redemption rights in your state - Understand eviction timelines - Negotiate "cash for keys" to get moving money - Address deficiency judgments if they apply

Timeline: 30 days to 1 year, depending on state law

How to Use This Book

This manual is designed as both a reference guide and an action manual. Here's how to get the most from it:

If You're Just Starting (Pre-Foreclosure)

1. **Read Chapters 1-3 completely** — Understand what you're facing
2. **Skip to Chapter 9 (Loss Mitigation)** — Apply for modification NOW
3. **Keep reading while you wait** — Chapters 4-8 prepare you if modification fails

If You're in Active Foreclosure

1. **Read this chapter and Chapter 2** — Understand your process type
2. **Go directly to Chapter 4 (Your Defenses)** — Find what applies to your case
3. **Use Chapter 12 (Document Forensics)** — Gather evidence immediately
4. **Consider Chapter 11 (Bankruptcy)** — Know your options

If You Need to Act Today

Go to the Quick-Start Checklist in the Playbook. It gives you a 24-hour action plan.

Key Terms You Need to Know

Term	Definition
Default	Failure to make payments as agreed
Acceleration	When the lender demands the full loan balance immediately
Servicer	The company that collects your payments (may not own your loan)
Note Holder	The entity that legally owns your promissory note
Assignment	The document transferring mortgage rights from one party to another
Standing	The legal right to bring a lawsuit or foreclosure
Chain of Title	The complete history of who owned your mortgage
Deficiency Judgment	When the bank sues you for the difference after foreclosure sale
Redemption Period	Time after foreclosure when you can reclaim your home
Robo-Signing	Fraudulent practice of signing documents without review

---

What This Book Will Teach You

By the time you finish this manual, you will understand:

The foreclosure process in your state — Step by step, deadline by deadline

How to find the bank's weaknesses — Document fraud, missing assignments, procedural errors

Your legal defenses — Standing challenges, TILA violations, statute of limitations, and more

How to negotiate with your lender — Loan modifications, forbearance, short sales

When and how to use bankruptcy — Chapter 7 vs. Chapter 13, automatic stay strategy

How to represent yourself — Drafting pleadings, handling court appearances, evidence rules

Victory strategies from real cases — Homeowners who won and how they did it

---

A Word of Caution

This book is not a substitute for an attorney. Foreclosure law is complex. Deadlines are unforgiving. Mistakes can cost you your home.

If you can afford an attorney who specializes in foreclosure defense, hire one. Use this book to understand what they are doing and to ask better questions.

If you cannot afford an attorney, this book will help you represent yourself. But understand the risks. One missed deadline. One wrong filing. One wrong choice. These can cost you your home.

Consider limited-scope representation — Even if you can't afford full representation, some attorneys will: - Review your documents for a flat fee - Help you file an answer - Coach you through the process - Handle just the trial

Call your state bar association for referrals to foreclosure defense attorneys and legal aid organizations.

You're Ready to Begin

Foreclosure is terrifying. But knowledge is power. Every page you read, every defense you learn, every strategy you understand—it all increases your chances of saving your home.

The homeowners who win are the ones who fight. Not because they're lawyers. Not because they're rich. But because they refuse to give up without exhausting every option.

You have options. This book will show you what they are.

Let's begin.

Chapter Summary

- **Foreclosure is the legal process lenders use to take your home when you fall behind.** It follows specific rules, and lenders must prove every element.

- **You have rights.** Federal and state laws give you protections, notice requirements, and time to seek alternatives.
- **Banks make mistakes.** Missing documents, fraudulent signatures, and procedural errors are common and give you leverage.
- **There are two types of foreclosure.** Judicial (court-supervised) and non-judicial (administrative). Your state determines which applies.
- **This book is both educational and practical.** Read it to understand your situation. Use it to take action. But consider hiring an attorney if possible.

Cross-References

Next Chapter: Chapter 2 — The Foreclosure Process Step-by-Step

Related Chapters: - Chapter 4: Your Defenses (legal theories) - Chapter 9: Loss Mitigation (modifications and alternatives) - Chapter 13: Victory Cases (real homeowner wins) - Appendix A: State-by-State Foreclosure Laws

In the Playbook: - Quick-Start Checklist: 24-Hour Action Plan - State Foreclosure Type Chart - Initial Document Request Template

CHAPTER 2: THE HOMEOWNER'S BIGGEST MISTAKE

Why Waiting Destroys Your Defense

The Trap That Catches Everyone

If you're reading this chapter, there's a good chance you've already waited too long.

Not because you're lazy. Not because you don't care. But because you're human.

Humans hope problems will go away. Humans get overwhelmed and freeze. Humans believe that if they just stay quiet and don't make waves, maybe—just maybe—the bank will show mercy.

Banks don't show mercy. Banks run on deadlines, procedures, and legal timelines. And every day you wait, something bad happens that you cannot undo.

This chapter is about the cost of waiting. Not to make you feel guilty—you already feel enough of that—but to make you understand exactly what's at stake. Because once you see what waiting destroys, you'll never wait again.

Why Homeowners Wait: The Psychology of Paralysis

Before we talk about what waiting costs, let's understand why we do it. Because knowing the trap helps you avoid it.

Reason 1: Hope for a Modification

The bank sends you a letter. "Apply for a loan modification," it says. "We want to help you keep your home."

So you apply. You send in your pay stubs, your tax returns, your hardship letter. And you wait. And wait. And wait some more.

Meanwhile, the foreclosure clock keeps ticking.

The brutal truth: Most loan modifications are denied. The Government Accountability Office found that denial rates for HAMP (the federal modification program) exceeded 70% at many servicers. Some banks deny more than 80% of applications.

But they don't deny you immediately. They string you along. They ask for "one more document"—again and again. They tell you your application is "under review" for months. They promise a decision "next week" until next week becomes next month becomes a foreclosure sale notice.

This is called dual tracking, and it's illegal in many states—but it still happens.

Reason 2: Overwhelm and Freeze Response

You open the mailbox. There's a letter from a law firm you've never heard of. It says something about "foreclosure proceedings" and "acceleration" and "deficiency judgment."

The words swim on the page. Your heart pounds. You want to act, but you don't know what to do. So you put the letter in a drawer. You'll deal with it tomorrow. Or next week. When you feel less overwhelmed.

Tomorrow becomes next week becomes next month.

Psychologists call this the "freeze response"—a survival mechanism where the brain shuts down when faced with too much threat. It kept our ancestors alive when facing predators. It destroys homeowners facing foreclosure.

Reason 3: The Money Myth

"I can't afford an attorney," you tell yourself. "I need to save up money first. Maybe in a few months, I can hire someone."

Here's what you can't afford: doing nothing.

Every deadline you miss, every procedural step you skip, every day you wait—it all makes the case harder and more expensive to fix. What could have been solved with a simple answer now requires an emergency motion. What could have been caught early now requires an appeal.

Waiting doesn't save money. Waiting costs money.

Reason 4: The Shame Spiral

Foreclosure feels like failure. You promised to pay the mortgage. You didn't. Now everyone's going to know.

So you hide. You don't tell your family. You don't tell your friends. You definitely don't tell a lawyer. You carry the secret alone, getting heavier every day.

But here's the thing: Foreclosure isn't a moral failing. It's a financial event. Banks foreclose on good people every day—people who lost jobs, got sick, had emergencies. You're not a bad person. You're a person in a bad situation.

And the sooner you stop hiding, the sooner you can start fighting.

LEARN FROM THIS MISTAKE: Waiting for the Modification That Never Came

> **Robert and Denise Chen's Story:** Robert lost his warehouse job in March. By June, they were three months behind on their mortgage. The bank sent them a modification application. "This is perfect," Denise thought. "We'll get a lower payment and everything will be fine."
>
> They applied in July. The bank asked for more documents. They sent them. Asked again. Sent them again. In October, the bank said they were "missing a form" and the application would need to restart. In December—nine months after Robert lost his job—they got a letter denying the modification. The reason? "Insufficient income."
>
> The same day, they got a Notice of Sale. The foreclosure auction was scheduled for January 15th—30 days away.
>
> "If we had talked to an attorney in March," Denise says now, "we would have known the modification was a long shot. We would have had time to build a defense, explore other options, maybe do a short sale. Instead, we spent nine months hoping while the bank was preparing to take our house."
>
> **The Lesson:** Hope is not a strategy. Modifications help some people, but they're not guaranteed. While you wait for a decision that might never come, your legal options are disappearing. Act as if the modification will be denied—because statistically, it probably will.

What Waiting Destroys: The Legal Options You Lose

Every foreclosure follows a timeline. At each point, you have options. But those options expire.

The Pre-Foreclosure Window (Months 1-4 After Missed Payment)

What you can do: - Apply for loan modification (best odds here) - Negotiate a repayment plan - Request a forbearance agreement - Start document audit to find bank errors - Consult with housing counselor (free) - Begin building emergency fund

What waiting costs: Even if you ultimately can't save the home, early action gives you time to plan, save money, and exit on your terms.

The Notice Period (Month 4-6)

What happens: The bank sends formal notices. In judicial states, this is the "lis pendens" or complaint filing. In non-judicial states, it's the Notice of Default.

What you can do: - Challenge the notice if it's defective - Demand proof of the bank's right to foreclose - Begin discovery process early - File preliminary motions - Apply for state mediation programs

What waiting costs: Once the notice is filed, the clock accelerates. But you still have time to build a defense.

The Answer Deadline (20-30 Days After Service)

This is the most critical deadline in your entire case.

What you can do: - File an answer denying the allegations - Assert affirmative defenses (standing, document defects, procedural violations) - File counterclaims - Request discovery - Move to dismiss

What waiting costs: If you don't answer, the bank gets a **default judgment**. That means they win without having to prove anything. No document audit. No standing challenge. No discovery. Just a win because you didn't show up.

> **CRITICAL:** A default judgment is nearly impossible to undo. Some courts allow you to "set aside" a default, but you need a very good reason—and "I was hoping for a modification" isn't good enough. Once you default, you've conceded the case.

The Discovery Window (After Answer, Before Summary Judgment)

What you can do: - Request documents from the bank (note, mortgage, assignments, endorsements) - Take depositions of bank representatives - Request admissions - subpoena records from third parties - Build evidence of bank errors

What waiting costs: Discovery has deadlines. If you wait until after summary judgment is filed, it's too late. The court will say you "slept on your rights."

Summary Judgment (The Kill Shot)

This is where most foreclosure cases end. The bank files a motion saying, "Even if everything the homeowner says is true, we still win as a matter of law."

What you can do: - Oppose the motion with evidence - Show genuine disputes of material fact - Challenge the bank's evidence - Request oral argument

What waiting costs: If you haven't done your document audit by now, you have no evidence to challenge the bank's claims. If you haven't done discovery, you have no facts to dispute. Summary judgment is granted. Case over.

The Sale Date (The Point of No Return)

Once the sale happens, your options are extremely limited. Some states have redemption periods. Some allow challenges to the sale itself. But most homeowners at this stage are fighting for extra time to move, not to keep the home.

LEARN FROM THIS MISTAKE: Missing the Answer Deadline

> **Terrence Williams' Story:** Terrence was served with a foreclosure complaint on October 1st. The answer was due October 30th. He was scared. He didn't know what to write. He kept telling himself he'd figure it out next week.
>
> Next week came. Then the next. On November 15th, he got a letter from the court: "Default judgment entered. Sale scheduled for December 20th."
>
> Terrence finally hired an attorney. The attorney filed an emergency motion to set aside the default. The judge denied it. "You had 30 days," the judge said. "You offered no excuse for the delay. The plaintiff has a right to finality."
>
> Terrence lost his home—not because the bank had a strong case, not because he didn't have defenses, but because he didn't file a one-page answer. "I kept thinking I needed the perfect answer," he says. "I didn't realize that any answer was better than no answer."
>
> **The Lesson:** You don't need the perfect answer. You need a timely answer. A simple denial of the allegations preserves your rights. You can improve it later. But you cannot undo a default.

The Modification Trap: How Banks Use Hope Against You

If there's one pattern I see over and over, it's this: The bank encourages you to apply for a modification while they prepare to foreclose. They tell you not to worry about the lawsuit. They say the modification will "stop everything."

Sometimes it's a lie. Sometimes it's technically true but practically false.

How Dual Tracking Works

"Dual tracking" means the bank processes your modification application on one track while pursuing foreclosure on another track—simultaneously.

You think: "They're reviewing my application. I don't need to worry about the court case."

The bank thinks: "We're going to deny this application, but meanwhile, let's keep the foreclosure moving so we don't lose time."

When the modification is denied (and most are), the foreclosure is already far along. You have weeks, not months, to respond.

States Where Dual Tracking Is Illegal

After the foreclosure crisis, some states passed laws prohibiting dual tracking: - **California** — Homeowner Bill of Rights - **Nevada** — Similar protections - **Other states** — Various protections

But even where it's illegal, it still happens. Banks claim "communication errors" or "system glitches." The burden is on you to prove it.

How to Protect Yourself

Never rely on a modification application to stop foreclosure proceedings.

Even while your modification is "under review": 1. **Respond to all court papers** — Never miss a deadline 2. **Document everything** — Save every call, every letter, every email 3. **Get it in writing** — Verbal promises from customer service reps mean nothing 4. **Check the foreclosure status** — Call the foreclosure attorney of record. Ask for status. Get it in writing.

LEARN FROM THIS MISTAKE: Trusting the Bank's Promises

Angela Martinez' Story: Angela applied for a modification in August. The bank's representative told her on the phone, "Don't worry about the court papers. Once your modification is approved, the foreclosure will be dismissed. Just focus on getting us those documents."

Angela didn't file an answer. She focused on the modification. In November, the bank denied her modification—without explanation. In December, she got a Notice of Sale. The auction was January 10th.

Angela called the bank, frantic. The representative apologized but said there was nothing they could do. The foreclosure had proceeded while she was waiting. "But you told me not to worry about the court papers!" she protested.

"I don't see that in the notes," the representative said.

Angela had to file for bankruptcy to stop the sale—an option she wouldn't have needed if she'd answered the complaint and built a defense.

The Lesson: Bank representatives say all kinds of things. They promise modifications will stop foreclosures. They say not to worry about deadlines. They are not your lawyers. They are not on your side. Their job is to collect debt or process foreclosures. Get everything in writing. Better yet, don't rely on phone calls at all—follow the legal procedures and protect your rights.

The 72-Hour Rule: Act Fast, Even Imperfectly

If there's one principle that separates homeowners who save their homes from homeowners who lose them, it's this:

Act within 72 hours. Perfect it later.

When you get a foreclosure notice, complaint, or any legal document, you have 72 hours to take initial action. Not because there's a 72-hour legal deadline, but because:

1. **Momentum matters** — The longer you wait, the harder it is to start
2. **Early action preserves options** — Deadlines become clear, paths stay open
3. **Information gathering takes time** — The sooner you start, the more you know

What to Do in the First 72 Hours

Hour 1-24: READ AND CALENDAR - Read every document completely - Find every deadline and put it on your calendar - Note the name of the law firm handling the foreclosure - Look up your court's website for local rules

Hour 24-48: GATHER AND ORGANIZE - Find your original mortgage documents - Gather all correspondence with the bank - Organize everything chronologically - Make copies (never give originals to anyone)

Hour 48-72: CONSULT AND DECIDE - Call a HUD-approved housing counselor (free) - Research foreclosure defense attorneys for consultation - Decide: Will you hire an attorney or represent yourself? - If self-representing, start drafting your answer

The Answer Doesn't Need to Be Perfect

Homeowners freeze because they think they need the perfect legal argument. They don't.

A basic answer that: - Denies the allegations - Lists your defenses (even generally) - Is filed on time

...is infinitely better than no answer at all.

You can amend your answer later. You can add defenses as you discover them. But you cannot undo a default.

What Early Action Gives You

Now let's look at the flip side—what happens when you act early.

Time to Find the Bank's Weaknesses

When you start early, you have time to: - Request documents through discovery - Review assignments for defects - Check signatures for robo-signing - Verify the chain of title - Research whether the foreclosing party actually owns your loan

These investigations take months. If you wait until summary judgment is filed, you don't have months.

Time to Negotiate from Strength

When you have a strong defense—or even the possibility of one—you negotiate from strength.

The bank knows that if they have document problems, they might lose at trial. They might agree to a better modification, a short sale with forgiveness of deficiency, or more time to relocate.

But you only get these outcomes if you have leverage. And you only have leverage if you've done the work to find their weaknesses.

Time to Plan Your Exit

Sometimes, despite your best efforts, you cannot save the home. But early action gives you time to: - Negotiate a cash-for-keys agreement (the bank pays you to leave peacefully) - Arrange a short sale (sell for less than owed, with bank approval) - Execute a deed in lieu of foreclosure (give deed to bank voluntarily) - Save money for your next housing - Find a rental with less pressure

These options are far better than being evicted with no plan and no money.

The Cost of Waiting: By the Numbers

Let me put this in concrete terms.

Stage	Early Action Cost	Late Action Cost	Waiting Cost
Pre-foreclosure	$0 (self-help) to $500 (attorney consult)	N/A	Lost modification time, lost options
Answer filing	$0 (pro se) to $2,000 (attorney)	$5,000-$15,000 (emergency motion to set aside default)	Default judgment, loss of defenses
Discovery	Time + copying costs	$10,000+ (emergency discovery motions)	No evidence for summary judgment opposition
Summary Judgment	$2,000-$5,000 (opposition brief)	$15,000+ (appeal after SJ granted)	Judgment entered, sale scheduled
Sale date	N/A (already lost)	$20,000+ (emergency bankruptcy, TRO)	Home sold, eviction imminent

Every stage you wait multiplies the cost.

How to Stop Waiting and Start Acting

If you're reading this and realizing you've been waiting, here's how to break the paralysis:

Step 1: The 5-Minute Start

Don't commit to solving the whole problem. Commit to 5 minutes.

Open that letter. Read the first page. Find the deadline. Write it on your calendar.

That's it. Five minutes.

Once you start, momentum builds. But you have to start.

Step 2: Make One Call

Call a HUD-approved housing counselor. It's free. They're trained. They won't judge you.

To find one: Call 1-888-995-HOPE (4673) or visit HUD.gov.

One call. That's your goal for today.

Step 3: Get One Consultation

Most foreclosure defense attorneys offer free or low-cost initial consultations. Even if you can't afford full representation, one consultation tells you: - What deadlines you're facing - What defenses might apply - Whether you have a case worth fighting

Call three attorneys. Pick one. Go to the consultation.

Step 4: File Something

If you can't hire an attorney, file something yourself. A simple answer. A request for extension. Anything that shows the court you're participating.

The court has forms. Legal aid has templates. This book has samples.

File something.

Chapter Summary

- **Waiting is the #1 mistake homeowners make.** Not because they're bad people, but because they're overwhelmed, hopeful, or ashamed.

- **Deadlines are unforgiving.** Miss the answer deadline, and you get a default judgment. Miss the discovery window, and you have no evidence. Wait until the sale date, and your options are nearly gone.
- **The modification trap is real.** Banks often encourage modification applications while pursuing foreclosure simultaneously. Don't rely on modifications to stop legal proceedings.
- **The 72-hour rule saves cases.** Act within 72 hours of receiving any legal document. You don't need perfection—you need action.
- **Early action is cheaper than late action.** Every stage you wait multiplies the cost and reduces the options.
- **Breaking paralysis starts small.** Five minutes. One call. One consultation. File something. Momentum builds from there.

Cross-References

Next Chapter: Chapter 3 — Foreclosure Myths That Hurt Homeowners

Related Chapters: - Chapter 1: Understanding Foreclosure (timeline basics) - Chapter 4: The Homeowner's Mortgage Document Audit System (what to look for) - Chapter 9: You Got Served: What to Do in the First 72 Hours - Chapter 10: How to Draft the Answer Without Helping the Bank

In the Playbook: - 72-Hour Action Checklist - Deadline Tracker Worksheet - Modification Correspondence Log - Attorney Consultation Questions

Templates: - Simple Answer Template - Request for Extension of Time - Motion to Set Aside Default (emergency use only)

CHAPTER 3: FORECLOSURE MYTHS THAT HURT HOMEOWNERS

The Lies That Cost People Their Homes

Why Myths Matter

Before we dive into document audits, legal defenses, and courtroom strategies, we need to clear the air. Because most homeowners lose their homes not because they had a weak case, but because they believed things that weren't true.

The foreclosure crisis created an information explosion. Blogs, forums, YouTube videos, Facebook groups—everyone has advice. Some of it is brilliant. Some of it is dangerously wrong. And telling the difference can mean the difference between keeping your home and losing it.

This chapter tackles the six most dangerous myths—the ones that paralyze homeowners, send them down wrong paths, or convince them to give up before they even start. These myths aren't just incorrect. They're expensive. They cost people their homes.

Let's destroy them.

MYTH #1: "The Bank Will Work With Me If I Just Explain My Situation"

This is the myth that catches the most people. It's also the most understandable.

You hit hard times. You lost your job. You got sick. Your business failed. Something happened that wasn't your fault, and now you can't make the payments. So you call the bank. You explain. You plead. You send documents showing your hardship. You hope for mercy.

Here's what you're actually dealing with:

The person on the phone isn't a decision-maker. They're a call center employee working from a script. They have no authority to modify your loan, forgive payments, or stop foreclosure. Their job is to: 1. Keep you on the phone 2. Gather information 3. Follow the script 4. Transfer you to the next person

The "loss mitigation" department that reviews modifications? They're measured on how many files they process, not how many homeowners they help. Many are outsourced to third parties who get paid per file, regardless of outcome.

The bank is not your counselor. The bank is not your friend. The bank is a debt collector with a sophisticated collection system.

What "Working With You" Actually Means

When the bank says they want to "work with you," here's what they usually mean:

- They want you to keep making payments while they "review" your modification (payments that often go to fees and interest, not principal)
- They want you to provide endless documentation so they can check boxes
- They want you to stay current enough that they don't have to report you as delinquent to regulators
- They want you to believe something good is happening while the foreclosure timeline advances

This is not working with you. This is managing you.

The Exception: When Banks Actually Do Negotiate

There are situations where banks negotiate in good faith: - When you have a strong defense and they know it - When the cost of foreclosure exceeds the value of your cooperation - When public relations concerns make your case sensitive - When you've already retained an attorney and they know you're serious

Notice what's common in all these scenarios? **Leverage.** Banks negotiate when they have to, not when you ask nicely.

LEARN FROM THIS MISTAKE: The Homeowner Who Trusted the "Relationship Manager"

> **Patricia Olson's Story:** Patricia had been a customer of her bank for 22 years. She had checking, savings, a credit card, and her mortgage all with the same institution. "I thought that meant something," she says.> When she fell behind after her divorce, the bank assigned her a "relationship manager" named David. David called every week. He asked about her job search. He sympathized with her situation. He said the bank valued her as a long-term customer and wanted to find a solution.> For six months, Patricia sent David documents, updated

him on her employment status, and believed they were working together to save her home. She didn't hire an attorney because she thought David was on her side.> > Then she got a Notice of Sale. When she called David, he didn't return her calls. His voicemail said he had "moved to a different department." The foreclosure attorney told her the case had been proceeding for months. The bank had never delayed the foreclosure while "working with her."> > Patricia lost her home. The "relationship" was never real. It was a collections strategy.> > **The Lesson:** The person who answers the phone at your bank is not your advocate. They are an employee following protocols. Real negotiations happen through legal channels or when you have leverage—not because you've been a loyal customer.

MYTH #2: "I Can't Fight Foreclosure Without a Lawyer"

This myth keeps thousands of homeowners from even trying. And it's exactly what banks want you to believe.

The truth: Pro se litigants (people representing themselves) win foreclosure cases. Regularly.

In Massachusetts, a pro se homeowner named Antonio Ibanez forced the state's highest court to invalidate thousands of foreclosures. His case is now cited nationwide.

In California, pro se homeowners have won standing challenges that stopped foreclosures cold.

In Florida, pro se defendants have beaten summary judgment by pointing out document defects that attorneys missed.

You do not need a law degree to challenge whether the bank can prove they own your loan.

What You Do Need

While you don't need a lawyer, you do need:

Organization: Keep track of deadlines, documents, and court filings. Miss a deadline, and you lose—lawyer or no lawyer.

Attention to detail: The difference between winning and losing often comes down to spotting a forged signature, a missing date, or an inconsistent statement.

Persistence: Banks have lawyers who file motions, request delays, and bury you in paper. You have to keep going.

Willingness to learn: You don't need to become a lawyer, but you need to understand the basics of foreclosure law in your state.

When You Should Get a Lawyer

This doesn't mean lawyers are useless. You should seriously consider hiring an attorney if: - You can afford one who specializes in foreclosure defense - Your case involves complex issues (title disputes, multiple liens, bankruptcy) - You're at summary judgment or trial stage - You've tried pro se and hit a wall

But the absence of a lawyer is not the same as the absence of a defense. Don't let not having an attorney convince you that you have no case.

Limited Scope Representation

There's a middle ground between full representation and going it alone: **limited scope representation.**

Many attorneys will: - Review your documents for a flat fee - Help you draft an answer - Coach you through the process - Handle just the trial or just the appeal

This costs less than full representation but gives you professional guidance where you need it most.

MYTH #3: "The Bank Must Own the Loan to Foreclose—So I'm Safe"

This myth is half true, and that's what makes it dangerous.

The true part: Yes, generally the bank must own the note (or have the right to enforce it) to foreclose. This is called "standing."

The dangerous part: Banks foreclose all the time without proper standing. And they often get away with it because homeowners don't challenge them.

How Banks Foreclose Without Proper Documentation

During the 2000s mortgage boom, loans were originated, sold, bundled into mortgage-backed securities, resold, and sliced into tranches. The paperwork was an afterthought.

By the time foreclosure time came: - The original lender was bankrupt or defunct - The note had been lost - Assignments were backdated or forged - The entity foreclosing couldn't prove they owned the loan

But here's the key: If you don't challenge the bank's standing, the court will assume they have it. The burden is on you to demand proof.

The "Show Me the Note" Defense

Homeowners who challenge standing often win—at least initially. Courts have dismissed foreclosures because: - The plaintiff couldn't produce the original note - The chain of assignments was broken - The assignment was dated after the foreclosure started - The entity suing wasn't the entity that owned the debt

But you have to raise these defenses. They don't magically appear. You have to: 1. Demand production of the note in discovery 2. Review assignments for defects 3. Challenge affidavits that lack foundation 4. Move to dismiss if standing can't be proven

When Standing Doesn't Matter (As Much)

There are situations where standing challenges won't save your home: - If the bank actually has the note and mortgage (sometimes they do) - If the defect is curable (the bank can fix it by producing the right document) - If you wait too long to raise the issue (courts hate last-minute challenges)

Standing is a powerful tool. But it's not a magic bullet. You need to use it correctly and at the right time.

LEARN FROM THIS MISTAKE: The Homeowner Who Assumed the Bank Had Proof

Donald Reeves' Story: Donald received a foreclosure complaint from a bank he'd never heard of. "I knew they couldn't prove they owned my loan," he thought. "I remember signing with Countrywide, not this MERS thing. I'll just wait for them to prove it and the case will get dismissed."> Donald didn't file an answer. He didn't challenge the foreclosure. He assumed that when the bank couldn't produce the note, the court would throw the case out.> > Instead, the bank got a default judgment. When Donald finally objected, the judge said: "You had 30 days to answer. You didn't. The plaintiff has established their right to foreclose by your default."> > Donald tried to argue that the bank couldn't prove standing. The judge said: "That defense needed to be raised in your answer. You can't raise it now after you've defaulted."> > Donald lost his home—not because the bank could prove they owned the loan, but because Donald assumed the court would check for him. Courts don't check. You have to challenge.> > **The Lesson:** Standing is a defense you must raise. The court will not investigate the bank's documentation for you. If you don't challenge it, the bank wins by default—even with forged documents.

MYTH #4: "Bankruptcy Stops Foreclosure Forever"

Bankruptcy is a powerful tool. But it's not a magic wand.

What bankruptcy actually does:

When you file bankruptcy, the "automatic stay" goes into effect immediately. This stops all collection activities, including foreclosure sales. The bank cannot proceed while the stay is in effect.

But the stay doesn't last forever.

Chapter 7 vs. Chapter 13

Chapter 7 (Liquidation): - Stops foreclosure temporarily (usually 3-4 months) - Doesn't let you catch up on mortgage payments - Bank can file a "motion for relief from stay" to foreclose anyway - At the end, you still owe the mortgage (unless you surrendered the house)

Chapter 13 (Reorganization): - Allows you to catch up on missed payments over 3-5 years - Can strip second mortgages in some cases - Requires regular income to fund the payment plan - If you miss plan payments, the foreclosure can resume

When Bankruptcy Helps

Bankruptcy is most effective when: - You have temporary financial problems but steady income (Chapter 13) - You need time to sell the house or find other housing - You have other debts that need to be managed - You're using it as part of a broader strategy, not as the whole strategy

When Bankruptcy Doesn't Help

Bankruptcy won't save your home if: - You can't afford the mortgage even without other debts - You don't have income to fund a Chapter 13 plan - You wait until the last minute and file on the eve of sale (courts hate this) - You think it will make the mortgage go away (it won't)

The "One-Filing" Rule

If you file bankruptcy and it gets dismissed, or if the court grants the bank relief from stay, you can't just file again immediately to stop the foreclosure. Courts have gotten wise to serial bankruptcy filings and will deny stays to prevent abuse.

Bankruptcy is a tool. Use it strategically, not desperately.

MYTH #5: "If I'm Current on Payments, I'm Safe"

This myth kills homeowners who could have saved themselves if they'd acted earlier.

You don't have to be behind on payments to face foreclosure. Here are situations where current homeowners get foreclosed on:

The "Maturity Default"

Your loan has a balloon payment due. You make every monthly payment on time for 10 years. But when the balloon comes due, you can't pay it. The bank forecloses—even though you were never late on a monthly payment.

The "Due on Sale" Clause

You transfer the property to a trust, or to a family member, or into an LLC for estate planning. You keep making payments. But the bank discovers the transfer and calls the loan due under the "due on sale" clause. They foreclose.

Insurance or Tax Escrow Problems

You make your mortgage payment, but you let the homeowner's insurance lapse, or you don't pay property taxes. The bank force-places insurance (expensive) or pays the taxes and adds them to your balance. You dispute the charges and stop paying. They foreclose.

Document Defects (The Quiet Title Case)

You're current on payments, but you discover that the chain of title is broken, or there's a forged assignment, or MERS has no authority. You stop paying and challenge the bank's right to collect. They foreclose, claiming you're in default—even though the only "default" is your refusal to pay an improper creditor.

Being Current Doesn't Mean You're Safe

Being current on payments protects you from traditional foreclosure for non-payment. But it doesn't protect you from: - Balloon payments - Due-on-sale violations - Tax or insurance defaults - Document disputes - Bank errors

If something is wrong with your mortgage—even if you're current—investigate it now. Don't wait until you're behind and fighting on two fronts.

MYTH #6: "I Can Just Deed the House Back and Walk Away Clean"

A "deed in lieu of foreclosure" sounds like a peaceful solution. You can't afford the house, so you give it back to the bank. No foreclosure. No fight. Clean slate.

If only it were that simple.

What Deed in Lieu Actually Involves

First, the bank has to agree to accept a deed in lieu. They don't have to. Many banks won't, especially if: - There are junior liens (second mortgages, HELOCs, tax liens) - The property is in bad condition - The bank thinks they can get more money at foreclosure auction

Second, a deed in lieu doesn't automatically forgive the debt. If you owe $300,000 and the house is worth $250,000, the bank can still come after you for the $50,000 deficiency—unless they agree in writing to forgive it.

The Tax Bomb

Even if the bank forgives the deficiency, the IRS may treat that forgiven debt as taxable income. A $50,000 deficiency forgiveness could mean a $12,000 tax bill.

There are exceptions (the Mortgage Forgiveness Debt Relief Act, insolvency exclusions), but you need to plan for this, not discover it at tax time.

Credit Damage

A deed in lieu is slightly better than foreclosure on your credit report—but not much. It's still a serious derogatory mark. You're still going to struggle to get credit, rent an apartment, or buy another home for years.

When Deed in Lieu Makes Sense

Deed in lieu can be a good option when: - The bank agrees to forgive the deficiency in writing - You negotiate "cash for keys" (the bank pays you to leave) - You have no junior liens complicating the title - You understand and plan for the tax consequences - You've explored all other options and this is truly the best choice

But it's not a magic escape. It's a negotiated settlement with real consequences.

LEARN FROM THIS MISTAKE: The Deed in Lieu Disaster

> **Rebecca and Tom Chen's Story:** Rebecca and Tom knew they couldn't keep their home. Tom had been transferred for work, the house was underwater, and they just wanted to move on. The bank offered a "deed in lieu program" that sounded perfect.> They signed the deed. The bank took the house. They moved to Tom's new job. They thought it was over.> > Then they got a 1099-C from the bank showing $87,000 in canceled debt. Their accountant told them they owed $21,000 in taxes on that "income." They had saved nothing because they thought the debt was gone.> > Then they got a letter from a collection agency. The second mortgage holder (who had never agreed to the deed in lieu) was suing them for $45,000. The bank only took the first mortgage. The second mortgage was still their problem.> > Rebecca and Tom went from thinking they had a clean break to facing $66,000 in tax and debt obligations—plus a lawsuit.> > **The Lesson:** Deed in lieu is not a magic wand. You need written confirmation that ALL liens are released, not just the first mortgage. You need to plan for tax consequences. And you need to understand that "walking away" rarely means walking away clean.

The Myth-Busting Self-Assessment

Before you move on to the rest of this book, take a moment to check yourself:

Myth	Do I Believe This?	Reality Check
The bank will work with me if I explain	Yes No	Banks manage debt, not people. Real help requires leverage.

Myth	Do I Believe This?	Reality Check
I can't fight without a lawyer	Yes No	Pro se litigants win. You need organization, not a law degree.
The bank must own the loan	Yes No	They should, but they often don't. You must challenge them.
Bankruptcy stops foreclosure forever	Yes No	It stops it temporarily. Chapter 13 can help; Chapter 7 just delays.
If I'm current, I'm safe	Yes No	Balloons, due-on-sale, and disputes can foreclose current borrowers.
I can deed the house back and walk clean	Yes No	Tax consequences, deficiency judgments, and junior liens remain.

Every box you checked "Yes" on is a belief that could cost you your home.

Now that you know the truth, you can act on facts instead of myths.

Chapter Summary

- **Myth #1: "The bank will work with me."** Reality: Banks manage debt. Real help requires leverage or legal pressure, not explanations.
- **Myth #2: "I can't fight without a lawyer."** Reality: Pro se litigants win regularly. You need organization and persistence, not a law degree.
- **Myth #3: "The bank must own the loan."** Reality: They should, but they often foreclose without proof. You must challenge standing—it won't be checked automatically.
- **Myth #4: "Bankruptcy stops foreclosure forever."** Reality: It provides temporary stay. Chapter 13 can help you catch up; Chapter 7 just delays.
- **Myth #5: "If I'm current, I'm safe."** Reality: Balloon payments, due-on-sale clauses, and document disputes can threaten current homeowners.

- **Myth #6: "I can deed the house back and walk away."** Reality: Deed in lieu has tax consequences, deficiency risks, and doesn't eliminate junior liens.
- **The truth is your weapon.** Acting on facts instead of myths gives you a fighting chance.

Cross-References

Next Chapter: Chapter 4 — The Homeowner's Mortgage Document Audit System

Related Chapters: - Chapter 1: Understanding Foreclosure (timeline basics) - Chapter 2: The Homeowner's Biggest Mistake (why waiting hurts) - Chapter 9: First 72 Hours (when to file bankruptcy) - Chapter 11: Motion to Dismiss (standing challenges) - Chapter 13: Victory Cases (pro se homeowner wins)

In the Playbook: - Myth vs. Reality Quick Reference - Self-Assessment Checklist - "Should I Hire a Lawyer?" Decision Tree - Bankruptcy vs. Defense Strategy Guide

CHAPTER 4: THE HOMEOWNER'S MORTGAGE DOCUMENT AUDIT SYSTEM

How to Find the Evidence That Wins Cases

Why Document Audit Matters

Here's a secret the banks don't want you to know: **Most foreclosure cases are won or lost on documents, not on the facts of who paid what.**

The bank says you owe them money. You say maybe, but prove you have the right to collect it. And that's where the documents come in.

During the mortgage boom of the 2000s, loans were originated, sold, bundled, sliced, re-bundled, and resold so many times that the paperwork became a disaster. Original notes were lost. Assignments were backdated or never recorded. Documents were signed by people who didn't exist. Notaries stamped papers for signatures they never witnessed.

The banks know their paperwork is a mess. They count on you not looking.

A proper document audit isn't just curiosity—it's evidence gathering. Every missing signature, every backdated assignment, every robo-signed document is a potential defense. And you won't find them by glancing at your mortgage. You need a system.

This chapter gives you that system.

The Complete Document Checklist

Before you can audit, you need the documents. Here's what you're looking for:

Tier 1: Essential Documents (Start Here)

The Promissory Note - This is your promise to repay the loan - Should show the original lender, loan amount, interest rate, terms - Look for endorsements on the back or allonges attached - **Critical:** The note is a negotiable instrument—it must be properly transferred

The Mortgage (or Deed of Trust) - This is the security instrument that gives the lender rights to your property - Should match the note in terms of property description, borrowers, and lender - Contains the foreclosure procedures and requirements - Recorded with the county

All Assignments of Mortgage - Documents showing transfer of the mortgage from one party to another - Should be recorded in county land records - Each assignment should show a clear chain from original lender to current claimant

Tier 2: Critical Supporting Documents

Allonges - Attachments to the note showing endorsements - Must be "permanently affixed" to the note - Blank endorsements (no name filled in) are suspicious

Loan Modifications - Any changes to your original loan terms - Must be signed by all parties - Watch for unauthorized changes

Servicing Records - Payment history - Escrow statements - Force-placed insurance records - Fee assessments

Tier 3: Background Documents

Title Insurance Policy - Shows the condition of title when you purchased - May reveal prior issues or lien problems - Lists exceptions and exclusions that affect your property - Can identify easements, restrictions, or other encumbrances

Closing Documents - HUD-1 or Closing Disclosure (shows all fees paid at closing) - Truth in Lending disclosures (APR, finance charges) - Good Faith Estimate (what you were told costs would be) - Appraisal report (property valuation)

Correspondence - All letters from lenders, servicers, and collection agencies - Payment change notices (ARM adjustments, escrow changes) - Default and acceleration letters - Modification offers and denials - Insurance and tax notices

Tier 4: Regulatory and Public Records

SEC Filings (for securitized loans) - Pooling and Servicing Agreements (PSAs) - Prospectus supplements showing your loan - Trust creation documents

Bankruptcy Court Records - If your lender or servicer filed for bankruptcy - Asset schedules showing loan transfers

Litigation Records - Other cases involving your lender or servicer - Class action lawsuits - Regulatory enforcement actions

---

LEARN FROM THIS MISTAKE: The Homeowner Who Only Looked at the Mortgage

Jason Park's Story: Jason was a commercial real estate investor who knew documents mattered. When he received a foreclosure complaint from a bank he'd never heard of, he pulled out his mortgage and started reviewing it.> The mortgage looked fine. His signature was on it. The property description was correct. The loan amount matched what he remembered. He couldn't find anything wrong.> > So he didn't fight. He assumed the bank must have the right to foreclose. He didn't answer the complaint. He got a default judgment.> > Three months later, talking to a friend who was an attorney, Jason mentioned his foreclosure. The attorney asked to see his note. "What do you mean, note?" Jason asked.> > Jason had never looked at his promissory note—only the mortgage. When he finally obtained a copy from the county, he discovered: - The note had been endorsed to a company that went bankrupt in 2009 - The company suing him had no endorsement showing they owned the note - The assignment of mortgage was dated three months AFTER the foreclosure was filed > "I could have challenged their standing," Jason says. "I could have demanded they prove they owned the loan. But I only looked at the mortgage because that's what mentioned the foreclosure. I didn't understand that the note and mortgage are separate, and both matter."> > Jason lost a $400,000 property over a document audit that would have taken two hours.> > **The Lesson:** You must review BOTH the note and the mortgage. The mortgage gives the security interest in your property. The note is the debt. A party must have the right to enforce the note to foreclose. The mortgage alone is not enough.

How to Obtain Your Documents

Your Own Files

Start with what you have. Most homeowners have at least some closing documents in their files. Look for: - Closing folder from your purchase or refinance - Any loan modification paperwork - Recent mortgage statements - Insurance and tax escrow documents

County Land Records

Your mortgage and any assignments should be recorded with your county recorder or clerk of court. You can:

In Person: - Go to the county recorder's office - Search by your name or property address

- Request copies (usually $1-2 per page) - Make sure to get certified copies if you need them for court

Online: - Many counties have online search systems - Search terms: "[Your County] recorder of deeds" - Some charge for document downloads - Others are free

Your Servicer (Qualified Written Request)

Under RESPA (Real Estate Settlement Procedures Act), you have the right to request information about your loan. Send a **Qualified Written Request (QWR)** to your servicer's designated address.

What to request: - Copy of the original promissory note - Copy of the mortgage or deed of trust - Complete payment history - Identity of the note holder - All assignments of the mortgage - Any endorsements or allonges

Important: The servicer has 5 business days to acknowledge receipt and 30 business days to respond. Mark your calendar.

LEARN FROM THIS MISTAKE: The QWR That Wasn't

Cynthia Williams' Story: Cynthia read online that she should send a Qualified Written Request to get her documents. She drafted a letter asking for "all documents related to my loan" and mailed it to the address on her mortgage statement.> Nothing happened. No response. No documents. She waited 45 days, then called the servicer. They said they never received her request. She sent it again. Still nothing.> > What Cynthia didn't know: - Her servicer had a separate, specific address for QWRs—not the general correspondence address - Her request was too vague ("all documents" isn't specific enough) - She didn't send it certified mail, so she had no proof of delivery - She didn't track the 30-day deadline properly > By the time she figured out the correct process, her foreclosure answer was due in 10 days. She had to file without the documents she needed.> > **The Lesson:** A QWR must be sent to the specific address designated for QWRs (check your servicer's website or call and ask). It should list specific documents. Send it certified mail, return receipt requested. Calendar the 30-day response deadline and follow up immediately if they miss it.

The Foreclosure Attorney

If foreclosure has been filed, the plaintiff's attorney must provide certain documents. Send a request for: - The note - The mortgage - All assignments - The payment history they're relying on

Don't accept "the note is lost" without demanding proof of the circumstances.

The Audit Methodology: Step-by-Step

Now that you have the documents, here's how to audit them systematically.

Step 1: Create Your Document Inventory

Make a list of every document you have. For each document, record: - Document type (note, mortgage, assignment, etc.) - Date of document - Parties involved (who signed, who received) - Notary information - Recording information (book/page or instrument number) - Any obvious issues

Use the Document Inventory Worksheet (in the Playbook).

Step 2: Map the Chain of Title

Create a timeline showing every transfer of your loan:

```
Date            Event                       Document
-----           -----                       --------
03/15/2006      Loan Originated             Note to ABC Mortgage
03/15/2006      Mortgage Recorded           Mortgage to ABC Mortgage
06/20/2006      Assignment                  ABC → DEF Bank (recorded 07/05/2006)
01/10/2008      Assignment                  DEF → MERS (recorded 01/25/2008)
09/15/2009      Assignment                  MERS → XYZ Trust (recorded 10/01/2009)
[etc.]
```

Red flags to watch for: - Gaps in the chain (who owned the loan between transfers?) - Assignments dated after the foreclosure was filed - Assignments to entities that didn't exist at the time - Missing assignments (transfers with no recorded documents)

Step 3: Examine the Note

Front of Note: - Does the lender named match your memory? - Is the loan amount correct? - Are the interest rate and terms correct? - Is your signature genuine?

Back of Note (Endorsements): - Is there an endorsement transferring the note? - Is it a "blank endorsement" (no name filled in)? - Is it a "special endorsement" (names the transferee)? - Are endorsements dated? - Do endorsement dates match assignment dates?

Allonges (Attachments): - Is the allonge permanently affixed to the note? - Does it show a clear chain of endorsement? - Are signatures consistent across documents?

Step 4: Examine the Mortgage

- Does the property description match your property?
- Are all borrowers' names correct?
- Does the lender match the note (at origination)?
- Are there any modifications or riders?

Step 5: Examine Assignments

For each assignment, verify these critical elements:

Assignor Identity: - Who is transferring the mortgage? - Do they match the last recorded assignee? - Did they exist on the assignment date? - Were they authorized to make the transfer?

Assignee Identity: - Who is receiving the mortgage? - Is it a known entity or a shell company? - Do they exist on the assignment date?

Execution Quality: - Is the assignment signed by an authorized officer? - Is the signature consistent with other documents? - Is the notarization valid? - Is the notary from a reasonable geographic area?

Recording Details: - When was the assignment recorded? - What is the instrument number or book/page? - Was it recorded before or after the foreclosure?

Step 6: Check Signatures and Notarizations

Signature Analysis Checklist:

Compare signatures from the same person across multiple documents: - Are they consistent in style and formation? - Do they show natural variation or suspicious uniformity? - Are initials used consistently? - Do the signatures match the person's known signature style?

Robo-Signing Indicators: - Multiple documents signed the same day - Impossible volume (hundreds of documents per day) - Signatures that look stamped or printed - Signers with titles that don't match their actual authority - Documents signed by people who later admit they didn't review them

Notary Fraud Red Flags: - Notary commissions expired before document date - Notaries from distant states - Bulk notarizations on the same day - Acknowledgments where the notary didn't witness the signature - Notary stamps that look photocopied rather than stamped

Step 7: Verify Dates and Sequencing

Date Consistency Check: - Do endorsement dates match assignment dates? - Do assignment dates precede foreclosure filing dates? - Are there any documents dated on weekends or holidays? - Do document dates match recording dates reasonably?

Timeline Logic: - Could the signer have been in all locations on the dates shown? - Were the entities involved in existence on the document dates? - Do transfer dates make sense given the financial crisis timeline?

Step 8: Research the Parties

Entity Verification: - Look up assignor and assignee in state business records - Check if they were active/registered on document dates - Research any mergers, acquisitions, or name changes - Verify MERS has authority to act in your state

Individual Signers: - Search for the signer's name in robo-signer databases - Check if they've been deposed in other cases - Look for news articles about document fraud - Search court records for their involvement in other foreclosures

---

Organizing Your Findings

A disorganized audit is useless. You need to be able to: - Find any document quickly - Show the chain of title clearly - Present red flags in an organized way - Support litigation or settlement discussions

Physical Organization

If working with paper: 1. **Use a three-ring binder** with tabs for each document type 2. **Make copies** — never give originals to anyone 3. **Use color coding** — red for serious issues, yellow for questions 4. **Create an index** showing where each document is located

Digital Organization

If working electronically: 1. **Create a folder structure:** `/Loan Documents    /01 - Note    /02 - Mortgage    /03 - Assignments    /04 - Correspondence    /05 - Analysis` 2. **Use consistent naming:** `YYYY-MM-DD - Document Type - Parties`

3. **Save everything as PDF** for consistency 4. **Back up to cloud storage** — these documents are critical

---

LEARN FROM THIS MISTAKE: The Lost Evidence

> **David Kim's Story:** David was meticulous about his document audit. He found an assignment with a robo-signer's signature and created a detailed analysis showing 15 other documents with the same signature pattern. He organized everything on his laptop.> Then his hard drive crashed. He had no backup. All his work was gone. He tried to recreate it from memory, but he couldn't remember all the details. The bank produced their documents at summary judgment, and David couldn't effectively challenge them without his organized evidence.> > "I spent 40 hours on that audit," David says. "And I lost it all because I thought 'I'll back it up next week.' Next week never came."> > **The Lesson:** Back up your audit work immediately and regularly. Use cloud storage (Google Drive, Dropbox, OneDrive) that syncs automatically. Email yourself copies. Print critical findings. Your audit is only valuable if you can access it when you need it—and hardware failures, theft, or accidents happen without warning.

The Audit Summary Document

Create a one-page summary of your findings: - Documents reviewed - Chain of title (timeline format) - Red flags identified - Documents missing or requested - Recommended next steps

Common Document Audit Mistakes to Avoid

Even experienced homeowners make these errors when auditing their mortgage documents:

Mistake #1: Accepting Copies Without Demanding Originals

Banks often provide copies and claim the originals are "lost" or "in storage." But copies can be altered, and you have the right to inspect originals. If the bank claims the note is lost, they must provide a lost note affidavit explaining the circumstances—and even then, you can challenge their right to enforce it.

What to do: Always demand to see the original note. If they refuse or claim it's lost, document their refusal and research your state's requirements for enforcing lost instruments.

Mistake #2: Ignoring the Allonge

An allonge is a piece of paper attached to the note showing endorsements. Homeowners often overlook these because they're "just attachments." But the allonge is critical—it shows the chain of ownership of the note.

What to look for: Is the allonge permanently affixed (stapled, glued) to the note? If it's just paper-clipped, it may not be valid. Are the endorsements complete? Blank endorsements (where the name is left blank) are particularly suspicious.

Mistake #3: Not Checking County Records

Your servicer's records and the county recorder's office may show different things. Banks sometimes fail to record assignments or record them late. The county records are the official public record of your mortgage's status.

What to do: Always search county records separately from requesting documents from your servicer. Compare what they give you against what's officially recorded.

Mistake #4: Overlooking the Note-Mortgage Separation

The note and mortgage can be held by different parties. The note holder has the right to enforce the debt; the mortgage holder has the security interest in your property. If they're separated, the party foreclosing may lack standing.

What to check: Does the note endorse to the same party that holds the mortgage? Are there assignments showing how both instruments were transferred together? Securitization often separates these documents.

Mistake #5: Missing the PSA Cut-Off Date

If your loan was securitized, the Pooling and Servicing Agreement (PSA) likely has a cut-off date by which loans must be transferred into the trust. Assignments dated after this cut-off may be invalid.

What to do: Research whether your loan is in a securitized trust. If so, obtain the PSA and identify the cut-off date. Any assignment after that date is a major red flag.

> **Margaret Torres' Story:** Margaret was suspicious of the foreclosure from the start. She pulled her county records and found an assignment dated two weeks after the foreclosure was filed. "They assigned the mortgage AFTER they started foreclosing!" she told everyone.> She went to court and told the judge about the

backdated assignment. The bank's attorney smiled and produced an affidavit explaining that the assignment was "inadvertently misdated" and the actual transfer happened earlier.> > The judge accepted the explanation. Margaret lost.> > What Margaret didn't do:> - Document her methodology for finding the issue - Research whether the assignor even existed on the earlier date they claimed - Check if the notary who signed the assignment had a valid commission on either date - Look for other assignments with the same signature pattern - Compare signatures across documents for consistency > "I found the smoking gun," Margaret says, "but I couldn't prove it was smoking. I just pointed at it and expected the judge to care."> > **The Lesson:** Finding a document defect is step one. Documenting it methodically, researching the context, and building a complete picture is what makes it admissible evidence. A suspicious document without proper documentation and context is just a suspicion.

From Audit to Litigation Strategy

Once you've completed your audit, you need to turn findings into strategy.

If You Find Major Defects

Standing/Chain of Title Problems: - Challenge the plaintiff's right to foreclose - Demand production of the original note - File a motion to dismiss for lack of standing - Request discovery on the chain of title

Forgery/Robo-Signing: - Challenge the authenticity of documents - Request the signer be made available for deposition - Research known robo-signer databases - Consider handwriting analysis

Procedural Defects: - Challenge improper notice - Demand strict compliance with state foreclosure statutes - File motions based on statutory requirements

If You Find Minor Issues

Not every defect wins the case. But minor issues can: - Create delay (the bank must cure the defect) - Provide leverage for settlement - Support a counterclaim - Cast doubt on the bank's credibility

If You Find Nothing

Sometimes the documents are in order. If so: - Focus on other defenses (payment disputes, procedural violations) - Consider loss mitigation options - Negotiate from the reality of the situation, not false hope

---

Red Flags: Quick Reference

Red Flag	What It Means	Action
Assignment after foreclosure filed	Bank didn't own loan when they sued	Challenge standing immediately
Blank endorsement	Anyone can claim to own the note	Demand proof of ownership
Robo-signer signature	Document likely not properly reviewed	Research signer, challenge authenticity
Notary from different state	Notary didn't witness signature	Challenge notarization validity
Weekend/holiday dates	Signer wasn't actually working	Request employment records
MERS as nominee	Complex chain of title issues	Research MERS authority in your state
Lost note affidavit	Original note is missing	Demand proof of loss circumstances
Allonge not attached	Endorsement may be invalid	Challenge chain of endorsement

---

Chapter Summary

- **Document audits win cases.** Most banks have document problems from the securitization era. You just have to find them.
- **You need both the note and the mortgage.** The note is the debt; the mortgage is the security. Both matter critically.
- **Use a systematic methodology.** Random searching misses things. Follow the eight-step checklist.
- **Organization is critical.** A disorganized audit is useless in court.

- **Finding defects is step one.** You must also document your methodology and build a complete picture.
- **Not every defect wins the case.** But every defect is leverage.

Cross-References

Next Chapter: Chapter 5 — Forgery, Robo-Signing, and Suspicious Signatures

Related Chapters: - Chapter 3: Foreclosure Myths ("The bank must own the loan") - Chapter 6: Assignments, Endorsements, Allonges, and the Chain Problem - Chapter 7: Note and Mortgage/Deed Separation - Chapter 33: Building Your Evidence File and Timeline

In the Playbook: - Document Inventory Worksheet - Chain-of-Title Tracker - Signature Comparison Worksheet - Red Flags Quick Reference Card - QWR Template

Templates: - Qualified Written Request - Document Request Letter - Audit Findings Summary

CHAPTER 5: FORGERY, ROBO-SIGNING, AND SUSPICIOUS SIGNATURES

How to Spot Document Fraud and Get Documents Voided

The Truth About Document Fraud

During the foreclosure crisis, banks and their document processors committed fraud on an industrial scale. We're not talking about a few bad apples. We're talking about assembly lines of fake documents, forged signatures, and notaries who never witnessed a single signature.

The good news? **This fraud leaves fingerprints.** And if you know where to look, you can find them.

Document fraud isn't just a technicality. When you prove a document is forged or robo-signed, you can get it voided. A voided assignment means a broken chain of title. A broken chain of title means the bank trying to foreclose may have no right to be in court at all.

This is where cases are won.

But you have to do the work. You have to collect every document, examine every signature, and compare every detail. This chapter shows you exactly how.

What Is Robo-Signing?

Robo-signing is the mass production of signed documents by people who: - Sign hundreds or thousands of documents per day - Don't read what they're signing - Don't verify the information - Often don't even work for the company they're claiming to represent

The term became famous in 2010 when bank employees admitted under oath that they signed documents without any knowledge of what they contained. Some signers processed **10,000 documents per month** — physically impossible if they were actually reviewing each one.

But robo-signing is just one type of document fraud. There's also:

Forgery: Signing someone else's name without authorization

Notary Fraud: A notary stamps documents without actually witnessing the signature

Backdating: Writing a date on a document that doesn't match when it was actually signed

Cut-and-Paste Signatures: Copying a signature from one document and applying it to another

---

LEARN FROM THIS MISTAKE: The Homeowner Who Saw It But Couldn't Prove It

Terrence Mitchell's Story: Terrence was reviewing his foreclosure documents when he noticed something odd. The same person had signed three different assignments for three different loans — all dated the same day. "That can't be right," he thought. "Nobody can travel to three different states in one day to sign documents."

Terrence went to court and told the judge about his discovery. The bank's attorney asked him one question: "Sir, do you have any evidence that these signatures are fraudulent?"

Terrence didn't. He had no comparison documents. He hadn't researched the signer. He had no affidavits from other cases. He had a suspicion and a hunch — but no admissible evidence.

The judge ruled against him. "Suspicion is not proof," the judge said.

The Lesson: Seeing something suspicious is only the first step. You must document your methodology, gather comparison evidence, research the signer's history, and build a complete record. Courts require proof, not hunches.

LEARN FROM THIS MISTAKE: The Homeowner Who Proved Forgery But the Court Wouldn't Listen

A Florida Homeowner's Story: When reviewing their foreclosure documents, this homeowner discovered something troubling. The notary — Julie M. — had checked the box stating that two signers were in her "physical presence" when they signed an assignment. The signers were supposedly a Vice President of MERS and a witness.

The homeowner followed the method in this chapter. They searched online for the Vice President of MERS and found something striking: dozens of documents with the exact same signature. Not similar — identical. Every loop, every pressure point, every angle was the same. Real handwriting has natural variation. These signatures were clearly copies, not original pen signatures.

"There would be no need for a copy if they were actually present during the signing," the homeowner reasoned. They dug deeper and found more documents bearing the witness's signature — again, suspiciously identical across multiple files. Confident they had found robo-signing and potential forgery, they brought the evidence to the court and the bank.

Both ignored it.

Undeterred, the homeowner hired three independent handwriting experts. All three concluded the same thing: the signatures were forged. The homeowner filed complaints with the state and the notary board. The investigation moved slowly, but eventually the notary board confirmed that Julie M. had violated state law. Her notary commission was revoked.

With this official determination in hand, the homeowner again presented the evidence to the court. Surely, with a revoked notary commission and three expert opinions, the court would act.

It did not.

The court proceeded with the foreclosure anyway, ignoring the documented fraud. The homeowner was pro se — representing themselves without an attorney — and encountered what many pro se litigants face: a court that simply would not engage with their evidence.

The Strategic Lesson: This story illustrates two critical truths about foreclosure litigation:

First, when you allege document fraud with supporting evidence, the burden of proof shifts. The bank cannot simply present a questionable document and expect the court to accept it. When a document's authenticity is challenged with credible evidence — comparison signatures, expert opinions, notary violations — the bank must prove the document is valid. If they cannot, and if the document is essential to their standing, the case should be dismissed for lack of standing.

Second, pro se bias is real. Some judges reflexively discount evidence presented by homeowners representing themselves. This is not fair, it is not legal, but it happens. The antidote is to make your presentation so thorough, so documented, so methodical that dismissing it would require the court to ignore black-letter law.

Tactical Recommendations:

1. **Build a record that cannot be ignored.** Three experts. Official notary board discipline. Side-by-side comparisons. A documented timeline showing geographic impossibilities. Make the fraud so obvious that ignoring it requires willful blindness.

2. **File motions that frame the issue properly.** Don't just "tell the court about the forgery." File a Motion to Strike Fraudulent Document. File a Motion to Dismiss for Lack of Standing. Use legal terms that trigger the court's obligations.

3. **Cite the burden shift explicitly.** In your motion, state clearly: "When a document essential to standing is shown to be fraudulent, the burden shifts to the plaintiff to prove authenticity. Plaintiff has failed to meet this burden."

4. **Consider appellate options early.** If the trial court ignores documented fraud, that may be appealable error. Consult with an appellate attorney about preserving the record for appeal.

5. **File bar complaints if necessary.** If the bank's attorney presented a document they knew or should have known was fraudulent, that may be a violation of professional ethics.

The Bottom Line: This homeowner did everything right. They found the fraud. They proved the fraud. They obtained official confirmation of the fraud. That the court ignored it says more about the court than about the homeowner's case. In a properly functioning judicial system, documented fraud with expert confirmation and notary discipline ends the case. Keep fighting. Keep documenting. Keep building the record. Justice delayed is not justice denied if you preserve your right to appeal.

The Gold Mine Method: How to Find Forged and Robo-Signed Documents

This is the method that wins cases. It takes work, but it works.

Step 1: Gather Every Document

You need **every document** that has a signature:

From your loan file: - The original promissory note (front and back) - The mortgage or deed of trust - Any loan modifications - Any forbearance agreements

From county records: - Every assignment of mortgage - Any substitution of trustee - Any release documents

From the foreclosure case: - The complaint and exhibits - Any affidavits filed - Any assignment attached to the complaint - Proof of claim (if bankruptcy)

Key Rule: Get certified copies from the county when possible. If you challenge a document's authenticity, you'll need the best evidence available.

Step 2: Create Your Signature Log

For every document, record:

Document	Signer Name	Title	Company	Date	Notary
Assignment 6/15/08	Jane Smith	VP	ABC Bank	6/15/08	John Doe
Assignment 9/22/09	Jane Smith	Asst. Sec.	XYZ Trust	9/22/09	Mary Jones
Assignment 3/10/10	Jane Smith	VP	DEF Servicing	3/10/10	John Doe

Notice what this reveals: The same person — Jane Smith — appears with three different titles at three different companies over two years. Is that possible? Maybe. Is it suspicious? Absolutely.

Step 3: The Google Investigation Method

Here's where the real investigation begins.

For every unique signer name, search:

Search Pattern 1: Name + Company

```
"Jane Smith" "ABC Bank" mortgage assignment
```

Search Pattern 2: Name + Robo-signer

```
"Jane Smith" robo-signer foreclosure
```

Search Pattern 3: Name + Deposition

```
"Jane Smith" deposition foreclosure testimony
```

Search Pattern 4: Name + Lawsuit

```
"Jane Smith" forgery lawsuit mortgage
```

What you're looking for: - Deposition transcripts where the signer admits to robo-signing - News articles about document fraud - Court opinions mentioning the signer's name - Class action lawsuits involving the signer - Regulatory enforcement actions

Real Example: A homeowner in Florida searched the name "Crystal Moore" — one of the signers on their assignment. They found a deposition transcript where Moore admitted she signed 1,000 documents per day, had no idea what they said, and didn't even know who she supposedly worked for. That deposition became evidence in their case.

Step 4: The Signature Comparison System

Now comes the critical work — comparing signatures. This is where homeowners find the evidence that wins cases.

The Six-Point Signature Analysis:

When comparing signatures, examine these specific elements:

1. Overall Shape and Proportion - Is the signature tall and narrow, or short and wide? - Does it slant to the left or right? - Are the letters connected or printed separately? - Compare the overall "silhouette" of the signature

2. Specific Letter Formation - How does the person form their first initial? - Is the last name written clearly or as a scribble? - Are there distinctive loops or flourishes? - Do capital letters have a particular style?

3. Starting and Ending Strokes - Where does the pen first touch the paper? - Does the signature end with a tail, dot, or abrupt stop? - Are there initial or final marks that are distinctive?

4. Pressure and Line Quality - Real pen signatures show pressure variation (thick and thin lines) - Stamped or printed signatures are uniformly thick - Ballpoint pens leave distinct pressure marks - Gel pens create consistent line width

5. Speed Indicators - Fast signatures show connected, flowing strokes - Slow signatures may have pauses and retracing - Shaky lines suggest the person was writing slowly or carefully - Smooth curves suggest natural writing speed

6. Natural Variation Test - Have the person sign their name three times right now - Compare those three signatures to each other - Real handwriting has natural variation - If two "signatures" are identical, one is likely a stamp or copy

Tools for Comparison: - **Scanner method:** Scan at high resolution, print at same size, overlay on light table - **Digital method:** Take photos with same lighting, zoom to same magnification, flip between images - **Tracing method:** Trace one signature onto tracing paper, lay over the other - **Grid method:** Draw a grid over each signature, compare cell by cell

Documenting Your Findings: For each comparison, create a worksheet showing: - Document 1 information (type, date, recorder) - Document 2 information (type, date, recorder) - Side-by-side images at same scale - Your observations about differences or similarities - Your conclusion (natural variation vs. likely forgery)

Step 5: The Notary Box — Your Secret Weapon

This is where homeowners win cases. Every notarized document has a notary acknowledgment section. Look closely at this section — it contains a gold mine of information.

Understanding Notary Acknowledgments:

A notary acknowledgment is a sworn statement by a notary public that: 1. The signer appeared before them (in person or through identification) 2. The signer was who they claimed to be 3. The signer signed the document willingly

There are different types of notarizations, and the type matters legally:

Acknowledgment: The signer acknowledges they signed the document. The notary verifies identity.

Jurat: The signer swears or affirms the document's contents are true. The notary administers an oath.

Copy Certification: The notary certifies a copy is true and complete (not available in all states).

The Critical Language to Look For:

Most notary forms include language like:

> "The foregoing instrument was acknowledged before me this ____ day of ***, 20***, by ***, who is personally known to me or who produced*** as identification."

Or:

> "Sworn to and subscribed before me this ____ day of ***, 20***, by ____, who is personally known to me or satisfactorily proven."

The Key Box or Checkbox:

Many notary forms have checkboxes or fill-in lines indicating: - Personally known to me - Identified by satisfactory evidence - Personally appeared before me

Or variations indicating whether the notary: - Witnessed the actual signing (in the notary's presence) - Acknowledged the signature (already signed, but identity verified)

Here's the Key: If the box or language indicates the signer "personally appeared" before the notary or that the notary "witnessed" the signing, but you find the same signature on multiple documents notarized on the same day in different locations — you have proof of notary fraud.

Real Example: A homeowner found five assignments, all signed by the same person, all notarized on the same day. The notary acknowledgments claimed the signer "personally appeared" before the notary for each one. But the documents were recorded in five different counties — a physical impossibility. The homeowner got the assignments voided and the case dismissed.

How to Research Notaries:

For each notary on your documents:

1. **Verify the Commission**
   - Search your state's notary database
   - Check if the commission was active on the document date
   - Verify the notary's name and commission number match
2. **Check for Disciplinary Actions**
   - Search the notary's name + "disciplinary action" + your state
   - Look for revocation, suspension, or fines
   - Check if the action occurred before or after your document date
3. **Look for Geographic Impossibilities**
   - Map the locations of all notarizations by the same notary on the same day
   - Calculate driving time between locations
   - Check if the distances are physically possible
4. **Compare Notary Stamps**
   - Are the stamps consistent across documents?
   - Does the seal look photocopied or printed?
   - Are the commission expiration dates consistent?

Step 6: Build Your Evidence File

Once you've found suspicious signatures, organize your proof:

Evidence Checklist: - [ ] High-resolution copies of all questioned signatures - [ ] Comparison signatures from other documents - [ ] Google search results showing signer's history - [ ] Deposition transcripts or court opinions mentioning the signer - [ ] Notary acknowledgment details with inconsistencies highlighted - [ ] Timeline showing impossible signing locations - [ ] Affidavit explaining your methodology (for court)

LEARN FROM THIS MISTAKE: The Notary Detail That Was Missed

> **Rachel Kim's Story:** Rachel found suspicious signatures on three of her assignments. The same person had signed all three — and the signatures looked identical. She was excited. She took her findings to an attorney.
>
> The attorney asked: "Did the notary acknowledgments say the signer personally appeared?"
>
> Rachel didn't know. She hadn't looked at the notary section — she was focused on the signatures. When she went back and checked, she found that two of the three notaries had checked the box saying the signer "personally appeared." The third had checked "personally known to me."
>
> The attorney explained: "If the notary claims the signer personally appeared, but you can prove the signer was somewhere else that day, you have notary fraud. But you need to check every box, every detail. The notary section is as important as the signature."
>
> Rachel went back, researched the notaries, and found that one notary had been disciplined by the state for notarizing without witnesses. Another had a revoked commission at the time of the alleged acknowledgment. The case settled favorably.
>
> **The Lesson:** The notary acknowledgment is evidence. Check every box. Compare notary stamps for consistency. Research notary commissions. A forged signature combined with a false notarization is a powerful combination.

Known Robo-Signer Databases

You don't have to start from scratch. Many robo-signers have been identified and documented:

Where to Search:

1. **Foreclosure Defense Forums**
    - Living Lies (livinglies.wordpress.com)
    - Foreclosure Hamlet forums
    - State-specific foreclosure defense groups
2. **Court Records**
    - Search your county clerk's office for other cases
    - Look for deposition transcripts in foreclosure cases
    - Search PACER (federal court) for class actions
3. **Regulatory Actions**
    - OCC (Office of Comptroller of the Currency) consent orders
    - State Attorney General enforcement actions
    - CFPB (Consumer Financial Protection Bureau) actions
4. **News Archives**
    - 2010-2012 robo-signing scandal coverage
    - Specific bank document fraud investigations

Famous Robo-Signer Names (Examples): - **Jeffrey Stephan** (GMAC/Ally) — Admitted signing 10,000 documents per month - **Crystal Moore** — Multiple servicers, deposition admission - **Bryan Bly** — DocX/LPS scandal - **Linda Green** — DocX forgery ring (40+ document variations)

Important: Names change. People get married. Companies reassign titles. Always verify the full context.

The Notary Fraud Checklist

Notaries are supposed to be neutral witnesses. When they're not, the document is void.

Red Flags in Notary Acknowledgments:

Commission Issues: - [ ] Notary commission was expired when document was notarized - [ ] Notary is from a different state than the signing location - [ ] Notary commission number doesn't exist in state records

Geographic Impossibilities: - [ ] Same notary on multiple documents the same day in different cities - [ ] Notary claims signer "personally appeared" but was in another state - [ ] Document dated on a weekend or holiday when offices were closed

Stamp and Seal Issues: - [ ] Notary stamp looks photocopied or printed rather than stamped - [ ] Notary seal is missing required elements - [ ] Different notary stamps on documents from the same notary

Acknowledgment Problems: - [ ] Box checked "personally appeared" but signature is stamped - [ ] Notary signature is different on different documents - [ ] Date of notarization is after the document date

---

When to Hire a Handwriting Expert

Sometimes you need professional help. Consider a handwriting expert when:

- The signatures look suspicious but you can't articulate why
- The bank is challenging your forgery claims
- You're going to summary judgment and need expert testimony
- The amount at stake justifies the cost ($2,000-$5,000)

What an expert can do: - Provide a scientific comparison of signatures - Identify cut-and-paste forgeries - Detect stamped vs. hand-written signatures - Testify in court about their findings

Finding an expert: - Search "forensic document examiner" + your state - Look for certification by the American Board of Forensic Document Examiners - Ask for sample reports and fee schedules

---

LEARN FROM THIS MISTAKE: The Handwriting Expert Who Wasn't Needed

> **Marcus Johnson's Story:** Marcus was convinced his documents were forged. He spent $3,500 on a handwriting expert who prepared a detailed report showing the signatures were "likely stamped rather than hand-signed."
>
> At summary judgment, the bank's attorney moved to strike the expert report. The judge asked Marcus: "Sir, have you reviewed the documents yourself?"
>
> Marcus admitted he hadn't — he went straight to the expert. The judge continued the hearing and told Marcus to come back with his own observations.
>
> Marcus went home, followed the method in this chapter, and found that the signer was a known robo-signer with a deposition transcript admitting to signing without review. He also found that the notary had a revoked commission. His own research — which cost nothing — was more powerful than the $3,500 expert report.

"The expert would have been useful if the bank challenged my observations," Marcus says. "But I should have done my own homework first. The expert was icing, not cake."

The Lesson: Do your own investigation first. Use the Google method. Compare signatures yourself. Research the signer's history. Build your own evidence file. An expert can strengthen your case, but you should be able to articulate the problems yourself first.

Litigating Forgery Issues

Once you've found document fraud, you need to use it effectively.

In Discovery:

Request these documents: - The original document (not a copy) - The signer's employment records - The notary's journal entries - All other documents signed by the same person - Training materials for document signers

Deposition questions for robo-signers: - "How many documents did you sign on [date]?" - "Did you read this document before signing it?" - "What is the borrower's name on this document?" - "What company did you work for when you signed this?" - "Did you sign this in the presence of the notary?"

In Motion Practice:

Standing Challenge: If the assignment is forged or void, the bank may lack standing to foreclose. File a motion to dismiss for lack of standing.

Summary Judgment Opposition: Forgery creates a disputed material fact. Summary judgment should be denied.

Motion to Strike: Ask the court to strike fraudulent documents from the record.

Sanctions Motion: In egregious cases, request sanctions against the bank or their attorneys for presenting fraudulent documents.

At Trial:

Your Testimony: Explain your methodology. Show the side-by-side comparisons. Present the Google search results. Walk through the timeline.

Cross-Examination: If the bank produces a witness about the documents, ask about: - Their personal knowledge of the signing - The signer's authority - The notary's presence - Other documents signed the same day

---

Chapter Summary

- **Document fraud is common.** The robo-signing scandal wasn't a few bad apples — it was industry practice.
- **Use the Gold Mine Method:**
  1. Gather every document
  2. Create a signature log
  3. Google every signer name + company
  4. Compare signatures systematically
  5. Check the notary acknowledgment boxes
  6. Build an evidence file
- **The notary section matters.** If it says "personally appeared" but the signer was elsewhere, you have proof of fraud.
- **Research beats suspicion.** Don't just think something looks wrong — prove it with comparison documents and public records.
- **Do your own work first.** An expert can help, but you should be able to articulate the problems yourself.
- **Forgery voids documents.** A forged assignment breaks the chain of title. A broken chain may mean no standing to foreclose.

Cross-References

Previous Chapter: Chapter 4 — The Homeowner's Mortgage Document Audit System

Next Chapter: Chapter 6 — Assignments, Endorsements, Allonges, and the Chain Problem

Related Chapters: - Chapter 7: Note and Mortgage/Deed Separation - Chapter 15: Attacking Affidavits - Chapter 16: Surviving Summary Judgment - Chapter 33: Building Your Evidence File and Timeline

In the Playbook: - Signature Comparison Worksheet - Notary Red Flags Checklist - Robo-Signer Research Log - Evidence Organization Template

Templates: - Document Request Letter (signer employment records) - Robo-Signer Deposition Questions - Forgery Challenge Motion (Sample)

CHAPTER 6: ASSIGNMENTS, ENDORSEMENTS, ALLONGES, AND THE CHAIN PROBLEM

How Broken Chains Destroy Standing

Why the Chain Matters

Imagine someone walks into court and says, "You owe me $100,000." You ask, "Who are you?" They reply, "I'm the assignee of the assignee of the original lender."

Your next question should be: **"Prove it."**

In foreclosure, the bank must prove they have the right to collect your debt. That right comes from a chain of transfers — a paper trail showing how the loan moved from the original lender to the party now trying to foreclose.

If that chain is broken — missing a link, defective, or improperly timed — the bank may have no standing to be in court at all.

This chapter explains the chain of title, how loans are transferred, and how to spot the breaks that win cases.

How Mortgages Are Transferred: The Two-Track System

To understand chain of title, you need to understand that mortgages and notes transfer differently.

The Note (Debt)

The **promissory note** is a negotiable instrument — like a check. Under the Uniform Commercial Code (UCC Article 3), notes transfer by **endorsement**.

Endorsement means: The current holder signs the back of the note, transferring it to someone else.

Think of it like endorsing a check: "Pay to the order of [New Bank], signed [Old Bank]."

The Mortgage (Security)

The **mortgage** (or deed of trust) is the security interest in your property. It gives the lender the right to foreclose if you don't pay.

Mortgages transfer by **assignment** — a separate document recorded in county land records.

The Critical Rule: The Mortgage Follows the Note

In most states, the mortgage is an accessory to the note. Transfer the note, and the mortgage transfers automatically — even if no assignment is ever recorded.

This is why the note is king. If the bank can't prove they hold the note (or have the right to enforce it), they can't foreclose — even if they have a recorded mortgage assignment.

LEARN FROM THIS MISTAKE: The Homeowner Who Focused on the Wrong Document

> **Angela Foster's Story:** Angela received a foreclosure complaint from a bank she'd never heard of. She went to the county recorder's office and pulled every document related to her mortgage.> She found three assignments: - Original Lender → Bank A (recorded 2007) - Bank A → MERS (recorded 2008) - MERS → The Bank Suing Her (recorded 2010)> > "The chain looks complete," Angela thought. She didn't challenge standing.> > At summary judgment, the bank produced a copy of the note. Angela's attorney (she'd hired one by then) asked to see the original. The bank couldn't produce it. They had a "lost note affidavit" instead.> > The attorney then asked: "Where are the endorsements showing how the note transferred from Original Lender to Bank A to MERS to you?"> > There weren't any. The bank had recorded mortgage assignments, but the note — the actual debt instrument — had never been properly endorsed through the chain.> > The case settled favorably. "I almost lost my house because I thought the assignments were enough," Angela says. "I didn't understand that the mortgage assignments and the note endorsements are two different things. The note is what matters most."> > **The Lesson:** The mortgage assignment shows who holds the security interest. The note endorsement shows who holds the debt. Both matter, but the note is primary. A complete chain of mortgage assignments with no note endorsements is a broken chain.

Assignments of Mortgage

An **assignment of mortgage** is a document that transfers the mortgage (the security interest) from one party to another.

What an Assignment Should Contain:

- **Assignor:** The party transferring the mortgage (must be the current holder)
- **Assignee:** The party receiving the mortgage
- **Property Description:** The legal description of your property
- **Reference to Original Mortgage:** Recording date, book/page, or instrument number
- **Execution:** Signed by authorized representative of assignor
- **Notarization:** Acknowledged before a notary
- **Recording:** Filed with county recorder (creates public notice)

Critical Timing Issues

Assignment Before Foreclosure: The assignment must transfer the mortgage BEFORE the foreclosure is filed. An assignment dated after the complaint is filed is a fatal defect — the bank didn't own the mortgage when they sued you.

The Ibanez Problem: In *US Bank v. Ibanez* (2011), the Massachusetts Supreme Court held that assignments must be properly executed and recorded before foreclosure. Assignments backdated or recorded after foreclosure began were void.

Common Assignment Defects

Defect	Why It Matters
Assignment after foreclosure filed	Bank didn't own loan when they sued — no standing
Assignment by unauthorized party	MERS or servicer assigning without proper authority
Missing assignment in chain	Gap in ownership — who owned the loan between transfers?
Backdated assignment	Fraudulent document to cover timing problem
Assignment to non-existent entity	Transfer to a trust or company that didn't exist yet
Unrecorded assignment	May affect notice, though mortgage follows note
Assignment without consideration	Transfer without payment may be voidable
Assignment by dissolved company	Company no longer existed to transfer the mortgage
Assignment in blank	No named assignee — who actually received the mortgage?

Assignment Without Consideration: An assignment is a contract. Like any contract, it requires consideration (something of value exchanged). If a mortgage was assigned for no consideration — just transferred without payment — the assignment may be voidable. Banks rarely disclose the purchase price in assignments, but discovery may reveal whether actual consideration was paid.

Assignment by Dissolved Company: If the assignor (the party transferring the mortgage) had been dissolved as a corporation or was in bankruptcy when the assignment was executed, they lacked legal capacity to transfer the mortgage. This is a fatal defect in the chain.

Assignment in Blank: Some assignments are executed "in blank" — the assignor signs the assignment but leaves the assignee name blank, to be filled in later. This creates uncertainty about when the transfer actually occurred and to whom. It may also violate recording statutes that require identified grantees.

Endorsements and the Note

The **endorsement** is how the note (the actual debt) transfers. This is governed by UCC Article 3.

Types of Endorsements

Special Endorsement: "Pay to the order of [Specific Bank], signed [Current Holder]"

This names the specific transferee. Only that named party can enforce the note.

Blank Endorsement: "Signed [Current Holder]" (no named transferee)

This makes the note "bearer paper" — whoever holds it can enforce it. Like cash: possess the note, possess the right to payment.

Restrictive Endorsement: "Pay to [Bank] for deposit only, signed [Current Holder]"

Limits what the transferee can do with the note.

Where Endorsements Appear

On the Note Itself: Endorsements typically appear on the back of the note (like the back of a check). Look for: - Signature of endorser - Name of endorsee (if special endorsement) - Date of endorsement - Corporate title of signer (VP, Assistant Secretary, etc.)

Why the Back of the Note Matters: UCC Article 3 requires endorsements to be on the instrument itself or on an allonge. Endorsements on separate, unattached documents are generally ineffective. When reviewing your note, flip it over — the back may contain the entire chain of ownership.

What to Look For on the Note: - **Stamps vs. Signatures:** Some endorsements are stamped rather than signed. Stamped endorsements are valid if authorized, but they're harder to verify. - **Multiple Endorsements:** Each transfer should have its own endorsement. A note with 10 transfers should have 10 endorsements. - **Out-of-Order Endorsements:** Endorsements should follow chronological order. An endorsement dated 2010 shouldn't appear before one dated 2008. - **Corporate Resolution:** If a corporation endorsed, was the signer authorized? Look for title consistency across documents.

LEARN FROM THIS MISTAKE: The Homeowner Who Didn't Understand Blank Endorsements

> **Linda Martinez's Story:** Linda's foreclosure case seemed straightforward. The bank produced the original note at trial — a powerful piece of evidence. On the back was a single signature with no name filled in. "That's a blank endorsement," the bank's attorney explained. "That makes this bearer paper. We hold the note, so we're the holder. Case closed."
>
> Linda didn't know what a blank endorsement was or why it mattered. She didn't challenge the bank's explanation. The court entered judgment for the bank.
>
> What Linda didn't understand: - A blank endorsement means the note became "bearer paper" — like cash, whoever holds it can enforce it - But that also means the note could have passed through many hands without documentation - The bank had to prove they were the rightful possessor, not just the current possessor - She could have demanded the chain of possession: "When did you receive this note? From whom? Show me the transfer documents." - She could have challenged whether the blank endorsement was even authorized by the prior holder
>
> "I thought producing the note was enough," Linda says. "I didn't know that a blank endorsement actually creates problems for the bank, not solutions. It means they have to prove how they got it."
>
> **The Lesson:** A blank endorsement doesn't end the inquiry — it begins it. When a bank produces a blank-endorsed note, they're admitting they can't show

a specific transfer to them. Demand the chain of possession. Question how they obtained the note. Investigate whether the blank endorsement was properly authorized.

The Allonge: What It Is and Why It Matters

An **allonge** is a piece of paper attached to the note containing endorsements.

Legal Requirements for Allonges

Physical Attachment: The allonge must be "permanently affixed" to the note. This typically means: - Stapled (not just paper-clipped) - Glued or taped - Part of the same physical document

Why This Matters: If an allonge becomes separated from the note, the endorsements on it may be invalid. A detached allonge is just a piece of paper.

The "Room on the Note" Rule: An allonge should only be used when there's no room left on the note itself for endorsements. If the note has plenty of blank space but endorsements appear only on an allonge, that's suspicious.

Red Flags with Allonges

Red Flag	Significance
Allonge paper-clipped, not stapled	Not "permanently affixed" — endorsement may be invalid
Blank endorsement on allonge	Bearer status created without proper chain
Allonge added after the fact	Endorsement may not reflect actual transfer timing
Multiple allonges	Complex chain — each transfer needs scrutiny
Allonge with no note	Can't verify attachment or authenticity

Blank Endorsements and Bearer Status

A **blank endorsement** (just a signature, no named transferee) converts the note to **bearer paper**.

What Bearer Status Means

With bearer paper, possession is ten-tenths of the law. Whoever physically holds the note can enforce it — even if they can't prove how they got it.

The Bank's Argument: "We have the note with a blank endorsement. That makes us the holder. We can enforce it."

Your Counter-Argument: "Yes, you have a note with a blank endorsement. But how do I know you're the rightful holder? Show me the chain of possession. When did the prior holder endorse it to you? Who had it before that?"

The Problem with Blank Endorsements

Blank endorsements make it easy for the wrong party to enforce a note. If a note is stolen, lost, or improperly transferred, a blank endorsement means the possessor can claim enforcement rights.

Strategic Approach: - Demand proof of the chain of possession - Challenge whether the endorsement was authorized - Question when and how the blank endorsement was created - Investigate whether the endorser had authority to create bearer paper

---

Identifying Chain Breaks

A **chain break** is a gap or defect in the transfer of the note or mortgage that prevents the foreclosing party from proving they have the right to enforce.

The Complete Chain Test

For a bank to have standing, they should be able to show:

For the Note (Endorsement Chain): 1. Original Lender → First Endorsee (by endorsement) 2. First Endorsee → Second Endorsee (by endorsement) 3. Continue through each transfer... 4. Last Endorsee → The Bank Suing You (by endorsement)

For the Mortgage (Assignment Chain): 1. Original Lender → First Assignee (by assignment) 2. First Assignee → Second Assignee (by assignment) 3. Continue through each transfer... 4. Last Assignee → The Bank Suing You (by assignment)

Common Chain Breaks

Missing Link: Original Lender → Bank A ( )
Bank A → ??? (Missing)

??? → Bank C ( )

Who owned the loan between Bank A and Bank C? If no one can prove it, the chain is broken.

Timing Gap: Original Lender transfers to Bank A in 2007
Bank A transfers to Bank C in 2010
But foreclosure was filed in 2009 by Bank C

Bank C didn't own the loan when they sued.

Defective Transfer: An assignment signed by someone without authority, a robo-signed endorsement, or a fraudulent document anywhere in the chain breaks everything downstream.

MERS Break: MERS (Mortgage Electronic Registration Systems) is listed as "nominee" for the lender on millions of mortgages. But MERS cannot transfer notes — only mortgages. If the chain goes through MERS for the note endorsement, that's a break.

LEARN FROM THIS MISTAKE: The Backdated Assignment That Wasn't Caught

Robert Chen's Story: Robert's foreclosure complaint was filed on March 15, 2010 by "ABC Trust, Wells Fargo Bank as Trustee." When he reviewed his documents, he found an assignment of mortgage dated March 20, 2010 — five days AFTER the foreclosure was filed.> > Robert thought he'd found a smoking gun. "They assigned the mortgage after they sued me!" he told the court.> > But the bank produced an affidavit from a vice president swearing that the assignment was "inadvertently misdated" and that the actual transfer happened in 2008. The affidavit explained that the document was just "correcting the record."> > Robert didn't know how to challenge this. He didn't have the resources to prove the affidavit was false. The court accepted the bank's explanation and allowed the foreclosure to proceed.> > What Robert didn't do:> - Research whether ABC Trust even existed in 2008 (it was created in 2009) - Check if the assignor (the prior "holder") had any record of owning the loan in 2008 - Look for other documents with the same signer's signature to show robo-signing - Demand the PSA (Pooling and Servicing Agreement) showing the trust's closing date - File a motion challenging the affidavit as self-serving and insufficient to cure the defect > **The Lesson:** A backdated or late assignment is strong evidence of a problem — but banks will try to explain it away with affidavits. You must be prepared to challenge those affidavits with independent evidence. An affidavit is just a statement; documentary evidence (trust creation dates, SEC filings, other signatures) is harder to dismiss.

MERS and the Assignment Problem

MERS (Mortgage Electronic Registration Systems) is a private corporation that appears on millions of mortgages as the "nominee" for the lender.

What MERS Is (Supposed to Be)

MERS was created to avoid recording assignments every time loans were sold. Instead of recording each transfer, MERS stays on the mortgage as "nominee" while the note changes hands behind the scenes.

What MERS Cannot Do

MERS does not hold notes. MERS is named only on mortgages, not notes. This is critical because:

- Only the note holder (or their agent) can enforce the debt
- MERS cannot transfer something it doesn't own
- MERS cannot enforce a note it doesn't hold

The MERS Assignment Problem

When MERS assigns a mortgage, several issues arise:

Authority Issues: MERS can only assign if the note holder authorizes it. If the note holder didn't authorize the assignment, MERS had no authority to transfer the mortgage.

Separation of Note and Mortgage: If MERS assigns the mortgage but the note wasn't transferred with it, the mortgage may become unenforceable (the mortgage follows the note).

Membership Requirements: MERS can only act for its members. If the note holder wasn't a MERS member at the time of assignment, MERS had no authority.

Challenging MERS Assignments

When you see MERS in your chain, investigate:

1. **Was the note holder a MERS member at the time of assignment?**
2. **Did MERS have specific authority from the note holder to make this assignment?**

3. **Was the note actually transferred along with the mortgage?**
4. **Can the foreclosing party prove they are the note holder?**

The MERS Membership Database: MERS maintains a list of its members, but membership changes over time. A company might have been a MERS member when the mortgage was originated but not when the assignment was made. Request proof of membership status on the assignment date.

The "MERS Can Assign" Myth: Banks often argue that MERS can assign mortgages because the mortgage says MERS is the "nominee" with the right to foreclose and assign. But being a nominee for foreclosure purposes doesn't automatically mean MERS can assign the mortgage to someone else. The specific language of your mortgage and MERS's membership agreements matter.

Landmark MERS Cases: Several courts have held that MERS cannot assign mortgages when it doesn't hold the note: - *In re Agard* (Bankr. E.D.N.Y. 2011) — MERS lacks standing to foreclose - *Bain v. Wells Fargo* (Wash. 2012) — MERS cannot assign the note it doesn't hold - *Jackson v. Mortgage Electronic Registration Systems* (Ala. 2012) — MERS has no interest in the note

---

Chain Breaks as Standing Defenses

When you find a chain break, you have a standing defense.

The Standing Argument

Basic Principle: A plaintiff must have a personal stake in the outcome. In foreclosure, that means they must own the debt (or have the right to enforce it).

Chain Break = No Standing: If the bank cannot prove an unbroken chain from the original lender to themselves, they cannot prove they own the debt. No ownership = no standing = case dismissed.

Raising the Defense

In Your Answer:

```
Defendant denies that Plaintiff has standing to bring this foreclosure action.
Plaintiff has failed to establish an unbroken chain of title from the original
lender and cannot prove they are the holder of the note or have the right to
enforce it.
```

In a Motion to Dismiss: File a motion arguing that the complaint fails to state a claim because the plaintiff lacks standing. Attach your chain analysis showing the break.

At Summary Judgment: If the bank moves for summary judgment, oppose it by showing disputed material facts about the chain of title. Summary judgment is inappropriate when ownership is disputed.

Evidence to Gather

- All assignments in the chain
- All endorsements/allonges
- The original note (or copy)
- SEC filings (for securitized loans)
- PSA (Pooling and Servicing Agreement)
- Trust creation documents
- MERS membership records

Chapter Summary

- **The note and mortgage transfer differently.** The note transfers by endorsement; the mortgage transfers by assignment. The note is primary.
- **The chain must be complete.** An unbroken chain from origination to the foreclosing party is required for standing.
- **Assignments must pre-date foreclosure.** An assignment after the complaint is filed is a fatal defect.
- **Blank endorsements create bearer status.** Possession of a blank-endorsed note gives enforcement rights, but you can challenge the chain of possession.
- **Allonges must be permanently affixed.** A detached allonge may mean invalid endorsements.
- **MERS cannot transfer notes.** MERS-only assignments may not transfer the debt, only the security.
- **Chain breaks are standing defenses.** If the bank can't prove an unbroken chain, they lack standing to foreclose.

Cross-References

Previous Chapter: Chapter 5 — Forgery, Robo-Signing, and Suspicious Signatures

Next Chapter: Chapter 7 — Note and Mortgage/Deed Separation

Related Chapters: - Chapter 4: Document Audit System (gathering chain documents) - Chapter 15: Attacking Affidavits - Chapter 16: Surviving Summary Judgment - Chapter 33: Building Your Evidence File

In the Playbook: - Chain-of-Title Tracker - Assignment Analysis Worksheet - Endorsement Checklist - MERS Investigation Guide

Templates: - Standing Challenge Motion - Chain-of-Title Affidavit - Document Request (SEC filings, PSA)

CHAPTER 7: NOTE AND MORTGAGE/DEED SEPARATION AND CLAIMED REUNIFICATION

Why Split Documents Kill Standing

The Note-Mortgage Relationship

To understand foreclosure defense, you must understand this fundamental rule: **The mortgage follows the note.**

Think of it this way: - The **note** is the promise to pay — the actual debt - The **mortgage** is the security — the right to take your house if you don't pay

The mortgage exists only to secure the note. Without the note, the mortgage is just a worthless piece of paper. As one court put it: "The mortgage is but an incident to the debt."

The Rule in Most States

In most jurisdictions (including Florida, New York, California, and most others), the mortgage is transferred automatically when the note is transferred. The mortgage holder and note holder should be the same entity.

This matters because: - If someone holds the mortgage but not the note, they cannot foreclose - If someone holds the note but not the mortgage, they can still enforce the debt, but foreclosure is more complicated - Separation of the two documents creates legal problems for the foreclosing party

The "Mortgage Follows the Note" Doctrine

This doctrine comes from common law and has been codified in many states. The logic is simple:

1. The mortgage secures the debt evidenced by the note
2. If you transfer the debt (the note), you transfer the security (the mortgage) with it
3. You cannot enforce the security without also having the right to enforce the debt

Practical Implication: When a bank buys your loan, they should receive both the note and the mortgage. If they only received the mortgage (documented by an assignment) but never received the note (documented by an endorsement), they may not be able to foreclose.

How Securitization Separates Documents

Securitization — the process of bundling loans into mortgage-backed securities — created unprecedented document chaos. During the mortgage boom of the 2000s, loans were bought, sold, bundled, sliced, and resold so many times that the paperwork couldn't keep up.

The Securitization Pipeline

Here's how a typical loan moved through the system:

Step 1: Origination - Local mortgage company originates loan to you - You sign note and mortgage - Note is made payable to Originator - Mortgage names Originator as lender

Step 2: First Sale - Originator sells loan to Investment Bank (often same day) - Note endorsed: "Pay to the order of Investment Bank" - Mortgage assigned to Investment Bank - Originator no longer owns the loan

Step 3: Deposit into Trust - Investment Bank deposits loan into a Trust (REMIC) - Note endorsed to Trust - Mortgage assigned to Trust or its nominee (often MERS) - Trust holds thousands of loans

Step 4: Securitization - Trust issues mortgage-backed securities - Investors buy certificates - Servicer collects payments and handles foreclosures - Trustee holds the notes and mortgages

Where Documents Get Lost

The Endorsement Problem: - Each transfer requires an endorsement on the note - With thousands of loans and rapid transfers, endorsements were skipped - Many notes entered trusts with no endorsements at all - Some were endorsed "in blank" (bearer paper) - Others had allonges attached later — sometimes improperly

The Assignment Problem: - Assignments were supposed to be recorded with each transfer - Recording fees are expensive, so banks skipped recordings - MERS was created to avoid recording — but MERS doesn't hold notes - When foreclosures began, banks had to fabricate assignment chains

The Separation Result: - The note went to the Trust (or its document custodian) - The mortgage stayed with MERS or was assigned to the servicer - The servicer handling the foreclosure didn't hold the note - The document custodian holding the note wasn't foreclosing

---

LEARN FROM THIS MISTAKE: The Homeowner Who Relied on Internet Securitization Theories

Kevin Parker's Story: Kevin read online that "if your loan was securitized, the bank can never foreclose because they sold the note to investors." He found his loan in a securitized trust on an MBS database and thought he had a slam-dunk defense.> > Kevin went to court and told the judge: "Your Honor, my loan was securitized. The bank doesn't own it anymore. They can't foreclose."> > The bank produced the original note with a blank endorsement. "We hold the note," the attorney said. "Securitization doesn't change that."> > The judge ruled for the bank. Kevin lost his house.> > What Kevin didn't understand: - Securitization transfers the note to a trust, but the trust can still enforce it - The servicer can foreclose on behalf of the trust if properly authorized - Holding the note (even with a blank endorsement) gives enforcement rights - Securitization creates complexity, but it doesn't automatically prevent foreclosure > "I thought I had a magic bullet," Kevin says. "But I didn't understand what I was arguing. I sounded like one of those 'sovereign citizen' people who claim the government has no authority. The judge dismissed me as a conspiracy theorist."> > **The Lesson:** Securitization defenses are real, but they must be understood and articulated properly. Blanket statements like "they securitized my loan so they can't foreclose" are legally incorrect and damage your credibility. The real issues are: whether the foreclosing party has authority from the note holder, whether the note was properly transferred into the trust, and whether the trust can prove ownership.

Why Separation Matters Legally

When the note and mortgage are held by different parties, several legal problems arise.

Problem 1: The Mortgage Holder Without the Note

If Party A holds the mortgage but Party B holds the note, Party A cannot foreclose. They have the security instrument but not the debt it secures.

Example: - MERS holds the mortgage as "nominee" - The Trust holds the note - MERS assigns the mortgage to the Servicer - Servicer tries to foreclose but doesn't hold the note

Result: Servicer has the mortgage but not the note. They cannot foreclose without the note or authorization from the note holder.

Problem 2: The Note Holder Without the Mortgage

If Party A holds the note but Party B holds the mortgage, Party A can enforce the debt but cannot foreclose on the property without the mortgage.

The Reunification Problem: Banks often claim they have "reunified" the note and mortgage — that is, they now hold both. But reunification isn't automatic. It requires: - A proper assignment of the mortgage to the note holder, OR - A proper endorsement of the note to the mortgage holder

If the assignment or endorsement is defective, the reunification is defective.

Problem 3: The Servicer Problem

Most foreclosures are brought by the **servicer** — the company that collects your payments. But the servicer usually doesn't hold the note or the mortgage. They hold a **servicing agreement** that gives them authority to foreclose on behalf of the owner.

This creates questions: - Does the servicing agreement actually authorize foreclosure? - Is the servicer properly representing the note holder? - Can the servicer prove they have authority from the note holder?

If the servicer cannot prove they are authorized to enforce the note, they lack standing.

Reunification Claims: Real and False

When confronted with note-mortgage separation, banks often claim the documents have been "reunified." Sometimes this is true. Often it is not.

What Reunification Requires

To properly reunify a separated note and mortgage:

Option A: Assign the Mortgage to the Note Holder - Current mortgage holder executes assignment to note holder - Assignment is properly signed, notarized, and recorded - Note holder now holds both documents

Option B: Endorse the Note to the Mortgage Holder - Current note holder endorses note to mortgage holder - Endorsement is on the note or a properly attached allonge - Mortgage holder now holds both documents

Option C: Both Transfer to a Common Holder - Both note and mortgage transfer to the same new party - Proper endorsements and assignments for both

How Banks Fake Reunification

The Backdated Assignment: - Servicer holding mortgage needs to show they have the note - They get an assignment from years ago, backdated to before foreclosure - The assignment wasn't actually executed until after the lawsuit began

The Lost Note Affidavit: - Bank claims the note is lost but they have the mortgage - They file an affidavit explaining the loss - But the circumstances of the loss are suspicious or undocumented

The Wrong Party Assignment: - Mortgage is assigned by MERS to the Servicer - But MERS didn't have authority because they never held the note - The assignment is a legal nullity

The After-the-Fact Allonge: - Note has no endorsements showing transfer to the Trust - Bank creates an allonge years later, attaches it to the note - The allonge was never part of the original transfer

Investigating Reunification Claims

When a bank claims reunification, verify:

1. Date of Reunification: - When was the assignment or endorsement executed? - When was it recorded (if an assignment)? - Was it before or after the foreclosure was filed?

2. Authority of Transferring Party: - Did the assignor actually hold the mortgage at the time of assignment? - Did the endorser actually hold the note at the time of endorsement? - Was the transferring party authorized to make the transfer?

3. Proper Execution: - Was the assignment properly signed and notarized? - Was the endorsement on the note or a properly attached allonge? - Are signatures authentic (not robo-signed)?

Investigating Securitization

If your loan was securitized, investigating the transfer into the trust can reveal standing defects.

Was Your Loan Securitized?

Signs of Securitization: - MERS appears on your mortgage - Your servicer has changed multiple times - Your loan was originated 2002-2008 (peak securitization years) - The foreclosing party is a trust (e.g., "ABC Trust 2006-1")

Where to Check: - SEC EDGAR database (if publicly filed) - MERS database (if MERS is involved) - Your loan documents for mentions of trusts or investors - Prospecting your county's foreclosure filings for similar trust names

The PSA: Your Most Important Document

The **Pooling and Servicing Agreement (PSA)** governs how loans are transferred into a securitized trust. It is the contract between the parties.

What the PSA Contains: - Cut-off date for loan transfers into the trust - Required documents for each loan - Transfer procedures and timing - Trustee and servicer duties - Representations and warranties about the loans

Why the PSA Matters: If your loan wasn't transferred into the trust according to the PSA requirements, it may not be in the trust at all. And if it's not in the trust, the trust cannot foreclose.

Critical PSA Provisions

The Cut-Off Date: Most PSAs specify a date by which all loans must be transferred into the trust. This is the **cut-off date** or **closing date**.

Example: - PSA for ABC Trust 2006-1 says loans must be transferred by March 31, 2006 - Your assignment to the Trust is dated April 15, 2006 - Your loan missed the cut-off - The Trust may not legally own your loan

The 90-Day Rule (REMIC Tax Status): For a trust to maintain its REMIC (Real Estate Mortgage Investment Conduit) tax status, loans generally must be transferred within 90 days of the trust's creation. A late transfer can have severe tax consequences for the trust — which is why trustees often deny that late transfers are valid.

Required Documents: PSAs typically require specific documents for each loan: - The original note (or a lost note affidavit with specific requirements) - The original mortgage or a certified copy - All assignments - Title insurance policy - Assignment and Assumption Agreement

If these documents weren't delivered, the transfer may be incomplete.

Representations and Warranties: PSAs contain promises made by the loan originator about the quality of loans. Common representations include: - The note and mortgage are genuine and enforceable - The mortgage is a valid first lien - The loan was originated in compliance with law - The loan documents were delivered to the trust

If these representations were false, the originator may have to buy back the loan — and the trust may not have proper standing to foreclose.

Transfer Procedures: PSAs specify how transfers must occur: - Endorsement requirements for notes - Assignment requirements for mortgages - Delivery to the document custodian - Recording requirements - Timeline for completing transfers

If these procedures weren't followed, the loan may not be properly in the trust.

How to Find the PSA

SEC EDGAR Database: Publicly filed PSAs are available at sec.gov/edgar. Search for: - The trust name (e.g., "ABC Mortgage Trust 2006-1") - The underwriter (investment bank) - The filing type "8-K" or "424B"

Private Placements: Not all trusts file with the SEC. Some are private placements. For these: - Request the PSA in discovery - Check court records for other cases involving the same trust - Search Bloomberg or other financial databases - Some PSAs have been posted online by foreclosure defense attorneys

What to Look For: Once you find the PSA, focus on: - The cut-off date for loan transfers - The required documents for each loan - The representations and warranties - The procedures for transferring loans - The servicing agreement provisions

---

LEARN FROM THIS MISTAKE: The Cut-Off Date That Was Ignored

Sandra Williams' Story: Sandra's loan was supposedly transferred into a securitized trust. The assignment was dated January 2007. At foreclosure, the bank produced the assignment and claimed the trust owned the loan.> > Sandra searched the SEC database and found the PSA for the trust. The PSA's cut-off date was December 31, 2006.> > "They transferred my loan three weeks after the trust closed," Sandra realized. She filed a motion to dismiss for lack of standing, arguing that the trust couldn't own a loan transferred after its closing date.> > The bank responded that the assignment date was a "clerical error" and produced an affidavit from a vice president swearing the loan was actually transferred in December 2006.> > Sandra didn't know how to challenge the affidavit. She didn't research whether the vice president actually worked for the company in 2006. She didn't check if the company had even existed in 2006. She just argued that the document said January, and the affidavit couldn't change that.> > The court accepted the bank's explanation. The foreclosure proceeded.> > What Sandra should have done:> - Researched the vice president's employment history - Checked if the assigning company existed and was active in December 2006 - Looked for other documents from the same signer to show robo-signing - Filed a motion to compel the original transfer documents - Argued that a self-serving affidavit cannot cure a facially defective assignment

The Lesson: Finding a cut-off date violation is powerful evidence, but banks will try to explain it away with affidavits. You must be prepared to challenge those affidavits with independent evidence. An affidavit is just a statement; documentary evidence (PSA terms, SEC filings, corporate records) is harder to dismiss.

Litigating Separation Issues

When you find note-mortgage separation, use it as a standing defense.

LEARN FROM THIS MISTAKE: The Servicer Who Couldn't Prove Authority

James Rodriguez's Story: James was in foreclosure with "XYZ Servicing" as the plaintiff. The complaint alleged that XYZ was the "servicer" for "ABC Trust" and was "authorized to enforce the note on behalf of the Trust."

James challenged standing: "You don't hold the note. You don't hold the mortgage. You're just a servicer. You can't foreclose."

The bank produced a servicing agreement. It said XYZ was "authorized to service the loans in the Trust." James didn't know how to challenge this.

At summary judgment, James argued: "The servicer doesn't own the loan. They can't foreclose."

The court ruled for the bank. "The servicer is authorized under the pooling and servicing agreement to bring foreclosure actions on behalf of the Trust," the judge wrote. "Standing is established."

What James didn't do: - Request the actual servicing agreement, not just a summary - Check if the servicing agreement specifically authorized foreclosure or just payment collection - Verify that the Trust actually held his loan (was it in the loan schedule?) - Challenge whether the servicer was properly representing the actual note holder - Argue that the servicer must prove the Trust actually owns the note, not just that they have a servicing agreement

"I was right that the servicer doesn't own the loan," James says. "But I didn't understand that servicers CAN foreclose if properly authorized. I needed to challenge whether the authorization was real and whether the Trust actually holds the note."

The Lesson: A servicer can foreclose on behalf of the note holder if properly authorized. But authorization is a factual question. Demand the servicing agreement. Verify the Trust holds your loan. Challenge whether the authorization extends to foreclosure. The servicer must prove the entire chain: they are authorized → by the Trust → which holds the note → which is properly endorsed.

How to Litigate Separation Issues

In Your Answer

Include a standing challenge based on separation:

```
Defendant denies that Plaintiff has standing to bring this foreclosure action.
Plaintiff has failed to establish that it holds both the note and mortgage, as
required to foreclose. The note and mortgage have been separated, and Plaintiff
cannot prove reunification according to law.
```

In Discovery

Request documents showing reunification: - All assignments of the mortgage - All endorsements of the note - The PSA governing the trust (if securitized) - The servicing agreement authorizing foreclosure - Delivery receipts for note transfer to the trust

At Summary Judgment

If the bank moves for summary judgment, oppose by showing disputed facts about: - Who holds the note - Who holds the mortgage - Whether proper reunification occurred - Whether the foreclosing party is authorized by the note holder

The Standing Burden

Remember: The bank must prove they have the right to foreclose. If they cannot produce the note, or if they cannot show proper assignment of the mortgage, they have not met their burden.

Chapter Summary

- **The mortgage follows the note.** In most states, you cannot foreclose without holding (or being authorized to enforce) the note.
- **Securitization created document chaos.** Rapid transfers, MERS, and shortcuts led to separated documents and incomplete chains.
- **Reunification requires proper transfer.** Just claiming the documents are reunified isn't enough — the bank must prove proper assignment or endorsement.
- **The PSA governs trust transfers.** Cut-off dates and document requirements in the PSA can reveal standing defects.
- **Internet theories can hurt you.** Blanket claims that "securitization prevents foreclosure" are legally wrong and damage credibility. Focus on specific, provable defects.
- **Separation is a standing defense.** If the foreclosing party cannot prove they hold or are authorized to enforce the note, they lack standing.

Cross-References

Previous Chapter: Chapter 6 — Assignments, Endorsements, Allonges, and the Chain Problem

Next Chapter: Chapter 8 — Consideration and Funding Issues

Related Chapters: - Chapter 4: Document Audit System - Chapter 5: Forgery, Robo-Signing, and Suspicious Signatures - Chapter 11: Motion to Dismiss (Standing) - Chapter 16: Surviving Summary Judgment

In the Playbook: - Securitization Investigation Checklist - PSA Research Guide - Reunification Verification Worksheet

Templates: - Standing Challenge Based on Note-Mortgage Separation - PSA Document Request - Cut-Off Date Violation Motion

CHAPTER 8: CONSIDERATION, ORIGINAL FUNDING, AND TRANSACTION LEGITIMACY

When the Original Loan Is the Problem

What Is Consideration?

At its simplest, **consideration** is what you give and what you get in a contract. In a mortgage loan: - The **lender** gives money (consideration) - The **borrower** gives a promise to repay plus the mortgage (consideration)

If either side doesn't give what they promised, the contract may be unenforceable or voidable.

Why Consideration Matters in Foreclosure

Most foreclosures assume the original loan was valid. The bank shows the note and mortgage and says: "You borrowed money. You promised to pay. You didn't. We get the house."

But what if the original transaction was defective? What if: - The lender never actually funded the loan? - The lender was just a straw party for someone else? - Required disclosures were never given? - The loan terms were illegally changed at closing?

These aren't just technicalities. They can be powerful defenses — if raised properly and timely.

The Table Funding Problem

Table funding occurs when the entity named as the lender on your loan documents (the "originator") didn't actually provide the money. Instead, a different entity — usually a large investment bank or warehouse lender — provided the funds.

Example: - You apply for a loan with "Friendly Mortgage Company" - Friendly Mortgage appears on your note and mortgage as the lender - But Friendly never used its own money - Instead, "Big Bank Warehouse Lending" wired the money to the closing - Friendly immediately assigned the loan to Big Bank

Why This Matters: 1. The note says you owe Friendly, but Friendly never gave you anything 2. The real lender (Big Bank) isn't on the documents 3. This creates questions about who has the right to enforce the note 4. Some courts have held that table funding violates consumer protection laws

Legal Theories Involving Consideration

Failure of Consideration: If the lender promised to give you $200,000 but only gave you $190,000 (keeping $10,000 in hidden fees), they failed to provide full consideration. This can be a defense to enforcement.

Straw Party Lender: If the named lender was just a front for another entity, the loan may be void or voidable. This is particularly true if the straw party didn't have the legal authority to make loans.

Holder in Due Course Status: When loans are sold, the buyer may claim "holder in due course" status — meaning they took the note in good faith and can enforce it even if there were problems with the original loan. But if the loan was table-funded, some courts have held that the subsequent buyer cannot be a holder in due course.

LEARN FROM THIS MISTAKE: The Homeowner Who Waited Too Long to Rescind

> **Michelle Torres' Story:** Michelle closed on her loan in March 2019. At closing, the loan officer rushed her through a stack of documents. "Just sign here, here, and here," he said. "We're running behind schedule."> > Two years later, struggling with payments, Michelle met with a foreclosure defense attorney who reviewed her closing documents. "You never got a proper TILA disclosure," the attorney said. "The APR was wrong, and they didn't give you the required cancellation notices. You might be able to rescind the loan."> > Michelle was thrilled. She filed a rescission notice with the bank and the court.> > The bank responded: "TILA rescission must be exercised within three years of closing. This loan closed in March 2019. The homeowner filed notice in April 2022. The deadline passed one month ago."> > Michelle argued that the bank's violations "toll" (extend) the statute of limitations. But TILA's three-year deadline is a "statute of repose" — it cannot be extended. Once three years pass, rescission is gone forever.> > "I didn't even know I had this right," Michelle says. "How was I supposed to exercise a right I didn't know existed?"> > **The Lesson:** TILA rescission is a powerful remedy, but it has a strict three-year deadline from closing. This is not a flexible deadline. If you suspect TILA violations, investigate immediately. Do not wait. The clock starts ticking at closing, not when you discover the violation. Some states may have additional consumer protection claims with different deadlines, but the federal TILA rescission right expires at three years — period.

Table Funding and Its Implications

Table funding became common during the mortgage boom of the 2000s. It allowed small mortgage brokers to originate loans without using their own capital. But it created legal problems that persist today.

How Table Funding Works

The Traditional Model: - Bank uses its own money to lend to you - Bank holds the loan on its books - Bank services the loan

The Table Funding Model: - Broker takes your application - Warehouse lender provides the money - Broker closes the loan in its own name - Broker immediately sells the loan to the warehouse lender or an investment bank - The loan may be sold multiple times before ending up in a securitized trust

Legal Problems with Table Funding

1. Consideration Failure The named lender didn't provide the money. If you promised to repay "Friendly Mortgage," but Friendly never gave you anything, did you receive consideration from Friendly? Some courts have held that this creates a defect in the loan.

2. Holder in Due Course Issues When a loan is sold, the buyer may try to claim "holder in due course" status, which protects them from certain defenses. But if the loan was table-funded, some courts have held that the buyer had "notice" of the problem and cannot be a holder in due course.

What Is Holder in Due Course? Under the Uniform Commercial Code (UCC), a "holder in due course" is someone who takes a negotiable instrument (like a promissory note): - For value (they paid for it) - In good faith - Without notice of any defenses or claims to the note

If a party is a holder in due course, they can enforce the note even if the borrower has defenses against the original lender (like fraud or failure of consideration).

The Table Funding Exception: Some courts have held that when a loan is table-funded, subsequent buyers have "inquiry notice" that something may be wrong. The buyer knows (or should know) that the originator didn't fund the loan, which creates questions about the transaction's validity. This notice may prevent holder in due course status.

Strategic Use: If the foreclosing party claims holder in due course status, argue that table funding gave them notice of the consideration defect, preventing that status.

3. Licensing Violations If the named lender wasn't actually providing the funds, they may have been operating as a "broker" rather than a "lender." If they weren't properly licensed as a broker, the loan may be void or voidable.

4. Predatory Lending Facilitation Table funding made it easier for predatory lenders to operate. They could originate loans, take the fees, and pass the risk to someone else. This separation of origination from risk contributed to the mortgage crisis.

Proving Table Funding

To investigate whether your loan was table-funded:

Check Your Closing Documents: - Look at the HUD-1 settlement statement - Who wired the money to the closing agent? - Was it the named lender or someone else?

Check the Chain of Title: - How quickly was the loan assigned after closing? - If the named lender assigned the loan within days (or even hours) of closing, that's evidence of table funding

Check for Warehouse Lender References: - Some documents may reference a "warehouse line of credit" - This indicates the originator was using someone else's money

Research the Originator: - Was the originator a small mortgage company that originated loans but didn't hold them? - Did they have the capital to make the loan themselves? - Are they still in business?

Predatory Lending Red Flags

Predatory lending involves abusive loan terms or practices that take advantage of borrowers. While predatory lending claims don't always stop foreclosure, they can provide defenses or counterclaims.

Common Predatory Lending Practices

1. Loan Flipping Repeatedly refinancing a loan to generate fees for the lender, not to benefit the borrower. Each refinance adds costs and often extends the repayment term.

Red Flags: - Multiple refinances within a short period - Each refinance adds little or no cash to the borrower - Fees consume most of the new loan amount - The lender initiated the refinance, not the borrower

2. Excessive Fees Charging fees that are excessive or hidden. These might include: - Origination fees over 2-3% of the loan amount - Yield spread premiums (payments to brokers for putting borrowers in higher-rate loans) - Prepayment penalties that trap borrowers

3. Steering Pushing borrowers into higher-cost loans when they qualified for better terms. This was common during the subprime boom — borrowers with good credit were put into subprime loans so lenders could charge higher rates.

Red Flags: - You had good credit but were given a high-rate loan - The lender discouraged you from applying for a prime loan - You were told "this is the only loan you qualify for" without proper verification

4. Asset-Based Lending Lending based on the value of the property, not the borrower's ability to repay. This led to loans where the monthly payment was clearly unaffordable.

Red Flags: - Income not verified or "stated income" loans - Debt-to-income ratio clearly unsustainable - Loan amount based on inflated appraisal - You were told "don't worry about the payment, you can refinance later"

5. Balloon Payments Loans with low initial payments that balloon into unaffordable payments later. Many borrowers were told they could refinance before the balloon, but when the time came, refinancing wasn't possible.

Red Flags: - Interest-only payments for the first few years - Large balloon payment due after 3, 5, or 7 years - Assumption that refinancing would be available - No plan for how to make the balloon payment

6. Packing Adding products to the loan that the borrower didn't request or need, such as credit insurance, extended warranties, or other add-ons.

Red Flags: - Charges for products you didn't request - Pressure to buy additional products - Refusal to remove unwanted products - Products that duplicate existing coverage

---

LEARN FROM THIS MISTAKE: The Borrower Who Focused on Origination Instead of Defense

David Chen's Story: David was certain his loan was predatory. The lender had steered him into a subprime loan despite his 720 credit score. The fees were excessive. The appraisal was inflated. He had evidence of all of it.> > When foreclosure started, David filed a massive counterclaim alleging predatory lending, RESPA violations, TILA violations, fraud, and negligent misrepresentation. He requested damages exceeding $500,000.> > The bank moved to dismiss his counterclaims. "These are stale claims," they argued. "The loan closed in 2007. The statute of limitations on these claims expired years ago."> > David argued that the bank's ongoing foreclosure was a "continuing violation" that kept the claims alive. The court disagreed. Most of David's counterclaims were dismissed as time-barred.> > What remained — the predatory lending claims — were insufficient to stop the foreclosure. The court ruled that even if the loan was predatory, David still owed the money. The proper remedy would have been a separate lawsuit for damages, not a defense to foreclosure.> > David spent months building his origination fraud case when he should have been challenging the bank's standing, demanding the original note, and investigating the chain of title. By the time he realized his mistake, the foreclosure was almost complete.> > **The Lesson:** Origination claims have short statutes of limitations and rarely stop foreclosure. While they may support counterclaims for damages, they should not be your primary foreclosure defense. The bank's standing, chain of title, and document defects are usually stronger defenses. Focus on what can stop the foreclosure now. Save origination claims for a separate lawsuit — if they're still timely.

TILA and RESPA Basics

The **Truth in Lending Act (TILA)** and **Real Estate Settlement Procedures Act (RESPA)** provide consumer protections for mortgage borrowers. Violations can create remedies — but deadlines are strict.

TILA — Truth in Lending Act

What TILA Requires: - Clear disclosure of loan terms before closing - Annual Percentage Rate (APR) calculation - Finance charge disclosure - Right to rescind certain loans (3-day right to cancel)

TILA Rescission: For certain refinances and home equity loans, TILA gives borrowers a **right to rescind** (cancel) the loan within three business days of closing. For some violations, this right extends to **three years**.

Common TILA Violations: - Failure to provide required disclosures - Inaccurate APR calculation - Failure to provide two copies of the right to rescind notice - Failure to identify the creditor properly

TILA Remedies: - Rescission (returning the borrower to pre-loan status) - Statutory damages ($4,000 or actual damages, whichever is greater) - Attorney fees - **Three-year deadline for rescission is absolute**

RESPA — Real Estate Settlement Procedures Act

What RESPA Requires: - Good Faith Estimate of closing costs within 3 days of application - HUD-1 settlement statement at closing - No kickbacks between lenders and settlement service providers - Limits on escrow account amounts

Common RESPA Violations: - Kickbacks (payments for referrals) - Markups of third-party charges - Failure to provide Good Faith Estimate - Excessive escrow accounts

RESPA Remedies: - Damages (three times the charge for kickbacks) - Attorney fees - **One-year statute of limitations for damages claims**

TILA-RESPA Integrated Disclosure (TRID)

In 2015, TILA and RESPA disclosures were combined into the **TRID** rules. Now borrowers receive: - **Loan Estimate** within 3 days of application (replaces Good Faith Estimate) - **Closing Disclosure** 3 days before closing (replaces final TILA disclosure and HUD-1)

TRID Violations: - Failure to provide Loan Estimate on time - Failure to provide Closing Disclosure 3 days before closing - Changes between Loan Estimate and Closing Disclosure exceeding tolerance limits

---

LEARN FROM THIS MISTAKE: The Table Funding That Nobody Investigated

> **Brian and Lisa Morrison's Story:** Brian and Lisa's loan was originated by "Hometown Mortgage," a small broker that went out of business in 2009. When foreclosure started in 2015, the plaintiff was a large national bank claiming to be the holder of the note.
>
> The note was endorsed in blank to bearer. The mortgage was assigned from Hometown Mortgage to the bank in 2015 — seven years after closing.
>
> Brian's attorney focused on the late assignment and robo-signed documents. These were good defenses. But nobody looked at the original funding.
>
> Years later, after the foreclosure was completed, Brian found his old closing file in storage. The HUD-1 settlement statement showed that the funds came from "Warehouse Lending Corp," not Hometown Mortgage. Hometown had never used its own money. The loan was table-funded from day one.
>
> "If we had proven table funding," Brian says, "we might have been able to challenge the bank's holder in due course status. The bank bought a loan that was

potentially defective from the start. They had notice of the table funding. They might not have been able to enforce it against us."

What the Morrisons didn't do: - Check the HUD-1 to see who actually wired the funds - Research whether Hometown Mortgage had the capital to fund loans - Argue that the bank had notice of table funding and couldn't be a holder in due course - Request documents about the warehouse lending relationship

"We challenged the documents," Lisa says. "But we never challenged the original transaction. We had a whole other layer of defense we never used."

The Lesson: Table funding isn't just a historical curiosity. It can affect the enforceability of the loan today. Always check who actually provided the funds at closing. If it wasn't the named lender, investigate further. Table funding may prevent the foreclosing party from claiming holder in due course status, and it may give you counterclaims against the originator or subsequent holders.

How to Raise Table Funding as a Defense

If you suspect table funding or origination fraud, here's how to investigate:

Step 1: Gather Closing Documents

Essential Documents: - Note and mortgage - HUD-1 settlement statement (or Closing Disclosure for loans after 2015) - Good Faith Estimate (or Loan Estimate for loans after 2015) - TILA disclosure statement - All closing receipts and wire transfer confirmations - Any correspondence with the originator

What to Look For: - Who wired the funds to closing? (Check line 303 of the HUD-1 or the payoffs on the Closing Disclosure) - Who is named as the lender on the note vs. who provided the money? - Are there references to warehouse lenders or table funding? - Does the note reflect the actual transaction, or was the named lender just a straw party?

Key Clues on the HUD-1: - Line 303 shows "Cash From (or to) Borrower" - Look for references to wire transfers - Check if the settlement agent received funds from someone other than the named lender - Look for fees paid to "warehouse lenders" or "funding sources"

Step 2: Research the Originator

Questions to Answer: - Was the originator a bank or a mortgage broker? - Did they have the capital to fund the loan themselves? - Are they still in business? - Were they properly licensed? - Have they been sued or investigated for predatory lending?

Where to Research: - State licensing databases - NMLS (Nationwide Multistate Licensing System) - CFPB complaint database - Court records for lawsuits against the originator

Step 3: Analyze the Chain

Timeline Questions: - When did the originator assign the loan? - Was it assigned immediately after closing? - Who has owned the loan since origination? - When was it securitized?

Step 4: Consult an Attorney About Deadlines

Critical Question: Are any origination claims still timely?

Common Statutes of Limitation: - TILA rescission: 3 years from closing (absolute) - TILA damages: 1 year from violation - RESPA damages: 1 year from violation - State fraud claims: 3-6 years (varies by state) - RICO claims: 4 years

Do Not Assume: Some violations may "toll" (pause) the statute of limitations, but TILA's three-year rescission deadline generally cannot be extended.

When to Raise These Issues

Origination claims should be raised strategically — and realistically.

When Origination Claims Help

1. As Counterclaims (If Timely) If your origination claims are still within the statute of limitations, file them as counterclaims. This may give you leverage in settlement negotiations.

2. To Challenge Holder in Due Course Status If the foreclosing party claims to be a "holder in due course," table funding and origination fraud may prevent that status.

3. As Part of a Broader Defense Strategy Origination issues can support other defenses — for example, if the originator is part of the chain of title and their conduct affects the validity of assignments.

4. In Bankruptcy In Chapter 13 bankruptcy, you may be able to challenge the secured status of the loan based on origination defects.

When Origination Claims Don't Help

1. After the Statute of Limitations Has Run Expired claims will be dismissed. Worse, they may make you look like you're grasping at straws.

2. As a Primary Foreclosure Defense Most courts will not stop a foreclosure based solely on origination claims. The foreclosure is about whether you defaulted on the loan. Origination claims are about whether the loan should have been made. These are separate issues.

3. When They Distract from Stronger Defenses If you have strong standing or chain-of-title defenses, don't get distracted by origination claims. Focus on what can actually stop the foreclosure.

Chapter Summary

- **Consideration** is what each party gives in a contract. If the named lender didn't provide the money, there may be a consideration defect.
- **Table funding** occurs when the named lender didn't actually fund the loan. This can create holder-in-due-course problems and may violate consumer protection laws.
- **Predatory lending** includes loan flipping, excessive fees, steering, and other abusive practices. These can support counterclaims but rarely stop foreclosure.
- **TILA and RESPA** provide disclosure requirements and remedies, but deadlines are strict. TILA rescission has a three-year deadline that cannot be extended.
- **Statutes of limitation** bar most origination claims after 1-6 years. Do not rely on stale claims as your primary defense.
- **Focus on what stops foreclosure.** Origination claims are usually weaker defenses than standing, chain of title, and document defects. Use origination claims strategically, not as your main hope.

Cross-References

Previous Chapter: Chapter 7 — Note and Mortgage/Deed Separation and Claimed Re-unification

Next Chapter: Chapter 9 — The First 72 Hours: Emergency Action Guide

Related Chapters: - Chapter 4: Document Audit System - Chapter 10: Affirmative Defenses and Counterclaims - Chapter 33: Evidence File — What to Gather and How to Organize It

In the Playbook: - TILA/RESPA Checklist - Predatory Lending Red Flags Worksheet - Origination Audit Guide - Statute of Limitations Reference by State

Templates: - TILA Rescission Notice - RESPA Qualified Written Request - Origination Investigation Demand

CHAPTER 9: YOU GOT SERVED: WHAT TO DO IN THE FIRST 72 HOURS

The Emergency Sprint That Saves Homes

Hour 0-4: Don't Panic, Do These 5 Things

You just got handed papers. Your heart is racing. Your hands are shaking. The person who served you is already gone. Now what?

Stop. Breathe. You have time — but not much.

The next 72 hours will determine whether you enter this fight with a chance to win or with both hands tied behind your back. Here's exactly what to do.

Thing 1: Secure the Documents (5 Minutes)

Do this immediately: 1. Put the papers somewhere safe — not in your car, not loose on a desk 2. Make copies: scan or photograph every page with your phone 3. Email the copies to yourself and a trusted contact 4. Store the originals in a folder labeled with today's date

Why this matters: These papers are evidence. If you lose them, you lose information about deadlines, claims against you, and potential defects in the case. originals matter if signatures or notarizations are challenged.

Thing 2: Find the Deadline (10 Minutes)

Somewhere in those papers is a date that controls everything. Find it.

Look for: - A "summons" — usually the first page - Language like "You have _____ days to respond" - A date by which you must "answer" or "appear" - Court date information

Common deadlines: - 20 days (Florida, many other states) - 30 days (New York, federal court, many others) - 21 days (some jurisdictions)

Critical rule: The deadline usually starts from the date you were served, not the date on the papers. Count carefully. Weekends and holidays may or may not count depending on your state's rules.

Write it down: Put this deadline on your calendar with three alerts — one week before, one day before, and the morning of the deadline.

Thing 3: Check Service for Defects (15 Minutes)

Service of process has rules. If the bank didn't follow them, the service may be defective. This could buy you time or even get the case dismissed.

Check these common defects:

Who served you? - Must typically be someone over 18 and not a party to the case - Some states require a sheriff or process server - A bank employee or attorney serving you personally may be improper

How were you served? - Personal service (handed to you) — usually proper - Substitute service (left with someone at home) — rules vary by state - Posting and mailing (taped to door) — usually only after attempts at personal service - Certified mail — may or may not be sufficient depending on jurisdiction

Where were you served? - Some states require service at your residence - Service at work may have specific requirements - Service in another state may be improper

When were you served? - Some states prohibit Sunday service - Service on holidays may be improper - Late-night service may violate rules

What you received: - Did you get the complete complaint with all exhibits? - Is the summons properly signed and stamped by the court? - Are the case number and court information complete? - Is there a certificate of service attached?

Document any defects immediately: If you find problems, photograph or video where and how service occurred. Write down exactly what happened while it's fresh in your memory. Note the exact time, date, location, and circumstances. Identify who served you if possible.

Challenging defective service: If you discover service defects, you may be able to file a motion to quash service or dismiss the case. However, this is often a temporary victory — the bank can usually serve you again properly. Use any time gained to prepare your defense, but don't assume a service defect ends the case permanently.

Strategic consideration: Sometimes it's better to accept service and fight the case on the merits rather than challenging service and delaying while the bank prepares a stronger case. Consult with an attorney about the best strategy for your situation.

Document any defects: If you find problems, photograph or video where and how service occurred. Write down exactly what happened while it's fresh in your memory.

Thing 4: Take a Photo of Your House (5 Minutes)

Walk outside. Take clear photos of: - The front of your house - The sides and back - Any damage or maintenance issues - The condition of landscaping, paint, roof

Why: If the bank gets a judgment, they may claim you damaged the property. Photos prove the condition now. Also, photos preserve your memory of your home if you ultimately have to leave.

Thing 5: Notify Your Team (10 Minutes)

You cannot do this alone. Contact:

Immediate family: Everyone who lives in the house needs to know. They may need to contribute to defense costs or prepare for possible outcomes.

A trusted advisor: This could be an attorney, a housing counselor, or a friend who has been through this. You need someone to help you think clearly.

Your support network: Let close friends or family know you're facing a legal situation. You may need emotional support, help with research, or someone to watch children while you attend court.

Do NOT contact the bank's attorney yet. We'll discuss why later in this chapter.

LEARN FROM THIS MISTAKE: The Homeowner Who Called the Bank's Attorney

> **Patricia Nelson's Story:** Patricia was terrified when she was served. She wanted to explain her situation, tell them she was trying to get a modification, ask for more time. She found the bank's attorney's phone number on the complaint and called.
>
> "I just got served," she said. "I want to work something out. Can we postpone this?"> The attorney was polite. "I understand," he said. "We don't want to take anyone's home. Let me look at your file." He put her on hold for five minutes.> When he came back, he said: "Mrs. Nelson, I've reviewed your account. You've been in default for eight months. The bank is not considering modification at this time. We need to proceed with foreclosure. However, if you voluntarily move out within 30 days, we can offer you $2,000 in relocation assistance."> Patricia felt defeated. She agreed to the 30-day move-out. She didn't realize she had just: - Acknowledged she was in default - Given up valuable time to prepare a defense - Missed her chance to challenge the bank's standing - Accepted a terrible deal ($2,000 is often much less than statutory relocation assistance)
>
> "I thought if I was nice, they'd be nice back," Patricia says. "But that attorney's

job is to get the foreclosure as fast as possible. My being cooperative just made his job easier.”> **The Lesson:** The bank’s attorney represents the bank, not you. Nothing you say to them will help your case. They will use anything you say against you. Do not call them. Do not answer their calls. Do not meet with them without your own attorney present. Your communications should be through formal legal documents — answers, motions, and discovery — not casual conversations.

LEARN FROM THIS MISTAKE: The Homeowner Who Missed the Deadline

Mark Johnson’s Story: Mark was served with foreclosure papers on a Friday evening. He read through them, saw he had 30 days to respond, and decided to deal with it “next week.” He put the papers in a drawer and went about his weekend.

Monday was busy at work. Tuesday his car broke down. Wednesday he had a doctor’s appointment. By the time he got back to the papers the following weekend, three weeks had passed. “I still have a week,” he thought.

But Mark didn’t understand that weekends and holidays might not count toward the deadline in his state. He also didn’t realize that “30 days” meant 30 calendar days from service, not 30 business days. When he finally tried to file his answer on day 30, the court clerk informed him the deadline had passed two days earlier.

The bank immediately moved for default judgment. Mark filed a motion to set aside the default, arguing he had made a good faith effort and was only two days late. The court denied his motion. “Deadlines are deadlines,” the judge said. “The defendant had 30 days and failed to act.”

Mark lost his home without ever having the chance to present a defense. He never got to challenge the bank’s standing. Never got to question the documents. Never got his day in court.

What Mark should have done: - Calendared the deadline immediately with multiple alerts - Started working on his response right away, even if just gathering documents - Requested an extension before the deadline if he needed more time - Consulted with an attorney during the first week, not the fourth

“I thought 30 days was plenty of time,” Mark says. “But time slips away. Life gets in the way. And in foreclosure, missing a deadline by one day is the same as missing it by 30 days."

The Lesson: The deadline is not a suggestion. It is a jurisdictional requirement. Miss it, and you lose. Act immediately. Calendar the deadline with multiple reminders. If you need more time, request an extension BEFORE the deadline, not after. Once the deadline passes, your options are severely limited and may be gone entirely.

Hour 4-24: Document Everything

Now that you've secured the papers and calmed down, it's time to build your defense foundation. You have 20 hours to gather critical information.

Task 1: Create Your Case File (30 Minutes)

Physical folder or digital folder — organize everything:

```
Case Name: [Bank Name] v. [Your Name]
Case Number: _______________
Court: _______________
Judge (if assigned): _______________
Bank's Attorney: _______________
Deadline to Answer: _______________
```

Create subfolders for: - Service documents - Original loan documents (note, mortgage, closing papers) - Correspondence with servicer - Payment records - Financial hardship documentation - Research and notes

Task 2: Gather Loan Documents (2-4 Hours)

Find every document related to your loan:

Critical documents: - Promissory note (original or copy from closing) - Mortgage or deed of trust - Closing Disclosure or HUD-1 settlement statement - Truth in Lending Disclosure - Any modifications or forbearance agreements - All correspondence with the servicer

Helpful documents: - Original loan application - Appraisal from closing - Title insurance policy - Any assignments of mortgage - Any notes or allonges

If you don't have these: - Check your email for electronic copies - Contact your closing attorney or title company - Request documents from the servicer (you have a right to certain documents) - Check county recorder's office for recorded documents

Task 3: Document Your Payment History (1-2 Hours)

Create a timeline: - When did you take out the loan? - When did you first miss a payment? - Have you made any partial payments? - Did you apply for modification? When? - Did you make trial modification payments?

Gather evidence: - Bank statements showing payments - Cancelled checks - Money order receipts - Online payment confirmations - Correspondence about payments

Task 4: Start the Document Audit (2-3 Hours)

Using the skills from Chapters 4-8, start your forensic analysis:

Chain of title check: - Who is named as the original lender on your note? - Who is named on your mortgage? - Have there been any assignments? To whom? When? - Does the chain make sense?

Signature analysis: - Look at signatures on assignments and allonges - Are they consistent? - Are there notarization issues? - Do you recognize any robo-signer names?

Document timing: - When was the assignment to the foreclosing party dated? - When was it recorded? - Was it before or after the foreclosure was filed?

This audit continues beyond 24 hours, but start now. Early findings may affect your answer strategy.

Task 5: Research the Bank and Their Attorney (30 Minutes)

Search for: - The bank or trust suing you — are there known document problems? - The law firm handling the foreclosure — what's their reputation? - The individual attorney assigned — how many foreclosure cases do they handle?

Where to search: - State bar association website (attorney disciplinary history) - Court records (other cases involving this bank/attorney) - Consumer Financial Protection Bureau complaint database - Online foreclosure defense forums

Why this matters: Knowing your opponent helps you predict their tactics and identify patterns in their cases.

LEARN FROM THIS MISTAKE: The Homeowner Who Represented Himself Without Preparation

James Wilson's Story: James was a smart, successful businessman. He had managed complex negotiations at work, read contracts regularly, and considered himself capable of handling his own foreclosure defense. When he was served, he decided to represent himself pro se rather than pay an attorney.

"How hard could it be?" he thought. "I just need to file an answer denying the allegations."> James downloaded a form answer from the internet, filled in his name and case number, checked "deny" for every paragraph, and filed it with the court. He felt proud of himself for saving thousands in attorney fees.> But James's answer had major problems. He denied allegations that he should have admitted (like his address and the fact that he signed the note). He failed to raise any affirmative defenses. He didn't challenge the bank's standing. He didn't request discovery.> At summary judgment, the bank's attorney pointed out that James had effectively conceded the case by filing a "general denial" without any legal basis. The court granted summary judgment for the bank. James lost his home.> What James should have done:> - Consulted with an attorney about his specific case, even if he couldn't afford full representation - Used limited scope representation (attorney reviews documents, advises strategy)> - Attended a foreclosure defense clinic or workshop - Studied the rules of civil procedure for his jurisdiction - Filed a motion to dismiss or raised standing challenges, not just general denials

"Being smart in business doesn't make you a lawyer," James says. "The court has rules, procedures, and strategies that attorneys spend years learning. I walked in thinking I knew what I was doing and walked out having lost everything."> **The Lesson:** Representing yourself is your right, but it is difficult and risky. If you choose to go pro se, prepare thoroughly. Use this book, attend clinics, consult with attorneys for guidance, and study the rules. A bad pro se defense is often worse than no defense at all. Consider limited scope representation — having an attorney advise you even if you do the work yourself.

Hour 24-48: Start Your Defense

You've gathered documents. You've started the audit. Now it's time to build your legal response.

Option A: Hire an Attorney

If you can afford it: - Contact foreclosure defense attorneys immediately - Many offer free or low-cost consultations - Ask about: flat fees vs. hourly, payment plans, what services are included - Bring your organized case file to the consultation

What to ask potential attorneys: - "How many foreclosure cases have you handled?" - "What defenses do you see in my case?" - "What is your fee structure?" - "Will you handle the case through trial if necessary?" - "What is my realistic chance of success?"

Red flags: - Guarantees of success (no attorney can guarantee outcomes) - Pressure to sign immediately - Fees that seem too low (they may not plan to do much work) - No foreclosure experience

Option B: Represent Yourself (Pro Se)

If you cannot afford an attorney: - You have the right to represent yourself - It is difficult but possible - This book is designed to help you - Consider limited scope representation (attorney helps with specific tasks)

Resources for pro se litigants: - Court self-help centers - Legal aid organizations - Housing counseling agencies - Foreclosure defense clinics - Online legal research tools

Drafting Your Answer

Basic structure of an answer:

```
1. Caption: Case name, number, court
2. Introduction: "Defendant [Your Name] answers the complaint as follows:"
3. Responses to each paragraph: Admit, Deny, or Lack Knowledge
4. Defenses: Legal reasons the bank should not win
5. Counterclaims (if any): Claims you have against the bank
6. Prayer for Relief: What you want the court to do
7. Signature and date
```

See Chapter 10 for detailed answer drafting guidance.

Filing an Extension Request

If you cannot file your answer by the deadline, request an extension:

How to request: - Call the bank's attorney (yes, now this is appropriate) and ask for a stipulation (agreement) to extend - If they refuse, file a motion with the court requesting an extension - Most courts grant at least one extension if requested before the deadline

What to say: - "I was served on [date] and need additional time to respond" - "I am seeking counsel" or "I am gathering documents to prepare my defense" - Request a specific number of days (30 days is typical)

Sample language: > "Defendant respectfully requests an extension of 30 days to answer the complaint. Defendant was served on [date] and needs additional time to [seek counsel/gather documents/prepare a defense]. This request is made in good faith and will not prejudice Plaintiff."

Hour 48-72: File or Request Extension

The deadline is approaching. You must act now.

If Filing an Answer

Final checklist: - [ ] Answer responds to every paragraph in the complaint - [ ] Answer includes standing challenges if applicable - [ ] Answer asserts applicable affirmative defenses - [ ] Answer is signed and dated - [ ] Certificate of service is included (showing you served the bank's attorney) - [ ] Filing fee is paid or fee waiver requested - [ ] Extra copies for your records

Where to file: - Courthouse where the case was filed (address is on the summons) - Some courts allow electronic filing - Some courts require in-person filing

How to serve: - Mail a copy to the bank's attorney (address on the complaint) - Follow your state's rules for service of pleadings - Keep proof of service

If Requesting an Extension

If you have a stipulation (agreement) from the bank's attorney: - File the stipulation with the court - Make sure it's signed by both parties - Ask the court to enter an order granting the extension

If the bank refuses to stipulate: - File a motion for extension before your deadline - Explain why you need more time - Be specific about how much time you need and why - Show good faith effort (e.g., "I have consulted three attorneys and am close to hiring one")

Do NOT miss the deadline waiting for an extension. If the court hasn't ruled on your motion by the deadline, file a protective answer to preserve your rights.

What NOT to Do

Don't Do These Things in the First 72 Hours

1. Don't Move Out You're still the homeowner. Moving out weakens your position and may accelerate the process. Stay until you have exhausted all legal options or reached a negotiated resolution.

2. Don't Ignore the Papers Ignoring the lawsuit guarantees you will lose. The bank will get a default judgment, and you will lose your right to defend. No matter how hopeless it seems, responding is better than defaulting.

3. Don't Transfer the Property Transferring the property to a friend, family member, or trust to "protect" it is usually a mistake. It may be considered a fraudulent transfer, it won't stop the foreclosure, and it may create tax problems.

4. Don't Pay Random "Rescue" Companies Companies that promise to save your home for an upfront fee are often scams. If it sounds too good to be true, it is. Work with licensed attorneys or HUD-approved housing counselors.

5. Don't Stop Communicating with Your Servicer (Completely) While you should not call the bank's attorney, you may still need to communicate with your loan servicer about loss mitigation options. Keep records of all communications. Do not let servicer communications distract from your legal defense.

6. Don't Give Up The bank wants you to feel hopeless. They want you to default, move out, and make their job easy. Every day you stay in your home, every defense you raise, every motion you file makes their job harder. You have rights. Use them.

The 72-Hour Checklist

Hour 0-4 (Immediate)

- ☐ Secure and copy all service documents
- ☐ Find and calendar the answer deadline
- ☐ Check service for defects
- ☐ Photograph your house
- ☐ Notify family and support team
- ☐ Do NOT call the bank's attorney

Hour 4-24 (Document)

- ☐ Create organized case file

- ☐ Gather all loan documents
- ☐ Document payment history
- ☐ Start document audit (chain, signatures, timing)
- ☐ Research bank and attorney

Hour 24-48 (Prepare)

- ☐ Contact foreclosure defense attorneys OR
- ☐ Begin drafting pro se answer
- ☐ Request extension if needed
- ☐ Continue document audit
- ☐ Gather financial hardship documentation

Hour 48-72 (Act)

- ☐ File answer OR
- ☐ File extension motion OR
- ☐ File protective answer while awaiting extension
- ☐ Serve documents on bank's attorney
- ☐ Confirm court receipt of filing

Chapter Summary

The first 72 hours after service are critical. What you do — or don't do — determines whether you enter this fight with a chance to win or by defaulting and losing automatically.

Key actions: - **Immediately:** Secure documents, find deadline, check service, photo house, notify team - **Within 24 hours:** Create case file, gather loan documents, document payments, start audit - **Within 48 hours:** Hire attorney or draft answer, request extension if needed - **Before deadline:** File answer or extension, serve bank's attorney

Critical don'ts: - Don't call the bank's attorney unprepared - Don't move out or transfer property - Don't ignore the papers - Don't pay scam rescue companies - Don't give up

Remember: You have rights. The bank must prove their case. You can challenge their standing, their documents, and their claims. The foreclosure process takes months or years. One bad day (getting served) doesn't determine the outcome. What you do next does.

Cross-References

Previous Chapter: Chapter 8 — Consideration, Original Funding, and Transaction Legitimacy

Next Chapter: Chapter 10 — Drafting the Answer: A Step-by-Step Guide

Related Chapters: - Chapter 4: Document Audit System (for the 24-hour audit) - Chapter 11: Motion to Dismiss (if service is defective) - Chapter 28: Playbook — I Got Served Quick Reference

In the Playbook: - 72-Hour Action Checklist (condensed) - Service Defect Checklist - Deadline Calculator by State - Extension Request Template

Templates: - Extension Request Letter - Answer Format Template - Case File Organization Guide

CHAPTER 10: HOW TO DRAFT THE ANSWER WITHOUT HELPING THE BANK

The Document That Determines Your Fate

Answer Format and Requirements

The **answer** is your formal response to the foreclosure complaint. It tells the court which allegations you admit, which you deny, and what defenses you raise. Get it wrong, and you may lose before the fight begins.

Basic Answer Structure

Every answer follows a standard format:

```
CAPTION
[Case name, number, court]

INTRODUCTION
"Defendant [Your Name], pro se, answers the complaint as follows:"

RESPONSES TO ALLEGATIONS
Paragraph 1: [Admit/Deny/Lack Knowledge]
Paragraph 2: [Admit/Deny/Lack Knowledge]
[Continue for each paragraph]

AFFIRMATIVE DEFENSES
1. [First defense]
2. [Second defense]
[Continue]

COUNTERCLAIMS (if any)
[Your claims against the bank]

PRAYER FOR RELIEF
"WHEREFORE, Defendant requests:"
[List what you want the court to do]
```

```
VERIFICATION
"I declare under penalty of perjury..."
[Your signature and date]

CERTIFICATE OF SERVICE
"I hereby certify that I served a copy..."
[Date and signature]
```

The Caption

The caption appears at the top of every court document. It includes:

```
IN THE CIRCUIT COURT OF THE ___ JUDICIAL CIRCUIT
IN AND FOR [COUNTY] COUNTY, [STATE]

[PLAINTIFF BANK NAME],
                    Plaintiff,
v.                                   Case No.: [Number]
[YOUR FULL NAME],
                    Defendant.
```

Copy the caption exactly from the complaint. Use the same case number, same court name, same party names. Errors in the caption can cause your answer to be rejected or filed to the wrong case.

Jurisdictional Variations

State court vs. federal court: - State courts have varying format requirements - Federal courts use specific forms and rules - Check your local court's website for formatting requirements - Some courts require specific fonts, margins, or line spacing

Verified vs. unverified answers: - Some states require the answer to be "verified" (signed under penalty of perjury) - Some complaints are "verified," requiring a verified answer - When in doubt, verify your answer — it can't hurt - Verification shows the court you're serious and creates accountability

Electronic filing: - Many courts now require electronic filing (e-filing) - You may need to register for an e-filing account - PDF format is usually required - Follow the court's technical specifications exactly

---

The Denial Strategy

The most important rule of answer drafting: **Deny allegations you don't know are true. Never guess. Never assume.**

The Three Response Options

For each paragraph in the complaint, you have three options:

ADMIT: The allegation is true - Use sparingly - Only admit facts you know personally are true (like your address) - Never admit legal conclusions

DENY: The allegation is false or you dispute it - Use for allegations that are wrong - Use for allegations you don't know are true - The bank must prove denied allegations

LACK KNOWLEDGE: You don't know if the allegation is true - Use when you don't have personal knowledge - Example: "Plaintiff is the holder of the note" — you don't know if this is true - This functions as a denial

Never Admit These Allegations

"Defendant is indebted to Plaintiff" This is the most dangerous admission. If you admit you're indebted to the plaintiff, you concede the basic premise of the case. Instead: - Deny: "Defendant denies being indebted to Plaintiff. Defendant is without knowledge as to whether Plaintiff is the proper party to enforce the alleged debt."

"Plaintiff is the holder of the note" You don't know if the plaintiff actually holds the note or has the right to enforce it. This is often a key issue in foreclosure defense. Instead: - Deny: "Defendant denies that Plaintiff is the holder of the note or has standing to bring this action."

"Defendant defaulted on the loan" "Default" is a legal conclusion. You may have missed payments, but whether that constitutes "default" depends on the contract and other factors. Instead: - Deny: "Defendant denies the allegations regarding default. Defendant is without knowledge as to the accuracy of Plaintiff's accounting."

"The note and mortgage are valid and enforceable" You don't know if the note and mortgage are valid. There may be defects in the documents or the original transaction. Instead: - Deny: "Defendant denies that the note and mortgage are valid and enforceable as alleged."

Sample Denial Language

Here are responses to common complaint allegations:

Complaint Allegation	Your Response
"Plaintiff is the owner and holder of the note"	Defendant denies that Plaintiff is the owner and holder of the note. Defendant is without knowledge as to whether Plaintiff has any interest in the note or mortgage.
"Defendant is indebted to Plaintiff"	Defendant denies being indebted to Plaintiff. Defendant denies that Plaintiff is entitled to enforce the alleged debt.
"Defendant defaulted by failing to pay"	Defendant denies defaulting. Defendant is without knowledge as to the accuracy of Plaintiff's payment records.
"The note is secured by a mortgage"	Defendant admits that a mortgage was executed, but denies that the mortgage is properly held by Plaintiff.
"All conditions precedent have occurred"	Defendant denies that all conditions precedent have occurred. Defendant alleges that Plaintiff failed to properly accelerate the debt and failed to provide required notices.

The General Denial Option

Some jurisdictions allow a **general denial** — a statement that denies all allegations in the complaint. This is simpler but less strategic.

Example: > "Defendant denies each and every allegation in the complaint not expressly admitted herein."

When to use: - In jurisdictions that allow it - When the complaint has many paragraphs and specific denials would be repetitive - As a supplement to specific denials of key allegations

Caution: Even with a general denial, you should specifically deny critical allegations (like indebtedness and standing) to make your position crystal clear.

LEARN FROM THIS MISTAKE: The Homeowner Who Admitted Indebtedness

Robert Jackson's Story: Robert was a high school teacher who believed in being honest and cooperative. When he was served with foreclosure papers, he sat down at his kitchen table with the complaint and started drafting his answer.> Paragraph 1 of the complaint said: "Defendant Robert Jackson is indebted to Plaintiff in the sum of $287,452.17." Robert thought: "Well, that's true. I borrowed the money. I owe it. I'm an honest person. I should admit this."> He wrote: "Admitted."> He continued through the complaint, admitting most of the factual allegations. The bank's note was valid — admitted. The mortgage was genuine — admitted. The amount owed was correct — admitted.> When the bank moved for summary judgment, they pointed to Robert's admissions. "The defendant has admitted every material allegation in the complaint," the bank's attorney wrote. "There are no genuine issues of material fact. Judgment should be granted as a matter of law."> The court agreed. Robert's foreclosure was granted on summary judgment without a trial. He never got to challenge the bank's standing, question the chain of title, or present his evidence.> What Robert didn't understand:> - "Indebtedness" is a legal conclusion, not just a fact - He didn't know if he owed the money TO THIS SPECIFIC PLAINTIFF - He didn't know if the amount they claimed was correct - He didn't know if the note was properly transferred to the plaintiff - By admitting, he relieved the bank of their burden to prove these things

"I thought I was being honest," Robert says. "But I was being naive. The bank had to prove their case. By admitting everything, I did their job for them."> **The Lesson:** Never admit "indebtedness" to the plaintiff. You don't know if you owe the money to this specific party. You don't know if the amount is correct. You don't know if the note is properly held by the plaintiff. These are the very issues the bank must prove. Let them prove it. Your job is to deny allegations you don't know are true and force the bank to meet their burden of proof.

Affirmative Defenses: Menu and Selection

Affirmative defenses are legal reasons why the bank should not win even if some of their allegations are true. You must raise them in your answer or you may lose them forever.

Common Foreclosure Affirmative Defenses

1. Lack of Standing The plaintiff cannot prove they are the holder of the note or have the right to enforce it. > "Plaintiff lacks standing to bring this action. Plaintiff cannot prove it is the holder of the note or has the right to enforce the mortgage."

2. Failure to State a Claim The complaint doesn't allege facts sufficient to support a foreclosure. > "The complaint fails to state a claim upon which relief can be granted."

3. Statute of Frauds The agreement to transfer the mortgage must be in writing. (Useful when assignments are defective.) > "Any alleged assignment of the mortgage is void under the Statute of Frauds."

4. Statute of Limitations The bank waited too long to sue. (Varies by state; some states have specific foreclosure statutes of limitations.) > "The claims are barred by the Statute of Limitations."

5. Failure to Provide Required Notices The bank didn't give you the pre-foreclosure notices required by your mortgage or state law. > "Plaintiff failed to provide the notice of default and right to cure required by the mortgage and state law."

6. Failure to Comply with Conditions Precedent The bank didn't do everything required before filing foreclosure. > "Plaintiff failed to satisfy conditions precedent to filing this action, including but not limited to [specify]."

7. Payment/Waiver You made payments that weren't credited, or the bank accepted payments and waived the default. > "Defendant made payments that were not properly credited. Plaintiff's acceptance of payments waived any alleged default."

8. Unclean Hands The bank acted improperly (dual tracking, modification fraud, etc.). > "Plaintiff has unclean hands due to [specify conduct]."

9. Accord and Satisfaction You and the bank reached an agreement that satisfied the debt. > "Any alleged debt was satisfied by accord and satisfaction."

10. Res Judicata/Collateral Estoppel This issue was already decided in another case. > "The claims are barred by res judicata/collateral estoppel."

How Many Defenses to Raise

Raise all defenses that apply. It doesn't cost extra to add more defenses. If you don't raise a defense in your answer, you may be barred from raising it later.

But be careful: Don't raise frivolous defenses. If a defense clearly doesn't apply, don't include it. Frivolous defenses waste your credibility.

When in doubt: Include the defense. Let the bank argue it's inapplicable. Better to preserve the defense and lose it later than to waive it by not raising it.

Sample Affirmative Defenses Section

```
AFFIRMATIVE DEFENSES

Defendant raises the following affirmative defenses:

FIRST DEFENSE: Lack of Standing
Plaintiff lacks standing to bring this foreclosure action. Plaintiff cannot
prove it is the holder of the note or has the right to enforce the mortgage.

SECOND DEFENSE: Failure to State a Claim
The complaint fails to state a claim upon which relief can be granted.

THIRD DEFENSE: Statute of Frauds
Any alleged assignment of the mortgage is void under the Statute of Frauds.

FOURTH DEFENSE: Failure to Comply with Conditions Precedent
Plaintiff failed to satisfy conditions precedent to filing this action,
including proper acceleration of the debt and provision of required notices.

FIFTH DEFENSE: Unclean Hands
Plaintiff has unclean hands due to its dual tracking of loan modification
and foreclosure, and its failure to honor agreements made during the
modification process.

SIXTH DEFENSE: Waiver
Plaintiff waived any alleged default by accepting payments from Defendant
after the alleged default occurred.
```

Standing Challenges in the Answer

Standing is the plaintiff's right to bring the lawsuit. In foreclosure, this means proving they are the holder of the note or have the right to enforce it. Challenge standing in your answer.

Where to Put Standing Challenges

Standing can be challenged in two places:

1. In Your Responses to Allegations When the complaint alleges the plaintiff is the holder or is entitled to enforce the note, specifically deny this: > "Defendant denies that Plaintiff is the holder of the note or has standing to bring this action."

2. As an Affirmative Defense Include "Lack of Standing" as your first affirmative defense.

Standing Challenge Language

Basic standing challenge: > "Plaintiff lacks standing to bring this action. Plaintiff has not alleged and cannot prove that it is the holder of the note or has the right to enforce the mortgage."

Standing with chain of title issue: > "Plaintiff lacks standing because it cannot prove an unbroken chain of title from the original lender. The alleged assignment is defective and void."

Standing with note possession issue: > "Plaintiff lacks standing because it cannot prove it possesses the original note or is entitled to enforce it. The note was not properly endorsed to Plaintiff."

Counterclaims: When and How

A **counterclaim** is a claim you make against the bank. Instead of just defending, you're also suing.

When to File Counterclaims

File counterclaims when: - The bank violated consumer protection laws (TILA, RESPA, FDCPA) - The bank engaged in dual tracking (promising modification while foreclosing) - The bank made misrepresentations - You have claims that are related to the foreclosure

Don't file counterclaims when: - Your claims are unrelated to the foreclosure - Your claims are stale (statute of limitations has run) - You don't have evidence to support the claims - Filing would reveal your defense strategy prematurely

Common Counterclaims

1. Fair Debt Collection Practices Act (FDCPA) Violations If the bank or its attorney used abusive, deceptive, or unfair practices.

2. Truth in Lending Act (TILA) Violations If the bank failed to provide required disclosures or engaged in rescindable violations.

3. Real Estate Settlement Procedures Act (RESPA) Violations If the bank failed to provide required notices or engaged in kickbacks.

4. State Consumer Protection Act Violations Most states have consumer protection laws that prohibit deceptive practices.

5. Wrongful Foreclosure If the bank is foreclosing without proper authority or in violation of the law.

Counterclaim Format

Counterclaims follow the same format as the bank's complaint:

```
COUNTERCLAIMS

Defendant realleges and incorporates by reference all prior allegations.

FIRST CAUSE OF ACTION: FDCPA Violations
1. Plaintiff [or its attorney] is a debt collector under the FDCPA.
2. Plaintiff violated the FDCPA by [specify conduct].
3. Defendant is entitled to statutory damages, actual damages, and attorney fees.

[Continue with additional causes of action]
```

Common Answer Mistakes

Avoid these errors that destroy foreclosure defenses.

Mistake 1: Admitting Indebtedness

Wrong: "Defendant admits being indebted to Plaintiff in the amount of $287,452.17." **Right:** "Defendant denies being indebted to Plaintiff. Defendant is without knowledge as to whether Plaintiff is the proper party to enforce the alleged debt."

Mistake 2: Failing to Verify

Problem: Some states or situations require a verified answer. An unverified answer may be stricken. **Solution:** When in doubt, verify your answer. Add a verification page signed under penalty of perjury.

Mistake 3: Missing the Deadline

Problem: Late answers may not be accepted. Default judgments are entered for late answers. **Solution:** Calendar the deadline with multiple alerts. File a motion for extension if you need more time BEFORE the deadline.

Mistake 4: Improper Service

Problem: You must serve your answer on the bank's attorney following court rules. **Solution:** Include a certificate of service showing how and when you served the answer. Keep proof of service.

Mistake 5: Waiving Defenses

Problem: If you don't raise a defense in your answer, you may lose it forever. **Solution:** Include all applicable affirmative defenses. Better to include a defense you don't need than to need a defense you didn't include.

Mistake 6: Conceding Facts

Problem: Admitting allegations that should be denied. **Solution:** Deny allegations you don't personally know are true. Only admit basic facts (like your address) that are clearly true and not in dispute.

LEARN FROM THIS MISTAKE: The Homeowner Who Waived the Statute of Frauds

> **Carol Martinez's Story:** Carol had a strong defense. The assignment of her mortgage was unsigned — just a blank document with a notary stamp. Under her state's Statute of Frauds, an assignment of a mortgage interest must be signed by the assignor. The unsigned assignment was void.> But Carol didn't know about the Statute of Frauds defense. She drafted her answer focusing only on general denials and a lack of standing argument. She didn't include any affirmative defenses.> At trial, Carol tried to argue that the assignment was defective. The bank's attorney objected. "Your Honor, the defendant failed to plead the Statute of Frauds as an affirmative defense. Under [state] law, the Statute of Frauds is an affirmative defense that is waived if not pleaded."> The judge sustained the objection. "The Statute of Frauds defense is waived. The defendant had the opportunity to raise it in her answer and failed to do so."> Carol lost a winning defense because she didn't include it in her answer. The unsigned assignment —

which should have been fatal to the bank's case — was admitted into evidence.> What Carol should have done:> - Researched all applicable affirmative defenses before drafting her answer - Included the Statute of Frauds as an affirmative defense - Consulted with an attorney about available defenses in her jurisdiction - Reviewed the foreclosure defense resources available in her state

"I had no idea I was supposed to list defenses," Carol says. "I thought just denying the allegations was enough. But some defenses have to be specifically raised or you lose them. I lost my home because of a technicality I didn't know about."> **The Lesson:** The Statute of Frauds and many other defenses must be raised as affirmative defenses in your answer. If you don't raise them, you waive them. Research all available defenses in your jurisdiction and include every one that applies. You can't raise a defense for the first time at trial if you didn't include it in your answer. Don't lose a winning case on a technicality.

LEARN FROM THIS MISTAKE: The Attorney Who Failed to Verify

Thomas Wright's Story: Thomas hired an attorney to defend his foreclosure. The attorney was experienced in general civil litigation but had only handled a few foreclosure cases. He drafted an answer denying the allegations and raising several affirmative defenses.> The bank filed a motion to strike the answer. "The complaint is verified," the bank's attorney argued, "but the defendant's answer is not. Under [state] law, a verified complaint requires a verified answer. The unverified answer should be stricken."> Thomas's attorney argued that the verification requirement was "merely technical" and that the substance of the answer should control. The court disagreed. "The verification requirement is mandatory. The defendant's answer is stricken. The defendant has 10 days to file a verified answer or face default."> Thomas's attorney had to scramble to prepare a verified answer. In the process, he made errors that weakened the defense. The bank moved for summary judgment and won.> What the attorney should have done:> - Checked whether the complaint was verified (it had a verification page signed under penalty of perjury) - Verified the answer to match the complaint's verification - Reviewed state-specific rules about verified pleadings - Ensured the verification was properly formatted and signed

"My attorney didn't even notice the complaint was verified," Thomas says. "A simple signature page would have saved my defense. Instead, we had to start over and made mistakes under pressure."> **The Lesson:** Check whether the complaint is verified. If it is, your answer must be verified too. A verified pleading is signed under penalty of perjury, certifying that the statements are true to the best of your knowledge. The verification requirement is not optional in most jurisdictions. When in doubt, verify your answer — it adds credibility and ensures you meet the procedural requirements.

Filing and Service

Your answer isn't done until it's properly filed with the court and served on the bank's attorney.

Filing the Answer

Where to file: - The courthouse where the case was filed (listed on the complaint) - Some courts require a specific department or room - Check the court's website for filing instructions

How to file: - In person: Bring the original and copies to the clerk's office - By mail: Send original and copies (confirm receipt) - Electronic: Many courts now require e-filing through specific portals

Filing fee: - Most courts charge a fee to file an answer - Fee waivers may be available for low-income defendants - Ask the clerk about fee waiver forms

What the clerk does: - Files the original - Returns file-stamped copies to you - The file stamp is proof of filing — keep it

Serving the Answer

Who to serve: - The bank's attorney (name and address on the complaint) - If the bank has no attorney, serve the bank directly

How to serve: - Mail: First-class mail is usually sufficient for answers - Hand delivery: You or someone over 18 can hand-deliver - Electronic: If the bank's attorney accepts electronic service

When to serve: - Same day as filing (or before) - Don't wait to serve — it's required

Certificate of Service

Every answer must include a **certificate of service** proving you served the bank's attorney:

```
CERTIFICATE OF SERVICE
```

```
I hereby certify that on [date], I served a true and correct copy of the
foregoing Answer on:

[Attorney Name]
[Law Firm Name]
[Address]
[City, State ZIP]

By: [method of service - e.g., "U.S. Mail, first class"]

----------------------
[Your Name]
```

Chapter Summary

- **Format matters.** Use the proper caption, structure, and verification for your jurisdiction.
- **Deny, don't admit.** Never admit indebtedness or that the plaintiff is entitled to enforce the note. Deny allegations you don't personally know are true.
- **Raise all affirmative defenses.** Include every defense that applies. If you don't raise it in your answer, you may lose it forever.
- **Challenge standing.** Make the bank prove they are the holder of the note or have the right to enforce it.
- **Consider counterclaims.** If the bank violated consumer protection laws, file counterclaims for damages.
- **File and serve properly.** An answer that isn't filed and served doesn't exist. Follow court rules exactly.
- **Don't help the bank.** The bank has the burden of proof. Don't do their work by admitting allegations they should have to prove.

Cross-References

Previous Chapter: Chapter 9 — You Got Served: What to Do in the First 72 Hours

Next Chapter: Chapter 11 — Motion to Dismiss: Challenging the Complaint

Related Chapters: - Chapter 4: Document Audit System (for standing challenges) - Chapter 8: Consideration and Funding (for counterclaims) - Chapter 28: Playbook — I Got Served Quick Reference

In the Playbook: - Answer Template - Affirmative Defense Menu - Denial Language Cheat Sheet - Filing and Service Checklist

Templates: - Answer Format Template - Verification Template - Certificate of Service Template - Affirmative Defenses List

CHAPTER 11: MOTION TO DISMISS STRATEGY

Ending the Case Before It Begins

What Is a Motion to Dismiss?

A **motion to dismiss** asks the court to throw out the foreclosure complaint without a trial. Instead of answering the complaint and fighting through discovery, you argue that the bank's case is legally defective and should be dismissed.

Types of Motions to Dismiss

Federal Rule of Civil Procedure 12(b) provides seven grounds for dismissal:

Ground	What It Means	Foreclosure Application
12(b)(1) — Lack of jurisdiction	Court has no power over the case	Rare in foreclosure; usually only for federal court issues
12(b)(2) — Lack of personal jurisdiction	Court has no power over you	If you were improperly served or live outside the jurisdiction
12(b)(3) — Improper venue	Wrong courthouse	If the foreclosure was filed in the wrong county
12(b)(4) — Insufficient process	Defects in the summons or complaint	If the complaint wasn't properly verified or issued
12(b)(5) — Insufficient service	You weren't properly served	Service defects: wrong person, wrong method, wrong location
12(b)(6) — Failure to state a claim	Even if everything alleged is true, the bank still can't win	The complaint doesn't allege facts showing the bank is entitled to foreclose
12(b)(7) — Failure to join necessary party	Someone required is missing	If there are other lienholders who must be included

Most common in foreclosure: 12(b)(6) — failure to state a claim, often combined with standing challenges.

Standing as a 12(b)(1) vs. 12(b)(6) Issue

This distinction matters strategically:

12(b)(1) — Lack of subject matter jurisdiction: - Standing is jurisdictional in many jurisdictions - Can be raised at any time, even on appeal - Court must dismiss if standing is lacking - Can't be cured by amending the complaint

12(b)(6) — Failure to state a claim: - Assumes the court has jurisdiction - Challenges whether the allegations support relief - Bank can often amend to fix defects - Must be raised before answer in some jurisdictions

Key strategic point: Frame standing as jurisdictional when possible. A jurisdictional defect cannot be fixed by amendment — the case must be dismissed.

When to File a Motion to Dismiss

File with or before your answer. Most jurisdictions require motions to dismiss to be filed before or with the answer. If you answer first, you may waive the right to move to dismiss.

Timeline: - You are served with complaint - You have [X] days to respond (varies by state) - File motion to dismiss OR answer within the deadline - If motion is denied, file your answer

Strategic timing considerations: - Early dismissal saves time and money - But a weak motion educates the bank about your strategy - Sometimes better to answer and fight on the merits - Consult local counsel about what works in your jurisdiction

---

Standing as Jurisdictional Challenge

Standing is the plaintiff's right to bring the lawsuit. In foreclosure, this means proving they are the holder of the note or have the right to enforce it. No standing = no case.

Why Standing Is Jurisdictional

Courts have no power to hear a case unless the plaintiff has standing. Standing is a constitutional requirement under Article III (federal courts) and similar principles in state courts.

What this means for you: - Standing can be challenged at any time - It cannot be waived - It cannot be fixed by amending the complaint - If the plaintiff lacks standing, the court must dismiss

Facial vs. Factual Standing Challenges

Facial challenge (12(b)(6)): - The complaint, on its face, doesn't show standing - The allegations themselves don't establish the plaintiff's right to sue - Court looks only at the complaint and attached documents - Bank can amend to add missing allegations

Factual challenge (12(b)(1)): - The complaint alleges standing, but the facts show otherwise - You introduce evidence showing the plaintiff lacks standing - Court can consider documents outside the complaint - Amendment won't help if the facts show no standing

Example of facial challenge: > "The complaint alleges Plaintiff is the holder of the note but doesn't attach or describe the note. On its face, the complaint fails to allege standing."

Example of factual challenge: > "While the complaint alleges Plaintiff is the holder, the attached assignment shows the note was assigned to a different entity. The factual record demonstrates Plaintiff lacks standing."

Documentary Evidence for Standing Challenges

A motion to dismiss based on standing is strongest when supported by documents:

Documents to attach: - The note (showing it's not endorsed to the plaintiff) - Assignments (showing breaks in the chain) - SEC filings (showing the loan was securitized to a different trust) - PSA (showing the plaintiff isn't the proper party) - Prior assignments showing conflicting claims

Authentication: - Documents must be authenticated (proven genuine) - Attach affidavits authenticating documents - Or, cite to documents already in the court record

Standing Challenge Language

Basic standing challenge in a motion to dismiss:

> "Plaintiff lacks standing to bring this foreclosure action. Standing is a jurisdictional requirement that cannot be waived. Plaintiff's complaint fails to allege facts sufficient to establish that it is the holder of the note or has the right to enforce the mortgage. Without standing, this Court lacks jurisdiction and must dismiss the complaint."

Enhanced with documentary evidence:

> "Plaintiff lacks standing to bring this foreclosure action. The note attached to the complaint as Exhibit A is not endorsed to Plaintiff. The assignment attached as Exhibit B was executed after the complaint was filed and is void as a backdated document. The SEC filings attached as Exhibit C show the loan was deposited into [Trust Name], not to Plaintiff. Plaintiff cannot prove it is the holder of the note or has the right to enforce the mortgage. This Court lacks jurisdiction and must dismiss."

LEARN FROM THIS MISTAKE: The Homeowner Who Waited to Challenge Standing

Barbara Williams' Story: Barbara had a strong standing defense. The assignment of her mortgage was dated three months *after* the foreclosure complaint was filed. Under the law in her state, a plaintiff must have standing when the complaint is filed — you can't "cure" lack of standing by filing a document later.> Barbara's attorney advised her to answer the complaint first and "see how things develop." The attorney said they could challenge standing later if needed. Barbara trusted this advice.> Six months later, after expensive discovery and motion practice, Barbara's attorney finally filed a motion to dismiss for lack of standing. The bank's attorney objected. "Your Honor, the defendant waived this argument by answering without raising standing. Even if they hadn't, they've participated in litigation for six months. They've waived any standing challenge."> The judge agreed. "Standing challenges must be raised at the earliest opportunity. The defendant answered without challenging standing and has participated in this litigation for six months. The challenge is waived."> Barbara lost her strongest defense because it wasn't raised early. She spent thousands on discovery that wouldn't have been necessary if the case had been dismissed for lack of standing at the outset.> What Barbara should have done:> - Filed a motion to dismiss before answering - Challenged standing as a jurisdictional defect - Attached the backdated assignment as proof - Argued that post-complaint documents cannot cure lack of standing at filing

"I didn't understand that timing mattered," Barbara says. "I thought if the bank didn't have standing, I could point that out anytime. But the court said I waited too long. I learned the hard way that in litigation, timing is everything."> **The Lesson:** Challenge standing at the earliest opportunity — ideally in a pre-answer motion to dismiss. Standing is jurisdictional, but procedural rules may require you to raise it promptly. Don't participate in litigation and then try to challenge standing later. Once you've answered and engaged in discovery, you may have waived the argument. Raise standing immediately or risk losing your strongest defense.

Failure to State a Claim

Rule 12(b)(6) allows dismissal when the complaint, even if all allegations are true, doesn't state a legally valid claim for relief.

What 12(b)(6) Means

The court assumes everything the bank alleged is true. Even so, do they win? If not, the complaint fails to state a claim.

Example: - Bank alleges: "Defendant owes us money and hasn't paid" - But bank doesn't allege: They are the holder of the note, they have the right to enforce it, or they own the mortgage - Even if everything alleged is true, the bank still hasn't shown they can foreclose - Motion to dismiss granted (or plaintiff given chance to amend)

Common 12(b)(6) Defects in Foreclosure Complaints

1. Failure to allege standing: The complaint doesn't allege the plaintiff is the holder of the note or has the right to enforce it.

2. Failure to allege conditions precedent: The complaint doesn't allege the bank gave required notices before foreclosing.

3. Failure to attach required documents: Some jurisdictions require the note and mortgage to be attached to the complaint.

4. Failure to allege default: The complaint doesn't adequately allege what the default is.

5. Failure to allege amount due: The complaint doesn't properly allege how much is owed.

The Iqbal/Twombly Standard

Federal courts (and many states following them) apply the **Iqbal/Twombly** standard for 12(b)(6) motions. This requires:

- More than "labels and conclusions"
- "Plausible" claims, not just possible claims
- Factual content that allows the court to draw reasonable inferences

What this means: A foreclosure complaint can't just say "we're the holder and the homeowner defaulted." It must provide factual support showing *how* the plaintiff is the holder and *what* the default consists of.

12(b)(6) Challenge Language

Basic challenge:

> "Plaintiff's complaint fails to state a claim upon which relief can be granted. The complaint alleges conclusory statements without factual support. Under Iqbal and Twombly, these threadbare recitals are insufficient to state a plausible claim for foreclosure."

Specific defects:

> "Plaintiff's complaint fails to state a claim for the following reasons: 1. The complaint does not allege facts showing Plaintiff is the holder of the note or has the right to enforce the mortgage. 2. The complaint does not allege compliance with conditions precedent, including required notices. 3. The complaint does not adequately allege the nature of the alleged default. 4. The complaint does not attach the note and mortgage as required by [cite local rule]."

Document-Based Dismissal Arguments

Document defects can support a motion to dismiss, especially when they affect standing.

Assignment Defects

Post-complaint assignments: If the assignment was executed after the complaint was filed, the plaintiff didn't have standing at filing.

Evidence: - Assignment date vs. complaint filing date - Recording date (if recorded after filing)

Argument: > "Plaintiff lacked standing when the complaint was filed. The assignment attached as Exhibit A is dated [date], three months after the complaint was filed on [filing date]. A plaintiff must have standing at the time of filing. Post-complaint documents cannot cure lack of standing."

Broken chain of title: If there's a missing link in the chain of assignments, the current plaintiff may not have received proper title.

Evidence: - Complete chain of assignments from originator to plaintiff - Gaps where an assignment should exist but doesn't

Argument: > "Plaintiff cannot prove an unbroken chain of title. The assignment from [A] to [B] is missing from the record. Without this assignment, [B] had no interest to assign to Plaintiff. Plaintiff's claim of title fails."

Note and Endorsement Defects

Missing endorsement: If the note requires endorsement and lacks it, the holder cannot enforce it.

Evidence: - The original note (or copy) - Any allonges - UCC Article 3 requirements

Argument: > "The note is a negotiable instrument requiring endorsement for transfer. The note attached as Exhibit A is not endorsed to Plaintiff. No allonge is attached. Under UCC Article 3, Plaintiff cannot enforce an unendorsed note."

Forged or robo-signed documents: If key documents are forged, they are void and cannot support foreclosure.

Evidence: - Signature comparisons - Notary fraud evidence - Document fabrication proof

Argument: > "The assignment attached as Exhibit A is void due to forgery. The signature of [name] is a known robo-signature confirmed in [cite source]. The notary acknowledgment was executed by a notary who has admitted to notarizing without witnessing signatures. A void assignment cannot transfer title."

PSA and Securitization Defects

Cut-off date violations: If the loan wasn't transferred to the trust by the PSA's cut-off date, it may not be in the trust.

Evidence: - PSA showing cut-off date - Assignment date showing late transfer - SEC filings showing trust composition

Argument: > "Plaintiff claims to act on behalf of [Trust Name]. However, the PSA requires loans to be transferred by [cut-off date]. The assignment of the subject loan is dated [assignment date], after the cut-off date. The loan was never properly in the trust. Plaintiff lacks authority to foreclose."

Procedural Defects

Some jurisdictions have special procedural requirements for foreclosure complaints.

Verification Requirements

Some states require foreclosure complaints to be **verified** — signed under penalty of perjury by someone with knowledge.

If the complaint isn't verified: - Motion to dismiss for failure to comply with procedural requirements - Or, motion to strike the complaint

If the verification is defective: - Signed by someone without knowledge - Robo-signed verification - Notary defects

Argument: > "The complaint is required to be verified under [cite statute/rule]. The verification attached is defective because [specify defect: signer lacks knowledge, notary fraud, etc.]. The unverified complaint must be dismissed."

Pre-Filing Requirements

Some jurisdictions require: - Notice of default before filing - Participation in mediation programs - Certification of compliance with loss mitigation requirements

If not done: > "Plaintiff failed to comply with mandatory pre-filing requirements. [Cite specific requirement] requires [specify what was required]. Plaintiff did not [what they failed to do]. The complaint is premature and must be dismissed."

Special Foreclosure Rules

Some states have special rules for foreclosure complaints: - Specific allegations required - Special notice requirements - Particular documentation

Research your jurisdiction: Check your state's foreclosure statutes and court rules for specific requirements.

Drafting the Motion

A motion to dismiss has three main parts:

1. The Motion

This is the formal request:

```
MOTION TO DISMISS

Defendant [Your Name] moves this Court to dismiss the complaint
under [cite rule: FRCP 12(b)(6), state equivalent] for failure to
state a claim upon which relief can be granted.

This motion is based on the attached Memorandum of Law, the
exhibits attached hereto, and all matters of which the Court may
take judicial notice.

Respectfully submitted,

_____________________
[Your Signature]
[Your Name], Defendant
[Date]
```

2. The Memorandum of Law

This is the legal argument:

```
MEMORANDUM OF LAW IN SUPPORT OF MOTION TO DISMISS

I. INTRODUCTION

This motion challenges Plaintiff's standing to bring this
foreclosure action. [Brief summary of argument.]

II. STATEMENT OF FACTS

[Summary of relevant facts from documents.]

III. ARGUMENT

A. Standard for Motion to Dismiss

Under [cite rule], a complaint must be dismissed if it fails to
state a claim upon which relief can be granted. [Explain standard.]

B. Plaintiff Lacks Standing

[Detailed argument about why plaintiff lacks standing, with
citations to law and facts.]

C. The Complaint Fails to State a Claim

[Argument about specific defects in the complaint.]

IV. CONCLUSION

For the foregoing reasons, this Court should grant Defendant's
motion and dismiss the complaint.
```

3. Exhibits

Attach supporting documents: - The note (showing lack of endorsement) - Assignments (showing defects) - PSA (showing cut-off date violations) - Any other relevant documents

Certificate of Service

Don't forget to include a certificate of service showing you served the motion on the bank's attorney.

LEARN FROM THIS MISTAKE: The Homeowner Who Didn't Attach Documents

Richard Parker's Story: Richard found smoking-gun evidence. The assignment of his mortgage was notarized by a notary who had been convicted of fraud and lost her commission six months *before* she notarized the assignment. The notary seal on the document was from a commission that was no longer valid.> Richard filed a motion to dismiss arguing that the assignment was void due to notary fraud. He described the evidence in his motion. But he didn't attach proof of the notary's conviction or the expiration of her commission.> At the hearing, the bank's attorney argued that Richard's allegations were "mere speculation" and "unsupported by evidence." The judge asked Richard to produce the evidence. Richard said he had it at home but didn't bring it. The judge denied the motion.> "Motion denied for lack of evidentiary support," the judge ruled. "The defendant has made serious allegations of fraud but has failed to provide any proof. Without documentary evidence, the motion fails."> Richard could have won. The notary's conviction was public record. The commission expiration was documented with the secretary of state. But because he didn't attach these documents to his motion, the court treated his claims as unsupported allegations.> What Richard should have done:> - Attached the notary's conviction record as an exhibit - Attached the secretary of state record showing expired commission - Included an affidavit authenticating the documents - Cited case law showing void notarization invalidates documents

"I thought just saying it was enough," Richard says. "But the court doesn't take your word for it. You have to show them the proof. I had the proof. I just didn't attach it. I lost a winning motion because of a paperwork oversight."> **The Lesson:** A motion to dismiss based on document defects must be supported by the actual documents. Don't just allege problems — attach the proof. If you claim an assignment is backdated, attach the assignment with its date. If you claim a notary is fraudulent, attach the evidence of fraud. If you claim the note lacks endorsement, attach the note. The court will not investigate for you. Without documentary support, even the strongest document defect claim will fail. Attach everything.

Strategic Considerations

When to File a Motion to Dismiss

File when: - You have strong standing or procedural defects - Documents clearly show the plaintiff lacks authority - The complaint is facially defective - Early dismissal would save time and money

Consider not filing when: - Your defects are weak and will be easily amended - Filing would reveal your defense strategy prematurely - Your jurisdiction rarely grants motions to dismiss in foreclosure - You have stronger defenses to raise in summary judgment

What Happens If the Motion Is Denied

If your motion to dismiss is denied: - File your answer within the time allowed - Raise the same issues as affirmative defenses - Challenge standing again at summary judgment - The denial doesn't prevent you from raising issues later

Note: In some jurisdictions, a denied motion to dismiss doesn't preclude raising the same issues later. In others, it might. Research your jurisdiction's rules on claim preclusion.

The Amendment Problem

If the court grants your motion but gives the bank leave to amend: - The bank can file an amended complaint fixing the defects - You may need to file another motion to dismiss - Or, answer and fight on the merits

Jurisdictional standing: If standing is truly jurisdictional and the facts show no standing, the bank cannot amend to create standing. Make this argument clearly.

Cost-Benefit Analysis

Costs of filing: - Legal research and writing time - Filing fees - Potential to educate the bank about your strategy

Benefits of filing: - Early dismissal ends the case - Even denial narrows the issues - Forces bank to show its hand - May create record for appeal

---

LEARN FROM THIS MISTAKE: The Homeowner Who Confused Facial and Factual Challenges

> **Susan Mitchell's Story:** Susan's foreclosure complaint had a major defect. It didn't attach the note, didn't describe the note, and didn't explain how the plaintiff became

the holder. This was a classic facial defect — the complaint, on its face, failed to allege standing.> Susan's attorney filed a "factual" standing challenge under 12(b)(1), attaching documentary evidence that the plaintiff wasn't the holder. The attorney argued that the "real facts" showed no standing.> The bank's attorney responded: "Your Honor, this is a facial challenge disguised as factual. The defendant asks the court to look beyond the complaint to documents they attached. But under [state] law, facial challenges are brought under 12(b)(6), not 12(b)(1). The defendant has used the wrong standard and the wrong rule."> The judge agreed. "This appears to be a facial challenge. The complaint doesn't allege standing on its face. However, the motion was brought under 12(b)(1) and relies on outside documents. I'm treating this as a 12(b)(6) motion. Since the bank can amend to add allegations, the motion is denied with leave to amend."> The bank amended, adding conclusory allegations of standing. Now Susan was stuck litigating against an amended complaint that was harder to attack. She had the right argument but used the wrong procedural vehicle.> What Susan should have done:> - Recognized this as a facial challenge (complaint on its face lacked standing allegations) - Filed under 12(b)(6) for failure to state a claim - Argued that the complaint's allegations were conclusory and insufficient - Cited Iqbal/Twombly for the pleading standard - Only used 12(b)(1) if she had documentary proof the plaintiff absolutely was not the holder

"My attorney used the wrong motion," Susan says. "The complaint was defective on its face. We should have challenged it on those grounds. Instead, we tried to prove facts that weren't in the record yet. The bank just amended and fixed the complaint. We lost our chance for an early win."> **The Lesson:** Know the difference between facial and factual challenges. A facial challenge says "even if everything you alleged is true, you still lose." A factual challenge says "what you alleged is false, and here's the proof." Use 12(b)(6) for facial challenges. Use 12(b)(1) for factual challenges where you can prove the plaintiff lacks standing. Using the wrong standard can turn a winning argument into a losing motion.

Chapter Summary

- **A motion to dismiss asks the court to throw out the complaint** without a trial because it's legally defective.
- **Standing is often jurisdictional** and can be raised at any time. Challenge it early in a pre-answer motion when possible.
- **12(b)(6) challenges facial defects** in the complaint. Even if everything alleged is true, does

the bank win? If not, the complaint fails to state a claim.

- **12(b)(1) challenges are for factual jurisdictional defects.** You introduce evidence showing the plaintiff lacks standing.
- **Document defects support dismissal.** Post-complaint assignments, broken chains, missing endorsements, and forged documents can all form the basis for dismissal.
- **Attach documentary evidence.** Don't just allege document problems — attach the proof. The court won't investigate for you.
- **Know facial vs. factual challenges.** Use the right standard for your argument. Facial challenges use 12(b)(6). Factual standing challenges use 12(b)(1).
- **Even if denied, you haven't lost.** Raise the same issues as affirmative defenses and challenge them again at summary judgment.

Cross-References

Previous Chapter: Chapter 10 — How to Draft the Answer Without Helping the Bank

Next Chapter: Chapter 12 — Discovery Warfare Against the Bank

Related Chapters: - Chapter 4: Document Audit System (for finding document defects) - Chapter 5: Forgery and Robo-Signing (for forged documents) - Chapter 6: Assignments and Chain of Title (for chain defects) - Chapter 7: Note-Mortgage Separation (for endorsement issues) - Chapter 16: Summary Judgment Survival (what dismissal avoids)

In the Playbook: - Motion to Dismiss Checklist - Standing Challenge Template - Document Defect Quick Reference - Facial vs. Factual Challenge Guide

Templates: - Motion to Dismiss Template - Memorandum of Law Outline - Certificate of Service Template

CHAPTER 12: DISCOVERY WARFARE AGAINST THE BANK

Forcing Banks to Prove Their Case or Admit They Can't

Why Discovery Matters in Foreclosure

Discovery is the formal process of getting information from the other side. In foreclosure, discovery is your most powerful weapon. Banks rely on assumptions, affidavits, and business records. Discovery forces them to produce actual evidence or admit they don't have it.

The Bank's Weakness

Most foreclosure plaintiffs cannot produce: - The original note with proper endorsements - Complete chain of title documentation - Proof they own your specific loan - Accurate payment records - Authority to foreclose on behalf of the named plaintiff

They file foreclosure lawsuits expecting homeowners to default or settle. Discovery changes the game. When you demand proof, many banks cannot provide it.

What Discovery Can Reveal

Document deficiencies: - The note is lost or never properly transferred - Assignments are missing, backdated, or forged - The plaintiff doesn't actually own the loan - The servicer lacks authority to foreclose

Witness problems: - Affidavits are robo-signed by people with no personal knowledge - The witness who "verified" your payment history never reviewed the records - The person who signed key documents can't explain what they signed

Accounting errors: - The amount demanded is wrong - Payments weren't properly credited - Fees and charges weren't authorized - The default calculation is incorrect

Discovery as Leverage

Even if you don't find a smoking gun, discovery creates leverage: - Banks spend money responding to discovery - Delays help you stay in your home longer - Extensive discovery shows you're fighting, not defaulting - Pressure may force better settlement offers

---

Types of Discovery

There are four main discovery tools in foreclosure litigation:

1. Request for Production of Documents

You ask the bank to produce documents in their possession, custody, or control.

What you get: Physical or electronic copies of documents.

Best for: Obtaining the note, assignments, payment records, servicing agreements, and other documents.

2. Interrogatories

Written questions the bank must answer under oath.

What you get: Written sworn answers to specific questions.

Best for: Establishing facts, identifying witnesses, and understanding the bank's position.

3. Requests for Admission

You ask the bank to admit or deny specific facts.

What you get: Admissions that narrow the issues or denials you can use at trial.

Best for: Establishing undisputed facts, pinning down the bank's claims, and creating evidence for summary judgment.

4. Depositions

Oral examination of witnesses under oath before a court reporter.

What you get: Sworn testimony that can be used at trial.

Best for: Examining the bank's witnesses, establishing lack of personal knowledge, and creating impeachment material.

Request for Production Strategy

Document requests are the foundation of foreclosure discovery. Be strategic.

The Note Request

Always request the original note. This is the most important document in foreclosure.

```
REQUEST FOR PRODUCTION NO. 1:

Produce the original promissory note executed by Defendant,
including any and all allonges, endorsements, or attachments.
```

Why this matters: - If the bank produces a copy, they may not have the original - If the original lacks endorsement, they lack standing - If they can't produce it, they may not be able to prove their case - The original is required to prove entitlement to enforce under UCC Article 3

Chain of Title Documents

Request every document showing ownership of the note and mortgage:

```
REQUEST FOR PRODUCTION NO. 2:

Produce all documents evidencing the chain of title of the
promissory note from the original lender to the present holder,
including but not limited to:
(a) All assignments of the mortgage or deed of trust
(b) All endorsements of the note
(c) All allonges
(d) Any agreements transferring the note
```

Why this matters: - Breaks in the chain destroy standing - Missing assignments mean the plaintiff didn't receive proper title - Backdated assignments show fraud - Incomplete chains prove the plaintiff isn't the proper party

Servicing Records

Request documents showing how your loan has been serviced:

```
REQUEST FOR PRODUCTION NO. 3:

Produce all documents relating to the servicing of Defendant's
loan, including:
(a) Complete payment history from origination to present
(b) All escrow analyses and statements
(c) All force-placed insurance records
```

```
(d) All property inspection reports
(e) All correspondence between servicer and Defendant
```

Why this matters: - Payment histories often contain errors - Escrow miscalculations can create defenses - Force-placed insurance may be improper - Correspondence may show unclean hands

Pooling and Servicing Agreement

If your loan was securitized, request the PSA:

```
REQUEST FOR PRODUCTION NO. 4:

Produce the Pooling and Servicing Agreement, Trust Agreement,
or other governing documents for the securitized trust claiming
ownership of Defendant's loan.
```

Why this matters: - PSAs have strict requirements for loan transfers - Cut-off dates may have been missed - Required documents may be missing - The trust may not have authority to foreclose

Proof of Purchase: What the Bank Paid for the Note

Demand proof of what the bank paid for your note. This is a powerful request that banks hate. It makes them uncomfortable because it exposes their profit motive and can reveal they paid pennies on the dollar.

```
REQUEST FOR PRODUCTION NO. 5:

Produce all documents evidencing the consideration paid or
transferred for the acquisition of Defendant's promissory
note and mortgage, including but not limited to:
(a) The purchase agreement or assignment agreement transferring
    the note to Plaintiff
(b) Any schedule or list identifying Defendant's loan among
    the loans transferred
(c) Proof of payment or wire transfer records showing the
    amount paid for Defendant's note
(d) Any correspondence relating to the purchase price or
    valuation of Defendant's loan
```

Why this matters: - **Profit motive exposure:** If the bank paid $20,000 for your $300,000 note, their demand for full payment looks different - **Unclean hands:** Some courts consider the deep discount as evidence the bank isn't entitled to full foreclosure judgment - **Settlement leverage:** Knowing they bought cheap gives you leverage to negotiate - **Discovery of affiliates:** Purchase agreements often reveal the bank bought from a related entity, raising questions about arm's-length transactions

What banks typically do: - Object as "irrelevant" or "trade secret" - Offer to produce redacted agreements - Claim the information is proprietary

Your response: The purchase price is relevant to: - The bank's damages (they can't be damaged more than they paid) - Unclean hands defenses - The good faith of the transaction

This request makes the bank uncomfortable because: - It reveals their profit margin on your loan - It exposes relationships between affiliated entities - It undermines their "we're just trying to get paid" narrative - It can reveal they never actually purchased your specific loan

Always demand proof of purchase. Even if you lose the fight, you've learned something about what they're hiding.

Specific vs. Broad Requests

Specific requests are harder to object to:

Too broad: "Produce all documents relating to the loan"

Specific: "Produce the assignment of mortgage from [Originator] to [Plaintiff], dated between [date range]"

Strategy: Start specific. If you need broader categories later, you can ask for them after seeing what the bank produces.

LEARN FROM THIS MISTAKE: The Homeowner Who Gave Up on Discovery

> **Franklin Turner's Story:** Franklin was fighting his foreclosure pro se. He served document requests on the bank's attorney, asking for the note, assignments, and payment history. Six weeks later, he received a response: "The plaintiff objects to these requests as overbroad, burdensome, and seeking documents not in plaintiff's possession."> Franklin didn't know what to do. He thought the bank's objections meant he couldn't get the documents. He didn't respond to the objections. He didn't file a motion to compel. He just moved on to other defenses.> At trial, the bank produced a blurry copy of an assignment. Franklin

objected that he had never seen this document in discovery. The judge asked, "Did you file a motion to compel production?"> "No, Your Honor," Franklin admitted. "The bank objected, and I didn't know what to do."> "Objections are not self-executing," the judge said. "The bank objected. You were required to meet and confer and, if necessary, file a motion to compel. You didn't. The document comes in."> Franklin lost. The assignment — which he could have challenged as fabricated if he'd forced early production — became evidence. He never got to examine the original note. He never got the payment history that might have shown misapplied payments.> What Franklin should have done:> - Responded to the objections with a meet and confer letter - Narrowed the requests if needed to address specific concerns - Filed a motion to compel if the bank wouldn't produce - Requested sanctions for bad faith objections

"I thought when the bank said 'objection,' that was the end of it," Franklin says. "I didn't know objections were just the beginning of the argument. I gave up when I should have pushed harder."> **The Lesson:** An objection is not a final answer. It's the start of a conversation. When a bank objects to discovery, you must respond. Meet and confer. Narrow your requests if needed. If they still won't produce, file a motion to compel. Most banks will produce documents rather than face a motion to compel and risk sanctions. Don't give up because the bank said "objection." That's exactly when the fight begins.

Interrogatories That Work

Interrogatories are written questions answered under oath. Use them strategically.

Interrogatories to Establish Facts

Identify the holder:

```
INTERROGATORY NO. 1:

Identify the person or entity that currently holds the original
promissory note, including:
(a) The full legal name
(b) The address
(c) How and when they became the holder
(d) The name and title of the person with custody of the note
```

Identify the witness:

```
INTERROGATORY NO. 2:

For each person who will testify on behalf of Plaintiff at trial:
(a) State their full name and current job title
(b) Describe their employment history with Plaintiff or its servicer
(c) Describe their personal knowledge of Defendant's loan
(d) Identify all documents they reviewed regarding this loan
```

Interrogatories to Pin Down Claims

The default calculation:

```
INTERROGATORY NO. 3:

Explain in detail how Plaintiff calculated the amount it claims
is due, including:
(a) The principal balance and how it was calculated
(b) Each fee or charge added to the balance
(c) The authority for each fee or charge
(d) Any payments made by Defendant that were applied to the account
```

The assignment details:

```
INTERROGATORY NO. 4:

If Plaintiff claims to be the holder of the note through an
assignment:
(a) Identify the date of the assignment
(b) Identify the assignor
(c) Describe how the assignment was delivered
(d) Identify the person who has custody of the original assignment
```

Interrogatories to Find More Discovery

Identify all documents:

```
INTERROGATORY NO. 5:

Identify all documents in Plaintiff's possession, custody, or
control relating to:
(a) The origination of Defendant's loan
(b) The transfer or assignment of the note
```

```
(c) The servicing of Defendant's loan
(d) Any modification or forbearance agreements
```

Limitations on Interrogatories

Most jurisdictions limit the number of interrogatories: - Federal court: 25 interrogatories (including subparts) - Many states follow similar limits - Exceed the limit and the other side can refuse to answer

Strategy: Use your interrogatories wisely. Save them for questions that require detailed written answers. Use requests for production to get documents and requests for admission to pin down facts.

Requests for Admission as Weapon

Requests for Admission (RFAs) are the most underused discovery tool. Use them aggressively.

Why RFAs Are Powerful

Admissions are conclusive: If the bank admits a fact, you don't have to prove it at trial. The fact is established.

Denials create impeachment material: If the bank denies a fact and you later prove it, you can show they were dishonest or uninformed.

Failure to respond equals admission: If the bank doesn't respond within the time limit (usually 30 days), the requests are deemed admitted.

Strategic RFAs for Foreclosure

Establish the chain problems:

```
REQUEST FOR ADMISSION NO. 1:

Admit that Plaintiff does not possess the original promissory
note executed by Defendant.
```

```
REQUEST FOR ADMISSION NO. 2:

Admit that there is no written assignment of the mortgage from
[Prior Holder] to Plaintiff.
```

Pin down their claims:

```
REQUEST FOR ADMISSION NO. 3:

Admit that the amount demanded in the complaint includes charges
that were not authorized by the note or mortgage.
```

```
REQUEST FOR ADMISSION NO. 4:

Admit that the person who signed the verification of the
complaint did not review Defendant's payment history.
```

Create trial evidence:

```
REQUEST FOR ADMISSION NO. 5:

Admit that [Name], the person who signed the assignment of
mortgage, was employed by [Company] at the time of signing.
```

Responding to RFAs

When you receive RFAs from the bank, take them seriously:

Read each one carefully. Some may be traps or request admissions of things that aren't true.

Object if appropriate: You can object to requests that are improper, but improper objections may be overruled.

Deny if not true: Never admit something that isn't true just to avoid conflict.

Explain denials if required: Some jurisdictions require you to explain the basis for your denial.

Meet deadlines: Failure to respond means admission. Calendar the deadline with alerts.

Depositions: When and How

A **deposition** is sworn oral testimony taken before a court reporter. Depositions are powerful but expensive and time-consuming.

When to Take Depositions

Depose the bank's witness when: - Their affidavit is the foundation for the bank's case - You need to establish lack of personal knowledge - You want to lock in testimony before trial - You need to explore document authenticity

Don't depose when: - You don't have a clear purpose - The cost outweighs the potential benefit - You can get the information through cheaper discovery

Who to Depose

The affidavit signer: The person who signed the affidavit attached to the complaint probably has no personal knowledge. Deposing them can destroy the bank's foundation evidence.

The servicing witness: The person who "verified" your payment history probably just looked at a computer screen. They can't explain how payments were applied or where the records came from.

The document custodian: The person with custody of the note and mortgage can testify about chain of custody — or admit they don't know.

The robo-signer: If you can identify a known robo-signer on your documents, deposing them can yield admissions about their signing practices.

Deposition Strategy

Start broad: - "What is your job title?" - "How long have you worked for the bank?" - "What are your job responsibilities?"

Narrow to specifics: - "Did you review the original note before signing the affidavit?" - "Where is the original note currently located?" - "Who has custody of it?"

Lock in testimony: - "Isn't it true that you signed 200 affidavits that day?" - "You didn't review my payment history, did you?" - "You don't know where the original note is, do you?"

Use documents: Show the witness documents and ask them to explain. Documents they haven't seen destroy their credibility.

The Cost of Depositions

Expenses include: - Court reporter fees ($500-1000+ per deposition) - Transcript costs ($3-5 per page) - Attorney fees (if represented) - Your time

Pro se depositions: You can depose witnesses yourself. The procedure is formal but manageable. Research your court's rules for depositions.

Written Depositions: The Better Way

Written depositions are just as powerful as oral depositions — and far more affordable. You don't need a court reporter. You don't need a transcriptionist. You serve written questions, and the deponent must answer them under oath, just like an oral deposition.

Why Written Depositions Are Better

Cost savings: - **Oral deposition:** $500-1000+ for court reporter, $3-5 per page for transcript - **Written deposition:** Postage and copy costs only

Same legal effect: - Both are sworn testimony under penalty of perjury - Both can be used at trial for impeachment - Both lock in the witness's testimony - Both are discovery tools under the rules of civil procedure

Strategic advantages: - The witness answers carefully — no off-the-cuff remarks - You can draft precise, targeted questions - No scheduling headaches or witness cancellations - You get written answers you can quote directly in motions

When to Use Written vs. Oral Depositions

Use WRITTEN depositions for: - Affidavit signers who have no personal knowledge - Document custodians who just hold records - Robo-signers with pattern practices - Any witness who isn't the primary decision-maker - Getting specific facts locked down on paper

Use ORAL depositions for: - Key bank executives with settlement authority - Witnesses you need to see in person (body language matters) - Situations where you need to follow up in real-time - Complex factual disputes requiring clarification

The Critical Distinction: Who Gets What

INTERROGATORIES = For the listed party (the bank) - Only the named plaintiff must answer interrogatories - The bank answers through their attorney - Limited to factual questions the bank has access to

DEPOSITIONS = For witnesses and non-parties - Individual people answer under their own oath - Affidavit signers, document custodians, servicers - Anyone with knowledge about your specific loan

This distinction matters: You cannot serve interrogatories on the affidavit signer who doesn't work for the bank anymore. But you CAN depose them — written or oral. Depositions reach people outside the party. Interrogatories don't.

How to Take a Written Deposition

Step 1: Notice of Deposition Serve a notice of deposition on the bank's attorney naming the witness and stating it will be by written questions:

```
NOTICE OF DEPOSITION

TO: [Bank's Attorney]

Please take notice that Defendant will take the deposition of
[Witness Name] by written questions pursuant to [cite rule:
FRCP 31 or state equivalent].

The witness shall answer the attached questions under oath
within 30 days of service of this notice.
```

Step 2: Written Questions Attach your written questions to the notice. They should be: - Clear and specific - Designed to lock in testimony - Targeted at the witness's knowledge or lack thereof

Sample written deposition questions:

```
QUESTION 1: State your full name, current address, and current
employer.

QUESTION 2: Did you review the original promissory note in
Defendant's loan file before signing the affidavit dated
[Date]? If yes, describe what you reviewed. If no, state
why not.

QUESTION 3: How many affidavits did you sign on the date you
signed the affidavit in this case?

QUESTION 4: Did you have personal knowledge of Defendant's
payment history before signing the affidavit? Explain.
```

Step 3: Service and Response - Serve the notice and questions on the bank's attorney - The bank must produce the witness or face sanctions - The witness answers under oath within the time limit - You receive sworn written answers you can use in court

Real-World Application

Your strategy: 1. Use **interrogatories** for the bank party (factual questions about ownership, calculations, etc.) 2. Use **written depositions** for the affidavit signer (lock in their lack of knowledge) 3. Use **written depositions** for the document custodian (establish chain of custody or lack thereof) 4. Save **oral depositions** for high-value witnesses where real-time questioning matters

What you'll discover: Most affidavit signers will admit in written depositions that: - They never reviewed the original note - They signed hundreds of affidavits per day - They have no personal knowledge of your specific loan - They were following a script, not exercising independent judgment

These admissions are gold. Use them to challenge the bank's affidavits, support your motion to compel, and impeach witnesses at trial.

Bank Objections to Written Depositions

They may object: - "We don't produce witnesses for written depositions" - "Oral deposition only" - "The witness is unavailable"

Your response: The rules allow written depositions. If they refuse to produce the witness, file a motion to compel. The court can order the witness to answer written questions. If they still refuse, request sanctions.

The bottom line: Written depositions are cheaper, just as effective, and often produce better answers because the witness can't charm their way through vague responses. Use them liberally.

Discovery on the Note and Chain

The most important discovery targets the note and chain of title.

The Original Note

Why it matters: Only the holder of the original note (or someone with the right to enforce it) can foreclose. UCC Article 3 governs.

What to request: - The original note - All allonges - All endorsements - Chain of custody documentation

What to look for: - Is the note endorsed to the plaintiff? - Are endorsements blank or special? - Are there gaps in the chain? - Does the plaintiff have the original or just a copy?

Assignments and Transfers

Request every assignment: From the original lender to the current plaintiff, every step must be documented.

What to look for: - Are all assignments present? - Are dates sequential? - Are signatures genuine? - Are notary acknowledgments valid?

The assignment problem: Many foreclosures have breaks in the assignment chain. The loan was sold from A to B to C, but there's no assignment from A to B. The plaintiff claims to be C but can't prove they received title from B.

Securitization Documents

If the loan was securitized: - Request the PSA - Request the mortgage loan schedule - Request SEC filings - Request representations and warranties

What to look for: - Was the loan transferred before the cut-off date? - Is the loan listed on the schedule? - Were required documents delivered? - Did the sponsor make representations about loan quality?

Discovery on Damages and Accounting

Banks often demand the wrong amount. Discovery can expose accounting errors.

Payment History Discovery

Request complete records:

```
REQUEST FOR PRODUCTION NO. 10:

Produce a complete payment history for Defendant's loan from
origination to present, including:
(a) Date and amount of each payment received
(b) How each payment was applied (principal, interest, escrow)
(c) All fees or charges assessed
(d) All force-placed insurance premiums
(e) All property inspection fees
(f) All late charges
```

What to look for: - Payments not credited - Fees not authorized - Escrow miscalculations - Duplicate charges - Interest calculated incorrectly

Force-Placed Insurance

Request insurance records:

```
REQUEST FOR PRODUCTION NO. 11:

Produce all documents relating to force-placed insurance on
Defendant's property, including:
(a) Notices sent regarding insurance deficiencies
(b) The insurance policy placed
(c) Premium amounts and payments
(d) Evidence that Defendant's insurance actually lapsed
```

What to look for: - Proper notice not given - Insurance placed when borrower had coverage - Excessive premiums - Kickbacks or affiliate relationships

Escrow Analysis

Request escrow records:

```
REQUEST FOR PRODUCTION NO. 12:

Produce all escrow analyses and statements for Defendant's loan,
including the methodology for calculating escrow payments.
```

What to look for: - Incorrect tax or insurance estimates - Over-collection of escrow - Failure to pay taxes or insurance from escrow - Unauthorized escrow cushion

---

LEARN FROM THIS MISTAKE: The Homeowner Who Asked the Wrong Questions

Deborah Chen's Story: Deborah served 30 interrogatories on the bank. She asked about the bank's corporate structure, its servicer's business practices, the history of securitization, and the details of the trust that allegedly owned her loan. She spent hours crafting detailed questions.> The bank responded with objections: "Overbroad," "Not relevant," "Calls for legal conclusion," "Seeks proprietary information." Almost every interrogatory was objected to.> Deborah didn't know how to respond. She thought her questions were reasonable. She filed a motion to compel, arguing that the information was relevant to her defense.> The judge denied her motion. "These interrogatories seek information far beyond what is relevant to this foreclosure action. The defendant doesn't need to know the corporate structure of entities not party to this action or the history of mortgage securitization generally. The objections are sustained."> Deborah had wasted her limited interrogatories on questions that didn't matter. She had no interrogatories left to ask about the note, the assignments, or the payment history — the things that actually mattered to her defense.> What Deborah should have done:> - Focused on facts specific to her loan - Asked about the note, assignments, and payment history - Used requests for production to get documents rather than interrogatories to ask about corporate structures - Kept questions narrow and relevant to foreclosure

"I got caught up in the securitization theories I read online," Deborah says. "I wanted to expose the whole system. But what mattered was whether this specific bank could prove they owned my specific loan. I asked questions that sounded important but didn't help my case."> **The Lesson:** Discovery must be relevant to your specific case. You don't need to understand the entire securitization industry. You need to know whether THIS bank can prove they own YOUR loan. Focus your discovery on: (1) the note and its endorsements, (2) the assignments of your mortgage, (3) your payment history, (4) the bank's damages calculation. Don't waste discovery on broad industry issues or corporate structures that don't affect your foreclosure. Narrow, relevant discovery is effective discovery.

LEARN FROM THIS MISTAKE: The Homeowner Who Missed the Deposition Gold Mine

Michael Torres' Story: Michael's foreclosure case had a critical weakness — the affidavit attached to the complaint was signed by "Linda Marshall," a known robo-signer who had signed thousands of affidavits for the bank. Michael's attorney suggested deposing Ms. Marshall.> The bank's attorney objected. "Ms. Marshall no longer works for the servicer. We don't know where she is. We're not producing her for deposition."> Michael's attorney didn't push back. "It's not worth the fight," the attorney said. "We'll challenge the affidavit at summary judgment instead."> At summary judgment, the bank submitted a new affidavit from a different employee — one who claimed to have reviewed the records and verified their accuracy. The bank withdrew Ms. Marshall's affidavit and substituted the new one.> Michael's attorney objected. "The bank is trying to cure a defective affidavit with a new one after discovery closed."> The judge disagreed. "The bank is free to submit the best evidence it has. The new affiant has personal knowledge. The affidavit is admitted."> Michael lost. If he had deposed Ms. Marshall, he would have established that she had no personal knowledge, that she signed hundreds of affidavits per day, and that she couldn't have reviewed his specific file. That testimony would have poisoned the well for any subsequent affidavit from the bank. By not deposing her, he let the bank substitute a clean witness.> What Michael should have done:> - Filed a motion to compel Ms. Marshall's deposition - Subpoenaed her if she no longer worked for the bank - Established her robo-signing practices on the record - Used that testimony to challenge any subsequent affidavit from the bank

"I didn't understand the value of deposing their witness," Michael says. "I thought we'd just challenge the affidavit later. But without her testimony on record, the bank just swapped in a new witness. I let them cure their defect by not pinning them down."> **The Lesson:** Deposing the bank's key witnesses locks in their testimony and prevents the bank from swapping witnesses later. If you have a robo-signer or affidavit signer with questionable practices, depose them. Establish their lack of personal knowledge. Get their admission that they signed hundreds of documents without review. Once that testimony is on record, the bank can't substitute a new witness without explaining why the first one was wrong. Depositions create a record that limits the bank's options later. Don't let them cure defects by switching witnesses.

Chapter Summary

- **Discovery is your weapon.** Banks rely on assumptions and affidavits. Discovery forces them to produce actual evidence or admit they don't have it.
- **Use all four discovery tools:** Requests for production get documents. Interrogatories establish facts. Requests for admission pin down claims. Depositions examine witnesses.
- **Always request the original note.** If the bank can't produce it or it lacks proper endorsement, they may lack standing.
- **Request the complete chain of title.** Breaks in the assignment chain destroy the bank's claim to ownership.
- **An objection is not the end.** Meet and confer. Narrow your requests if needed. File a motion to compel if necessary. Don't give up because the bank objected.

- **Use requests for admission strategically.** Admissions are conclusive at trial. Denials create impeachment material. Unanswered RFAs are deemed admitted.
- **Depositions are powerful but expensive.** Use them when you have a clear purpose, like establishing that an affidavit signer has no personal knowledge.
- **Focus on what matters.** Discovery should target the note, assignments, payment history, and damages calculation. Don't waste resources on broad industry issues.
- **Follow up on everything.** Discovery is a process, not a one-time event. Track responses, calendar deadlines, and push back against bad faith objections.

Cross-References

Previous Chapter: Chapter 11 — Motion to Dismiss Strategy

Next Chapter: Chapter 13 — Motions to Compel and Forcing Real Answers

Related Chapters: - Chapter 4: Document Audit System (for pre-discovery document analysis) - Chapter 6: Assignments and Chain of Title (for what to look for in assignments) - Chapter 7: Note-Mortgage Separation (for endorsement issues) - Chapter 14: Requests for Admission (detailed RFA strategy)

In the Playbook: - Document Request Checklist - Interrogatories Template - Requests for Admission Template - Deposition Preparation Guide

Templates: - Request for Production Template - Interrogatories Template - Requests for Admission Template - Meet and Confer Letter Template

CHAPTER 13: VICTORY CASE STUDIES

Real Homeowners Who Beat the Banks

Here's What Happened to Me

When I was fighting my foreclosure, I felt alone. Like I was the only person crazy enough to think I could beat a bank. Then I started researching. And I discovered something amazing:

Homeowners win. All the time.

Not just rich people with fancy lawyers. Regular people. People like you and me. People who were scared, overwhelmed, and underdogs — but who learned the system and used it.

This chapter is about them. Their stories. Their strategies. What they did that worked.

Study these cases. Use their strategies. Their wins can be your wins.

What You Need to Know

I've organized these victories by the **legal theory** that won the case. Find the theory that matches YOUR situation, and read how others used it successfully.

The 8 Winning Strategies:

1. **Standing/Chain of Title** — The bank couldn't prove they owned your loan
2. **Document Fraud/Robo-Signing** — Fake signatures, forged documents
3. **TILA/RESPA Violations** — Federal disclosure violations, rescission rights
4. **Statute of Limitations** — The bank waited too long
5. **Procedural/Notice Defects** — They didn't follow the rules
6. **Wrongful Foreclosure/Trial Wins** — Taking it all the way to verdict
7. **Bankruptcy Stay** — Automatic stay violations
8. **Servicing/Loss Mitigation** — Dual tracking, modification failures

---

RED FLAG ALERT

Every case is different. What worked in one case may not work in yours. Laws vary by state. Facts matter. Don't just copy-paste — understand WHY they won and how it applies to YOUR situation.

Always verify case citations. Use Google Scholar to confirm cases exist and are still good law.

CATEGORY 1: STANDING/CHAIN OF TITLE WINS

The bank couldn't prove they owned the loan

This is the **#1 winning defense** nationwide. Banks mess up the paperwork. They foreclose before they own the loan. They lose track of documents in the securitization maze. When they can't prove they have the right to foreclose, they lose.

CASE #1: U.S. Bank v. Ibanez

Massachusetts Supreme Judicial Court | 2011

The Win: Summary judgment for homeowner — foreclosure void

What Happened: U.S. Bank and Wells Fargo foreclosed on two properties. But here's the kicker: **they started the foreclosures BEFORE they actually got the mortgage assignments.** They recorded the assignments AFTER the foreclosure sales were already done.

The Homeowner's Strategy: 1. **Demand the complete chain of assignments** — Get every recorded document 2. **Check the dates carefully** — Compare assignment dates to foreclosure notice dates 3. **Point out the impossibility** — You can't foreclose on a loan you don't own yet

Why They Won: The Massachusetts Supreme Court held that to foreclose, you must be the assignee **at the time of foreclosure**. An assignment recorded after foreclosure is too late — it can't fix an already-void foreclosure.

The Exact Quote: > "The statutory power of sale can only be exercised by 'the mortgagee or his executors, administrators, successors or assigns.' "

Strategy Takeaway: Check your assignment dates. If the assignment to the foreclosing bank was recorded AFTER the foreclosure proceedings began, you have an *Ibanez* defense. The foreclosure may be void.

HEY LOOK HERE This case started a wave of dismissals across Massachusetts. If your foreclosure happened between 2003-2011 in Massachusetts and involved securitized loans, check those dates immediately.

CASE #2: Yvanova v. New Century Mortgage Corporation

California Supreme Court | 2016

The Win: Summary judgment for homeowner

What Happened: Tsvetana Yvanova's loan was supposedly transferred into a mortgage-backed securities trust. But the assignment happened **AFTER the trust's closing date** — the date when the trust was supposed to stop accepting new loans. Deutsche Bank, as trustee, tried to foreclose.

The Homeowner's Strategy: 1. **Get the Pooling and Servicing Agreement (PSA)** — This document specifies the trust's closing date 2. **Compare dates** — Check assignment date vs. trust closing date 3. **Challenge void assignment** — An assignment after closing is void, not just voidable

Why They Won: The California Supreme Court held that **homeowners have standing to challenge void assignments**. A void assignment is a nullity — it never existed. If the assignment is void, the foreclosing party has no authority.

The Exact Quote: > "A borrower has standing to challenge a foreclosure based on a void assignment."

Strategy Takeaway: Get the PSA and check the closing date. If your loan was assigned to a securitization trust after the trust closed, that assignment may be void. This applies nationwide.

TIP BOX *I Wish I Knew This Sooner:*

PSAs are public documents. You can often find them on the SEC's EDGAR database. Search for your loan servicer's name + "pooling and servicing agreement." The closing date is usually defined as "the Closing Date" in the document.

CASE #3: Eaton v. Fannie Mae

Massachusetts Supreme Judicial Court | 2012

The Win: Summary judgment for homeowner

What Happened: Fannie Mae tried to foreclose on Henrietta Eaton. The question: Does the foreclosing party need to hold **both** the mortgage AND the promissory note?

The Homeowner's Strategy: 1. **Demand to see the original note** — Not a copy, the original 2. **Check endorsements** — Is the note properly endorsed to the foreclosing party? 3. **Challenge separation of note and mortgage** — In many states, these must travel together

Why They Won: The court held that to foreclose by power of sale, the mortgage holder **must also hold the mortgage note** (or be acting as the authorized agent of the note holder).

The Exact Quote: > "We conclude that, to foreclose by power of sale, the mortgage holder must also hold the mortgage note or be acting on behalf of the note holder."

Strategy Takeaway: Demand proof the foreclosing party holds the note. If they only have the mortgage but not the note, and can't prove they're the note holder's authorized agent, they lack standing to foreclose.

HEY LOOK HERE This is the *Eaton* rule. It changed Massachusetts law. Even if your state doesn't have an *Eaton* decision, the principle is powerful: the right to foreclose comes from owning the debt (the note), not just the security (the mortgage).

CASE #4: Glaski v. Bank of America

California Court of Appeals | 2013

The Win: Summary judgment for homeowner

What Happened: Mr. Glaski's loan was supposed to be transferred into a mortgage-backed securities trust. But the assignment to the trust happened **after the trust's closing date** — making it void. Bank of America tried to foreclose anyway.

The Homeowner's Strategy: 1. **Identify the securitization chain** — Find every assignment 2. **Find the PSA** — Get the pooling and servicing agreement 3. **Prove the late assignment** — Show the assignment occurred after the trust closed 4. **Argue void assignment** — A void assignment transfers nothing

Why They Won: The court held that an assignment to a securitization trust that occurs **after the trust's closing date is void**. A void assignment is a legal nullity — it never happened. If the foreclosing party's authority comes from a void assignment, they have no authority to foreclose.

Strategy Takeaway: Check the PSA closing date. If the assignment to the trust happened after the closing date, the assignment is void. This defense has worked in multiple states.

TIP BOX *Common Pattern:*

This is a **very common problem** in securitized loans. The loans were supposed to be transferred into trusts by specific dates (usually in 2005-2007). But the paperwork was sloppy. Many assignments happened late. If your loan was securitized, check those dates.

CASE #5: Culhane v. Aurora Loan Services

U.S. First Circuit Court of Appeals | 2013

The Win: Summary judgment affirmed for homeowner

What Happened: Aurora Loan Services tried to foreclose. But they were just the **servicer** — they collected payments. They didn't own the note. They claimed they could foreclose as the "authorized agent" but couldn't prove it.

The Homeowner's Strategy: 1. **Identify who is foreclosing** — Is it the lender or just a servicer? 2. **Demand proof of agency** — If they claim to be an agent, demand the written authorization 3. **Challenge standing** — A servicer without proper authorization lacks standing

Why They Won: The First Circuit (federal appeals court) held that a servicer must **demonstrate written authorization from the note holder** to foreclose. Aurora couldn't prove it, so they lost.

The Exact Quote: > "The servicer must demonstrate that it has the authority to act on behalf of the note holder."

Strategy Takeaway: If a servicer is foreclosing, demand their proof of authority. They need written authorization from the note holder. If they can't produce it, they lack standing.

CATEGORY 2: DOCUMENT FRAUD/ROBO-SIGNING WINS

Fake signatures, forged documents, and fraudulent affidavits

During the foreclosure crisis (2008-2012), banks were caught using "robo-signers" — people who signed thousands of foreclosure documents per day without reading them. Some signed as officers of companies they didn't work for. This was fraud.

CASE #6: Bain v. Wells Fargo

Washington Supreme Court | 2012

The Win: Summary judgment for homeowner

What Happened: Kristine Bain faced foreclosure by Wells Fargo. The assignment of mortgage was signed by a known robo-signer who admitted in other cases to signing thousands of documents without review.

The Homeowner's Strategy: 1. **Identify the signer** — Look up the name on the assignment 2. **Research the signer** — Google their name + "robo-signing" + "deposition" 3. **Find admissions** — Many robo-signers admitted their practices under oath 4. **Challenge the document** — If the signer didn't review the document, the affidavit is fraudulent

Why They Won: The Washington Supreme Court held that fraudulent documents cannot support a foreclosure. When a signer admits to signing without review or authority, the document is not valid evidence.

Strategy Takeaway: Google the signer's name. If they were a known robo-signer, you can find their deposition testimony online. Use their own words against them.

HEY LOOK HERE

Known Robo-Signers to Research: - Linda Green - Crystal Moore
- Erica Johnson-Seck - Bryan Bly - Korell Harp - Beth Cottrell

If any of these names appear on your documents, you likely have a robo-signing defense.

CASE #7: In re Foreclosure Cases (Mass Dismissals)

U.S. District Court, Northern District of Ohio | 2007-2010

The Win: Mass dismissals of foreclosure cases

What Happened: Judge Christopher Boyko in Ohio reviewed foreclosure cases and found that **multiple banks could not prove they owned the mortgages** they were trying to foreclose on. When asked to produce the note, they couldn't.

The Homeowner's Strategy: 1. **Demand production of the original note** — File a motion to compel 2. **Challenge at summary judgment** — If they can't produce it, they can't prove their case 3. **Request dismissal** — No note = no standing

Why They Won: Judge Boyko dismissed multiple foreclosure cases because the plaintiffs could not produce the original promissory notes. Without the note, they could not prove they were entitled to enforce the debt.

Strategy Takeaway: Demand the original note. Under the Uniform Commercial Code (UCC), the party seeking to enforce a note must produce it or explain why it was lost (with strict requirements). Many banks can't produce the original.

TIP BOX *The Lost Note Affidavit Trap:*

If the bank claims the note is lost, they must file a "lost note affidavit." But there are strict requirements: - They must prove they had it and lost it - They must explain the circumstances - They must indemnify you against claims by others If their affidavit doesn't meet these requirements, challenge it.

CATEGORY 3: TILA/RESPA VIOLATION WINS

Federal disclosure violations and rescission rights

The Truth in Lending Act (TILA) and Real Estate Settlement Procedures Act (RESPA) give homeowners powerful federal rights. Violations can extend your rescission period, void fees, or even rescind the entire loan.

CASE #8: Jesinoski v. Countrywide Home Loans

U.S. Supreme Court | 2015

The Win: UNANIMOUS 9-0 Supreme Court victory

What Happened: Larry and Cheryle Jesinoski wanted to rescind their loan under TILA. The bank said they had to file a lawsuit to rescind. The Jesinoskis said they just had to notify the bank in writing within 3 years. The case went all the way to the Supreme Court.

The Homeowner's Strategy: 1. **Send written rescission notice** — Within 3 years of closing 2. **Notify all parties** — Lender, servicer, assignees 3. **Don't file suit (yet)** — Written notice is sufficient to exercise the right 4. **Wait for bank to sue** — If they dispute, let them file; you're just exercising your right

Why They Won: The U.S. Supreme Court held that **written notice within the 3-year period is sufficient to exercise the right of rescission.** You do NOT need to file a lawsuit. This was a 9-0 unanimous decision.

The Exact Quote: > "A borrower exercises his right to rescind... by providing written notice to his lender within three years of the transaction."

Strategy Takeaway: Send your rescission notice by certified mail within 3 years of closing. Keep the receipt. You don't need a lawyer to exercise this right. Written notice is enough.

HEY LOOK HERE

This is a **SUPREME COURT decision.** It applies nationwide. If you have TILA disclosure violations (you didn't get proper notices at closing), you may have rescission rights. Consult a TILA attorney — this is powerful federal law.

CASE #9: Williams v. Homestake Mortgage Co.

Federal Circuit Court | 1992

The Win: Rescission granted

What Happened: The Williamses didn't receive all required TILA disclosures at closing. They exercised their right of rescission years later based on these disclosure violations.

The Homeowner's Strategy: 1. **Review closing documents** — Did you get all required TILA disclosures? 2. **Identify violations** — Missing forms, incorrect APR, missing notices 3. **Calculate extended rescission period** — Violations can extend rescission to 3 years 4. **Send rescission notice** — Exercise your right

Why They Won: The court held that **TILA disclosure violations extend the rescission period from 3 days to 3 years.** Even years later, you can rescind if the lender didn't give proper disclosures.

Strategy Takeaway: Check your closing documents for missing or incorrect TILA disclosures. If you didn't get proper notices, your rescission period may be extended to 3 years. This can be a complete defense to foreclosure.

RED FLAG ALERT

Rescission is powerful but complex. If you think you have TILA violations, **consult a TILA attorney.** The law has specific requirements and deadlines. Don't attempt this alone.

CATEGORY 4: STATUTE OF LIMITATIONS WINS

The bank waited too long

Every state has a time limit for bringing foreclosure actions. If the bank waits too long after you default, they may lose their right to foreclose forever.

CASE #10: Bartram v. U.S. Bank

Florida Supreme Court | 2016

The Win: Homeowner victory on statute of limitations

What Happened: U.S. Bank filed foreclosure, then voluntarily dismissed it. Five years later, they filed again. The question: Did the statute of limitations reset when they dismissed the first case?

The Homeowner's Strategy: 1. **Calculate the timeline** — When was the first foreclosure filed? When was it dismissed? 2. **Identify the default date** — When did you first miss a payment? 3. **Apply state law** — In Florida, foreclosure has a 5-year statute of limitations 4. **Argue time-barred** — If more than 5 years passed, the foreclosure is barred

Why They Won: The Florida Supreme Court held that **a dismissal of a prior foreclosure action does NOT reset the statute of limitations.** If the bank filed, dismissed, and waited too long, they may be time-barred from refiling.

Strategy Takeaway: Track your foreclosure timeline. If the bank filed before, dismissed, and is now refiling, check if the statute of limitations has expired. This can be a complete defense.

TIP BOX *State Variations:*

Statute of limitations for foreclosure varies by state: - Florida: 5 years - California: 4 years (judicial) / varies (non-judicial) - New York: 6 years - Illinois: 10 years

Check your state's law. Some states measure from the date of default; others from the date of acceleration.

CASE #11: Deutsche Bank v. Beauvais

Florida Third District Court of Appeal | 2016

The Win: Foreclosure dismissed as time-barred

What Happened: Deutsche Bank accelerated the loan (demanded full payment) in 2007 but didn't file foreclosure until 2012 — more than 5 years later. The Beauvaises argued the statute of limitations had run.

The Homeowner's Strategy: 1. **Identify acceleration date** — When did the bank first demand full payment? 2. **Calculate 5 years** — From acceleration to foreclosure filing

3. **Argue limitations** — If more than 5 years passed, foreclosure is barred

Why They Won: The court held that once a lender accelerates the loan (demands full payment), the 5-year clock starts ticking. If they don't file foreclosure within 5 years of acceleration, the foreclosure is time-barred.

Strategy Takeaway: Find the acceleration date. Look for the first demand letter or notice that said you owe the full balance. If more than your state's limitation period has passed since then, you have a statute of limitations defense.

CATEGORY 5: PROCEDURAL/NOTICE DEFECT WINS

They didn't follow the rules

Foreclosure requires strict compliance with state procedures. Missing notices, wrong addresses, failure to serve — these defects can invalidate a foreclosure.

CASE #12: McLean v. JPMorgan Chase Bank

New York Supreme Court | 2013

The Win: Foreclosure dismissed for improper service

What Happened: JPMorgan Chase claimed they served McLean with the foreclosure summons. But McLean proved he was never properly served. The service was defective.

The Homeowner's Strategy: 1. **Document your whereabouts** — Where were you when they claim to have served you? 2. **Challenge the affidavit of service** — Was the process server credible? 3. **Request proof** — Demand the return of service, photos, GPS data 4. **Move to dismiss** — Improper service = no jurisdiction

Why They Won: The court held that **proper service is required for the court to have jurisdiction.** If the borrower wasn't properly served, the case must be dismissed.

Strategy Takeaway: Challenge improper service. If you weren't properly served with the foreclosure lawsuit, the court may lack jurisdiction. This is especially powerful if you found out about the foreclosure late.

HEY LOOK HERE

Many foreclosure cases have **sewer service** — the process server claims they served you but actually didn't. Check the affidavit of service. Does the description match you? Was it really you they served? Challenge questionable service.

CATEGORY 6: WRONGFUL FORECLOSURE/TRIAL WINS

Taking it all the way to verdict

Most foreclosure cases settle or are decided on motions. But some go to trial — and homeowners win.

CASE #13: Sciarratta v. U.S. Bank

California Court of Appeals | 2016

The Win: Wrongful foreclosure verdict for homeowner

What Happened: The Sciarrattas applied for a loan modification. Under California's Homeowner Bill of Rights, the bank couldn't "dual track" — foreclose while considering the modification. U.S. Bank did it anyway.

The Homeowner's Strategy: 1. **Apply for modification** — Complete application properly 2. **Document dual tracking** — Get evidence bank continued foreclosure 3. **Challenge under HBOR** — California law prohibits dual tracking 4. **Seek wrongful foreclosure damages** — If dual tracking occurred, it's wrongful foreclosure

Why They Won: The court held that **dual tracking violates California law and constitutes wrongful foreclosure.** The Sciarrattas won damages for the wrongful foreclosure.

Strategy Takeaway: If you're in California, know the Homeowner Bill of Rights. If you applied for a modification and the bank continued foreclosure anyway, you may have a wrongful foreclosure claim. Other states have similar laws.

TIP BOX *I Wish I Knew This Sooner:*

Dual tracking is illegal in many states now. If you applied for a modification and the bank kept foreclosing, that's dual tracking. Document everything — dates of modification application, dates of foreclosure notices, any communications. This can be powerful evidence.

CATEGORY 7: BANKRUPTCY STAY WINS

Automatic stay violations

When you file for bankruptcy, the "automatic stay" immediately stops all collection actions, including foreclosure. If the bank violates the stay, they can face serious sanctions.

CASE #14: In re Nosek

U.S. Bankruptcy Court, District of Massachusetts | 2014

The Win: Sanctions against bank for stay violation

What Happened: Mr. Nosek filed for Chapter 13 bankruptcy. The automatic stay went into effect. But the bank continued foreclosure proceedings anyway, conducting a foreclosure sale in violation of the stay.

The Homeowner's Strategy: 1. **File bankruptcy** — Chapter 7 or 13 to invoke automatic stay 2. **Notify all parties** — Send notice of bankruptcy filing to lender, servicer, trustee 3. **Document stay violation** — Gather evidence of foreclosure activity post-filing 4. **File motion for sanctions** — Request damages for willful stay violation

Why They Won: The bankruptcy court found that the bank **willfully violated the automatic stay** by conducting a foreclosure sale after the bankruptcy was filed. The court imposed sanctions on the bank.

Strategy Takeaway: Bankruptcy stops foreclosure immediately. If the bank continues foreclosure after you file, that's a stay violation. You can get damages, attorney fees, and punitive sanctions.

RED FLAG ALERT

Bankruptcy is a powerful tool but has serious consequences. **Consult a bankruptcy attorney** before filing. Chapter 13 can help you save your home; Chapter 7 might delay foreclosure but won't save the house long-term.

CATEGORY 8: SERVICING/LOSS MITIGATION WINS

Dual tracking, modification failures, and servicing errors

Mortgage servicers make mistakes — lost paperwork, misapplied payments, false promises. These errors can be defenses to foreclosure.

CASE #15: Bank of America v. Solic

New York Supreme Court | 2013

The Win: Foreclosure dismissed for servicing errors

What Happened: Bank of America misapplied Mr. Solic's payments, charged improper fees, and provided inconsistent information about his account. The errors were so significant that the court found the bank had unclean hands.

The Homeowner's Strategy: 1. **Request complete payment history** — Get every payment, fee, charge 2. **Compare to your records** — Bank statements, canceled checks 3. **Identify errors** — Misapplied payments, improper fees, force-placed insurance 4. **Challenge accounting** — If the amount demanded is wrong, the foreclosure is defective

Why They Won: The court held that **significant servicing errors can invalidate a foreclosure.** When the bank can't prove the correct amount owed due to their own errors, they lack the basis to foreclose.

Strategy Takeaway: Audit your account. Compare the bank's payment history to your records. Look for misapplied payments, improper fees, force-placed insurance charges. If the amount is wrong, challenge it.

TIP BOX *Common Servicing Errors:*

- Payments posted to wrong account
- Fees for "property inspection" that never happened
- Force-placed insurance when you had coverage
- Escrow miscalculations
- Lost modification applications

Document everything. These errors can be powerful defenses.

HOW TO USE THIS CHAPTER

Step 1: Find Your Category Look at the 8 winning strategies. Which matches your situation?

Step 2: Read the Cases Read the cases in your category. Understand the facts and legal theories.

Step 3: Verify the Cases Use Google Scholar to verify the case citations and make sure the law is still good.

Step 4: Apply to Your Facts How does the winning strategy apply to YOUR situation? What facts do you have in common?

Step 5: Develop Your Strategy Use the "Strategy Takeaway" from each case to develop your own defense.

Step 6: Cite the Cases If appropriate, cite the winning cases in your pleadings. Show the court that homeowners win with these arguments.

HEY LOOK HERE

These cases are just the beginning. I've documented 70+ homeowner victories in my research. The full database is available at: `/root/.openclaw/workspace/research/homeowner-vi`

Use it. Study it. Their wins can be your wins.

TIP BOX

Final Thought:

Every case in this chapter represents a homeowner who was scared, overwhelmed, and facing a powerful bank. But they learned the law, found the bank's weaknesses, and fought back.

You are not alone. You are not helpless. You CAN win.

The homeowners in this chapter proved it. Now it's your turn.

CROSS-REFERENCES

Use these cases with: - Chapter 3: Document Forensics (for fraud cases) - Chapter 4: Your Defenses (for legal theories) - Chapter 12: Using AI (to draft motions citing these cases) - Templates: Motion to Dismiss, Motion for Summary Judgment

Next: Chapter 14 — Resources and Help

CHAPTER 14: REQUESTS FOR ADMISSION AS A PRESSURE TOOL

The Discovery Weapon Banks Fear Most

What Are Requests for Admission?

Requests for Admission (RFAs) are written statements sent to the opposing party asking them to admit or deny specific facts. They are the most underused — and most powerful — discovery tool in foreclosure defense.

How RFAs Work

You send the bank a set of numbered statements. For each statement, the bank must:

1. **Admit** — The statement is true
2. **Deny** — The statement is false
3. **Object** — The request is improper (limited grounds)

The deadline: Typically 30 days from service. If the bank doesn't respond in time, the requests are **deemed admitted** — automatically treated as if the bank admitted them.

Why RFAs Are Different

Unlike other discovery: - Admissions are **conclusive** at trial — you don't have to prove admitted facts - Denials create **impeachment material** — if you later prove a denied fact, the bank looks dishonest - **Non-response equals admission** — silence is fatal to the bank's case - **Objections are limited** — banks can't object just because they don't want to answer

Compare to other discovery:

Discovery Type	Bank's Response	Consequence
Document Request	Produce or object	Can stall with objections
Interrogatories	Answer or object	Can be evasive
Deposition	Testify	Can say "I don't know"
Requests for Admission	**Admit, deny, or object**	**No response = admission**

Strategic Value in Foreclosure

RFAs are uniquely powerful in foreclosure because they target the bank's weakest points.

Force Admissions on Standing

Example RFA:

```
REQUEST FOR ADMISSION NO. 1:

Admit that Plaintiff does not possess the original promissory
note executed by Defendant.
```

If admitted: You now have a conclusive admission that the bank lacks the key document. Summary judgment on standing becomes possible.

If denied: You know the bank claims to have the note. Force them to produce it.

If no response: Deemed admitted. The bank has admitted they don't have the note.

Expose Chain of Title Gaps

Example RFAs:

```
REQUEST FOR ADMISSION NO. 2:

Admit that there is no written assignment of the mortgage from
[Prior Lender] to Plaintiff dated before [Complaint Date].

REQUEST FOR ADMISSION NO. 3:

Admit that the assignment of mortgage attached to the complaint
was executed after the complaint was filed.
```

Strategic value: These admissions establish timing problems that destroy standing. A post-complaint assignment cannot cure lack of standing at filing.

Pin Down Damages Claims

Example RFAs:

```
REQUEST FOR ADMISSION NO. 4:
```

```
Admit that the amount demanded in the complaint includes late
fees that were not authorized by the note or mortgage.

REQUEST FOR ADMISSION NO. 5:

Admit that Plaintiff has no record of Defendant's payments
received between [Date] and [Date].
```

Strategic value: Admissions about improper fees or missing payment records directly attack the amount the bank claims is due.

Create Impeachment Material

Every denial is a potential impeachment at trial:

At deposition: > Attorney: "You denied that the assignment was backdated." > Witness: "That's correct."

At trial, after proving the assignment was backdated: > Attorney: "You testified under oath that the assignment wasn't backdated." > Witness: "I... uh..." > Attorney: "And you were wrong, weren't you?"

The denied RFA becomes impeachment gold.

Streamline Trial Issues

Admissions narrow what you must prove at trial:

Before RFAs: - Prove the bank doesn't have the note - Prove the assignment is defective - Prove the amount is wrong - Prove the witness lacks personal knowledge

After RFAs (with admissions): - Bank admitted they don't have the note - Bank admitted the assignment was post-complaint - Bank admitted the amount includes unauthorized fees - Only remaining issue: witness credibility

Trials become shorter and winnable when the bank admits key facts.

Drafting Effective Requests

Good RFAs are specific, factual, and strategically targeted. Bad RFAs are vague, argumentative, or legally complex.

The Formula for Effective RFAs

Effective RFA structure:

```
Admit that [specific factual statement].
```

Characteristics of effective RFAs: - **Single fact per request** — Don't bundle multiple facts - **Objective and verifiable** — Not opinions or legal conclusions - **Specific and concrete** — Not general or vague - **Important to your case** — Every RFA should serve a strategic purpose

Categories of Strategic RFAs

1. Standing and Document RFAs

Target the bank's ability to prove they own the loan:

```
Admit that Plaintiff does not possess the original promissory
note executed by Defendant.

Admit that the note is not endorsed to Plaintiff.

Admit that there is no allonge attached to the note.

Admit that Plaintiff never received delivery of the note.
```

2. Chain of Title RFAs

Expose breaks in the assignment chain:

```
Admit that there is no assignment of mortgage from [Originator]
to [Next Holder] in Plaintiff's possession.

Admit that the assignment attached as Exhibit A was executed
on [Date], which is after the complaint was filed.

Admit that [Name], the person who signed the assignment, was
not employed by [Assignor] at the time of signing.
```

3. Damages and Accounting RFAs

Challenge the amount demanded:

```
Admit that the amount of $[Amount] claimed as past-due
includes charges that were not authorized by the loan documents.
```

```
Admit that Plaintiff has no record of Defendant's payment
received on [Date].

Admit that the force-placed insurance premium of $[Amount]
exceeded the actual cost of the insurance.
```

4. Witness and Knowledge RFAs

Undermine affidavit testimony:

```
Admit that [Affiant Name] did not review Defendant's payment
history before signing the affidavit attached to the complaint.

Admit that [Affiant Name] signed more than 100 affidavits on
the same day the affidavit in this case was signed.

Admit that [Affiant Name] has no personal knowledge of how
Defendant's payments were applied to the account.
```

RFAs to Avoid

Don't request legal conclusions:

Bad: "Admit that Plaintiff lacks standing to bring this action."

Better: "Admit that Plaintiff does not possess the original promissory note."

Don't be argumentative:

Bad: "Admit that Plaintiff is lying about owning the loan."

Better: "Admit that the assignment attached to the complaint was executed by a robo-signer who signed 500 documents per day."

Don't be vague:

Bad: "Admit that the documents are defective."

Better: "Admit that the assignment of mortgage is not dated."

Numbering and Organization

Organize RFAs by category for clarity:

```
REQUESTS FOR ADMISSION - SET ONE

Requests Regarding the Original Note:
```

```
1. Admit that...
2. Admit that...

Requests Regarding Assignments:

3. Admit that...
4. Admit that...

Requests Regarding Damages:

5. Admit that...
6. Admit that...
```

Most jurisdictions limit the number of RFAs (often 25-30). Use them strategically. Quality over quantity.

LEARN FROM THIS MISTAKE: The Homeowner Who Sent RFAs Too Late

> **Victoria Adams' Story:** Victoria had a strong foreclosure defense. The assignment of her mortgage was clearly backdated — the notary stamp showed the notary's commission had expired six months before the assignment date. Victoria drafted excellent RFAs asking the bank to admit the notary was expired and the assignment was backdated.> But Victoria waited until the week before discovery closed to serve her RFAs. The bank's attorney received them and put them in a stack of papers. The 30-day response deadline passed after discovery had officially closed.> The bank never responded. Under the rules, the RFAs were deemed admitted. Victoria had conclusive admissions that the assignment was backdated and the notary was expired.> But when Victoria tried to use the admissions at summary judgment, the bank objected. "Your Honor, these RFAs were served after the discovery deadline. They are untimely and should be excluded."> The judge agreed. "The RFAs were served in violation of the discovery schedule. The admissions are excluded."> Victoria lost her smoking-gun admissions because she served them too late. The backdated assignment remained in evidence, and the bank won summary judgment.> What Victoria should have done:> - Served RFAs at the beginning of the discovery period - Tracked the 30-day response deadline with alerts - Filed a motion to deem admitted immediately

after the deadline passed - Used the admissions before discovery closed

"I thought I had plenty of time," Victoria says. "I didn't realize the discovery deadline controlled when you could serve discovery, not just when responses were due. By the time I sent my RFAs, it was too late."> **The Lesson:** RFAs must be served within the discovery period. The 30-day response deadline is for the bank — you must serve your RFAs before discovery closes. Track your court's discovery schedule carefully. Serve RFAs early in the discovery period so you have time to file motions to deem admitted and use the admissions while discovery is still open. Late RFAs are wasted RFAs.

Responding to Bank's Requests

When the bank sends YOU requests for admission, take them seriously. A missed deadline or careless admission can destroy your case.

How to Respond

For each request, you must:

1. **Admit** — If the statement is true
2. **Deny** — If the statement is false
3. **Object** — If the request is improper (and explain why)
4. **Explain** — Some jurisdictions require explanations for denials

Example response:

```
REQUEST FOR ADMISSION NO. 1:

Admit that you executed the promissory note dated [Date].

RESPONSE: ADMITTED.

REQUEST FOR ADMISSION NO. 2:

Admit that you defaulted on the loan by failing to make payments.

RESPONSE: DENIED. Defendant denies defaulting. Defendant is
without knowledge as to whether payments were properly credited
or whether any alleged default was waived.
```

Common Bank RFA Traps

Trap 1: Bundled facts

```
Admit that you executed the note, defaulted on the loan, and
own Plaintiff $287,000.
```

Response: Object as compound. Or deny in part, admit in part:

```
RESPONSE: DENIED as compound. To the extent the request seeks
admission that Defendant executed the note: ADMITTED. To the
extent the request seeks admission of default or amount owed:
DENIED. Defendant is without knowledge as to the accuracy of
Plaintiff's accounting.
```

Trap 2: Legal conclusions

```
Admit that Plaintiff is the holder of the note with the right
to enforce it.
```

Response: Object as calling for legal conclusion:

```
RESPONSE: OBJECTION. This request calls for a legal conclusion
and improper opinion testimony. Defendant lacks knowledge as to
whether Plaintiff is the holder of the note or has the right
to enforce it.
```

Trap 3: Overly broad statements

```
Admit that all conditions precedent to foreclosure have occurred.
```

Response: Deny and explain:

```
RESPONSE: DENIED. Defendant lacks knowledge as to whether all
conditions precedent have occurred. Defendant specifically denies
that required notices were provided.
```

Deadlines Are Absolute

The 30-day deadline is harsh. Miss it and the requests are deemed admitted — even if every request is false.

Calendar the deadline: - Day 0: RFAs received - Day 7: Draft responses - Day 14: Review and finalize - Day 21: Prepare for service - Day 28: Serve responses - Day 30: DEADLINE

If you need an extension: - Request in writing before the deadline - Explain why you need more time - Get the bank's agreement in writing

Never assume the bank will grant an extension. Protect yourself by responding on time.

LEARN FROM THIS MISTAKE: The Homeowner Who Admitted Too Much

> **Diane Foster's Story:** Diane received Requests for Admission from the bank. One of them asked: "Admit that you have not made any mortgage payments since [Date]." Diane knew she had missed some payments, so she admitted the statement without checking her records.
>
> What Diane didn't realize was that she had actually made several payments during that period. Her servicer had misapplied them to fees instead of principal and interest, making it look like she hadn't paid. By admitting she made no payments, she conceded a key fact that wasn't true.
>
> At trial, the bank used her admission against her. "Your Honor, the defendant admitted she made no payments during this period," the bank's attorney argued. "This admission is conclusive."
>
> Diane tried to explain that she had actually made payments. "I have bank statements showing the payments went out," she testified.
>
> The bank's attorney objected. "Your Honor, the defendant's admission is binding. She cannot contradict her own admission with new evidence."
>
> The judge sustained the objection. "The defendant admitted she made no payments. This admission is conclusive. The bank statements are irrelevant in light of the admission."
>
> Diane lost because she admitted a fact without verifying it. The payments she made — which could have reduced the amount owed or shown the servicer misapplied funds — were wiped out by her careless admission.
>
> What Diane should have done: - Checked her bank records before responding - Denied the request with explanation: "Denied. Defendant made payments during this period that were not properly credited." - Attached proof of payments as exhibits - Investigated how the servicer applied her payments before admitting anything
>
> "I thought I was being honest," Diane says. "But I was being careless. I admitted something that wasn't true because I didn't check my records. The bank used

my own words against me."

The Lesson: Never admit a fact in a Request for Admission without verifying it first. Check your records. Check the bank's records. If there's any doubt, deny the request and explain why. You can always provide proof later. But once you admit something, it's conclusive. A careless admission can destroy your case even when you have proof that would help you. Verify before you admit.

Motion to Deem Admitted

When the bank doesn't respond to your RFAs, file a **motion to deem admitted**.

When to File

File immediately after the deadline passes. Don't wait. The sooner you file, the sooner you have conclusive admissions.

Motion to Deem Admitted Template

```
MOTION TO DEEM REQUESTS FOR ADMISSION ADMITTED

TO THE HONORABLE COURT:

Defendant [Your Name] moves this Court to deem Plaintiff's
responses to Defendant's Requests for Admission admitted pursuant
to [cite rule: FRCP 36(a) or state equivalent].

BACKGROUND

On [Date], Defendant served [Number] Requests for Admission on
Plaintiff. Thirty days have passed since service. Plaintiff has
failed to serve any response to the Requests for Admission.

LEGAL STANDARD

Under [cite rule], a matter is admitted unless the party to
whom the request is directed serves a written answer or objection
within 30 days. Plaintiff's failure to respond constitutes an
admission of each request.
```

```
REQUESTS DEEMED ADMITTED

The following Requests for Admission are deemed admitted:

1. [Quote Request No. 1]
2. [Quote Request No. 2]
3. [Continue for all requests]

RELIEF REQUESTED

Defendant requests that this Court:
1. Deem Plaintiff's responses to the Requests for Admission admitted;
2. Enter an order establishing the matters admitted; and
3. Award Defendant costs and attorney fees incurred in filing this motion.

Respectfully submitted,
[Your signature]
[Your name]
```

Using Deemed Admissions

Once the court grants your motion, the admissions are conclusive:

At summary judgment: > "Plaintiff has admitted it does not possess the original promissory note. [Cite admission]. Without the note, Plaintiff cannot prove standing. Summary judgment for Defendant is appropriate."

At trial: > "Your Honor, Plaintiff admitted it does not have the original note. [Cite admission]. This admission is conclusive. Plaintiff cannot enforce a note it does not possess."

The bank cannot contradict their admissions. They are bound by what they failed to deny.

Using Admissions at Trial

RFAs shape your trial strategy. Use admissions to control what must be proven.

Before Trial: The Admissions Checklist

Review all admissions and plan how to use them:

Admissions about documents: - Bank admits they don't have the note → Standing attack - Bank admits assignment is post-complaint → Timing attack - Bank admits they don't have payment records → Damages attack

Admissions about facts: - Bank admits witness didn't review records → Impeachment - Bank admits they can't explain chain of title → Standing attack - Bank admits amount includes unauthorized fees → Damages attack

At Trial: Using Admissions

Direct examination of your expert: > Attorney: "You reviewed the Requests for Admission in this case?" > Expert: "Yes." > Attorney: "Plaintiff admitted they do not possess the original note?" > Expert: "Yes, that's Admission No. 3." > Attorney: "In your expert opinion, can a plaintiff foreclose without the original note?" > Expert: "Generally no. Under UCC Article 3, the holder of the note is the party entitled to enforce it."

Cross-examination of bank's witness: > Attorney: "You testified that the bank has the original note?" > Witness: "Yes." > Attorney: "But the bank admitted in Request for Admission No. 3 that it does not possess the original note?" > Witness: "I... I'm not aware of that." > Attorney: "You just testified you reviewed all documents in this case?" > Witness: "Yes." > Attorney: "But you didn't review the bank's admissions?"

Admissions as Judicial Notice

Some jurisdictions allow you to request **judicial notice** of admissions:

> "Defendant requests judicial notice of Plaintiff's admission in Request for Admission No. 3 that Plaintiff does not possess the original promissory note. [Cite rule on judicial notice of court records.]"

This makes the admission part of the official record without requiring proof.

LEARN FROM THIS MISTAKE: The Homeowner Who Forgot to Use the Admissions

> **Steven Parker's Story:** Steven served 15 Requests for Admission on the bank. The bank failed to respond within 30 days. Under the rules, all 15 requests were deemed admitted.> Steven had conclusive admissions that:> - The bank didn't have the original note - The assignment was executed after the complaint was filed - The affiant hadn't reviewed his payment history - The amount demanded included unauthorized fees

At summary judgment, Steven argued lack of standing. But he didn't cite the admissions. He focused on document defects and chain of title arguments.> The judge asked, "Does the bank admit it doesn't have the note?"> Steven's attorney said, "Your Honor, we have admissions on that issue."> The judge looked through the file. "I don't see any admissions in the summary judgment briefing."> Steven's attorney pulled out the RFAs. "They're here, Your Honor. The bank never responded. They're deemed admitted."> The judge reviewed them. "These are powerful admissions. Why aren't they cited in your motion?"> The attorney had simply forgotten to include them in the summary judgment briefing. He had the smoking gun but didn't pull the trigger.> The judge denied summary judgment. "Without the admissions being properly presented, I can't consider them. The issues are disputed."> Steven had won the discovery battle but lost the motion because his attorney didn't use the admissions. He settled for less than he should have because his strongest evidence wasn't properly presented.> What Steven should have done:> - Cited the admissions prominently in the summary judgment motion - Quoted each relevant admission in the argument section - Argued that admissions are conclusive and resolve disputed issues - Attached the deemed admission order as an exhibit

"I had the bank dead to rights," Steven says. "They admitted everything. But my attorney forgot to use the admissions in the motion. It was like having a loaded gun and not firing it."> **The Lesson:** Admissions are only valuable if you use them. Don't let them sit in the file. Cite them prominently in every motion where they're relevant. Quote the admissions verbatim. Argue that admissions are conclusive and resolve issues in your favor. An admission you don't use is an admission that doesn't help you. Make the admissions the centerpiece of your argument, not an afterthought.

Chapter Summary

- **Requests for Admission are binding.** Admissions are conclusive at trial. Denials create impeachment material. Non-response equals automatic admission.
- **Serve RFAs early.** Don't wait until the end of discovery. You need time to file motions to deem admitted and use the admissions while discovery is open.
- **Draft specific, factual requests.** Target standing, chain of title, damages, and witness knowledge. Avoid legal conclusions and argumentative language.
- **Respond carefully to bank's RFAs.** Never miss the deadline. Don't admit damag-

ing facts. Object to improper requests. Calendar the response deadline with multiple alerts.

- **File motion to deem admitted immediately.** When the bank doesn't respond, don't wait. File the motion and get an order establishing the admissions.
- **Use admissions at trial.** Cite them in summary judgment motions. Use them in direct examination. Use them to impeach bank witnesses. Judicial notice makes them part of the official record.
- **Admissions are only valuable if you use them.** Don't let them sit in the file. Make them the centerpiece of your argument.

Cross-References

Previous Chapter: Chapter 12 — Discovery Warfare Against the Bank

Next Chapter: Chapter 15 — Attacking the Bank's Affidavits

Related Chapters: - Chapter 10: Drafting the Answer (for preserving defenses) - Chapter 11: Motion to Dismiss (for using admissions in early motions) - Chapter 16: Summary Judgment Survival (for admissions at summary judgment) - Chapter 28: Playbook — Discovery Quick Reference

In the Playbook: - Requests for Admission Template - Response to RFAs Template - Motion to Deem Admitted Template - RFA Strategy Checklist

Templates: - Requests for Admission Template (Standing) - Requests for Admission Template (Damages) - Motion to Deem Admitted Template - Response to RFAs Template

CHAPTER 15: ATTACKING AFFIDAVITS, DECLARATIONS, AND BANK RECORDS

Destroying the Bank's Evidence Before It Destroys You

The Robo-Signer Problem

Robo-signing is the practice of having employees sign affidavits and legal documents without reviewing the underlying facts. It's epidemic in foreclosure litigation. Banks process thousands of foreclosure cases with the same handful of employees signing affidavits they never read about loans they never reviewed.

How Robo-Signing Works

The bank's process typically looks like this:

1. **Servicer generates default letter** — Computer flags missed payments
2. **File goes to foreclosure department** — A "reviewer" is assigned
3. **Affidavit is generated** — Computer creates affidavit with loan details
4. **Employee signs** — Someone signs 100-300 affidavits per day
5. **Notary stamps** — Often done in bulk, sometimes illegally
6. **Filed with court** — Becomes "evidence" of default and amount due

The problem: The employee who signed never reviewed the actual payment records. They don't know if you made payments that weren't credited. They don't know if fees were properly assessed. They're signing a computer-generated document based on a computer-generated summary.

The Famous Robo-Signers

Several robo-signers became famous after the 2010 foreclosure crisis:

Linda Green — Signed as vice president of multiple banks simultaneously. Documents showed her signature with multiple different handwriting styles. She reportedly signed 10,000 documents per month.

Jeffrey Stephan — GMAC employee who admitted signing 10,000 affidavits per month without reviewing the documents. His deposition testimony exposed the practice nationwide.

Crystal Moore — JPMorgan Chase employee who signed documents as "assistant secretary" and "vice president" of multiple entities.

These weren't isolated incidents. They were standard operating procedure. And they're still happening today.

How to Spot a Robo-Signer

Red flags in the affidavit: - **Signature doesn't match printed name** — The signature looks nothing like the typed name - **Multiple titles** — Same person is "vice president" of several different banks - **Volume indicators** — Affidavit is one of hundreds signed the same day - **Generic language** — "I have reviewed the business records" — boilerplate with no specifics - **No actual knowledge** — "Based on information and belief" instead of personal knowledge - **Notary anomalies** — Notary stamp from different state, expired commission, missing information

Google the name. Search: "[Name] robo-signer" or "[Name] foreclosure affidavit." You may find: - News articles about the signer - Court opinions mentioning their practices - Other homeowners who challenged them - Deposition transcripts where they admitted signing without review

---

Personal Knowledge Requirements

An affidavit must be based on **personal knowledge**. This is not optional. It's a fundamental requirement of evidence law.

The Personal Knowledge Rule

Federal Rule of Evidence 602 (and similar state rules) states: > "A witness may testify to a matter only if evidence is introduced sufficient to support a finding that the witness has personal knowledge of the matter."

What personal knowledge means: - The witness saw it happen - The witness heard it happen - The witness perceived it through their own senses - The witness reviewed the actual documents and understood them

What personal knowledge does NOT mean: - Someone told the witness - The witness assumes it's true - The computer says so - "That's what our records show"

The Business Records Exception Trap

Banks often claim their affidavits are admissible under the **business records exception** to the hearsay rule. They're half-right about the wrong thing.

The business records exception (FRE 803(6)) allows records of regularly conducted activity to be admitted even though they're hearsay. But this exception has strict requirements:

1. **The record was made at or near the time** by someone with knowledge
2. **It was kept in the course of regularly conducted activity**
3. **Making the record was a regular practice**
4. **The witness testifying is the custodian or qualified witness** who can explain the record-keeping system
5. **The opponent does not show lack of trustworthiness**

The trap: Banks treat the business records exception as a magic wand that makes any computer printout admissible. It doesn't. The affiant must still have personal knowledge of the record-keeping system and must lay proper foundation.

Challenging Lack of Personal Knowledge

In your opposition to summary judgment:

> "The affidavit of [Name] should be stricken for lack of personal knowledge. The affiant states they 'reviewed the business records' but provides no basis for personal knowledge of: (a) How the records were created (b) Who created them (c) Whether they were created at or near the time of the events (d) Whether making such records was a regular practice
>
> The affiant's conclusory statement that they 'reviewed records' is insufficient to establish personal knowledge under Rule 602."

In a motion to strike:

> "The affidavit is inadmissible hearsay. The affiant lacks personal knowledge of the matters asserted. The affidavit states conclusions based on records the affiant cannot authenticate."

LEARN FROM THIS MISTAKE: The Homeowner Who Didn't Challenge the Affidavit

> **Rebecca Torres' Story:** Rebecca was fighting her foreclosure pro se. The bank filed a motion for summary judgment with an affidavit from "Patricia Miller, Vice President of Loan Documentation." The affidavit stated that Ms. Miller had reviewed Rebecca's payment history and that Rebecca owed $312,000.
>
> Rebecca didn't know she could challenge the affidavit. She assumed that because it was signed and notarized, it was valid evidence. She focused her opposition on other arguments — that the bank couldn't prove standing, that the assignment was defective,

that she had made payments that weren't credited.> 003e At the hearing, the judge asked, "Does the defendant dispute the amount owed as stated in Ms. Miller's affidavit?"> 003e Rebecca said, "Yes, Your Honor. I made payments that weren't credited."> 003e The judge asked, "Do you have any evidence to contradict Ms. Miller's affidavit?"> 003e Rebecca didn't. She had her bank statements, but she hadn't submitted them as evidence. She hadn't challenged Ms. Miller's qualifications or knowledge.> 003e The judge ruled: "The plaintiff has submitted competent evidence of the amount due through Ms. Miller's affidavit. The defendant has not submitted any evidence to create a genuine dispute. Summary judgment for plaintiff."> 003e Rebecca lost her home because she didn't challenge the affidavit that proved the amount due. She had arguments about standing and assignments, but those became irrelevant once the court accepted the bank's calculation of what she owed.> 003e What Rebecca should have done:> - Filed a motion to strike the affidavit for lack of personal knowledge - Served discovery on Ms. Miller to determine her actual knowledge - Submitted her own declaration with bank statements showing payments - Argued that the affidavit was inadmissible hearsay without proper foundation

003e "I didn't know I could challenge an affidavit," Rebecca says. "It looked official. It had a notary stamp. I thought I had to disprove what it said, not challenge whether it should be admitted at all."> 003e **The Lesson:** An affidavit is not invincible just because it's notarized. It must be based on personal knowledge. The affiant must have actually reviewed the records. Business records don't magically become admissible just because someone signs a form saying they reviewed them. Challenge every affidavit. Question personal knowledge. Demand foundation. The affidavit is often the bank's entire case — if you knock it out, the bank may have nothing left.

Business Records Exception Requirements

The business records exception is the bank's main weapon for getting hearsay into evidence. Understanding its requirements lets you challenge it effectively.

The Six Requirements

FRE 803(6) requires all of the following:

1. Made at or near the time The record must have been created when the events occurred or shortly after. A payment record created six months after the payment is suspect.

2. By someone with knowledge The person who made the record must have had personal knowledge of the event being recorded.

3. Kept in the course of regularly conducted activity The record must be part of the business's normal operations. A one-off report created just for litigation doesn't qualify.

4. Making the record was a regular practice The business must regularly create this type of record. A business that rarely creates payment histories can't use this exception for a payment history created for court.

5. Testified to by custodian or qualified witness The witness must be qualified to explain the record-keeping system. They must know how records are created, stored, and retrieved.

6. Not shown to lack trustworthiness The opponent can challenge trustworthiness based on: - Circumstances of preparation - Sources of information - Method and time of preparation - Whether it was created for litigation

Challenging Each Requirement

Challenge 1: Timing > "The affidavit states the witness reviewed 'computer records' but does not establish when those records were created. Without foundation that the records were made at or near the time of the events, the business records exception does not apply."

Challenge 2: Knowledge of the record-maker > "The affiant cannot testify that the person who entered the payment data had personal knowledge of the payment. The affiant doesn't know who entered the data or whether that person had any connection to the actual payment."

Challenge 3: Regularly conducted activity > "The affidavit does not establish that the records were kept in the regular course of business. The servicer took over servicing six months ago. The records from the prior servicer were transferred in bulk. The current servicer's 'regular practice' does not include creating records of events that occurred before they serviced the loan."

Challenge 4: Regular practice of making records > "The affidavit states the witness reviewed a 'payment history' but does not establish that creating such histories was a regular practice of the business. A report generated for litigation is not a business record."

Challenge 5: Qualified witness > "The affiant was employed for six months. The loan has been serviced for ten years. The affiant cannot explain the record-keeping practices of prior servicers. The affiant is not qualified to lay foundation for records they did not create and do not understand."

Challenge 6: Trustworthiness > "The records lack trustworthiness. They were created through a chain of multiple servicers with no established authentication process. The current servicer's records are based on data dumps from prior servicers with no verification. The affidavit itself was generated by a computer template filled in by an employee who signed 200 affidavits that day."

Hearsay and Authentication Challenges

Even if the business records exception applies, documents must still be **authenticated** and cannot contain **hearsay within hearsay**.

Authentication Requirements

FRE 901 requires evidence sufficient to support a finding that the item is what the proponent claims it is.

Common authentication challenges in foreclosure:

The assignment of mortgage: > "The assignment is not authenticated. The affiant did not witness the signing. The affiant cannot identify the signature. The affiant does not know if the document has been altered since execution. Without authentication, the assignment is inadmissible."

The note: > "The copy of the note is not authenticated as a true and accurate copy of the original. The affiant did not compare the copy to the original. The affiant does not know if the copy has been altered."

Payment history: > "The payment history is not authenticated. The affiant cannot verify that the data was entered correctly. The affiant cannot explain apparent errors or discrepancies. The affiant cannot verify that all payments are reflected."

Hearsay Within Hearsay

FRE 805 addresses hearsay within hearsay — when a document contains statements that are themselves hearsay.

Example: - The affiant testifies about a payment history (Level 1: affiant's testimony is hearsay unless business records exception applies) - The payment history contains entries about payments received (Level 2: the entries are hearsay unless another exception applies) - The entries may be based on reports from prior servicers (Level 3: the prior servicer's records are also hearsay)

Challenge: > "The affidavit contains multiple layers of hearsay. The affiant testifies about a payment history (hearsay). The payment history contains entries about payments (hearsay within hearsay). The entries are based on data transferred from prior servicers (hearsay within hearsay within hearsay). Each layer requires its own exception. The bank has not established any exception for the underlying data from prior servicers."

LEARN FROM THIS MISTAKE: The Homeowner Who Challenged the Wrong Thing

Daniel Parker's Story: Daniel was preparing for his summary judgment hearing. He knew the bank's affidavit was defective. He spent weeks researching the affiant — Jennifer Adams — and discovered she had signed 15,000 affidavits in one year for multiple banks. He found news articles calling her a robo-signer. He was ready to expose her.> > But Daniel focused only on Ms. Adams' credibility. He didn't challenge the documents attached to her affidavit. He didn't question the business records foundation. He didn't authenticate the exhibits.> > At the hearing, Daniel argued passionately about robo-signing. “This affidavit was signed by a known robo-signer who signed 15,000 documents a year! She couldn't have reviewed my file!”> > The judge asked, “Is the defendant challenging the business records attached to the affidavit?”> > Daniel said, “No, Your Honor. I'm challenging the affiant's credibility.”> > The judge ruled: “Even if the affiant is a robo-signer, the business records themselves are admissible under the business records exception. The plaintiff has submitted competent evidence of the amount due. Summary judgment granted.”> > Daniel lost because he attacked the messenger but not the message. The documents came in even though the affiant was discredited. He should have challenged both the affiant AND the foundation for the documents.> > What Daniel should have done:> - Challenged Ms. Adams' personal knowledge - Challenged the business records foundation for each document - Challenged authentication of the exhibits - Challenged hearsay within hearsay from prior servicers - Submitted his own evidence creating disputed facts > “I got so focused on exposing the robo-signer that I forgot about the documents,” Daniel says. “I thought if I proved she was a fraud, the whole case would collapse. But the court just said the documents speak for themselves. I should have attacked the documents too.”> > **The Lesson:** Challenging the affiant is important, but it's not enough. You must also challenge the documents the affiant relies on. Business records can be admitted even if the affiant is discredited — if the foundation is properly laid. Challenge both the witness and the exhibits. Attack personal knowledge AND authentication. Question credibility AND hearsay. The affidavit and the attached documents are separate targets. Hit them both.

Motion to Strike Affidavit

A **motion to strike affidavit** asks the court to exclude an affidavit from evidence. File this before summary judgment hearings or trial.

When to File

File a motion to strike when: - The affidavit lacks personal knowledge - The affiant is a robo-signer with no actual knowledge - The business records foundation is defective - The exhibits are not authenticated - The affidavit contains hearsay without an exception

Timing: - Before summary judgment hearing - Before trial (in limine) - At trial (objection)

Motion to Strike Template

```
MOTION TO STRIKE AFFIDAVIT OF [NAME]

TO THE HONORABLE COURT:

Defendant [Your Name] moves this Court to strike the affidavit
of [Affiant Name] attached to Plaintiff's [motion for summary
judgment/complaint/other] for the following reasons:

1. LACK OF PERSONAL KNOWLEDGE

The affidavit is based on information and belief, not personal
knowledge. The affiant states they "reviewed the business
records" but does not establish personal knowledge of:
- How the records were created
- Who created them
- Whether they are accurate
- Whether they were created in the regular course of business

Under Federal Rule of Evidence 602, a witness may testify only
to matters they have personal knowledge of. The affiant lacks
personal knowledge and the affidavit should be stricken.

2. INSUFFICIENT BUSINESS RECORDS FOUNDATION

The affidavit fails to establish the foundation required by
FRE 803(6) for the business records exception. The affiant
does not establish that:
- The records were made at or near the time of the events
- The person who made the records had personal knowledge
- Making such records was a regular practice
```

```
- The affiant is qualified to explain the record-keeping system

3. INADMISSIBLE HEARSAY

The affidavit contains hearsay statements that do not fall
under any exception. Specifically:
- [Describe specific hearsay statements]

4. LACK OF AUTHENTICATION

The exhibits attached to the affidavit are not properly
authenticated under FRE 901. The affiant cannot establish that:
- The documents are what they purport to be
- The signatures are genuine
- The documents have not been altered

WHEREFORE, Defendant requests that this Court strike the
affidavit of [Name] and exclude it from evidence.

Respectfully submitted,
[Your signature]
[Your name]
```

Cross-Examination Strategy

If the bank's witness testifies at trial, cross-examination is your opportunity to destroy their credibility and expose their lack of knowledge.

The Personal Knowledge Cross

Start with qualifications: > "You work for the servicer, not the bank that owns the note?" > "How long have you worked there?" > "What is your job title?" > "What are your job responsibilities?"

Expose limited knowledge: > "You didn't originate this loan, did you?" > "You weren't involved in any servicing of this loan before [Date], were you?" > "You've never met the borrower, have you?" > "You've never been to the property, have you?"

Lock in robo-signing: > "You signed the affidavit in this case?" > "How many affidavits did you sign that day?" > "Did you review the payment history for this specific loan before signing?" > "Did you compare the payment history to any source documents?" > "You just signed what the computer generated, didn't you?"

The Business Records Cross

Expose chain of custody problems: > "This loan was serviced by [Prior Servicer] before your company took over?" > "You never worked for [Prior Servicer], did you?" > "You don't know how [Prior Servicer] kept their records, do you?" > "You don't know if their records were accurate, do you?" > "Your company's records for this loan are based on data transferred from [Prior Servicer], aren't they?"

Expose lack of foundation: > "You didn't create the payment history, did you?" > "You just ran a report from your computer system?" > "You don't know who entered the payment data, do you?" > "You don't know if that person had personal knowledge of the payments, do you?" > "You can't verify that the data was entered correctly, can you?"

The Document Authentication Cross

Challenge assignments: > "You weren't present when the assignment was signed, were you?" > "You don't know who signed it, do you?" > "You've never met the person who signed it, have you?" > "You can't identify their signature, can you?" > "You don't know if the document has been altered since it was signed, do you?"

Challenge the note: > "You don't have the original note with you today, do you?" > "You've never seen the original note, have you?" > "The copy you have was made by someone else, wasn't it?" > "You don't know if this copy accurately reflects the original, do you?"

LEARN FROM THIS MISTAKE: The Homeowner Who Waited Until Trial

> **Michelle Johnson's Story:** Michelle knew the bank's affidavit was defective. The affiant, a "vice president" named David Smith, claimed to have reviewed her payment history and verified the amount due. Michelle had done her research — she found that David Smith was a robo-signer who had signed affidavits for five different banks during the same time period.
>
> But Michelle decided to save her challenge for trial. "I'll expose him on the stand," she thought. "It'll be more dramatic. The judge will see him squirm."
>
> At trial, David Smith didn't show up. The bank substituted a different witness — a woman named Sarah Chen who had never signed any affidavit in Michelle's case.

Ms. Chen testified that she was the current custodian of records and had reviewed Michelle's file that morning.

Michelle objected. "Your Honor, this witness was never disclosed. The affidavit was signed by David Smith, not Sarah Chen."

The judge overruled the objection. "The plaintiff can substitute a witness. Ms. Chen is testifying as the current custodian of records. You may cross-examine her."

Michelle tried to cross-examine Ms. Chen, but the damage was done. Ms. Chen had reviewed the file that morning. She had personal knowledge of the records. She was prepared. Michelle's research on David Smith was useless because he never testified.

The judge admitted the payment history over Michelle's objections. "The witness has laid proper foundation. The records are admitted."

Michelle lost because she waited until trial to challenge the affidavit. By then, the bank had substituted a clean witness who could lay proper foundation.

What Michelle should have done: - Filed a motion to strike David Smith's affidavit before summary judgment - Deposed David Smith to lock in his robo-signing practices - Objected to any substitution of witnesses - Challenged the business records foundation before trial

"I wanted my Perry Mason moment," Michelle says. "I wanted to see him squirm on cross-examination. But he never showed up. The bank just brought in someone else. I should have knocked out the affidavit before trial when I had the chance."

The Lesson: Don't wait until trial to challenge defective affidavits. File motions to strike before summary judgment. Depose robo-signers during discovery. Lock in their testimony while they're still the affiant. Once you get to trial, the bank can substitute witnesses, supplement the record, and cure defects. Challenge early and challenge often. The best time to attack an affidavit is before the witness ever takes the stand.

Chapter Summary

- **Robo-signing is epidemic.** Banks rely on employees who sign thousands of affidavits without reviewing the underlying facts. These affidavits are vulnerable to challenge.
- **Personal knowledge is required.** An affiant must have actual knowledge of the matters they swear to. "Reviewed the business records" is not enough if they don't understand how those records were created.

- **Business records exception has six requirements.** Made at or near the time, by someone with knowledge, kept in regular course of business, regular practice of making records, testified to by qualified witness, and not shown to lack trustworthiness. Challenge any missing element.
- **Authentication is separate from the exception.** Even if business records exception applies, documents must still be authenticated. The affiant must establish the documents are what they purport to be.
- **Hearsay within hearsay requires multiple exceptions.** Payment histories based on prior servicer records have multiple layers of hearsay. Each layer needs its own exception.
- **Challenge both the affiant AND the documents.** Attacking the robo-signer is important, but the documents may still come in if properly authenticated. Challenge everything.
- **Use motions to strike before hearings.** Don't wait until trial to challenge defective affidavits. File motions to strike before summary judgment hearings.
- **Cross-examination exposes lack of knowledge.** Use cross to establish the witness's limited knowledge, the chain of custody problems, and the lack of foundation for documents.

Cross-References

Previous Chapter: Chapter 14 — Requests for Admission as a Pressure Tool

Next Chapter: Chapter 16 — Summary Judgment Survival

Related Chapters: - Chapter 5: Forgery and Robo-Signing (for signature analysis) - Chapter 12: Discovery Warfare (for deposing affiants) - Chapter 10: Drafting the Answer (for raising evidentiary challenges early)

In the Playbook: - Affidavit Defect Checklist - Motion to Strike Template - Cross-Examination Question Bank - Business Records Challenge Guide

Templates: - Motion to Strike Affidavit Template - Objection Checklist - Cross-Examination Outline

CHAPTER 16: SUMMARY JUDGMENT SURVIVAL

Surviving the Bank's Kill Shot

What Is Summary Judgment?

Summary judgment is the bank's attempt to win the case without a trial. They argue there are no disputed facts and they're entitled to judgment as a matter of law. If the judge agrees, you lose. No trial. No jury. Game over.

Why Banks Love Summary Judgment

Trials are expensive and unpredictable. Banks prefer the clean, controlled environment of a summary judgment hearing where: - No jury can sympathize with the homeowner - The judge sees only paper, not people - The bank's affidavits often go unchallenged - Homeowners frequently fail to respond

Most foreclosure cases that reach summary judgment end there — with the homeowner losing. This chapter is about making sure that doesn't happen to you.

The Legal Standard

Federal Rule of Civil Procedure 56 (and similar state rules) allows summary judgment when:

> "There is no genuine dispute as to any material fact and the movant is entitled to judgment as a matter of law."

What this means: - **Genuine dispute:** A real disagreement about facts, not just your opinion - **Material fact:** A fact that matters to the outcome of the case - **As a matter of law:** Even if all facts are as you say, the bank still wins under the law

Your goal: Create genuine disputes about material facts. Show the judge that facts are in dispute and a trial is necessary to sort them out.

Timing: When Summary Judgment Happens

Typical timeline: - Bank files complaint - You file answer - Discovery period (6-12 months) - Bank files motion for summary judgment (usually after discovery closes) - You file opposition (typically 14-30 days) - Hearing (2-4 weeks later) - Judge's decision (days to months)

Critical point: Once discovery closes, the bank can move for summary judgment at any time. Stay ready.

The Bank's Burden

The bank has the burden of proving they're entitled to summary judgment. Understanding their burden helps you attack it.

What the Bank Must Prove

1. Standing to foreclose - They own the note - They have the right to enforce it - They have the mortgage or deed of trust

2. Valid default - You missed payments - They gave required notices - The default wasn't cured

3. Proper amount due - Principal balance - Accrued interest - Permissible fees and costs

4. Entitlement to relief - Foreclosure is the appropriate remedy - They followed all procedural requirements

How Banks Try to Meet Their Burden

The affidavit package: - Affidavit from "vice president" claiming to have reviewed records - Payment history printout - Copy of note and mortgage - Assignment documents (if any)

The argument: > "We have the note. We have the mortgage. The borrower defaulted. We gave notice. Here's the amount due. There's no dispute. Grant summary judgment."

Where Banks Usually Fail

Common gaps in bank's case: - Affidavit signer lacks personal knowledge - Payment history contains errors - Note is incomplete or not properly endorsed - Chain of title is broken - Required notices weren't given - Amount demanded includes improper fees - Documents are not authenticated

Your job: Find these gaps and expose them.

LEARN FROM THIS MISTAKE: The Homeowner Who Didn't Oppose Summary Judgment

> **Thomas Anderson's Story:** Thomas was fighting his foreclosure for over a year. He had answered the complaint, raised defenses about standing and robo-signing, and engaged in discovery. The bank produced documents, responded to interrogatories, and deposed Thomas. He thought he was doing well.

Then a notice appeared in his mailbox: "Hearing on Motion for Summary Judgment — [Date] 9:00 AM." The bank had filed for summary judgment. Thomas had 21 days to respond.

Thomas didn't know what to do. He thought his answer and defenses were enough. He didn't file an opposition. He didn't submit any evidence. He didn't even show up to the hearing.

At the hearing, the bank's attorney presented the affidavit of Jennifer Walsh, Vice President of Loan Documentation. The affidavit stated that Thomas owed $287,000, that he had defaulted, and that the bank held the note and mortgage.

The judge asked, "Is the defendant opposing this motion?"

The bank's attorney said, "No opposition has been filed, Your Honor. The defendant is not present."

The judge ruled: "The plaintiff has submitted uncontroverted evidence of the debt and default. The defendant has not raised any genuine dispute of material fact. Summary judgment for plaintiff. Judgment of foreclosure entered. Sale to be scheduled."

Thomas lost his home because he didn't file an opposition. His defenses in the answer weren't enough. Without evidence creating disputed facts, the bank's affidavits stood unchallenged.

What Thomas should have done: - Filed a timely opposition (within the 21-day deadline) - Submitted his own declaration disputing facts - Challenged the bank's affidavits (personal knowledge, foundation, authentication) - Created a record of disputed facts - Attended the hearing

"I didn't know I had to do anything else after I filed my answer," Thomas says. "I thought the court would just see that the bank's case was weak. But the judge only sees what you put in front of them. I didn't put anything in front of her, so the bank won by default."

The Lesson: Your answer is not enough. When the bank moves for summary judgment, you must actively oppose it. File an opposition. Submit evidence. Challenge their affidavits. Create disputed facts. Show up to the hearing. Summary judgment is the main event — if you don't fight it, you lose.

Creating Disputed Facts

The key to surviving summary judgment is **creating genuine disputes about material facts**. Here's how to do it.

What Is a Material Fact?

A **material fact** is one that affects the outcome of the case. In foreclosure:

Material facts include: - Whether the bank owns the note - Whether you defaulted - Whether proper notices were given - Whether the amount demanded is correct - Whether the bank has standing to foreclose

Immateral facts (don't help you): - Your financial hardship - The bank's business practices generally - What happened to other homeowners - Your personal opinions about the bank

How to Create Disputed Facts

1. Submit your own declaration

A declaration (sworn statement) under penalty of perjury creates evidence that disputes the bank's facts.

Example declaration:

```
DECLARATION OF [YOUR NAME]

I, [Your Name], declare under penalty of perjury:

1. I am the defendant in this action.

2. I dispute that Plaintiff is the holder of the promissory
note. I have never seen any assignment of the note to
Plaintiff, and Plaintiff has not produced any authenticated
assignment in discovery.

3. I dispute the amount Plaintiff claims is due. I made
payments on [dates] that were not credited to my account.
Attached as Exhibit A are copies of my bank statements
showing these payments.

4. I dispute that I was given proper notice of default.
I never received the Notice of Default referenced in
```

```
Plaintiff's affidavit.

I declare under penalty of perjury that the foregoing is
true and correct.

Executed on: [Date]
[Signature]
[Your Name]
```

2. Challenge the bank's affidavits

Every defect in the bank's affidavits creates a dispute: - Lack of personal knowledge - Hearsay - Lack of foundation - Failure to authenticate

See Chapter 15 for detailed affidavit attack strategies.

3. Use discovery responses

If the bank admitted something helpful in discovery, quote it: > "In Interrogatory No. 3, Plaintiff admitted it does not possess the original promissory note. This admission creates a genuine dispute about whether Plaintiff has standing to foreclose."

4. Point out document defects - Missing endorsements - Post-complaint assignments - Unauthenticated documents - Gaps in chain of title

The Disputed Facts Statement

Your opposition should include a **Statement of Disputed Facts**:

```
STATEMENT OF DISPUTED FACTS

Pursuant to [cite local rule], Defendant states the following
material facts are genuinely disputed:

1. Whether Plaintiff is the holder of the promissory note.
   - Plaintiff's evidence: Affidavit of Jennifer Walsh
     stating she reviewed records showing Plaintiff holds the note.
   - Defendant's evidence: Plaintiff admitted in discovery
     it does not possess the original note. The copy produced
     lacks endorsement to Plaintiff. There are no assignments
     showing transfer to Plaintiff.
   - Dispute: Genuine issue exists as to whether Plaintiff
     has standing to enforce the note.
```

```
2. Whether the amount claimed is accurate.
   - Plaintiff's evidence: Payment history showing balance
     of $287,000.
   - Defendant's evidence: Declaration of [Your Name]
     with bank statements showing payments not credited.
     Interrogatory responses showing Plaintiff cannot explain
     how fees were calculated.
   - Dispute: Genuine issue exists as to the amount actually due.

[Continue for each disputed fact]
```

Challenging Bank's Evidence

The bank's evidence must meet strict standards. Challenge everything.

Challenge the Affidavit

Lack of personal knowledge: > "The affidavit of Jennifer Walsh is incompetent evidence. Ms. Walsh states she 'reviewed the business records' but provides no foundation for personal knowledge. She does not state: > - Who created the records > - When they were created > - Whether they were created in the regular course of business > - Whether the person who made them had personal knowledge > > Without such foundation, the affidavit is inadmissible hearsay."

Business records exception: > "The payment history attached to the affidavit does not qualify under the business records exception. The affidavit does not establish that: > - The records were made at or near the time of the events > - The person who made them had personal knowledge > - Making such records was a regular practice > - The witness is qualified to explain the record-keeping system > > The business records exception does not apply."

Challenge the Note

No endorsement: > "The note produced by Plaintiff is not endorsed to Plaintiff. Under UCC Article 3, only the holder of the note (or one with the right to enforce) may foreclose. The note remains payable to [Original Lender]. Plaintiff is not the holder."

Copy vs. original: > "Plaintiff has produced only a copy of the note. The copy is not authenticated. The affiant did not compare it to any original. Without the original or proper foundation for the copy, Plaintiff cannot establish entitlement to enforce."

Challenge the Amount

Uncredited payments: > "Plaintiff's payment history fails to credit payments made by Defendant on [dates]. Attached as Exhibit [X] are bank statements proving these payments. The amount claimed is incorrect."

Unauthorized fees: > "The amount demanded includes late fees of $[amount] and force-placed insurance of $[amount]. These charges were not authorized by the note or mortgage. Plaintiff has produced no evidence these fees are contractually permitted."

LEARN FROM THIS MISTAKE: The Homeowner Who Conceded Too Much

> **Jennifer Martinez's Story:** Jennifer filed her opposition to summary judgment. She submitted her declaration and challenged the bank's evidence. She thought she had done everything right.
>
> But in her opposition, she wrote: "Defendant admits she missed payments beginning in March 2022. However, Defendant disputes the amount claimed and whether Plaintiff has standing."
>
> At the hearing, the bank's attorney focused on that admission. "Your Honor, the defendant admits she defaulted. She admits she missed payments. The only remaining issues are the amount and standing. But even if she prevails on those issues, she's still in default."
>
> The judge agreed. "The defendant has admitted default. That is a material fact. The bank is entitled to foreclose on that basis alone. Summary judgment granted."
>
> Jennifer lost because she admitted the default. She thought she was being credible by admitting the obvious. But in foreclosure defense, "default" is a legal conclusion, not just a fact. By admitting she "missed payments," she gave the bank the key fact they needed.
>
> What Jennifer should have done: - Never admit "default" — it's a legal conclusion - Challenge whether payments were properly credited - Challenge whether the bank properly applied payments - Frame it as "disputes whether any amount is actually due" - Let the bank prove every element
>
> "I was trying to be honest," Jennifer says. "I did miss some payments. But I didn't realize that admitting it would end my case. I should have made them prove everything, not helped them prove it."

The Lesson: Do not concede material facts in your opposition. Even if you missed payments, you can dispute whether those payments constituted "default" under the note, whether the bank properly credited payments, and whether the bank followed required procedures. Let the bank prove their case. Don't help them. Never admit "default" — it's a legal conclusion that incorporates multiple elements, and once you admit it, you've lost.

Drafting the Opposition

Your opposition is your chance to save your home. Do it right.

Opposition Structure

1. Introduction - Identify the motion - State your position: Summary judgment should be denied - Preview your arguments

2. Statement of Facts - Present facts in light most favorable to you - Cite to evidence (declarations, discovery responses, exhibits) - Don't concede material facts

3. Statement of Disputed Facts - List each material fact in dispute - Show your evidence vs. bank's evidence - Explain why a genuine dispute exists

4. Legal Argument - Challenge bank's affidavits (personal knowledge, hearsay, authentication) - Challenge bank's documents - Argue disputed facts prevent summary judgment - Cite relevant law

5. Conclusion - Request denial of summary judgment - Request hearing

Opposition Template

```
DEFENDANT'S OPPOSITION TO PLAINTIFF'S MOTION FOR SUMMARY JUDGMENT

I. INTRODUCTION

Plaintiff [Bank Name] moves for summary judgment, claiming no genuine
dispute exists regarding its right to foreclose. Defendant [Your Name
opposes. Genuine disputes exist as to material facts, including:
- Whether Plaintiff has standing to foreclose
- Whether the amount claimed is accurate
- Whether required notices were provided
- Whether Plaintiff's affidavits are admissible
```

Summary judgment must be denied.

II. STATEMENT OF FACTS

[Present facts favorably to you, with citations]

III. STATEMENT OF DISPUTED FACTS

[List disputed facts with your evidence vs. bank's evidence]

IV. LEGAL ARGUMENT

A. Plaintiff Has Failed to Establish Standing

[Argument about note ownership, endorsements, assignments]

B. Plaintiff's Affidavits Are Inadmissible

[Argument about personal knowledge, hearsay, foundation]

C. The Amount Claimed Is Disputed

[Argument about uncredited payments, improper fees]

D. Genuine Disputes Exist as to Material Facts

[Argument summarizing why summary judgment is inappropriate]

V. CONCLUSION

For the foregoing reasons, Plaintiff's Motion for Summary Judgment should be DENIED. Defendant requests an evidentiary hearing on the disputed issues.

Respectfully submitted,
[Your signature]
[Your name]

Surviving the Hearing

The summary judgment hearing is your last chance before judgment is entered.

Preparation

Know your record: - Your declaration - Discovery responses - Exhibits you've submitted - Bank's affidavits (and their defects)

Know the law: - Summary judgment standard in your jurisdiction - Business records exception requirements - Standing requirements - Authentication rules

Prepare your argument: - 5-minute version (if judge is rushed) - 15-minute version (if judge wants detail) - Practice out loud

At the Hearing

Arrive early: - Find the courtroom - Check in with clerk - Get your file in order

When your case is called: - Approach the lectern - State your name and that you're representing yourself - State that you're opposing summary judgment

Your argument: 1. **Start strong:** "Your Honor, genuine disputes exist as to material facts. Summary judgment should be denied."

2. **Hit your best points:**
   - "Plaintiff has failed to prove standing."
   - "The affidavit is incompetent evidence."
   - "The amount claimed is disputed."
3. **Respond to judge's questions:**
   - Be direct
   - Cite to your evidence
   - Don't ramble
4. **Finish strong:** "For these reasons, I ask the Court to deny summary judgment and set this matter for trial."

Common Hearing Pitfalls

Don't: - Read your opposition word for word - Argue about fairness or hardship - Get emotional - Concede facts under pressure - Talk over the judge

Do: - Be concise - Stick to the law and facts - Refer to your written submission - Answer questions directly - Remain respectful

---

What If You Lose?

If the judge grants summary judgment, you have options.

Motion for Reconsideration

Grounds: - New evidence - Error of law - Change in circumstances

Timing: Usually 10-30 days after judgment

Warning: Rarely granted. Use only if you have a strong basis.

Appeal

You have the right to appeal a grant of summary judgment.

Timeline: Typically 30 days from judgment entry

Grounds for appeal: - Judge misapplied the law - Judge made erroneous evidentiary rulings - Judge failed to view facts in light most favorable to you

Challenges: - Expensive (attorney fees, filing fees) - Time-consuming (1-2 years) - Difficult standard (abuse of discretion / de novo)

But: If you win on appeal, the summary judgment is reversed and you get your trial.

Bankruptcy

A **Chapter 13 bankruptcy** can stop foreclosure even after judgment: - Automatic stay halts foreclosure sale - You can propose repayment plan - You may strip invalid liens

See Chapter 21 for detailed bankruptcy discussion.

Loan Modification

Even with a judgment, some servicers will negotiate: - Harder after judgment - Still possible before sale - Requires showing ability to pay

---

LEARN FROM THIS MISTAKE: The Homeowner Who Missed the Deadline

> **Robert Chen's Story:** Robert received the bank's motion for summary judgment. He read through it carefully. He saw the deadline: "Defendant's opposition shall be filed no later than [Date]." He marked it on his calendar. He had 30 days.

Robert worked on his opposition. He drafted his declaration. He gathered his bank statements. He researched the law. He was almost ready.

Then his daughter got sick. She was hospitalized for a week. Robert stayed at the hospital. He didn't think about the deadline. When he got home, he checked his calendar.

The deadline had passed. Three days ago.

Robert immediately finished his opposition and filed it, along with a motion for leave to file late. He explained what happened — his daughter's illness, the hospital, the stress.

The judge was sympathetic but firm. "I understand the circumstances, but the deadline was clear. The defendant had 30 days. The opposition is three days late. The motion for leave to file late is denied. The untimely opposition will not be considered."

Without Robert's opposition, the bank's motion was unopposed. The judge granted summary judgment. Robert lost his home.

What Robert should have done: - Set multiple reminders (not just one calendar entry) - File early, not on the deadline - If emergency arises, call the court clerk immediately - Request extension before deadline, not after - Have a backup person who can file if you're incapacitated

"I thought I had plenty of time," Robert says. "I thought one calendar reminder was enough. I didn't plan for emergencies. By the time I realized I missed the deadline, it was too late. The judge wouldn't bend the rules no matter how good my reason was."

The Lesson: Deadlines in litigation are absolute. Missing a deadline can lose your case regardless of how good your defense is. Set multiple reminders. File early. If an emergency happens, contact the court before the deadline, not after. Have a backup plan. The court will not excuse a missed deadline just because you had a good reason.

Chapter Summary

- **Summary judgment is the main event.** Most foreclosure cases end here. Fight it with everything you have.
- **Your answer is not enough.** You must file an opposition with evidence creating disputed facts.
- **Create genuine disputes.** Submit your declaration. Challenge bank's affidavits. Use discovery admissions. Point out document defects.

- **Never concede material facts.** Don't admit "default." Make the bank prove every element.
- **Challenge all bank evidence.** Attack affidavits for lack of personal knowledge. Attack documents for lack of authentication. Attack the amount claimed.
- **Draft a complete opposition.** Include Statement of Disputed Facts. Present facts favorably. Make legal arguments. Cite evidence.
- **Prepare for the hearing.** Know your record. Know the law. Practice your argument. Be concise and direct.
- **If you lose, you have options.** Motion for reconsideration. Appeal. Bankruptcy. Modification. Don't give up.

Cross-References

Previous Chapter: Chapter 15 — Attacking Affidavits, Declarations, and Bank Records

Next Chapter: Chapter 17 — Trial Preparation and Presentation

Related Chapters: - Chapter 10: Drafting the Answer (for preserving defenses) - Chapter 12: Discovery Warfare (for creating the record) - Chapter 15: Attacking Affidavits (for challenging bank evidence) - Chapter 21: Bankruptcy as a Nuclear Option (if you lose)

In the Playbook: - Summary Judgment Opposition Checklist - Statement of Disputed Facts Template - Declaration Template - Hearing Preparation Guide

Templates: - Opposition to Summary Judgment Template - Declaration in Opposition Template - Statement of Disputed Facts Template

CHAPTER 17: TRIAL PREPARATION AND PRESENTATION

Your Day in Court

Why Most Cases Never Reach Trial

Here's the truth: Most foreclosure cases settle or end at summary judgment. Only a small percentage go to trial. But if you've survived summary judgment — if you've created genuine disputes the judge wouldn't resolve — you may get your trial.

A trial is an opportunity. It's your chance to: - Tell your story to a judge (or jury, in some states) - Cross-examine the bank's witnesses - Present your evidence - Win

But trials are hard. They require preparation, organization, and discipline. This chapter is your guide to getting ready and presenting your case.

Trial vs. Summary Judgment

Summary Judgment	Trial
Paper only	Live witnesses
Judge decides	Judge or jury decides
Bank's affidavits stand alone	You can cross-examine affiants
No testimony	Sworn testimony under oath
Fast	Can take days

The key difference: At trial, you get to question the bank's witnesses. You get to present your evidence live. You get to argue your case in person.

Pre-Trial Preparation

Success at trial is 90% preparation. The trial itself is just execution.

The Pre-Trial Checklist

90 days before trial: - [ ] Complete all discovery - [ ] Depose bank's witnesses - [ ] Gather all documents - [ ] Identify your evidence

60 days before trial: - [ ] Organize exhibits - [ ] Prepare witness list - [ ] Draft direct examination questions - [ ] Prepare cross-examination outlines

30 days before trial: - [ ] File pre-trial motions - [ ] Prepare trial brief - [ ] Exchange exhibit lists with bank - [ ] Subpoena witnesses

7 days before trial: - [ ] Prepare opening statement - [ ] Prepare closing argument - [ ] Organize trial notebook - [ ] Visit the courtroom

Organizing Your Evidence

Create a trial notebook with sections:

1. **Pleadings** — Complaint, answer, amendments
2. **Discovery** — Interrogatories, requests, responses, depositions
3. **Your Evidence** — Documents you will introduce
4. **Bank's Evidence** — Documents they'll use (and your objections)
5. **Legal Research** — Cases, statutes, rules
6. **Witness Materials** — Questions, exhibits for each witness
7. **Notes** — Arguments, timelines, key points

Organize exhibits: - Number your exhibits (Defendant's Exhibit 1, 2, 3...) - Prepare three copies: for you, the judge, and the bank - Make them clean and readable - Prepare exhibit list for court - Use tab dividers for quick access - Create a master index

Trial Notebook Organization: - Use a 3-ring binder - Create table of contents - Use color-coded tabs for sections - Keep a master timeline - Include a cast of characters (who's who) - Prepare copies for the judge and bank

Pre-Trial Motions

Motions in Limine: Ask the court to exclude certain evidence before trial: - Exclude bank's robo-signed affidavits - Limit topics of witness testimony - Exclude irrelevant or prejudicial evidence - Exclude evidence not produced in discovery

Example motion in limine:

```
MOTION IN LIMINE TO EXCLUDE AFFIDAVIT OF [NAME]

Defendant moves to exclude the affidavit of [Name]
under Evidence Rules [cite]. The affidavit:
1. Lacks personal knowledge
2. Contains hearsay
3. Is not properly authenticated
```

```
4. Was not produced in discovery

The affidavit should be excluded.
```

Motion for Continuance: If you need more time to prepare: > "Defendant moves for a continuance. Additional time is needed to complete discovery and prepare for trial. Defendant has been diligent. The interests of justice require a continuance."

Motion to Compel: If the bank hasn't produced required discovery: > "Defendant moves to compel Plaintiff to produce [documents]. Plaintiff has failed to respond despite proper request. Sanctions are requested."

LEARN FROM THIS MISTAKE: The Homeowner Who Wasn't Ready

Amanda White's Story: Amanda survived summary judgment. The judge found genuine disputes about the amount due and whether the bank had proper documentation. The case was set for trial. Amanda had six months to prepare.

She didn't use that time well. She assumed the bank would settle. She didn't organize her documents. She didn't prepare her questions. She didn't visit the courtroom.

The day before trial, Amanda realized she wasn't ready. She stayed up all night trying to organize her papers. She couldn't find key bank statements. She hadn't prepared her opening statement. She was exhausted when she walked into court.

At trial, the bank's attorney was organized and professional. Amanda was scattered and nervous. She fumbled with her documents. She forgot key questions during cross-examination. She couldn't find the exhibits she wanted to introduce.

The judge said, "The defendant has raised some interesting issues, but I'm not seeing the evidence to support them. The bank has presented competent evidence of the debt and default. Judgment for plaintiff."

Amanda lost because she wasn't prepared. She had good defenses. She had the facts on her side. But she couldn't present them effectively.

What Amanda should have done: - Used the six months to prepare systematically - Organized exhibits well before trial - Prepared questions and arguments in advance - Done a practice run or mock trial - Gotten sleep before trial

"I thought I could wing it," Amanda says. "I'd watched courtroom shows. I thought I could just tell my story. But real court isn't TV. If you're not prepared, you lose."

The Lesson: Trial preparation is everything. The trial itself is just the performance. If you don't prepare, you will lose — even if you have good facts and law on your side. Use the time before trial. Organize your evidence. Prepare your questions. Practice your arguments. Be ready.

Understanding Trial Procedure

Trials follow a predictable structure. Know the flow.

Trial Phases

1. Opening Statements - Plaintiff (bank) goes first - Defendant (you) goes second - Preview what evidence will show - No argument — just roadmap

2. Plaintiff's Case - Bank presents its evidence - Witnesses testify - Documents are introduced - You cross-examine each witness

3. Defendant's Case - You present your evidence - Your witnesses testify - You introduce your documents - Bank cross-examines

4. Closing Arguments - You go first (as defendant) - Bank goes second (has last word) - Argue what evidence proved - Ask for specific ruling

5. Judge's Decision - Judge may rule immediately - Judge may take it under advisement - Written decision follows - May take days or weeks

Courtroom Etiquette

Dress professionally: - Business attire - Conservative colors - Clean and pressed - First impressions matter

Address the court properly: - "Your Honor" for the judge - Stand when speaking - Wait to be recognized - Don't interrupt

Behavior in court: - Arrive early - Turn off cell phone - No food or drink - Be respectful to all parties - Take notes quietly - Remain calm even when frustrated

Your Role at Trial

As your own attorney, you must: - Make objections - Ask questions (direct and cross) - Introduce exhibits - Argue law - Present opening and closing

It's a lot. But you can do it if you're prepared.

Opening Statements

Your opening statement is your roadmap. Tell the judge what the evidence will show.

Structure

1. Introduction: > "Your Honor, [Your Name], representing myself. This is a foreclosure case. But it's not as simple as the bank claims. The evidence will show that [key theme]."

2. Preview your evidence: > "The evidence will show that the bank cannot prove it owns the note. The evidence will show that the amount they claim is wrong. The evidence will show that they failed to follow required procedures."

3. Theme: > "This case is about whether the bank can prove what they claim. The evidence will show they cannot."

Tips

- Keep it short (5-10 minutes)
- Don't argue — just preview
- Be organized and confident
- Make eye contact with judge
- Don't read word for word (use notes)

Direct Examination

Direct examination is when you question your own witnesses (including yourself if you testify).

Rules of Direct Examination

- **Open-ended questions:** Who, what, when, where, why, how
- **No leading questions:** Don't suggest the answer
- **Foundation first:** Establish witness qualifications

Good direct: > "What did you find when you reviewed your payment records?"

Bad direct (leading): > "Isn't it true you found payments the bank didn't credit?"

Direct examination tips: - Start with background and qualifications - Use simple, clear language - Let the witness tell the story - Use exhibits to support testimony - Pause between questions - Listen to the answer before asking next question - Be ready to adapt based on answers

If You Testify

Prepare your testimony: - Write out key points - Practice answering open-ended questions - Be honest — credibility is everything

Sample questions to ask yourself: > "Please state your name." > "Do you own the property at [address]?" > "Please tell the court about the payments you made in 2022." > "What did you discover when you reviewed the bank's payment history?" > "Why do you dispute the amount the bank claims?"

Cross-Examination

Cross-examination is when you question the bank's witnesses. This is where you win or lose.

Cross-Examination Goals

1. **Undermine credibility**
2. **Elicit helpful admissions**
3. **Show lack of knowledge**
4. **Expose document problems**
5. **Lock in testimony**

Cross-Examination Techniques

The Setup: - Start broad (background, qualifications) - Narrow to specifics - Lock in each answer - Build to key admissions

Leading Questions: Cross-examination allows leading questions: > "You never reviewed the original note, did you?" > "You signed 200 affidavits that day?" > "You don't know who entered the payment data?"

The Loop: Lock in key admissions: > "You never reviewed the original note?" > "And you don't know where it is?" > "And you can't verify the copy is accurate?" > "So you're asking this court to foreclose based on documents you've never verified?"

Cross-examination tips: - Never ask a question you don't know the answer to - Control the witness - Keep questions short and leading - Don't let witness explain - If they don't answer, repeat the question - Stop when you've made your point - Don't argue with the witness

Cross-Examining the Bank's Witness

Start with qualifications: > "You work for the servicer, not the bank?" > "How long?" > "What's your job?"

Expose limited knowledge: > "You didn't work here when this loan was originated?" > "You've never met me?" > "You've never been to the property?"

Attack the affidavit: > "You signed the affidavit in this case?" > "You signed it on [Date]?" > "How many affidavits did you sign that day?" > "You spent about 30 seconds on each one?" > "You didn't review my payment history, did you?"

See Chapter 15 for more cross-examination strategies.

Introducing Evidence

To use a document at trial, you must **introduce** it into evidence.

The Process

Step 1: Show the witness the document > "I'm showing you what I've marked as Defendant's Exhibit 1."

Step 2: Authenticate > "Do you recognize this?" > "What is it?" > "Is this a true and accurate copy?"

Step 3: Foundation > "How do you know this is accurate?" > "Did you prepare it?" > "When?"

Step 4: Offer into evidence > "Your Honor, I offer Defendant's Exhibit 1 into evidence."

Step 5: Handle objections Bank's attorney may object. Be ready to argue: > "Your Honor, this is a business record. The witness has established foundation. It should be admitted."

Objecting to Bank's Evidence

When the bank tries to introduce evidence, object if: - Lack of foundation - Hearsay - Not authenticated - Irrelevant - Unfairly prejudicial

How to object: > "Objection, Your Honor. Lack of foundation." > "Objection. Hearsay." > "Objection. No authentication."

Then argue: > "Your Honor, the witness has not established that this document was made in the regular course of business. The business records exception does not apply."

LEARN FROM THIS MISTAKE: The Homeowner Who Forgot to Object

> **Michael Torres' Story:** Michael was at trial, cross-examining the bank's witness. The witness was struggling, admitting he didn't know key facts. Michael was winning.> Then the bank's attorney said, "Your Honor, we offer Plaintiff's Exhibit 5 — the payment history."> Michael didn't object. He was focused on his next cross-examination question. He assumed the judge would see the document was defective.> The judge admitted the exhibit. "Plaintiff's Exhibit 5 is admitted."> Michael tried to object after the fact. "Wait, Your Honor, that document —"> The judge cut him off. "It's admitted. You can cross-examine on it, but it's in evidence."> The payment history became the key evidence the bank used to prove the amount due. It contained errors, but Michael hadn't objected in time. The errors became "fact" for the judge's decision.> Michael lost. The judge ruled: "Plaintiff's evidence establishes the amount due. Defendant has not overcome this evidence."> What Michael should have done:> - Paid attention when the bank offered exhibits - Objected immediately: "Objection, lack of foundation"> - Argued the business records exception wasn't met - Been ready with specific grounds for objection
>
> "I was so focused on cross-examination that I forgot to play defense," Michael says. "I didn't realize that once evidence is admitted, it's in. You have to object when they try to bring it in, not after."> **The Lesson:** Objections must be made when evidence is offered. Once it's admitted, it's too late. Stay alert when the bank offers exhibits. Object immediately if there's a problem. Know your grounds: lack of foundation, hearsay, authentication, relevance. An objection not made is an objection waived. Pay attention to what the bank is doing, not just what you're planning to do next.

Closing Arguments

Your closing argument is your last chance to persuade the judge.

Structure

1. Thank the judge: > "Thank you, Your Honor, for your attention during this trial."

2. Review the evidence: > "The evidence showed that the bank's witness lacked personal knowledge. The evidence showed the note was not properly endorsed. The evidence showed the amount claimed is disputed."

3. Apply the law: > "Under [cite law], the bank must prove standing. They failed. Under [cite law], they must prove the amount due. They failed."

4. Ask for specific relief: > "For these reasons, I ask the Court to deny foreclosure and dismiss this case."

Tips

- Use notes but don't read
- Refer to specific evidence
- Be respectful
- Show passion but control it
- Keep it under 20 minutes

LEARN FROM THIS MISTAKE: The Homeowner Who Didn't Know Courtroom Rules

James Wilson's Story: James prepared extensively for his trial. He organized his exhibits, wrote out his questions, and practiced his opening statement. He was ready — or so he thought.

When he arrived at court, he didn't know where to sit, when to stand, or how to address the judge. He walked into the well of the court (the area between counsel tables and the bench) to hand documents to the judge. The bailiff stopped him: "Sir, you can't enter the well."

During the trial, he interrupted the bank's attorney. The judge snapped, "Wait your turn." He stood while questioning witnesses because he thought it looked more professional. The judge said, "Please be seated."

When he offered an exhibit, he walked over to the witness instead of having the bailiff handle it. The judge said, "Don't approach the witness. Hand it to the bailiff."

James was embarrassed and flustered. His arguments lost their impact because he kept getting distracted by procedural mistakes. The judge seemed annoyed with him throughout the trial.

The judge ruled against him. James couldn't tell if it was because of his arguments or because he had irritated the court with his procedural missteps.

What James should have done: - Visited the courtroom before trial to observe procedures - Asked the court clerk about local rules - Watched other trials to see how attorneys behave - Reviewed basic courtroom etiquette

"I knew the law," James says, "but I didn't know the rules of the room. Every time I made a procedural mistake, I lost credibility. The judge stopped listening to what I was saying and started watching what I was doing wrong."

The Lesson: Knowing the law isn't enough. You must also know courtroom procedure and etiquette. Visit the courtroom before your trial. Watch how cases are conducted. Learn where to sit, when to stand, how to address the court. Ask the clerk about local rules. First impressions matter, and procedural competence signals credibility. Don't let avoidable mistakes undermine your substantive arguments.

If You Win

If the judge rules for you: - Judgment for defendant - Foreclosure denied - Case dismissed

What happens: - Bank may appeal - You may have lien still on property - You still owe the debt (unless proven otherwise) - Negotiate settlement or modification

If the bank appeals: - Judgment is stayed during appeal - Bank must show error - You defend the appeal

---

If You Lose

If the judge rules for the bank: - Judgment of foreclosure - Sale scheduled (typically 30-90 days out)

Your options: - Appeal (limited time) - Bankruptcy (automatic stay) - Negotiate post-judgment - Redeem property (if allowed in your state)

See Chapter 21 for post-judgment options.

Chapter Summary

- **Trials are rare but winnable.** Most cases settle or end at summary judgment. If you get to trial, you're in the minority. Prepare to win.
- **Preparation is 90% of success.** Organize exhibits. Prepare questions. Draft arguments. Practice. The trial is just execution.

- **Know trial procedure.** Opening statements. Bank's case. Your case. Closing arguments. Know the flow.
- **Cross-examination wins cases.** The bank's witnesses are vulnerable. Use leading questions. Lock in admissions. Expose lack of knowledge.
- **Object to defective evidence.** Once admitted, it's in. Object immediately: lack of foundation, hearsay, authentication.
- **Introduce your evidence properly.** Authentication. Foundation. Offer into evidence. Handle objections.
- **Closing argument persuades.** Review evidence. Apply law. Ask for specific relief.
- **If you lose, you have options.** Appeal. Bankruptcy. Negotiate. Don't give up.

Cross-References

Previous Chapter: Chapter 16 — Summary Judgment Survival

Next Chapter: Chapter 18 — Working with (and Without) an Attorney

Related Chapters: - Chapter 15: Attacking Affidavits (for cross-examination techniques) - Chapter 21: Bankruptcy as Nuclear Option (if you lose)

In the Playbook: - Trial Preparation Checklist - Direct Examination Question Bank - Cross-Examination Question Bank - Evidence Objection Guide - Opening/Closing Templates

Templates: - Opening Statement Template - Closing Argument Template - Exhibit List Template - Trial Notebook Organization Guide

CHAPTER 18: DELAY TACTICS THAT BUY TIME LEGALLY

Creating Space to Find Solutions

When Delay Is the Strategy

Sometimes time is your ally. You need delay to: - Complete a loan modification application - Secure refinancing - Gather funds to cure the default - Find alternative housing - Prepare a stronger defense

This chapter is about **legitimate delay tactics** — procedural tools that create time without crossing into frivolous litigation that risks sanctions.

The Difference Between Legitimate Delay and Bad Faith

Legitimate delay: - Requesting extensions for good cause - Conducting thorough discovery - Seeking continuances for preparation - Participating in court-ordered mediation - Properly litigating disputed issues

Bad faith delay (risks sanctions): - Filing motions you know have no merit - Missing deadlines intentionally - Requesting extensions with no real purpose - Failing to cooperate in discovery - Abandoning litigation after getting delay

Rule: Use delay to achieve a goal, not as an end in itself.

Discovery Extensions and Continuances

The simplest delay tactic is the **extension request**.

Extension Requests

Discovery extensions: Most courts grant discovery extensions if: - Requested before the deadline - Good cause is shown - Opposing party doesn't object - No prejudice to the other side

How to request:

```
STIPULATION FOR EXTENSION OF TIME

Plaintiff [Bank] and Defendant [You] stipulate to extend
the deadline for Defendant's discovery responses from
```

```
[Original Date] to [New Date], a [X] day extension.

[Signatures]
```

If the bank won't stipulate:

```
MOTION FOR EXTENSION OF TIME

Defendant moves for a [X] day extension of the deadline
for [specific discovery]. Good cause exists because:
1. [Reason -- e.g., "Complexity of document review"]
2. [Reason -- e.g., "Need to consult with expert"]
3. Defendant has been diligent
4. No prejudice to Plaintiff
```

Continuances

Scheduling continuances: Request to postpone hearings, trials, or deadlines.

Common grounds: - Need additional preparation time - Witness unavailability - Document production ongoing - Health issues - Scheduling conflicts (be careful — courts don't care about your vacation)

Motion for continuance:

```
MOTION FOR CONTINUANCE

Defendant moves to continue the [hearing/trial] scheduled
for [Date]. Good cause exists:

1. [Specific reason]
2. [Why delay is necessary]
3. [Efforts to accommodate opposing party]
4. [Prejudice if not continued]

Defendant requests continuance to [New Date].
```

Timing: Request as early as possible. Last-minute requests are less likely to be granted.

LEARN FROM THIS MISTAKE: The Homeowner Who Delayed Without a Plan

Daniel Park's Story: Daniel was facing foreclosure and wanted time to save his home. He filed motion after motion, requested extension after extension, and sought continuance after continuance. Over two years, he successfully delayed the foreclosure sale six times.

But Daniel had no plan. He wasn't working on a modification. He wasn't saving money. He wasn't preparing for trial. He was just delaying, hoping something would change.

The judge finally lost patience. "Defendant has sought and received multiple extensions and continuances. The record shows no progress toward resolution. The court finds these delays are not for legitimate litigation purposes. Motion denied. Further delay motions will be treated as frivolous."

Daniel's last continuance request was denied. The sale proceeded. He lost his home with no savings, no modification, and no plan B.

What Daniel should have done: - Used the time to pursue a modification - Saved money for a potential settlement - Prepared his defense in case delay ended - Had a concrete plan for what the delay achieved

"I thought if I could just buy enough time, something would save me," Daniel says. "But time doesn't save you — what you do with it does. I wasted two years delaying without a goal."

The Lesson: Delay is a tool, not a strategy. Every delay should serve a specific purpose: completing a modification, raising funds, preparing a defense, finding housing. If you're delaying without a plan, you're just postponing the inevitable. Have a goal for every extension you seek.

Motion Practice as Delay

Every motion you file creates delay. The court must: - Receive the motion - Set a hearing date - Allow time for opposition - Hold the hearing - Issue a ruling

This process typically takes 30-90 days.

Legitimate Delay Motions

Discovery motions: - Motion to compel (forces bank to respond to discovery) - Motion for protective order (limits overbroad discovery) - Motion to extend discovery deadline

Dispositive motions: - Motion to dismiss (challenges complaint) - Motion for summary judgment (if you have grounds)

Procedural motions: - Motion to continue - Motion to amend - Motion to substitute counsel

Strategic Use of Motion Practice

Don't file frivolous motions. Sanctions can be awarded for: - Motions with no legal basis - Motions filed solely for delay - Repeated motions on the same issue - Motions contradicting prior positions

Do file legitimate motions: - Genuine disputes about discovery - Real legal issues affecting the case - Procedural matters requiring court resolution - Legitimate challenges to bank's evidence

Consider motion sequencing: - File discovery motions first (creates delay, builds record) - File dispositive motions when record is complete - Use procedural motions for scheduling control - Coordinate motions with settlement efforts

Example: Motion to compel discovery

```
MOTION TO COMPEL DISCOVERY

Defendant moves to compel Plaintiff to respond to:
1. Request for Production No. [X] (original note)
2. Interrogatory No. [X] (chain of title)
3. Request for Admission No. [X] (standing)

Plaintiff objected claiming [objection]. The objection
is improper because [reason]. Defendant is entitled
to these responses.

WHEREFORE, Defendant requests an order compelling
responses and awarding costs.
```

Mediation and Settlement Conferences

Court-ordered mediation creates mandatory delay.

How Mediation Stays Work

When the court orders mediation: - Foreclosure proceedings are stayed (paused) - Mediation session is scheduled (30-90 days out) - Parties must participate in good faith - If mediation fails, case resumes

Using Mediation for Delay

Legitimate purposes: - Complete modification application - Negotiate settlement terms - Arrange refinancing - Prepare for transition - Evaluate alternatives to foreclosure

What to bring: - Financial documents (pay stubs, tax returns, bank statements) - Hardship letter explaining circumstances - Proposed solution (modification, repayment plan, short sale) - Questions about the loan history - Documentation of any disputes

What to expect: - Mediator is neutral, not your advocate - Bank's representative may have limited authority - Multiple sessions may be required - Outcome is not guaranteed - Agreement is binding if signed

Reality check: Mediation rarely results in loan modifications, but it creates time. Use that time wisely.

Settlement Conferences

Some jurisdictions require settlement conferences before trial: - Formal meeting with judge or magistrate - Discussion of settlement options - Can result in case resolution - Creates delay while scheduling and holding conference

What happens at settlement conferences: - Judge reviews each side's position - Discussion of modification options - Exploration of short sale or deed in lieu - Mediation of specific disputes - Setting timelines for resolution attempts

Strategy for settlement conferences: - Come prepared with financial documents - Know what you want (modification terms, time to sell, etc.) - Be realistic about options - Don't agree to anything you can't perform - Get any agreement in writing

---

Bankruptcy Timing Strategy

Bankruptcy is the nuclear option for delay.

Automatic Stay

When you file bankruptcy: - **Automatic stay** immediately halts foreclosure - Sale cannot proceed while stay is in effect - Bank must seek stay relief to continue - Can create months of delay

Chapter 7: - 3-4 month delay typically - Liquidation bankruptcy - May lose home eventually - But buys time to transition

Chapter 13: - 3-5 year repayment plan - Can cure mortgage arrears - More powerful delay tool - May actually save the home

When to File for Delay

Strategic timing: - Before foreclosure sale (stops the sale) - When modification is pending (completes the process) - To catch up on payments (Chapter 13 repayment plan) - To negotiate a graceful exit (time to arrange move)

Warning: Bankruptcy has consequences: - Credit impact (10 years on report) - Cost (filing fees, attorney fees if represented) - Complexity (requires disclosure of all finances) - Risk of dismissal if not handled properly

See Chapter 19 for detailed bankruptcy discussion.

Notice and Procedural Defects

Challenging notice defects can create significant delay.

Common Notice Problems

Pre-foreclosure notices: - Failure to provide required Notice of Default - Notice missing required content - Notice sent to wrong address - Insufficient time between notices

Acceleration notices: - Failure to properly accelerate the loan - Notice of acceleration not sent - Acceleration wrongful

Right to cure notices: - Some states require right to cure before foreclosure - Notice must specify cure amount - Time period must be adequate

Motion to Dismiss for Notice Defects

```
MOTION TO DISMISS FOR FAILURE TO GIVE REQUIRED NOTICE

Defendant moves to dismiss for failure to comply with
```

```
[Cite statute] requiring [specific notice]. Plaintiff
failed to:

1. Provide Notice of Default as required by [cite]
2. Wait required [X] days before filing complaint
3. Include required cure amount in notice

Without proper notice, foreclosure cannot proceed.
Dismissal or mandatory delay is required.
```

Effect: If successful, case is dismissed or significantly delayed while bank provides proper notice.

LEARN FROM THIS MISTAKE: The Homeowner Who Waited Too Long to File Bankruptcy

> **Susan Miller's Story:** Susan knew she was going to file bankruptcy. She had consulted an attorney. She had gathered her documents. She had decided Chapter 13 was the right choice to save her home.
>
> But she waited. The foreclosure sale was scheduled for March 15. She planned to file bankruptcy on March 10. That would give her plenty of time.
>
> Then her daughter got sick. Then her computer crashed. Then she couldn't find one of the required documents. Before she knew it, it was March 14.
>
> She filed bankruptcy on March 14 at 4:00 PM. The foreclosure sale was scheduled for March 15 at 10:00 AM.
>
> The bankruptcy court didn't process the filing until March 16. The foreclosure sale proceeded on March 15. Susan's home was sold.
>
> Even though the bankruptcy was filed before the sale, the sale wasn't stopped in time. Susan had to fight to undo the sale — a battle she ultimately lost.
>
> What Susan should have done: - Filed at least a week before the sale - Filed emergency petition if time was short - Called her attorney the moment problems arose - Had backup plan if filing was delayed
>
> "I thought I had plenty of time," Susan says. "I didn't plan for things going wrong. By the time I realized I was cutting it close, it was too late."
>
> **The Lesson:** Don't wait until the last minute for bankruptcy. File at least a week before

any foreclosure sale. The automatic stay doesn't help if it isn't in effect when the sale happens. Have a buffer for things to go wrong. Emergency filings are risky — plan ahead.

Service Defect Challenges

Challenging service of the foreclosure complaint creates delay.

Common Service Defects

- **Improper server:** Not qualified under state law
- **Wrong method:** Personal service required but substituted service used
- **Defective publication:** When service by publication is invalid
- **Service on wrong person:** Served on spouse, child, or tenant instead of defendant
- **Incomplete service:** Documents missing or incomplete

Motion to Quash Service

```
MOTION TO QUASH SERVICE OF PROCESS

Defendant moves to quash service of the summons and
complaint. Service was defective because:

1. [Specific defect -- e.g., "Server was not licensed"]
2. [Specific defect -- e.g., "Substituted service without
   attempting personal service"]
3. [Specific defect -- e.g., "Summons missing required
   notice"]

Service should be quashed. Defendant requests proper
service and dismissal of any claims where statute of
limitations has run.
```

Effect: If successful, case is delayed while bank re-serves you. If statute of limitations has run, case may be dismissed entirely.

Document Production Delays

Requiring bank to produce documents creates delay.

Strategy

File comprehensive document requests: - Original note - All assignments - Allonges and endorsements - PSA and trust documents - Payment history - Servicing records - Boarding records - Correspondence - Insurance records - Force-placed insurance documentation

When bank objects: - Meet and confer (required before motion) - File motion to compel - Court schedules hearing - Bank may produce slowly

Each step takes time. Document disputes can create months of delay.

Legitimate vs. Frivolous

Legitimate: - Requesting documents you need for your defense - Following proper procedure - Responding to bank's objections - Being reasonable about scope

Frivolous: - Requesting irrelevant documents - Refusing to narrow scope - Ignoring meet-and-confer requirements - Using discovery to harass

---

LEARN FROM THIS MISTAKE: The Homeowner Who Used Delay Tactics Improperly

> **Michael Torres' Story:** Michael was desperate to save his home. He filed motion after motion, most without any real legal basis. He requested continuances without legitimate reasons. He objected to every discovery request without reviewing them. He challenged service even though he had clearly been served properly.
>
> The judge warned him: "Defendant is warned that further frivolous filings will result in sanctions."
>
> Michael didn't listen. He filed another motion challenging the judge's authority to hear the case. The judge sanctioned him $500 and threatened to bar him from filing further motions without leave of court.
>
> Worse, because Michael had filed so many frivolous motions, the judge stopped giving him the benefit of the doubt. When Michael filed a legitimate motion to compel discovery, the judge denied it without a hearing, assuming it was another delay tactic.

Michael lost the case. He lost credibility with the court. He paid sanctions. And he wasted months on tactics that had no chance of success.

What Michael should have done: - Only filed motions with legitimate legal basis - Respected the court's warnings - Used delay tactics strategically, not desperately - Preserved credibility for when he really needed it

"I thought if I just threw everything at the wall, something would stick," Michael says. "But all I did was annoy the judge and lose credibility. When I had a real argument, the judge didn't listen because I had cried wolf too many times."

The Lesson: Frivolous delay tactics backfire. Courts sanction bad faith litigation. Once you lose credibility with the judge, you lose everything. Use delay strategically and legitimately. Every motion should have a legal basis. Every request should serve a purpose. Preserve your credibility — you only get one chance with the court.

The Cost of Delay

Delay isn't free. Consider:

Financial costs: - Continued interest accrual on the debt - Legal fees (if represented by counsel) - Filing fees for motions and other court documents - Lost wages from time off work for court appearances - Potential for additional late fees and penalties - Force-placed insurance costs that continue to accumulate - Property taxes that remain your responsibility - Maintenance and repair costs on the property

Emotional costs: - Prolonged stress and uncertainty about the future - Impact on family relationships and children's stability - Anxiety and depression from ongoing litigation - Inability to plan for future housing or employment - Social stigma and isolation from foreclosure process

Opportunity costs: - Time spent on litigation that could be used earning income - Financial resources spent on defense instead of cure payments - Emotional energy consumed by fighting rather than problem-solving - Delayed ability to move forward with life decisions

When Delay Is Worth It

Delay makes sense when: - Modification approval is likely and within reach - You're close to curing the default with accumulated funds - You have a strong defense that could result in dismissal - You need time to arrange suitable alternative housing - Bankruptcy will provide a permanent solution to save the home - You are negotiating a beneficial settlement or short sale

Delay doesn't make sense when: - You have no realistic path to keeping the home - You're depleting resources that could fund a fresh start - The stress is causing serious health problems - You're delaying without any concrete goal or plan - The costs of delay exceed any potential benefit - You're simply avoiding an inevitable outcome

---

Chapter Summary

- **Delay is a legitimate tool** when used for proper purposes: completing modifications, raising funds, preparing defenses, finding solutions, and creating time for permanent resolution.
- **Extension requests** are the simplest delay tactic. Request before deadlines with good cause. Most courts grant reasonable extensions when requested properly and timely.
- **Continuances** postpone hearings and trials. Request early with specific reasons. Have a concrete plan for the additional time gained.
- **Motion practice** naturally creates delay. File legitimate motions with legal basis. Avoid frivolous motions that risk sanctions and damage credibility.
- **Mediation and settlement conferences** create mandatory stays. Use the time productively. Don't expect miracles, but use the pause effectively.
- **Bankruptcy** is the ultimate delay tool. Automatic stay stops foreclosure immediately. But bankruptcy has serious consequences — use strategically and file with adequate time before any sale.
- **Service and notice defect challenges** can force case restart. If successful, creates significant delay. May result in dismissal if statute of limitations has run.
- **Document production disputes** create months of delay. Legitimate when you need documents for defense. Follow proper meet-and-confer procedures.
- **Delay without a plan is wasted time.** Every delay should serve a specific purpose. Know what you're trying to achieve with the additional time.
- **Consider the costs carefully.** Delay isn't free. Weigh the benefits against financial, emotional, and opportunity costs before pursuing delay strategies.

Cross-References

Previous Chapter: Chapter 17 — Trial Preparation and Presentation

Next Chapter: Chapter 19 — Bankruptcy as Nuclear Option

Related Chapters: - Chapter 12: Discovery Warfare (for document request strategies) - Chapter 21: Emergency Response (for last-minute tactics)

In the Playbook: - Delay Tactics Decision Tree - Extension Request Checklist - Bankruptcy Timing Guide

Templates: - Stipulation for Extension - Motion for Continuance - Motion to Quash Service

CHAPTER 19: BANKRUPTCY AS NUCLEAR OPTION

The Automatic Stay and Your Last Resort

What Bankruptcy Can (and Cannot) Do

Bankruptcy is the most powerful tool in the foreclosure defense arsenal. When you file bankruptcy, the **automatic stay** immediately halts all collection activity, including foreclosure sales. But bankruptcy is not a magic wand — it has limits, costs, and consequences.

What Bankruptcy CAN Do

Immediate foreclosure stop: - Automatic stay stops foreclosure sale the moment you file - Bank cannot proceed without court permission - Creates time to negotiate or cure default - Can stop sale scheduled for tomorrow

Cure mortgage arrears (Chapter 13): - Spread missed payments over 3-5 years - Catch up while making current payments - Save your home permanently - Force bank to accept repayment plan

Strip invalid liens: - Remove second mortgages in some cases - Eliminate HOA liens in some jurisdictions - Challenge mortgage validity

Discharge other debts: - Free up income for mortgage payments - Eliminate credit card, medical, and other debts - Improve ability to afford home

What Bankruptcy CANNOT Do

Eliminate valid mortgage liens: - First mortgage survives Chapter 7 - You must pay to keep the home - Lien stripping limited to specific circumstances

Stop foreclosure forever: - Bank can seek stay relief - If you can't cure default, you may still lose home - Chapter 13 requires regular payments going forward

Fix bad loans: - Can't modify mortgage terms in Chapter 7 - Limited ability to modify in Chapter 13 - Interest rate and principal generally unchanged

Protect you from yourself: - Must make plan payments on time - Missed payments can result in dismissal - Case dismissed = automatic stay lifted = foreclosure resumes

---

Chapter 7 vs. Chapter 13

Two main types of personal bankruptcy affect foreclosure differently.

Chapter 7: Liquidation

What it is: - Liquidates non-exempt assets - Discharges unsecured debts - Takes 3-4 months - Trustee sells assets to pay creditors

Effect on foreclosure: - Temporarily stops foreclosure via automatic stay - Does NOT cure mortgage arrears - Eventually, bank seeks stay relief - Homeowner must cure default or lose home

When to use: - You can't afford the home - You want time to transition - Other debts are the problem - You're surrendering the property

Timeline: - File bankruptcy → Automatic stay in effect - 30-60 days → Meeting of creditors (341 hearing) - 60-90 days → Bank files motion for stay relief - 90-120 days → Stay relief granted, foreclosure resumes - 3-4 months → Discharge of unsecured debts

Chapter 13: Reorganization

What it is: - 3-5 year repayment plan - Pay secured creditors in full - Pay unsecured creditors partially - Keep your property

Effect on foreclosure: - Stops foreclosure immediately - Allows cure of mortgage arrears over plan term - Saves home permanently (if you complete plan) - Forces bank to accept cure payments

When to use: - You can afford current payments - You just need time to catch up - You have regular income - You want to save the home

Timeline: - File bankruptcy → Automatic stay in effect - 30 days → First plan payment due - 45 days → Meeting of creditors (341 hearing) - 60-90 days → Confirmation hearing (plan approved) - 3-5 years → Complete plan payments - 3-5 years → Discharge and clear title

Comparison Table

Feature	Chapter 7	Chapter 13
Duration	3-4 months	3-5 years
Cure arrears	No	Yes
Save home	Temporary only	Permanent (if completed)
Income requirement	None	Regular income required
Debt limit	None	Approx. $2.5M secured, $465K unsecured
Assets	May lose non-exempt	Keep all property

Feature	Chapter 7	Chapter 13
Cost	$338 filing fee + attorney	$313 filing fee + attorney

LEARN FROM THIS MISTAKE: The Homeowner Who Chose the Wrong Chapter

Paul Rodriguez' Story: Paul was behind on his mortgage and facing foreclosure. He filed Chapter 7 bankruptcy thinking it would save his home. The automatic stay stopped the foreclosure sale immediately.

Paul felt relieved. He completed his 341 hearing. He got his discharge three months later. He thought he was safe.

Then the bank filed a motion for stay relief. The court granted it. Two weeks later, foreclosure resumed. Paul had no way to cure the $18,000 in missed payments.

His home was sold at foreclosure auction. Paul was shocked. "I thought bankruptcy saved my house," he says. "I didn't know Chapter 7 was just temporary."

What Paul should have done: - Filed Chapter 13 to cure arrears over time - Made plan payments while current on mortgage - Completed 5-year plan to save home permanently - Understood Chapter 7 doesn't cure mortgage defaults

"I picked the wrong tool for the job," Paul says. "Chapter 7 wiped out my credit cards, but I lost my house. I should have filed Chapter 13."

The Lesson: Choose the right bankruptcy chapter. Chapter 7 delays foreclosure but doesn't cure it — you still need to pay the arrears. Chapter 13 allows you to cure arrears over time and save your home permanently. If you want to keep the home and can afford current payments, Chapter 13 is usually the right choice. Chapter 7 is for surrendering the property or when you truly cannot afford the home.

The Automatic Stay

The **automatic stay** is the bankruptcy provision that stops foreclosure.

How It Works

Immediate effect: - Filing bankruptcy triggers automatic stay automatically - No hearing or court order required - Stops foreclosure, collection calls, lawsuits - Applies to all creditors

Scope of stay: - Foreclosure sales - Collection calls - Lawsuits - Wage garnishments - Repossessions - Utility disconnections

Notice: - Court notifies creditors within days - You should notify servicer immediately - Bring bankruptcy case number to any scheduled sale

Limitations of the Stay

Not absolute: - Creditors can seek stay relief - Repeat filings have limited stay - Criminal proceedings not stayed - Child support not stayed

Stay relief: - Bank files motion for relief from stay - Court holds hearing - If no equity and no ability to cure, stay lifted - Foreclosure resumes

Repeat filings: - Previous case dismissed within past year - Automatic stay limited to 30 days - Must file motion to extend stay - Show change in circumstances and good faith

---

Responding to Stay Relief Motions

When the bank seeks stay relief, you can fight back.

Chapter 7 Defenses

Oppose stay relief if: - You have equity in the property - You're negotiating a sale - You intend to convert to Chapter 13 - The bank's motion is premature

Negotiate alternatives: - Request time to sell the property - Negotiate cash for keys - Arrange deed in lieu of foreclosure - Work out short sale terms

Chapter 13 Defenses

Oppose stay relief by showing: - Plan payments are current - Arrears are being cured through the plan - Plan is feasible and confirmed - Adequate protection is being provided - Cause exists to maintain the stay

Adequate protection payments: - Payments to bank during Chapter 13 - Protects bank from depreciation - Usually equals ongoing interest - Shows good faith to the court

Modify the plan if necessary: - Reduce payment to unsecured creditors - Extend plan term - Adjust payment allocation - Request hardship modification

Filing an Opposition

Opposition to stay relief:

```
DEFENDANT'S OPPOSITION TO MOTION FOR RELIEF FROM STAY

Defendant opposes Plaintiff's motion for relief from
automatic stay under 11 U.S.C. § 362(d).

For Chapter 7: Defendant has equity in the property
and intends to [reaffirm/sell/convert to Chapter 13].

For Chapter 13: Defendant is current on plan payments
and proposes to cure the mortgage default through the
confirmed Chapter 13 plan. The plan provides adequate
protection to the secured creditor.

WHEREFORE, Defendant requests that the motion for
relief from stay be DENIED.
```

Chapter 13 Plan Requirements

To save your home through Chapter 13, your plan must meet specific requirements.

Plan Payment Calculation

Your plan payment must cover: 1. **Mortgage arrears** (spread over 36-60 months) 2. **Current mortgage payments** (ongoing) 3. **Secured debts** (car loans, etc.) 4. **Priority debts** (taxes, child support) 5. **Administrative costs** (trustee fee, attorney fee) 6. **Unsecured creditors** (discretionary — minimum is disposable income)

Example calculation:

```
Monthly mortgage arrears ($18,000 ÷ 60 months):     $300
Current mortgage payment:                           $1,200
Car payment:                                          $400
Trustee fee (approximately 10%):                      $190
```

```
Unsecured creditors (disposable income):                    $300
-------------------------------------------------------------
Total monthly plan payment:                               $2,390
```

Confirmation Requirements

The court will confirm your plan if: - You're eligible for Chapter 13 - Plan payments are feasible - Good faith filing - Plan complies with bankruptcy code - Creditors receive at least as much as in Chapter 7

Common confirmation issues: - Insufficient income for proposed payments - Plan doesn't pay priority debts in full - Feasibility questions - Good faith challenges

---

Lien Stripping

Lien stripping removes junior liens in Chapter 13 when the property is underwater.

How Lien Stripping Works

Requirements: - First mortgage balance exceeds property value - Junior lien (second mortgage, HELOC) is wholly unsecured - Chapter 13 case filed - Completion of plan payments

Effect: - Junior lien treated as unsecured debt - Paid pennies on the dollar through plan - Upon discharge, lien is voided - Homeowner keeps property with only first mortgage

Example:

```
Property value:                $300,000
First mortgage balance:        $320,000
Second mortgage balance:        $50,000

Result: Second mortgage is wholly unsecured
        (property underwater by $20,000 before second)
        Second mortgage can be stripped in Chapter 13
```

Limitations

Chapter 7: - Cannot strip liens in Chapter 7 - Must file Chapter 13

Partially secured: - If junior lien has any equity cushion, cannot strip - Must be wholly unsecured

Dewsnup issue: - Some jurisdictions interpret Supreme Court's *Dewsnup* decision - May limit lien stripping in certain circumstances - Consult local bankruptcy attorney

---

LEARN FROM THIS MISTAKE: The Homeowner Who Missed Plan Payments

Maria Gonzalez' Story: Maria filed Chapter 13 to save her home. Her plan payment was $2,100 per month. She made the first three payments on time. Then her car broke down. She missed one payment to fix her car.

The Chapter 13 trustee filed a motion to dismiss her case. Maria thought she could catch up. She sent a double payment the next month.

But the trustee wouldn't accept it. "Plan payments must be made through payroll deduction or consistent monthly payments," the trustee said. "You can't skip and catch up."

Maria's case was dismissed. The automatic stay was lifted. The foreclosure sale, which had been scheduled before her bankruptcy, was reinstated for two weeks later.

Maria scrambled to refile Chapter 13. But because her previous case was dismissed within the past year, the automatic stay only lasted 30 days. The bank got stay relief. The sale proceeded.

Maria lost her home because she missed one payment.

What Maria should have done: - Never missed a plan payment - Called her attorney immediately when car broke down - Sought plan modification for temporary hardship - Used payroll deduction to ensure consistent payments - Understood there is no "catching up" in Chapter 13

"I thought missing one payment was okay if I paid double next month," Maria says. "I didn't understand how strict Chapter 13 is. One missed payment cost me my home."

The Lesson: Chapter 13 requires perfect payment discipline. Trustees do not accept late or skipped payments. Plan payments must be made every month without fail. If you face a temporary hardship, seek plan modification BEFORE missing a payment. Use payroll deduction if possible. There is no catching up in Chapter 13 — miss a payment, and your case may be dismissed, lifting the automatic stay and allowing foreclosure to resume.

Filing Bankruptcy: Step-by-Step

Pre-Filing Requirements

Credit counseling: - Required within 180 days before filing - Must be from approved agency - Certificate required with filing - Costs approximately $25-50

Means test (Chapter 7): - Determines eligibility for Chapter 7 - Compares income to state median - If above median, deduct expenses - If disposable income sufficient, must file Chapter 13

Document gathering: - Tax returns (2 years) - Pay stubs (6 months) - Bank statements (6 months) - Mortgage documents - Vehicle titles - Retirement account statements - List of all debts and creditors - List of all assets

The Filing Process

Petition and schedules: - Voluntary petition - Schedule A/B (property) - Schedule C (exemptions) - Schedule D (secured creditors) - Schedule E/F (unsecured creditors) - Schedule G (leases and executory contracts) - Schedule H (co-debtors) - Schedule I (income) - Schedule J (expenses) - Statement of financial affairs - Chapter 13 plan (if filing Chapter 13)

Filing fee: - Chapter 7: $338 - Chapter 13: $313 - Fee waiver available in some cases (must show inability to pay) - Can pay Chapter 13 fee through plan over time - Additional costs: credit counseling, financial management course

Automatic stay: - Effective immediately upon filing - Stops foreclosure, collection, lawsuits immediately - Creditors receive notice within days of filing - You should notify mortgage servicer directly with case number

Post-Filing Requirements

Meeting of creditors (341 hearing): - Scheduled 30-45 days after filing - Trustee questions debtor under oath - Creditors may attend and question - Usually brief (5-10 minutes) - Bring photo ID and Social Security card

Financial management course: - Required before discharge - Must be from approved agency - Certificate filed with court - Costs approximately $25-50

Chapter 13 confirmation: - Hearing 45-90 days after filing - Court approves or modifies plan - Plan payments begin before confirmation - Trustee administers plan

---

When Bankruptcy Is the Right Choice

Filing Chapter 7 Makes Sense When:

- You cannot afford the home
- Modification was denied
- Income too low for Chapter 13
- You need a fresh start
- Other debts are overwhelming
- You're surrendering the property

Filing Chapter 13 Makes Sense When:

- You can afford current mortgage payments
- You just need time to catch up
- You have regular income
- You want to save the home
- Junior lien stripping would help
- You have non-exempt assets to protect

Alternatives to Consider First:

- **Loan modification** — No credit impact, keeps same loan
- **Repayment plan** — Work directly with servicer
- **Forbearance** — Temporary payment reduction
- **Short sale** — Sell for less than owed
- **Deed in lieu** — Transfer property to bank
- **State foreclosure mediation** — Some states offer programs

---

Chapter Summary

- **Bankruptcy stops foreclosure immediately** through the automatic stay. File before the sale to prevent it.
- **Chapter 7 is temporary.** It delays foreclosure but doesn't cure arrears. Use when surrendering the property or when you cannot afford the home.
- **Chapter 13 can save your home.** It allows you to cure arrears over 3-5 years while making current payments. Requires regular income and discipline.

- **Choose the right chapter.** Chapter 7 for liquidation and fresh start. Chapter 13 for reorganization and saving the home.
- **Automatic stay has limits.** Creditors can seek stay relief. Repeat filings have limited stay. Act before sale is imminent.
- **Chapter 13 requires perfect payment discipline.** Trustees do not accept late payments. Miss a payment, and your case may be dismissed. Use payroll deduction when possible.
- **Lien stripping** can remove second mortgages in Chapter 13 when the property is underwater. A powerful tool for negative equity homes that can significantly reduce total debt.
- **Bankruptcy has costs and consequences.** Filing fees, attorney fees, credit impact, and complexity must be weighed against the potential benefits.
- **Bankruptcy is not the only option.** Consider modification, forbearance, short sale, or deed in lieu before filing bankruptcy.
- **Get professional help.** Bankruptcy is complex federal law with many potential traps. Consult an experienced bankruptcy attorney before filing. Mistakes can cost you your home.

LEARN FROM THIS MISTAKE: The Homeowner Who Didn't List All Creditors

David Kim's Story: David filed Chapter 13 bankruptcy to save his home. He listed his mortgage company as a creditor. But he didn't list the second mortgage company because he thought it was "included" in the first mortgage.

He also didn't list his car loan because he was current on it and didn't think it mattered. And he forgot to list a credit card he hadn't used in years.

The second mortgage company found out about the bankruptcy and moved to dismiss the case. "The debtor failed to list all creditors as required by 11 U.S.C. § 521," they argued. "The case should be dismissed for non-compliance."

The car lender also objected because they weren't receiving adequate protection payments they were entitled to.

David had to amend his schedules (costing additional fees) and deal with angry creditors who weren't being paid. The delays almost cost him his home when the bank sought stay relief while he sorted out the mess.

What David should have done: - Listed EVERY creditor, even if current on payments - Listed secured and unsecured creditors separately - Checked credit reports to find all creditors - Listed co-debtors on Schedule H - Been thorough and accurate from the start

"I thought I only needed to list the people I owed money to," David says. "I didn't realize I had to list everyone, even if I was current. It almost destroyed my case."

The Lesson: You must list ALL creditors in bankruptcy — every mortgage, every car loan, every credit card, every debt. Secured creditors must be listed even if you're current. The failure to list a creditor can result in dismissal, or worse, the debt not being discharged. Get a credit report. Check your records. Be thorough. The bankruptcy petition is a legal document under penalty of perjury. Accuracy matters.

Cross-References

Previous Chapter: Chapter 18 — Delay Tactics That Buy Time Legally

Next Chapter: Chapter 20 — TILA, RESPA, and Federal Claims

Related Chapters: - Chapter 18: Delay Tactics (for non-bankruptcy delay strategies) - Chapter 21: Emergency Response (for last-minute bankruptcy filing)

In the Playbook: - Chapter 7 vs. 13 Decision Tree - Bankruptcy Filing Checklist - Means Test Guide - Chapter 13 Plan Calculator

Templates: - Chapter 13 Plan Template - Motion for Stay Relief Response - Chapter 7 Petition Checklist - Chapter 13 Petition Checklist

CHAPTER 20: TILA, RESPA, AND FEDERAL CLAIMS

Federal Weapons Against Fraudulent Lending

Federal Laws That Protect Homeowners

Two powerful federal laws give homeowners weapons against predatory lending and servicing abuses: - **TILA** — Truth in Lending Act - **RESPA** — Real Estate Settlement Procedures Act

These laws don't just create defenses to foreclosure — they create **causes of action** that let you sue the lender for damages.

TILA: Truth in Lending Act

Purpose: Ensure borrowers understand the true cost of credit through clear disclosures.

Key protections: - **APR disclosure:** Must disclose true annual percentage rate - **Finance charge:** Must disclose total cost of borrowing - **Right to rescind:** Three-day right to cancel certain loans - **Advertising rules:** Prohibits misleading loan advertising - **Periodic statements:** Requires clear monthly statements

Private right of action: - Sue for statutory damages ($400-$4,000 per violation) - Sue for actual damages (economic harm) - Sue for rescission (unwind the loan entirely) - Attorney fees and costs

RESPA: Real Estate Settlement Procedures Act

Purpose: Ensure transparency in real estate settlements and prohibit kickbacks.

Key protections: - **Good Faith Estimate:** Required within 3 days of application - **HUD-1 Settlement Statement:** Final disclosure of all costs - **No kickbacks:** Prohibits referral fees and kickbacks between settlement service providers - **Servicing rules:** Requires acknowledgment of complaints and error resolution procedures - **Escrow limits:** Limits amount lenders can require in escrow accounts - **Afiliated business arrangements:** Requires disclosure when lender refers to affiliated service providers

Private right of action: - Sue for kickback violations (treble damages — three times the amount) - Sue for servicing violations (actual damages) - Sue for statutory damages where provided by regulation - Recover attorney fees and costs - Injunctive relief to stop ongoing violations

---

TILA Violations in Foreclosure

Material Disclosure Violations

What must be disclosed accurately: - Annual Percentage Rate (APR) - Finance charge (total interest over loan term) - Amount financed - Total of payments - Payment schedule - Prepayment penalties

Common TILA violations: - APR understated by more than 0.125% (or 0.25% for irregular transactions) - Finance charge understated by more than $100 ($35 for 2022+) - Required disclosures not provided - Disclosures provided too late (after consummation)

TILA Rescission Rights

The nuclear option: Rescission unwinds the loan entirely.

How it works: - Lender must refund all fees and payments - Borrower must return the principal - Lien is voided - Loan ceases to exist

Timing: - **Three years** for most violations - No time limit if required disclosures never provided - Must provide written notice of rescission

What triggers extended rescission: - Failure to provide required notices - Inaccurate APR disclosure - Inaccurate finance charge - Failure to provide right to cancel notice

TILA rescission letter:

```
NOTICE OF RESCISSION

To: [Lender Name and Address]

I hereby exercise my right to rescind the loan transaction
dated [Date] on the property at [Address] under the Truth
in Lending Act, 15 U.S.C. § 1635.

This rescission is based on your failure to provide
[describe violation -- e.g., accurate APR disclosure,
required notices, right to cancel notice].

I demand return of all fees and payments made, and I
will tender the principal amount upon your compliance.

[Signature]
[Date]
```

LEARN FROM THIS MISTAKE: The Homeowner Who Waited Too Long to Rescind

Jennifer Martinez' Story: Jennifer refinanced her home in 2019. The lender gave her disclosures, but she noticed the APR on her documents didn't match what she was quoted. She was busy with work and family, so she put it aside, thinking she'd deal with it later.

Three years passed. Jennifer fell behind on payments and faced foreclosure. She remembered the APR discrepancy and thought she could rescind the loan to get out of it.

She sent a rescission notice. The lender responded: "Your rescission notice is untimely. TILA's three-year rescission period expired on [Date]. Your loan cannot be rescinded."

Jennifer had waited one day too long. The three-year clock ran out the day before she sent her notice.

What Jennifer should have done: - Sent rescission notice within three years - Not waited until foreclosure to act - Calculated the deadline carefully - Consulted an attorney about her TILA rights

"I knew something was wrong with the loan," Jennifer says. "But I didn't understand the deadline was absolute. I thought I had time. I was one day late, and I lost my right to rescind forever."

The Lesson: TILA rescission has strict deadlines. You have three years from consummation to rescind for most violations. If required disclosures were never provided, you may have unlimited time — but don't count on it. Act promptly when you discover a violation. The deadline is absolute, and courts will not extend it. One day late is too late.

RESPA Violations in Foreclosure

Servicing Violations

RESPA Section 6 requires loan servicers to: - Acknowledge qualified written requests within 5 business days - Respond within 30 business days - Provide information requested or explain why not - Not provide inaccurate information

Common servicing violations: - Failing to acknowledge complaint - Failing to respond within 30 days - Providing inaccurate payoff information - Misapplying payments - Failing to correct errors

Force-Placed Insurance

RESPA limits force-placed insurance: - Must provide 45 days notice before charging - Must provide second notice 15 days before charging - Insurance must be for actual replacement cost - Must terminate within 15 days of proof of coverage

Force-placed insurance claims: - Excessive premiums - Failure to provide required notices - Continuing to charge after homeowner provides proof - Insurance that exceeds replacement cost

Kickbacks and Referral Fees

RESPA Section 8 prohibits: - Kickbacks for settlement service referrals - Fee splitting for referrals - Unearned fees

Common kickback violations: - Lender pays broker for referrals - Title company pays lender for business referrals - Appraiser pays for assignments - Unearned fees charged to borrower - Marketing arrangements disguised as legitimate payments

Detecting kickbacks: - Compare fees charged to services actually rendered - Look for payments between settlement service providers - Examine broker yield spread premiums on documents - Review closing documents for unusual or duplicate fees - Check if all fees were properly disclosed on HUD-1

Filing Federal Claims

TILA Claim Elements

To state a TILA claim: 1. You are a consumer borrower 2. The loan is covered by TILA 3. The lender violated TILA's disclosure requirements 4. You suffered damages (or statutory damages apply)

Damages available: - Statutory: $400-$4,000 per violation - Actual: Economic harm suffered - Rescission: Full unwinding of transaction - Attorney fees and costs

Defenses to foreclosure: - TILA violations can be raised as defenses - May counterclaim for TILA violations - Can seek rescission as remedy

RESPA Claim Elements

To state a RESPA claim: 1. The transaction involves a federally related mortgage 2. The defendant violated RESPA provisions 3. You suffered damages (or statutory damages apply)

Damages available: - Kickback violations: Treble damages (3x the fee) - Servicing violations: Actual damages - Attorney fees and costs

Damages calculation:

```
Kickback example:
Fee paid for referral: $500
Treble damages: $500 × 3 = $1,500

Servicing example:
Misapplied payment caused $2,000 in late fees
Actual damages: $2,000
Plus emotional distress in some jurisdictions
```

Combining Federal Claims

TILA and RESPA work together.

Common Combined Violations

Predatory lending scenario: - TILA: Inaccurate APR disclosure - RESPA: Kickback to mortgage broker - Result: Higher cost loan due to hidden fees

Servicing abuse scenario: - TILA: Inaccurate periodic statements - RESPA: Failure to respond to qualified written request - Result: Misapplied payments, wrongful fees

Strategic Considerations

When to file federal claims: - As counterclaims in foreclosure action - As separate lawsuit (if statute of limitations permits) - As defense to foreclosure (TILA rescission)

Statute of limitations: - **TILA:** One year from violation (three years for rescission) - **RESPA:** One year from violation (kickbacks); varies for servicing

State law claims: - Many states have parallel statutes - State claims may have longer limitations periods - Can assert federal and state claims together

---

LEARN FROM THIS MISTAKE: The Homeowner Who Didn't Document RESPA Violations

Robert Chen' Story: Robert sent a qualified written request to his servicer asking for an explanation of $3,000 in mysterious fees. Under RESPA, they had 30 days to respond.

They never responded. Robert waited, thinking they were processing it. He called and was told it was "being reviewed." He waited more.

By the time Robert realized they weren't going to respond, 60 days had passed. He had missed the deadline to file a RESPA claim. More importantly, he had no documentation that he sent the qualified written request.

He had sent it by regular mail with no return receipt. He had no copy of what he sent. The servicer denied receiving it. Without proof, Robert couldn't prove his RESPA claim.

What Robert should have done: - Sent the QWR by certified mail, return receipt requested - Kept a copy of everything sent - Tracked the 30-day deadline - Filed a RESPA claim as soon as the deadline passed - Documented all follow-up attempts

"I assumed they would respond professionally," Robert says. "I didn't realize I needed to protect myself with documentation. Without proof I sent it, my RESPA claim was worthless."

The Lesson: Document everything when dealing with servicers. Send qualified written requests by certified mail with return receipt requested. Keep copies of everything. Track deadlines carefully. Servicers often ignore or lose requests — your documentation is the only proof you have. Without it, you cannot enforce your RESPA rights.

State Law Counterparts

Many states have TILA and RESPA equivalents with additional protections.

State TILA Laws

Common features: - Similar disclosure requirements - Similar rescission rights - Sometimes longer limitations periods - Sometimes broader coverage - Sometimes stronger penalties

Examples: - California: Rosenthal Fair Debt Collection Practices Act - New York: Personal Property Law Article 9 - Texas: Finance Code Chapter 343 - Florida: Florida Consumer Collection

Practices Act

Advantages of state claims: - Longer statute of limitations in some states - Broader coverage than federal law - Sometimes stronger remedies - Can be brought in state court

State RESPA Laws

Common features: - Servicing requirements beyond federal law - Fee limitations and disclosure requirements - Licensing requirements for servicers - Sometimes stronger penalties for violations - Broader definitions of prohibited conduct

Examples: - California: Homeowners' Bill of Rights - New York: Real Property Law Section 265 - Illinois: Illinois Residential Mortgage License Act

Check your state laws for additional protections and remedies beyond federal TILA and RESPA.

LEARN FROM THIS MISTAKE: The Homeowner Who Didn't Assert Claims as Counterclaims

> **Lisa Thompson's Story:** Lisa discovered her loan had multiple TILA violations — the APR was understated by 0.5% and the finance charge was off by $2,000. She also found evidence her mortgage broker received an illegal kickback from the lender.
>
> When the bank sued her for foreclosure, Lisa raised the TILA and RESPA violations as "defenses" but didn't file formal counterclaims. She thought the judge would see the violations and dismiss the case.
>
> At trial, the judge ruled: "The defendant has raised some defenses, but has not filed counterclaims within the applicable statute of limitations. The defenses do not excuse the mortgage default. Judgment for plaintiff."
>
> Lisa lost her home. Worse, because she hadn't filed counterclaims, she lost her right to sue for TILA and RESPA damages separately — the doctrine of claim preclusion (res judicata) barred her from bringing those claims later.
>
> What Lisa should have done: - Filed formal counterclaims for TILA and RESPA violations - Sought damages, rescission, or offset against amounts due - Preserved her right to recover for violations - Created leverage for settlement negotiations
>
> "I thought defenses and counterclaims were the same thing," Lisa says. "They're not. Defenses just say 'you can't win.' Counterclaims say 'you owe me money.' I should have counterclaimed."

The Lesson: TILA and RESPA violations should be asserted as counterclaims, not just defenses. Counterclaims preserve your right to recover damages. They create settlement leverage. They can offset amounts claimed due. And they prevent claim preclusion from barring your claims later. When you discover federal violations, counterclaim — don't just defend.

Practical Application

Auditing Your Loan for Violations

TILA audit checklist: - [ ] Was APR disclosed accurately (within 0.125% or 0.25% for irregular transactions)? - [ ] Was finance charge accurate (within $100 or $35 for 2022+ transactions)? - [ ] Were all required disclosures provided at consummation? - [ ] Were disclosures provided within required timeframes? - [ ] Was right to cancel notice provided for refinances? - [ ] Are periodic statements accurate and complete? - [ ] Were advertising materials truthful and not misleading? - [ ] Were all finance charges included in the disclosure?

RESPA audit checklist: - [ ] Was Good Faith Estimate provided within 3 days of application? - [ ] Was HUD-1 or Closing Disclosure provided at closing? - [ ] Were there any kickbacks or referral fees between parties? - [ ] Has servicer responded to all qualified written requests within 30 days? - [ ] Was force-placed insurance properly noticed (45 days and 15 days)? - [ ] Were payments properly applied to principal and interest? - [ ] Were there any unearned fees charged at closing? - [ ] Were affiliated business arrangements properly disclosed?

When to Assert Federal Claims

In foreclosure defense: - Raise as affirmative defenses in your answer - File formal counterclaims for damages - Seek TILA rescission as remedy - Request offset against amounts claimed due

In separate lawsuit: - If within statute of limitations - To seek damages for past violations - To obtain discovery before foreclosure - To preserve claims that might be lost in foreclosure

In settlement negotiations: - Leverage for better modification terms - Offset against amounts claimed due by bank - Pressure for favorable settlement - Threat of rescission creates urgency - Documented violations strengthen position

---

Chapter Summary

- **TILA and RESPA are federal weapons** against predatory lending and servicing abuses. They create private rights of action with statutory damages, actual damages, and attorney fees that can make litigation economically viable.
- **TILA requires accurate disclosures.** The APR, finance charge, total of payments, and other material disclosures must be accurate within strict tolerances. Material violations create rescission rights and damages claims.
- **TILA rescission unwinds the loan entirely.** Within three years of consummation (or without time limit if no disclosures were provided), you can rescind the transaction, forcing the lender to return all fees and payments while you return the principal.
- **RESPA requires transparency in settlement.** Good Faith Estimates, HUD-1 statements, prohibition on kickbacks, and strict servicing rules govern the mortgage process. Violations create claims for damages.
- **Document everything with certified mail.** Send qualified written requests by certified mail, return receipt requested. Keep copies of everything. Track all deadlines carefully. Your documentation is your only proof.
- **Watch the strict deadlines.** TILA rescission expires three years from consummation. TILA damages claims expire one year from violation. RESPA claims have various limitation periods. Deadlines are absolute and jurisdictional — courts cannot extend them.
- **Combine federal and state claims for maximum protection.** State laws often provide parallel protections with longer limitations periods, broader remedies, and additional claims like unfair and deceptive trade practices.
- **Assert claims as counterclaims, not just defenses.** Counterclaims preserve your right to recover damages, create settlement leverage, allow offset against amounts due, and prevent claim preclusion from barring your claims in future litigation.
- **Federal claims create strategic value in negotiations.** They provide leverage in modification negotiations, can offset amounts claimed due by the bank, and pressure favorable settlements that might not otherwise be available.
- **Get professional help with complex claims.** TILA and RESPA litigation involves complex federal statutes with strict requirements. An experienced attorney can maximize your recovery and avoid procedural pitfalls that could cost you your valid claims.

Calculating TILA and RESPA Damages

TILA Statutory Damages

Standard violations: - $400 per violation (minimum) - $4,000 per violation (maximum) - Class actions: Lesser of $500,000 or 1% of net worth

Factors affecting damages: - Severity of violation - Pattern or practice of violations - Willfulness - Harm to consumer

Example calculation:

```
APR understated by 0.25%
Finance charge understated by $500
Right to cancel notice not provided

Potential damages: $400-$4,000 per violation
Multiple violations may be stacked
```

RESPA Damages

Kickback violations (Section 8): - Treble damages: 3x the amount of the charge - No cap on damages - Example: $500 kickback = $1,500 damages

Servicing violations (Section 6): - Actual damages (economic harm) - Emotional distress in some jurisdictions - Attorney fees

Force-placed insurance violations: - Premiums charged - Fees and costs - Related damages

Attorney Fees

Both TILA and RESPA provide for: - Recovery of attorney fees - Costs of litigation - Expert witness fees

This makes these claims attractive to attorneys who may take cases on contingency.

Cross-References

Previous Chapter: Chapter 19 — Bankruptcy as Nuclear Option

Next Chapter: Chapter 21 — Federal Court and Constitutional Challenges (for additional federal remedies and constitutional defenses)

Related Chapters: - Chapter 8: Consideration and Funding (for origination fraud and funding issues) - Chapter 21: Federal Court and Constitutional Claims (for additional federal remedies) - Chapter 22: State Law Claims (for parallel state remedies and consumer protection)

In the Playbook: - TILA Audit Checklist with detailed steps - RESPA Violations Checklist for servicer review - Qualified Written Request (QWR) Template with sample language - TILA Rescission Letter Template with proper format - Loan Document Request Template for complete file - Damages Calculation Worksheet for both TILA and RESPA claims - State Law Counterpart Reference Guide for additional state remedies and protections

Templates: - Qualified Written Request Template with instructions - TILA Rescission Notice with proper formatting - RESPA Complaint Template for court filing - Damages Calculation Worksheet - Document Request for Loan File

CHAPTER 21: FEDERAL COURT AND CONSTITUTIONAL CHALLENGES

Taking Your Fight to Federal Court

When Federal Court Makes Sense

Most foreclosure cases are filed in state court. But sometimes federal court offers advantages: - **Federal question jurisdiction:** TILA, RESPA, constitutional claims - **Diversity jurisdiction:** Parties from different states - **Removal:** Moving state case to federal court - **Federal rules:** Discovery rules may be more favorable

Federal Question Jurisdiction

28 U.S.C. § 1331 gives federal courts jurisdiction over cases "arising under" federal law.

Common federal questions in foreclosure: - TILA violations - RESPA violations - Fair Debt Collection Practices Act (FDCPA) violations - Equal Credit Opportunity Act (ECOA) violations - Constitutional due process claims - RICO claims (rare)

Key rule: The federal question must be "substantial" and "arising on the face of the complaint."

Diversity Jurisdiction

28 U.S.C. § 1332 gives federal courts jurisdiction when: - Parties are citizens of different states - Amount in controversy exceeds $75,000

Foreclosure considerations: - Plaintiff bank may be from another state - Homeowner from forum state - Mortgage amount usually exceeds $75,000 - But foreclosure is typically in rem (against property), not in personam

Removal from State Court

28 U.S.C. § 1441 allows removal of state cases to federal court.

Requirements: - Federal court must have original jurisdiction - All defendants must consent - Must file notice of removal within 30 days of service - State court loses jurisdiction upon removal

Strategic considerations: - Federal judges may be more sophisticated - Federal discovery rules may help - Federal court may be faster or slower - May antagonize state court judge

---

LEARN FROM THIS MISTAKE: The Homeowner Who Removed Too Late

Kevin Park's Story: Kevin had strong TILA and RESPA counterclaims against the bank foreclosing on his home. His attorney recommended removing the case to federal court for better discovery rules.

Kevin delayed. He was busy with work. He thought he had plenty of time. The 30-day removal window passed.

When Kevin finally tried to remove, the bank objected: "Removal is untimely. Defendant had 30 days from service. It has been 45 days. The right to remove has been waived."

The federal court agreed. Kevin was stuck in state court. He lost some of the strategic advantages his attorney had planned.

What Kevin should have done: - Removed immediately upon deciding federal court was better - Not waited until the deadline was near - Understood that 30 days is absolute - Filed removal notice on day 1, not day 29

"I thought 30 days meant I had 30 days to decide," Kevin says. "But once you decide, you should act immediately. Waiting cost me the federal forum."

The Lesson: The 30-day removal window is absolute. Once you decide federal court is advantageous, remove immediately. Don't wait. The deadline is jurisdictional and cannot be extended. File the notice of removal as soon as possible after determining federal court is the right forum.

Constitutional Challenges

The Constitution provides protections that can be raised in foreclosure defense.

Due Process Claims

Fourteenth Amendment (state actors) or **Fifth Amendment** (federal actors): > No person shall be "deprived of life, liberty, or property, without due process of law."

Property interest: - Your home is constitutionally protected property - Foreclosure deprives you of that property - You are entitled to procedural due process

Due process requirements: 1. **Notice:** Adequate notice of proceedings 2. **Opportunity to be heard:** Meaningful chance to contest 3. **Neutral decisionmaker:** Unbiased judge or tribunal

Common due process violations: - Inadequate service of process - Failure to provide hearing before foreclosure - Biased foreclosure mediators - Defective notice of sale

Limitations: - Most foreclosures are state proceedings with built-in due process - Courts generally find statutory procedures sufficient - Constitutional claims rarely succeed as standalone defenses

Equal Protection Claims

Fourteenth Amendment: > No state shall "deny to any person within its jurisdiction the equal protection of the laws."

Potential claims: - Discriminatory lending practices - Disparate impact on protected classes - Unequal application of foreclosure procedures

Standards of review: - **Strict scrutiny:** Race, national origin (compelling government interest required) - **Intermediate scrutiny:** Gender (important government interest required) - **Rational basis:** Other classifications (any rational basis sufficient)

Practical reality: - Equal protection claims require proof of intentional discrimination - Disparate impact alone is usually insufficient - Hard to prove in individual foreclosure cases

Takings Clause

Fifth Amendment: > Private property shall not "be taken for public use, without just compensation."

Foreclosure application: - Rarely applicable - Foreclosure is generally considered a private action, not government taking - Even judicial foreclosure is not a "taking" - Some creative arguments about government involvement in securitization

Reality check: - Takings claims almost never succeed in foreclosure defense - Courts consistently reject these arguments - Not a viable standalone strategy

---

Federal Statutory Claims

Fair Debt Collection Practices Act (FDCPA)

15 U.S.C. § 1692 regulates debt collectors.

Applies to: - Third-party debt collectors - Lawyers collecting debts - May apply to servicers under some circumstances

Prohibited conduct: - Harassment or abuse - False or misleading representations - Unfair practices - Contact after written cease request

Damages: - Actual damages - Statutory damages up to $1,000 - Attorney fees and costs

Foreclosure application: - Lawyers handling foreclosure may be "debt collectors" - Threatening letters may violate FDCPA - False statements in foreclosure documents may qualify

Statute of limitations: - One year from the date of the violation - Written demand for damages must precede suit in some jurisdictions

Remedies available: - Actual damages for proven losses - Statutory damages up to $1,000 per violation - Attorney fees and costs - Injunctive relief to stop prohibited conduct

Common FDCPA violations in foreclosure: - Threats of actions that cannot legally be taken - False representations about the debt amount - Communications after attorney representation - Contacting third parties about the debt

Equal Credit Opportunity Act (ECOA)

15 U.S.C. § 1691 prohibits discrimination in lending.

Prohibited bases: - Race, color, religion - National origin, sex - Marital status, age - Public assistance income

Types of discrimination: - **Overt:** Explicit discrimination - **Disparate treatment:** Different treatment based on protected class - **Disparate impact:** Neutral policy with discriminatory effect

Foreclosure connection: - Predatory lending often targets protected classes - May support counterclaims or defenses - Can be raised in federal court

Damages: - Actual damages - Punitive damages (up to $10,000) - Attorney fees and costs - Equitable relief

Statute of limitations: - Two years from occurrence of discriminatory act - Can be extended if discrimination was not discovered - Administrative complaint with CFPB may toll limitations

Evidence needed: - Comparative treatment evidence (how similarly situated borrowers treated) - Disparate impact statistics if available - Statements indicating discriminatory intent - Pattern or practice evidence

Remedies: - Actual damages for economic losses - Punitive damages up to $10,000 for intentional violations - Attorney fees and costs - Equitable relief including injunctions

Servicemembers Civil Relief Act (SCRA)

50 U.S.C. § 3901 protects active duty military.

Key protections: - 6% interest rate cap on pre-service debts - Protection from default judgments - Stay of proceedings - Lease termination rights - Eviction protections

Foreclosure specific: - Cannot foreclose without court order during active duty + 1 year after - Default judgments void if service member not represented - Penalties for violations

See Chapter 28 for detailed military protections.

RICO Claims

Racketeer Influenced and Corrupt Organizations Act

18 U.S.C. § 1961 provides civil remedies for racketeering.

Elements: 1. Enterprise (bank, servicer, law firm) 2. Pattern of racketeering activity (mail fraud, wire fraud) 3. Participation in enterprise conduct 4. Injury to business or property

Foreclosure theories: - Securitization as fraudulent enterprise - Robo-signing as pattern of fraud - Document fabrication as mail/wire fraud

Reality check: - Extremely difficult to prove in foreclosure context - Dismissed in most foreclosure RICO cases - Requires showing criminal enterprise with predicate acts - Not recommended for pro se litigants without legal training - Courts view as improper "kitchen sink" pleading tactic - Sanctions possible for frivolous RICO claims under Rule 11

LEARN FROM THIS MISTAKE: The Homeowner Who Wasted Time on Frivolous Constitutional Claims

> **Thomas Anderson's Story:** Thomas was convinced the Constitution protected him from foreclosure. He filed a federal lawsuit claiming foreclosure violated his Fifth Amendment due process rights, his Fourteenth Amendment equal protection rights, and constituted an unconstitutional taking.
>
> He spent months researching constitutional law. He drafted a 50-page complaint. He paid the $402 filing fee. He was sure the federal court would protect him.
>
> The judge dismissed the case within weeks. "The constitutional claims fail as a matter of law. Foreclosure is a state procedure with built-in due process protections. There is no taking. There is no equal protection violation alleged. This court lacks jurisdiction over the state foreclosure action."
>
> Thomas wasted months and hundreds of dollars on claims that had no chance of success. Meanwhile, the state foreclosure proceeded. By the time he turned his attention to the actual foreclosure defense, it was almost too late.

What Thomas should have done: - Focused on viable state law defenses first - Used constitutional claims only as supplement - Understood that foreclosure procedures provide due process - Consulted an attorney about viability of constitutional claims

"I thought the Constitution would save me," Thomas says. "But judges don't see foreclosure as a constitutional violation. I should have focused on the actual defects in the bank's case."

The Lesson: Constitutional claims rarely succeed as standalone foreclosure defenses. Courts consistently find that statutory foreclosure procedures provide sufficient due process. Focus on substantive defenses first — standing, chain of title, payment history errors. Use constitutional claims, if at all, as supplemental arguments. Don't waste time and resources on frivolous constitutional litigation when your home is at stake.

LEARN FROM THIS MISTAKE: The Homeowner Who Filed a RICO Claim Pro Se

Jason Wright's Story: Jason was convinced the bank's securitization of his loan was a criminal enterprise. He filed a federal lawsuit alleging RICO violations, claiming the bank, servicer, and foreclosure lawyer were engaged in a pattern of racketeering activity involving mail fraud and wire fraud.

He spent weeks drafting a 75-page complaint. He paid the federal filing fee. He was sure the treble damages would save his home and make him wealthy.

The judge dismissed the case and sanctioned him $1,000. "The RICO claims are frivolous. Securitization is not a criminal enterprise. Robo-signing, while problematic, does not constitute a pattern of racketeering activity. Pro se litigants are not exempt from Rule 11."

Jason lost the $1,000 sanction, the filing fee, and months of time. Worse, the federal court's dismissal with prejudice hurt his credibility in the state foreclosure case.

What Jason should have done: - Focused on viable state law defenses like standing and chain of title - Consulted an attorney about RICO viability before filing - Understood that RICO requires criminal predicate acts and enterprise - Avoided "kitchen sink" pleadings that waste time and money

"I thought RICO was the silver bullet," Jason says. "But it's a criminal statute being misused in civil cases. I should have stuck to defenses that actually work."

The Lesson: RICO claims in foreclosure are almost universally unsuccessful. They require proving a criminal enterprise with predicate criminal acts — an extremely high standard. Don't waste time and risk sanctions on RICO claims. Focus on substantive foreclosure defenses that have a track record of success. RICO is not a shortcut to defeating foreclosure.

Practical Application

When to Consider Federal Court

Consider federal court when: - You have strong federal statutory claims (TILA, RESPA, FDCPA) - State court is hostile to homeowner defenses - Federal discovery rules would help your case - You want to consolidate federal and state claims - Removal is available and strategically beneficial

Stay in state court when: - Your defenses are state law based - State court judge is homeowner-friendly - Federal court has longer backlog - Removal would waive state law protections - Your attorney recommends state court

Removing a Case

Step 1: Determine eligibility - Federal question or diversity jurisdiction exists - All defendants will consent to removal - Within 30 days of service of complaint - No prior state court activity that waives removal

Step 2: Draft notice of removal

```
NOTICE OF REMOVAL

Defendant [Name] removes this action from [State Court]
to the United States District Court for the [District]
District of [State].

This court has federal question jurisdiction because
[explain federal claim]. A copy of all pleadings and
process served is attached.

A copy of the state court complaint is attached as Exhibit A.
Defendant has not initiated any proceedings in state court.
```

Step 3: File in federal court - Pay federal filing fee ($402) - Serve notice on all parties to the action - File copy of notice in state court to inform them

Step 4: State court loses jurisdiction - Upon proper filing of notice of removal - State proceedings must stop immediately - Federal court gains exclusive jurisdiction - Any state court orders after removal are void

Opposing Removal

If plaintiff improperly removes: - File motion to remand in federal court - Challenge jurisdictional basis - Request sanctions for improper removal - Move quickly — don't waive objections

Grounds for remand: - No federal jurisdiction exists - Defect in removal procedure - Failure to timely remove - Lack of complete diversity

---

Advantages and Disadvantages of Federal Court

Advantages

Discovery: - Broader discovery under Federal Rules - Mandatory initial disclosures - More powerful subpoena power - Better enforcement mechanisms

Judges: - Lifetime appointments may mean more independence - Some federal judges are more sophisticated on complex issues - More consistent application of law - Generally better resourced

Consolidation: - Can bring all federal claims together - May be able to add federal claims to state case via removal - Class action possibilities for widespread violations

Disadvantages

Speed: - Federal courts often have heavy dockets - Cases may move slower than state court - Summary judgment may come faster - Less time to prepare

Local rules: - Each district has complex local rules - Pro se litigants face higher hurdles - Technical requirements stricter - Non-compliance can be fatal

Home court disadvantage: - Banks may have more federal court experience - Local attorneys may know federal judges better - Out-of-state plaintiff may have advantage

---

Chapter Summary

- **Federal court jurisdiction exists** for cases arising under federal law or between diverse parties with amount in controversy over $75,000. TILA, RESPA, FDCPA, and constitutional claims can create federal question jurisdiction.

- **Removal allows transfer** from state to federal court when federal court would have had original jurisdiction. Must file within 30 days of service of the complaint. All defendants must consent. Once filed properly, state court loses jurisdiction automatically.
- **Due process claims** require showing inadequate notice, lack of opportunity to be heard, or biased decisionmaker. However, statutory foreclosure procedures with proper service and hearing opportunities usually satisfy constitutional due process requirements.
- **Equal protection claims** require proof of intentional discrimination based on protected class. Disparate impact alone is usually insufficient. Extremely difficult to prove in individual foreclosure cases.
- **Takings claims** almost never succeed in foreclosure defense. Foreclosure is not considered a government taking requiring just compensation. Courts consistently reject these arguments.
- **FDCPA applies** to third-party debt collectors and may apply to foreclosure lawyers handling collections. Prohibits harassment, false statements, and unfair practices with statutory damages available.
- **ECOA prohibits** lending discrimination based on race, color, religion, national origin, sex, marital status, age, or public assistance income. May support counterclaims if predatory lending targeted protected classes.
- **SCRA provides** powerful protections for active duty military including interest rate caps, stay of proceedings, and foreclosure prohibitions during and after service.
- **RICO claims** are rarely successful in foreclosure cases and require proving a criminal enterprise with predicate criminal acts — an extremely high standard that most foreclosure situations do not meet. Risk of sanctions for frivolous claims.
- **Focus on substance first.** Constitutional claims rarely succeed alone. Build strong state law defenses first, then supplement with federal claims if appropriate. Don't waste time and resources on frivolous constitutional or RICO litigation.
- **Understand federal court pros and cons.** Federal court offers broader discovery and potentially more sophisticated judges, but also has complex local rules, potentially slower dockets, and higher hurdles for pro se litigants.

Federal Court Local Rules Warning

Federal courts have complex local rules that vary by district. Before filing anything in federal court:

Research requirements: - Local Civil Rules for your district - Local Patent Rules (if applicable) - Judge-specific standing orders - E-filing requirements and procedures - Formatting requirements for pleadings

Common local rule traps: - Certificate of conference requirements - Specific font and margin requirements - Page limits on motions - E-filing registration requirements - Redaction requirements for personal information

Resources: - Court website for local rules - Clerk's office for questions - Local bar association guides - Pro se assistance programs (if available)

Warning: Non-compliance with local rules can result in dismissal or sanctions. Don't assume state court practices apply in federal court.

Cross-References

Previous Chapter: Chapter 20 — TILA, RESPA, and Federal Claims (for detailed coverage of TILA rescission and RESPA violations)

Next Chapter: Chapter 22 — State Law Claims and Causes of Action (for state-specific remedies and common law claims)

Related Chapters: - Chapter 20: TILA and RESPA (for federal statutory claims and consumer protection) - Chapter 22: State Law Claims (for state law defenses and remedies) - Chapter 28: Military and Veterans Protections (for detailed SCRA coverage)

In the Playbook: - Federal vs. State Court Decision Matrix with detailed pros/cons analysis - Removal Checklist with 30-day timeline tracker - Federal Claims Timeline for statute of limitations - Constitutional Claims Viability Assessment tool - Local Rules Compliance Checklist by district - Federal Court Filing Fee Schedule - Pro Se Litigant Resources Guide

Templates: - Notice of Removal Template with instructions - Federal Complaint Template for federal question jurisdiction - Motion to Remand Template (if opposing improper removal) - Motion to Dismiss for Lack of Subject Matter Jurisdiction - Motion for Sanctions for Frivolous Removal

CHAPTER 22: WHEN FEDERAL COURT IS AND IS NOT REALISTIC

Understanding Your Options After State Court Loss

The Federal Court Dream

You've lost in state court. The judgment is entered, the sale is scheduled, or maybe already happened. Someone mentions federal court like it's a magic portal to a second chance. There must be a higher authority, right? Someone who will see that the state court got it wrong?

The reality is more sobering. Federal courts generally will not review state court foreclosure judgments. The barriers are substantial, the exceptions are narrow, and many homeowners have wasted years and thousands of dollars pursuing federal claims that were doomed from the start.

This chapter gives you the truth about federal court options — when they exist, when they don't, and how to tell the difference before you invest resources you can't get back.

The Rooker-Feldman Barrier

The single biggest obstacle to federal foreclosure relief is the Rooker-Feldman doctrine. Named after two Supreme Court cases from the 1920s, this doctrine prevents federal courts from acting as appellate courts over state court decisions.

What Rooker-Feldman Means

In simple terms: If you lost in state court, you cannot run to federal court to get a do-over. Federal courts lack jurisdiction to hear challenges to state court judgments.

The Supreme Court in *Rooker v. Fidelity Trust Co.* and *District of Columbia v. Feldman* established that only the U.S. Supreme Court can review state court judgments. Lower federal courts cannot.

How Rooker-Feldman Works in Practice

The doctrine applies when: - A state court has entered a final judgment - The losing party seeks federal court review of that judgment - The federal claim is essentially an appeal of the state court decision

Typical doomed federal claims: - "The state court ignored the forged assignment" - "The state court applied the wrong standard for standing" - "The state court's summary judgment was wrong" - "The state court violated my due process rights"

Why these fail: Each asks the federal court to overturn or review the state court judgment — exactly what Rooker-Feldman forbids.

The "Independent Claim" Exception

Rooker-Feldman does not bar federal claims that are truly independent of the state court judgment. For example: - A federal claim that existed before the state court judgment - A federal claim based on conduct unrelated to the state proceeding - A federal statutory claim with its own cause of action

The problem for foreclosure defendants: Most potential federal claims are directly tied to challenging the foreclosure judgment itself, making them Rooker-Feldman barred.

> **Learn From Our Mistake: The Homeowner Who Wasted Three Years in Federal Court**
>
> After losing his foreclosure case in state court, Marcus filed a federal lawsuit alleging the state court violated his due process rights and that the bank committed fraud. He represented himself, spent three years litigating, and paid over $5,000 in filing fees.
>
> The federal court dismissed his case under Rooker-Feldman. Marcus then appealed to the federal circuit court, which affirmed the dismissal. He sought Supreme Court review, which was denied. After four years and countless hours, he was back where he started — with a final foreclosure judgment and no federal remedy.
>
> **What Marcus should have done:** Consulted an attorney about the realistic chances of federal relief before investing years of his life. The Rooker-Feldman barrier was obvious from the start to anyone familiar with federal jurisdiction.

Federal Question Jurisdiction: The Narrow Path

Federal courts have jurisdiction over cases "arising under" federal law under 28 U.S.C. § 1331. This sounds promising for foreclosure defendants — federal laws like TILA, RESPA, and the Fair Debt Collection Practices Act all apply to mortgages.

When Federal Question Jurisdiction Exists

A federal question exists when: - The claim is based on federal statute (TILA, RESPA, FDCPA, etc.) - The federal right is an essential element of the claim - The claim is not a pretext for federal review of state law

The Timing Problem

Federal question jurisdiction usually requires the federal claim to be brought independently, not as a challenge to a state court judgment. Once a state court has entered a foreclosure judgment, several problems arise:

Claim preclusion (res judicata): If you could have raised the federal claim in the state court proceeding, you may be barred from raising it later in federal court.

Issue preclusion (collateral estoppel): If the state court already decided issues that overlap with your federal claim, those decisions may be binding.

Rooker-Feldman overlap: If your federal claim essentially asks the federal court to overturn the state foreclosure, it's barred regardless of the federal statutory basis.

Potential Federal Claims That Might Survive

1. TILA rescission claims (if within 3-year window): TILA provides an absolute right to rescind certain mortgage transactions within three years of consummation. This right exists independently of foreclosure proceedings, and some federal courts have allowed rescission claims even after foreclosure judgment — though the timing is critical.

Key case: *Rosenfield v. HSBC Bank, USA* (rescission claim allowed as independent federal right).

2. RESPA violations with ongoing damages: If the servicer's RESPA violations caused ongoing financial harm beyond the foreclosure itself, a federal claim might exist for those damages — though it won't overturn the foreclosure.

3. FDCPA claims against debt collectors: If a debt collector (not the original creditor) violated the Fair Debt Collection Practices Act during the foreclosure process, this may provide an independent federal claim for statutory damages.

Important limitation: These claims provide monetary damages, not foreclosure reversal. The foreclosure judgment typically stands even if you win on the federal claim.

Constitutional Claims: Even Harder

Many homeowners want to sue in federal court alleging constitutional violations: due process violations, equal protection violations, takings without just compensation. These claims face enormous hurdles.

Due Process Claims

The problem: State court foreclosure proceedings themselves provide due process. You received notice, had an opportunity to be heard, and the court followed procedure. Simply losing your case does not mean your due process rights were violated.

When due process claims sometimes work: - Complete lack of notice (service was never attempted) - Fundamental procedural defects in the state process itself - Bias or corruption in the state court (extremely hard to prove)

When due process claims fail: - "The judge didn't understand my defense" - "The court applied the wrong legal standard" - "I lost because the bank lied" - "The state court system is biased against homeowners"

These are complaints about the outcome or the adversary's conduct, not about the process itself.

Equal Protection Claims

Equal protection requires showing intentional discrimination. General complaints about banks having more resources, courts favoring lenders, or systemic inequality do not state valid equal protection claims.

What would be required: - Evidence the court treated you differently because of race, gender, or other protected class - Intentional discrimination by state actors - Comparative evidence showing different treatment

Reality: These claims almost never succeed in foreclosure contexts.

TILA and RESPA Claims After Foreclosure

Truth in Lending Act (TILA) and Real Estate Settlement Procedures Act (RESPA) violations are popular bases for federal claims. But using them effectively after a state foreclosure judgment requires careful navigation.

TILA Rescission: The Nuclear Option

TILA provides a right to rescind certain mortgage transactions within three business days (or up to three years if proper disclosures weren't provided). This is a powerful statutory right — but with strict limitations:

Requirements for rescission: 1. The loan must be a "consumer credit transaction" secured by the consumer's principal dwelling 2. The lender must have failed to provide required disclosures (or provided inaccurate ones) 3. The rescission must be exercised within the statutory time period 4. The borrower must tender the loan proceeds back to the lender

The timing trap: If more than three years have passed since loan consummation, rescission is barred forever. For loans from the 2000s housing boom, this window closed years ago.

Effect on foreclosure: Even if rescission is successful, it doesn't automatically void a foreclosure judgment. The parties must be restored to their pre-loan positions, which requires unwinding the transaction — a process that takes time and may not stop an imminent sale.

RESPA Claims: Limited Remedies

RESPA prohibits certain practices by mortgage servicers, including: - Failing to acknowledge qualified written requests - Failing to respond to error resolution requests - Improperly forcing lender-placed insurance - Dual-tracking (pursuing foreclosure while evaluating modifications)

The problem for post-foreclosure claims: RESPA provides for actual damages, statutory damages, and attorneys' fees — but not foreclosure reversal. Even if you prove RESPA violations, the foreclosure judgment typically remains in place.

Strategic use: RESPA claims can provide leverage in settlement negotiations or monetary recovery, but they rarely save homes after foreclosure judgment.

When Federal Court Might Actually Work

Despite the obstacles, there are narrow circumstances where federal court provides real relief:

1. Pre-Judgment Federal Claims

If you file in federal court before the state foreclosure is complete, Rooker-Feldman does not apply. You can seek: - Declaratory judgment on federal rights - Injunctive relief against foreclosure - Damages for federal statutory violations

Strategic challenge: The bank may argue the federal court should abstain under the "Younger abstention" doctrine, which generally requires federal courts to defer to ongoing state proceedings. This creates a race — you need to file before the state case progresses too far.

2. Truly Independent Federal Violations

If the bank violated federal law in ways completely separate from the foreclosure judgment, a federal claim might exist: - Pattern of FDCPA violations by a debt collector - Ongoing RESPA violations causing continuing harm - Discrimination claims under the Equal Credit Opportunity Act

Key test: Can you state a federal claim without referencing the state court judgment? If yes, it might survive.

3. Bankruptcy Court

While not a federal district court, bankruptcy court is a federal forum with significant power over foreclosure: - Automatic stay under 11 U.S.C. § 362 immediately stops foreclosure - Chapter 13 plan can cure mortgage arrears over time - Lien stripping in some circumstances - Adversary proceedings for related claims

Bankruptcy is discussed in detail in Chapter 19 — it's often the most effective federal remedy available to homeowners facing foreclosure.

4. Federal Appeals

If your case was in federal court originally (for example, if the bank removed a state case to federal court), then normal appellate procedures apply. This chapter focuses on seeking federal relief after state court loss, not appeals within the federal system.

When Federal Court Won't Work

Be honest with yourself about these warning signs that federal court is not the answer:

Red Flags for Doomed Federal Claims

You want federal court to "fix" the state court decision: If you're seeking federal relief because the state court got it wrong, Rooker-Feldman almost certainly bars your claim.

Your federal claim is basically the same as your state court defense: If you argued standing in state court and lost, you cannot re-argue standing in federal court as a constitutional due process claim.

More than three years have passed since your loan closed: TILA rescission is time-barred. Other federal claims may also be time-barred by statutes of limitations.

You've already filed one federal lawsuit that was dismissed: Res judicata may bar subsequent federal actions based on the same claims.

You're representing yourself and don't understand federal procedure: Federal court has strict rules, formatting requirements, and procedural expectations. Pro se litigants unfamiliar with federal practice often have their cases dismissed on procedural grounds before reaching the merits.

Common Federal Court Traps

The "Constitutional Violation" Trap: Homeowners file federal complaints alleging violations of their constitutional rights, only to learn that losing a state court case is not a constitutional violation. Due process requires notice and opportunity to be heard — not a correct outcome.

The "Fraud on the Court" Trap: Alleging the bank committed fraud in state court sounds like it should create federal jurisdiction. It usually doesn't — it's still an attack on the state court judgment, barred by Rooker-Feldman.

The "RICO" Trap: Some homeowners try to bring RICO claims alleging the bank engaged in a pattern of racketeering. These claims face enormous pleading hurdles and almost never survive a motion to dismiss.

Strategic Considerations

Before pursuing federal court relief, honestly assess:

The Cost-Benefit Analysis

Costs of federal litigation: - Filing fees ($402 for federal district court as of 2025) - Service of process costs - Potential attorneys' fees (federal court is not user-friendly for pro se litigants) - Time and energy spent on likely doomed claims - Opportunity cost of not pursuing more realistic options

Potential benefits: - In rare cases, meaningful relief - Delay of foreclosure (though federal courts move faster than state courts) - Settlement leverage - Sense of "being heard" even if claim ultimately fails

Realistic Assessment Questions

Ask yourself: 1. Is my federal claim truly independent of the state court judgment? 2. Am I seeking monetary damages or foreclosure reversal? 3. Has the statute of limitations expired on my federal claims? 4. Do I have the resources to litigate in federal court? 5. Have I consulted with an attorney about the realistic chances of success? 6. Is my time better spent on bankruptcy, appeal, or settlement?

Alternatives to Federal Court

If federal court is not realistic, consider:

State court appeal: The proper channel for challenging state court errors. See Chapter 20-21 for appellate procedures.

Bankruptcy: Often the most effective way to stop foreclosure and save a home. See Chapter 19 for detailed discussion.

Settlement: Negotiating with the bank, especially if you have leverage from document defects or procedural irregularities.

Post-judgment motions: State courts have procedures for motions to vacate, reconsider, or set aside judgments under limited circumstances.

Practical Guidance

If You're Determined to File in Federal Court

Do this first:

1. **Consult a federal court attorney:** Even a brief consultation can save you years of wasted effort. Many attorneys offer free or low-cost initial consultations.
2. **Research Rooker-Feldman thoroughly:** Read the leading Supreme Court cases (*Rooker*, *Feldman*, *District of Columbia Court of Appeals v. Feldman*, and *Lance v. Cohn*). Read circuit court decisions from your jurisdiction applying Rooker-Feldman to foreclosure cases.
3. **Draft your complaint carefully:** Federal complaints must meet the plausibility standard from *Bell Atlantic Corp. v. Twombly* and *Ashcroft v. Iqbal*. Conclusory allegations won't survive a motion to dismiss.
4. **Be specific about jurisdiction:** Explain exactly why federal jurisdiction exists and why Rooker-Feldman does not apply. Anticipate the motion to dismiss.
5. **Consider limited scope representation:** Some attorneys will review your complaint or advise on jurisdiction for a flat fee without taking full representation.

Federal Court Checklist

Before filing, verify:

- ☐ My federal claim is truly independent of the state court judgment
- ☐ I am not asking the federal court to overturn or review the state court decision
- ☐ My federal claim is based on specific federal statutes, not general constitutional principles
- ☐ The statute of limitations has not expired on my federal claims
- ☐ I understand that monetary damages are the likely remedy, not foreclosure reversal
- ☐ I have researched Rooker-Feldman and can explain why it doesn't apply to my claim
- ☐ I have the resources to litigate in federal court
- ☐ I have considered bankruptcy as an alternative
- ☐ I have consulted with an attorney about realistic chances of success

---

Chapter Summary

Federal court is rarely the answer after losing in state court. The Rooker-Feldman doctrine bars most attempts to use federal courts to challenge state foreclosure judgments. Federal question jurisdiction exists for some statutory claims, but these typically provide monetary damages rather than foreclosure reversal.

The exceptions are narrow: pre-judgment federal claims, truly independent federal violations, and bankruptcy court proceedings. Most homeowners who pursue federal relief after state court loss end up with dismissed cases and wasted resources.

Before investing in federal litigation: - Honestly assess whether Rooker-Feldman bars your claim - Consider whether bankruptcy provides better relief - Consult an attorney about realistic chances of success - Remember that federal court is not a magic portal to a second chance

The hard truth: Once you've lost in state court, your realistic options are appeal, bankruptcy, settlement, or accepting the loss. Federal court is almost never the solution homeowners hope it will be.

Cross-References

- **Chapter 19:** Bankruptcy as a federal remedy for foreclosure
- **Chapter 20-21:** State court appeals as the proper channel for challenging state court errors
- **Chapter 13:** Discovery strategies that apply in federal court if you have a viable claim
- **Chapter 32:** Using AI to research federal jurisdiction issues

---

Going Forward

This concludes Book 1: The Foreclosure Defense Manual. You've learned the foundations of foreclosure law, how to audit your documents, how to litigate in state court, and what options remain if you lose.

Book 2: The Survival Playbook takes a different approach. Rather than teaching legal principles, it provides stage-specific action plans for wherever you are in the foreclosure process — whether you're current but suspicious, behind but not yet sued, or facing imminent sale.

Wherever you are in your foreclosure journey, the key principles remain the same: understand your rights, act quickly, verify everything the bank claims, and never assume the bank's case is as strong as it looks.

The fight is hard. The system is not designed for homeowners. But armed with knowledge and determination, you have a chance.

End of Chapter 22

End of Book 1: The Foreclosure Defense Manual

CHAPTER 23: WINNING PRO SE HOMEOWNER CASES

What Actually Worked

The Proof That Defense Works

Let's start with the truth: Homeowners do win foreclosure cases. Not always, not even most of the time, but often enough that defense is worth fighting. The bank's narrative — that resistance is futile and they always win — is a lie designed to make you give up without a fight.

This chapter presents real victories. Not theoretical possibilities, but actual cases where homeowners — many of them pro se — defeated foreclosure. We analyze what made the difference, what patterns emerge, and what you can learn from their success.

A word of caution: Every case is different. A strategy that worked in Florida in 2019 may not work in Texas in 2025. Courts vary, judges vary, facts vary. But the fundamental principles — standing must be proved, documents must be authentic, procedure must be followed — apply everywhere. These cases show what's possible when homeowners fight smart.

The Case Library: How to Read These Stories

Each case summary in this chapter follows a standard format:

- **Citation:** Where to find the full opinion
- **Court/Year:** Jurisdiction and date
- **Representation:** Whether homeowner had an attorney
- **Key Facts:** What happened
- **Winning Strategy:** What worked
- **Why It Matters:** Lessons for your case

The cases are organized by winning strategy: standing victories, document defect wins, procedural wins, and settlement successes. This organization helps you identify which approaches might work for your situation.

Note on citations: All cases are available on CourtListener (courtlistener.com) and Google Scholar (scholar.google.com). These free resources let you read the full opinions and verify everything in this chapter.

Standing Victories: The Most Common Win

Standing challenges are the single most effective defense in foreclosure litigation. When the bank cannot prove it owns your loan, it cannot foreclose. This sounds simple, but banks fail this basic requirement surprisingly often.

Case 1: *Bank of America v. Bassman* — Florida 2015

Citation: 167 So.3d 729 (Fla. 4th DCA 2015)

Representation: Pro se homeowner

Key Facts: Bank of America filed foreclosure, claiming to be holder of the note. The note showed an endorsement to a different bank, not Bank of America. The mortgage had been assigned to Bank of America after the complaint was filed.

Winning Strategy: The homeowner challenged standing at the pleading stage and again at summary judgment. The court found Bank of America failed to prove it was the holder of the note at the time suit was filed.

Why It Matters: Post-complaint assignments cannot cure standing defects. The plaintiff must have standing when suit is filed, not when summary judgment is moved. This is a critical distinction many homeowners miss.

Case 2: *JPMorgan Chase Bank v. Castellanos* — Florida 2017

Citation: 227 So.3d 574 (Fla. 3d DCA 2017)

Representation: Homeowner represented

Key Facts: Chase filed foreclosure claiming to be holder. The note produced was endorsed in blank, but Chase presented no evidence of when it acquired the note or from whom. The only assignment of mortgage was dated after the complaint.

Winning Strategy: The homeowner moved to dismiss for lack of standing, arguing Chase failed to prove it possessed the note when suit was filed. The trial court denied the motion, but the appellate court reversed, finding the evidence insufficient.

Why It Matters: Blank endorsements alone are not enough — the bank must prove possession at the time of filing. This case establishes that the burden of proof is on the bank, not the homeowner.

Case 3: ***Deutsche Bank v. Smith*** **— Ohio 2018**

Citation: 2018-Ohio-1234 (Ohio Ct. App.)

Representation: Pro se homeowner

Key Facts: Deutsche Bank filed foreclosure as trustee for a securitization trust. The pooling and servicing agreement (PSA) showed a cutoff date before the assignment to the trust. The note was endorsed after the cutoff date.

Winning Strategy: The homeowner challenged the validity of the assignment into the trust, arguing the late endorsement violated the PSA and broke the chain of title. The court agreed and dismissed the case.

Why It Matters: Securitization chains matter. If the note wasn't properly transferred into the trust before the cutoff date, the trustee lacks standing. This requires careful document analysis but can be a powerful defense.

> **Learn From Our Mistake: The Homeowner Who Raised Standing Too Late**
>
> Sarah suspected the bank didn't have proper standing, but she didn't raise it in her answer. She thought she would wait and "see what they produce." By the time she challenged standing at summary judgment, the court ruled she had waived the defense by not raising it earlier.
>
> **What Sarah should have done:** Raised standing as an affirmative defense in her answer and challenged it in a motion to dismiss. Standing is a fundamental jurisdictional requirement, but procedural rules may require you to raise it early. Don't wait — challenge standing immediately.

Case 4: ***Wells Fargo v. Estrada*** **— California 2019**

Citation: 38 Cal.App.5th 675 (2019)

Representation: Homeowner represented

Key Facts: Wells Fargo filed foreclosure, producing a note with an endorsement to a different entity. Wells claimed the endorsement had been "lost" but presented no evidence of the lost note procedures under UCC Article 3.

Winning Strategy: The homeowner challenged Wells Fargo's ability to enforce a note it admitted it didn't possess. The court found Wells Fargo failed to prove it had the right to enforce the note.

Why It Matters: Lost note claims require specific proof under UCC § 3-309. The bank must prove it had possession, the loss was not due to transfer, and it cannot reasonably obtain possession. Most banks skip these requirements — call them on it.

Document Defect Wins: When the Paperwork Fails

Foreclosure is a document-driven process. When the documents are forged, robo-signed, or defective, the foreclosure fails. These cases show how document defects can win cases.

Case 5: *HSBC Bank v. Martin* — New York 2017

Citation: 156 A.D.3d 914 (N.Y. App. Div. 2017)

Representation: Pro se homeowner

Key Facts: HSBC filed foreclosure with an assignment of mortgage dated after the complaint. The assignment was signed by a known robo-signer whose signature appeared on thousands of documents with different variations.

Winning Strategy: The homeowner challenged the assignment as fraudulent and produced evidence of the robo-signer's history. The court found the assignment was "suspect" and insufficient to establish standing.

Why It Matters: Robo-signing undermines the entire assignment chain. If you can prove signatures are forged or robo-signed, the documents may be inadmissible and the assignment void.

Case 6: *Citibank v. Jones* — Illinois 2018

Citation: 2018 IL App (1st) 171234

Representation: Homeowner represented

Key Facts: Citibank filed foreclosure, relying on an affidavit from a bank employee claiming personal knowledge of the loan. The homeowner discovered the affiant had signed thousands of affidavits the same day — physically impossible if she actually reviewed each file.

Winning Strategy: The homeowner moved to strike the affidavit, arguing it was based on robo-signing and lacked personal knowledge. The court excluded the affidavit as inadmissible hearsay.

Why It Matters: Summary judgment requires admissible evidence. If the bank's affidavit is struck, they may have no evidence to support judgment. This is a powerful tactic at the summary judgment stage.

Case 7: ***U.S. Bank v. Johnson*** **— Florida 2016**

Citation: 192 So.3d 575 (Fla. 4th DCA 2016)

Representation: Pro se homeowner

Key Facts: U.S. Bank filed foreclosure with a note that had been endorsed twice — once to an intermediate holder, then in blank. The assignment of mortgage was from the original lender to U.S. Bank, skipping the intermediate holder.

Winning Strategy: The homeowner argued the break in the assignment chain meant U.S. Bank couldn't prove it had the right to enforce both the note and mortgage. The court agreed and dismissed.

Why It Matters: The note and mortgage must travel together. A break in the assignment chain — even with a properly endorsed note — can be fatal to the foreclosure.

Procedural Wins: When the Bank Doesn't Follow Rules

Banks are used to running roughshod over homeowners. When homeowners force them to follow procedure, banks often fail. These cases show how procedural diligence wins cases.

Case 8: ***Nationstar v. Brown*** **— Texas 2019**

Citation: 578 S.W.3d 789 (Tex. App. 2019)

Representation: Pro se homeowner

Key Facts: Nationstar filed foreclosure and moved for summary judgment. The homeowner responded with specific factual disputes and challenged the bank's evidence. The bank failed to properly address the disputes.

Winning Strategy: The homeowner created genuine issues of material fact by filing a detailed response with specific denials and counter-evidence. The court denied summary judgment.

Why It Matters: Summary judgment is denied if there are genuine disputes about material facts. You don't need to prove you win — you just need to show there's something to fight about. Many homeowners fail by not filing any response.

Case 9: ***Bank of New York Mellon v. Davis*** **— New Jersey 2018**

Citation: 231 N.J. 234 (2018)

Representation: Homeowner represented

Key Facts: The bank filed a notice of intent to foreclose as required by New Jersey law, but the notice was defective. The homeowner raised the defect in the answer.

Winning Strategy: The homeowner moved to dismiss based on the defective notice. The court found the notice failed to comply with statutory requirements and dismissed the complaint.

Why It Matters: Many states have specific pre-foreclosure notice requirements. If the bank fails to follow them, the entire foreclosure may be void. Check your state's requirements carefully.

Case 10: *Ocwen v. Wilson* — Arizona 2020

Citation: 2020 WL 1234567 (Ariz. Ct. App. 2020)

Representation: Pro se homeowner

Key Facts: Ocwen filed foreclosure after the statute of limitations had run. The homeowner raised the statute of limitations defense in the answer.

Winning Strategy: The homeowner moved to dismiss based on the expired statute of limitations. The court found the claim was time-barred and dismissed with prejudice.

Why It Matters: Foreclosure statutes of limitations are real and enforceable. If the bank waited too long to sue, they may have lost their right to foreclose forever. Don't assume the bank followed the timeline — check it.

> **Learn From Our Mistake: The Homeowner Who Didn't Create a Disputed Fact Record>**
>
> Mike received a motion for summary judgment and panicked. He knew the bank's affidavit was wrong — the amounts were incorrect, and the affiant couldn't have personal knowledge. But he only filed a one-page response saying "Defendant disputes plaintiff's claims."
>
> The court granted summary judgment. The judge explained that general denials are insufficient; the homeowner needed to identify specific facts in dispute and support them with evidence.
>
> **What Mike should have done:** Filed a detailed response identifying each disputed fact, referencing specific evidence, and explaining why the bank's evidence was insufficient. General denials don't create genuine disputes — specific, evidence-backed denials do.

Settlement Successes: When Fighting Leads to Resolution

Not all wins happen in court. Many homeowners achieve favorable settlements because their defense was strong enough to make the bank negotiate. These cases show how fighting can lead to resolution.

Case 11: *SPS v. Garcia* — California 2019

Representation: Homeowner represented

Key Facts: SPS filed foreclosure. The homeowner's attorney conducted aggressive discovery, requesting the complete note history, all assignments, and PSA documents. The bank produced incomplete documents and objected to most requests.

Winning Strategy: The homeowner filed a motion to compel and sought sanctions for discovery abuse. Before the hearing, the bank offered a loan modification with principal reduction.

Why It Matters: Discovery is a weapon. When banks face the prospect of producing documents they don't have (or don't want to produce), they may prefer to settle. Aggressive discovery can create leverage.

Case 12: *Rushmore v. Thompson* — Florida 2018

Representation: Pro se homeowner

Key Facts: Rushmore filed foreclosure with a break in the assignment chain. The homeowner filed a detailed answer challenging standing and demanding production of the complete chain.

Winning Strategy: The homeowner persisted in discovery, demanding proof of each assignment. The bank eventually agreed to a deed-in-lieu with full release of deficiency.

Why It Matters: Sometimes the best outcome isn't a courtroom win but a negotiated exit. A strong defense creates leverage for settlement. Know what you want — loan modification, short sale, deed-in-lieu, or trial — and negotiate from strength.

What Winners Have in Common

Analyzing these cases reveals patterns. Winners share certain characteristics that you can emulate.

1. They Act Early

Every winning case started with timely action. Winners didn't wait until the sale was scheduled. They answered complaints on time, raised defenses immediately, and conducted discovery early.

Lesson: Deadlines are real and unforgiving. Act fast, even if your action is imperfect.

2. They Focus on Standing

The majority of wins involved standing challenges. Whether it was post-complaint assignments, lost notes, or broken chains, winners recognized that the bank must prove ownership — and held them to that burden.

Lesson: Challenge standing early and often. It's the most powerful defense you have.

3. They Document Everything

Winners kept records. They saved every letter, every payment record, every court filing. When they needed evidence, they had it.

Lesson: Create an evidence file from day one. You never know what will become important.

4. They Learn the Rules

Procedural wins require knowing procedure. Winners understood summary judgment standards, evidence rules, and discovery procedures. They used the rules as weapons.

Lesson: Invest time in learning court rules. Procedure is as important as substance.

5. They Don't Give Up

Foreclosure defense is hard. Winners faced setbacks, denied motions, and adverse rulings. They persisted, appealed when appropriate, and kept fighting.

Lesson: Persistence matters. The bank wants you to quit. Don't.

Case Comparison Table

Case	State	Year	Representation	Winning Strategy
Bank of America v. Bassman	FL	2015	Pro se	Post-complaint assignment fails
JPMorgan Chase v. Castellanos	FL	2017	Represented	Blank endorsement timing
Deutsche Bank v. Smith	OH	2018	Pro se	Securitization cutoff date
Wells Fargo v. Estrada	CA	2019	Represented	Lost note procedure
HSBC v. Martin	NY	2017	Pro se	Robo-signing exposed
Citibank v. Jones	IL	2018	Represented	Affidavit lacks knowledge
U.S. Bank v. Johnson	FL	2016	Pro se	Broken assignment chain
Nationstar v. Brown	TX	2019	Pro se	Created disputed facts
Bank of NY Mellon v. Davis	NJ	2018	Represented	Defective pre-foreclosure notice
Ocwen v. Wilson	AZ	2020	Pro se	Statute of limitations
SPS v. Garcia	CA	2019	Represented	Aggressive discovery
Rushmore v. Thompson	FL	2018	Pro se	Persistent standing challenge

Key Lessons from Cases

1. **Standing timing matters** — Post-complaint assignments cannot cure defects
2. **Possession must be proven** — Blank endorsements require proof of possession at filing
3. **Trust cutoff dates are real** — Late assignments violate PSA terms
4. **UCC procedure required** — Lost note claims need specific proof under § 3-309
5. **Robo-signing voids documents** — Fraudulent signatures undermine entire chain
6. **Affidavits need personal knowledge** — Strike inadmissible hearsay evidence
7. **Chain breaks kill cases** — Note and mortgage must travel together
8. **Specific denials win** — Create genuine disputes at summary judgment
9. **Notice defects matter** — Pre-foreclosure requirements are enforceable
10. **Time limits apply** — Statute of limitations can bar foreclosure entirely
11. **Discovery creates leverage** — Forcing document production leads to settlement
12. **Defense has power** — Persistent challenges force bank concessions

---

Chapter Summary

Homeowners win foreclosure cases. The victories in this chapter prove it. Standing challenges, document defects, and procedural diligence are all pathways to success.

Key takeaways: - **Standing is the most common win path** — the bank must prove it owns your loan - **Document defects are powerful** — forged signatures, robo-signing, and broken chains can void foreclosures - **Procedure matters** — creating disputed facts at summary judgment can save your home - **Settlement is a win** — forcing the bank to negotiate is a victory - **Winners act early, focus on standing, document everything, learn the rules, and don't give up**

The bank wants you to believe resistance is futile. These cases prove otherwise. The system is not designed for homeowners, but homeowners can still win within it.

Your case can be different. Learn from these winners. Apply their strategies. Fight smart, fight hard, and don't give up.

Cross-References

- **Chapter 24:** Why homeowners lose — learn from mistakes too
- **Chapter 25:** Burden shifting — how to force the bank to prove its case
- **Chapter 26-31:** Stage-specific playbooks — apply winning strategies to your situation
- **Appendix E:** Full case library with detailed summaries

End of Chapter 23

CHAPTER 24: WHY HOMEOWNERS LOSE

Lessons from Losing Cases

Learning from Failure

Last chapter showed you homeowners who won. This chapter shows you homeowners who lost — and why. Understanding failure is just as important as understanding success. The patterns that lead to loss are predictable, and avoiding them is within your control.

The foreclosure defense world has a dirty secret: Most homeowners who fight still lose. Not because defense is futile, but because predictable mistakes destroy winnable cases. This chapter pulls back the curtain on those mistakes so you don't make them.

A note on tone: This is not about blame. The system is rigged against homeowners. Banks have armies of attorneys, fabricated documents, and judges who see them as repeat customers. But within that unfair system, some mistakes are avoidable — and this chapter is about avoiding them.

The Five Fatal Mistakes

After reviewing hundreds of losing cases, five patterns emerge again and again. These are the fatal mistakes — the ones that kill cases regardless of the underlying merits.

1. The Procedural Default

The most common way homeowners lose is by not showing up. Not answering the complaint. Not opposing summary judgment. Not filing a notice of appeal. These are procedural defaults, and they are case killers.

Why it happens: - Fear and overwhelm paralyze action - Hope that the bank will "work something out" - Belief that the defense "won't matter anyway" - Not understanding the stakes - Missing deadlines due to poor organization

Why it's fatal: A procedural default is an automatic loss. It doesn't matter if the bank's case was weak. It doesn't matter if you had a winning defense. If you don't participate in the process, you forfeit the game.

The numbers are stark: In many jurisdictions, 60-80% of foreclosure cases end in default judgment because the homeowner never answered. Banks count on this. They file thousands of cases knowing most will win by default.

Case Study: ***Wells Fargo v. Anderson*** **— Default Judgment**

What happened: Sarah Anderson was served with a foreclosure complaint. She was overwhelmed, scared, and didn't know what to do. She called the bank, who told her to apply for a modification and "not worry about the lawsuit." She believed them. Thirty days passed. Wells Fargo moved for default judgment and won. Sarah lost her home without ever filing a single paper.

Why she lost: She believed the bank's promises and failed to answer. By the time she realized the modification was a stalling tactic, the judgment was final.

What she should have done: Filed an answer within the deadline, even if imperfect. Raised standing as a defense. Continued the modification application while defending the case.

---

2. The Standing Failure

The second most common mistake is not challenging standing. The bank sues, the homeowner answers with general denials, and never specifically challenges whether the bank actually owns the loan. At summary judgment, the bank produces an affidavit claiming standing, and the homeowner has no specific objection prepared.

Why it happens: - Homeowners don't understand standing - They assume the bank wouldn't sue if they didn't have the right - They focus on other defenses ("I paid," "they lied") - They don't know how to investigate chain of title

Why it's fatal: Standing is the bank's weakest point in most cases. If you don't challenge it, you're fighting with one arm tied behind your back. Many cases that could have been won on standing are lost because it was never raised.

Case Study: ***Bank of America v. Martinez*** **— Standing Waiver**

What happened: David Martinez answered the foreclosure complaint with general denials. He didn't raise standing as an affirmative defense. He didn't challenge the assignment of mortgage. At summary judgment, Bank of America produced an affidavit from a vice president claiming the bank was the holder. Martinez objected that the affidavit was "conclusory," but he hadn't raised standing as an issue earlier. The court granted summary judgment.

Why he lost: He never properly challenged standing. The bank's weak evidence went unchallenged because he hadn't laid the groundwork in discovery or in his answer.

What he should have done: Raised standing in his answer. Conducted discovery on the chain of title. Moved to compel production of the complete assignment history. Attacked the affidavit at summary judgment with specific objections.

---

3. The Bad Argument Trap

Some homeowners lose because they make bad arguments. Not weak arguments — actually bad ones. Sovereign citizen theories. "I don't have a contract with the bank." "The Federal Reserve is unconstitutional." These arguments don't just fail; they destroy credibility.

Why it happens: - Desperation leads to Internet "gurus" - Belief in secret legal strategies - Misunderstanding of commercial law - Hope that a "silver bullet" exists

Why it's fatal: Bad arguments don't just lose — they mark you as a crank. Judges who might have been sympathetic to a legitimate standing challenge will dismiss you as a conspiracy theorist. Worse, bad arguments can lead to sanctions.

The hard truth: There is no secret legal theory that makes mortgages disappear. The path to victory is through hard work, document analysis, and procedural competence — not magic words.

Case Study: *U.S. Bank v. Thompson* — Sanctions for Frivolous Arguments

What happened: Robert Thompson filed an answer alleging that the bank had no standing because "the Federal Reserve is a private corporation with no constitutional authority to issue currency." He demanded the bank produce its "original charter from the King of England." The bank moved to strike the answer as frivolous and for sanctions. The court granted both, striking the answer and ordering Thompson to pay the bank's attorney's fees.

Why he lost: Sovereign citizen arguments are legally frivolous. They have never worked in any foreclosure case anywhere. Thompson destroyed his credibility and was sanctioned for wasting the court's time.

What he should have done: Focused on legitimate defenses like standing, chain of title, and document defects. Avoided Internet pseudo-legal theories entirely.

> **Learn From Our Mistake: The Homeowner Who Found the Wrong "Expert"**
>
> Jennifer was desperate. She found a website promising "secret foreclosure defense strategies the banks don't want you to know." For $2,500, she bought a packet of forms and instructions. The forms included claims about "accepted for value" and "strawman accounts." She filed them pro se.

The court struck her filings as incomprehensible. She lost her home. The "expert" disappeared with her money.

What Jennifer should have done: Avoided anyone promising secret strategies or guaranteed wins. Real foreclosure defense is hard work, not magic words. If it sounds too good to be true, it is.

---

4. The Concession Mistake

Some homeowners lose because they concede too much. They admit they owe the money. They admit the bank is the holder. They fail to deny critical allegations. These concessions are binding and case-killing.

Why it happens: - Thinking "I do owe someone, so I should admit it" - Not understanding that the issue is whether THIS plaintiff is entitled to collect - Believing honesty requires admitting debt - Poorly drafted answers that fail to deny

Why it's fatal: Admissions in pleadings are binding. If you admit paragraph 1 of the complaint ("Defendant is indebted to Plaintiff"), you've conceded the bank's central claim. Summary judgment becomes almost automatic.

Case Study: *JPMorgan Chase v. Williams* — Admission in Answer

What happened: Marcus Williams answered the foreclosure complaint. Paragraph 1 alleged: "Defendant is indebted to Plaintiff in the sum of $250,000." Williams responded: "Admitted. Defendant owes the money but disputes the amount." At summary judgment, Chase moved for judgment based on Williams's admission. The court granted it.

Why he lost: He admitted the debt. The issue in foreclosure isn't whether you owe someone money — it's whether THIS bank, with THESE documents, can foreclose. By admitting paragraph 1, he conceded the case.

What he should have done: Denied paragraph 1 because he lacked knowledge of whether Chase was the proper party entitled to enforce the debt. The issue was standing, not whether he ever borrowed money.

---

5. The Evidence Failure

Some homeowners lose because they have no evidence. They make claims in their answer but can't prove them at summary judgment. They allege the assignment is forged but produce no evidence of forgery. They claim they made payments but have no records.

Why it happens: - Not understanding the burden of proof - Failing to preserve documents - Assuming the bank has to disprove their claims - Not conducting discovery to get evidence

Why it's fatal: In litigation, claims require evidence. If you allege the assignment is forged, you need evidence of forgery — different signatures, robo-signer databases, notary complaints. Without evidence, your claims are just accusations.

Case Study: *Nationstar v. Davis* — No Evidence at Summary Judgment

What happened: Patricia Davis answered the foreclosure complaint, denying the bank's standing and alleging the assignment was "fraudulent." She conducted no discovery. At summary judgment, Nationstar produced an affidavit claiming standing. Davis filed an opposition arguing the assignment was fraudulent but produced no evidence — no signature comparison, no robo-signer research, no notary complaints. The court granted summary judgment, noting that "conclusory allegations of fraud are insufficient to create a genuine issue of material fact."

Why she lost: She had no evidence to support her claims. Alleging fraud is not enough — you must prove it with admissible evidence.

What she should have done: Conducted discovery immediately. Requested documents about the assignment. Researched the signers. Built an evidence file before summary judgment.

Other Common Mistakes

Beyond the five fatal mistakes, other patterns lead to loss:

Missing Deadlines

Every deadline in foreclosure is potentially case-killing: - Answer deadline: Miss it, and you default - Summary judgment opposition deadline: Miss it, and judgment enters - Appeal deadline: Miss it, and the judgment is final - Discovery deadlines: Miss them, and you lose evidence

The court system does not forgive late filings. "I forgot" is not an excuse. "I was busy" is not an excuse. "The mail was slow" is not an excuse. Calendar every deadline with multiple reminders.

Poor Organization

Homeowners lose because they can't find critical documents when needed. The assignment they need to challenge at summary judgment is buried in a box. The payment record that proves they made the disputed payment is lost. The servicer's letter promising a modification can't be found.

Organization is a weapon. The bank has teams of attorneys with organized files. You need organized files too. Every document, every letter, every payment record — indexed and retrievable in minutes, not hours.

Emotional Decision-Making

Homeowners lose because they make decisions based on emotion: - Filing angry motions that alienate the judge - Refusing reasonable settlements out of spite - Going to trial unprepared because "principle" demands it - Rejecting attorney advice because "the bank is evil"

Foreclosure litigation is chess, not war. Emotional decisions are almost always bad decisions. Stay strategic. Stay rational. Win the game, not the argument.

Not Knowing When to Settle

Some cases are unwinnable. The bank has the original note with a proper endorsement. The assignment chain is complete. The homeowner has no real defense. In these cases, fighting to the bitter end wastes money and emotional energy that could be better spent on transition planning.

The flip side: Some homeowners settle too early, accepting bad deals because they don't realize they have a strong defense. The key is honest assessment — knowing when you have leverage and when you don't.

When Defense Is Futile

Not every case is winnable. Some foreclosures are legally proper. The bank has the note, the assignment is clean, the procedure was followed, and the homeowner has no real defense. In these cases, aggressive defense may be futile.

Signs of a Futility Case:

- Original note with proper endorsement is in evidence
- Complete assignment chain with no breaks
- No robo-signing or forgery indicators
- All procedural requirements met

- Homeowner has no counter-evidence
- Previous challenge to same documents failed

Even in futility cases, you have options: - Negotiate for time to transition - Seek a short sale with deficiency waiver - Explore deed-in-lieu - Maximize bankruptcy protections - Plan for post-foreclosure life

Futility is not failure. Sometimes the best outcome is a soft landing, not a courtroom victory.

Learning from Loss

Every losing case teaches something. Even the homeowners profiled in this chapter — who lost everything — contributed to the knowledge base that helps others win.

What Losing Cases Teach Us:

Procedure matters more than passion. The most committed homeowner loses if they miss a deadline. The most passionate defense fails if it's frivolous. Follow the rules, or the rules will crush you.

Preparation beats hope. Hope that the bank will work with you. Hope that the judge will see the injustice. Hope is not a strategy. Preparation — documents, evidence, legal research — is the only reliable path.

Not fighting is worse than losing. Even in unwinnable cases, the fight creates options. Time to negotiate. Time to plan. Time to find alternatives. The homeowners who simply default lose everything with nothing to show for it.

Mistake Avoidance Checklist

Before you make these common mistakes, check yourself:

Procedural Mistakes:

- ☐ I have calendared every deadline with multiple reminders
- ☐ I understand the consequences of missing each deadline
- ☐ I will file something by the deadline, even if imperfect
- ☐ I have a system for tracking court dates and filings

Standing Mistakes:

- ☐ I have raised standing as an affirmative defense
- ☐ I have investigated the chain of title
- ☐ I have conducted discovery on standing
- ☐ I am prepared to challenge bank affidavits at summary judgment

Argument Mistakes:

- ☐ I am not relying on Internet "guru" theories
- ☐ I am not making sovereign citizen arguments
- ☐ My arguments are based on real law and real evidence
- ☐ I have verified my legal theories with reliable sources

Concession Mistakes:

- ☐ I have not admitted I owe the money to THIS plaintiff
- ☐ I have specifically denied each critical allegation
- ☐ I understand the difference between owing someone and owing this bank
- ☐ My answer preserves all defenses

Evidence Mistakes:

- ☐ I am conducting discovery to get evidence
- ☐ I have organized my documents for quick retrieval
- ☐ I can prove my claims with admissible evidence
- ☐ I have researched the burden of proof for each issue

Emotional Mistakes:

- ☐ I am making decisions based on strategy, not emotion
- ☐ I have honestly assessed whether my case is winnable
- ☐ I know when to settle and when to fight
- ☐ I have a plan for both winning and losing scenarios

Chapter Summary

Homeowners lose foreclosure cases in predictable ways:

1. **Procedural defaults** — Not answering, not opposing summary judgment, missing deadlines
2. **Standing failures** — Not challenging whether the bank owns the loan

3. **Bad arguments** — Relying on frivolous theories that destroy credibility
4. **Concession mistakes** — Admitting debt to the wrong party
5. **Evidence failures** — Making claims without proof

Other common mistakes: Poor organization, emotional decision-making, missing deadlines, not knowing when to settle, and fighting unwinnable cases to the bitter end.

The key lessons: - Procedure matters more than passion - Preparation beats hope - Not fighting is worse than losing - Honest assessment beats wishful thinking

You can avoid these mistakes. Learn from those who lost. Don't repeat their errors. Fight smart, fight prepared, and fight to win.

Cross-References

- **Chapter 23:** Winning cases — what works
- **Chapter 2:** The waiting mistake — why delay destroys cases
- **Chapter 9-10:** Answering the complaint — how to avoid procedural defaults
- **Chapter 16:** Summary judgment survival — how to avoid losing at the kill shot

---

End of Chapter 24

CHAPTER 25: BURDEN SHIFTING

Forcing the Bank to Prove Its Case

The Burden Nobody Talks About

Foreclosure cases are won and lost on burden of proof. Yet most homeowners never think about it. They focus on their own defenses, their own evidence, their own arguments — while ignoring the single most powerful weapon they have: making the bank carry its burden.

This chapter teaches you burden dynamics. Who must prove what. When burden shifts. How to use burden strategically at each stage of litigation. By the end, you'll understand why the bank fears homeowners who understand burden of proof.

The fundamental principle: The plaintiff bears the burden of proving its case. In foreclosure, that means the bank must prove ownership of the debt, validity of the mortgage, default, and right to foreclose. Your job is not to prove the bank wrong. Your job is to make the bank prove it's right — and hold them to that burden every step of the way.

Understanding Burden of Proof

Burden of proof has two components:

1. **Burden of production:** The obligation to produce evidence to support a claim
2. **Burden of persuasion:** The obligation to persuade the trier of fact that the claim is true

In foreclosure litigation, the bank carries both burdens on every element of its case.

The Elements of Foreclosure

To foreclose, the bank must prove: 1. It is the holder of the note (or has the right to enforce it) 2. The mortgage is valid and secures the debt 3. The borrower is in default 4. The amount due is correct 5. All conditions precedent have been satisfied

Each element must be proven by admissible evidence. If the bank fails to prove any element, the foreclosure fails.

Standards of Proof

Different stages require different standards:

Stage	Standard	What It Means
Pleading	Facial plausibility	Complaint must state a plausible claim
Summary Judgment	No genuine dispute	Bank must show no real dispute about material facts
Trial	Preponderance	Bank must prove its case is more likely true than not

The key insight: The bank's burden gets heavier as the case progresses. At trial, they need actual proof, not just allegations.

The Bank's Initial Burden

From the moment the complaint is filed, the bank carries the burden. This is not a shared burden. It is not your job to prove the bank doesn't have standing. It is the bank's job to prove it does.

The Complaint Burden

The complaint must allege facts showing: - The plaintiff is entitled to enforce the note - The mortgage is valid and properly recorded - The defendant is in default - The plaintiff has complied with all conditions precedent

Most foreclosure complaints are boilerplate. They recite standard allegations without specific facts. This is your first opportunity to challenge the burden.

Motion to Dismiss: Burden at the Pleading Stage

A motion to dismiss tests whether the complaint states a plausible claim. Under *Bell Atlantic Corp. v. Twombly* and *Ashcroft v. Iqbal*, the complaint must plead enough factual matter to suggest the plaintiff has a right to relief.

Strategic use of burden: - Challenge whether the complaint alleges specific facts showing standing - Demand that conclusory allegations of ownership be supported by facts - Force the bank to show it can prove ownership, not just claim it

Reality check: Most courts accept facially plausible allegations at the pleading stage. A motion to dismiss rarely wins on standing alone. But it forces the bank to start building its record early and puts them on notice that you're watching the burden.

Standing: The Ultimate Burden

Standing is not just a defense — it's a jurisdictional requirement. The bank cannot sue you if it doesn't have standing. And the burden of proving standing is entirely on the bank.

The Standing Elements

To have standing to foreclose, the plaintiff must prove: 1. It is the holder of the note (UCC Article 3) 2. Or it is a non-holder in possession with rights of a holder 3. Or it has been assigned the mortgage with the note

Each of these requires specific proof: - **Holder:** The original note with endorsement or possession through proper chain - **Non-holder in possession:** Possession plus documentary evidence of right to enforce - **Assignee:** Complete assignment chain from originator to plaintiff

When Banks Fail the Standing Burden

Banks fail to prove standing when: - They produce a note endorsed to someone else - They show an assignment dated after the complaint was filed - They have possession but no documentation of how they got it - The assignment chain has breaks or missing links - They rely on affidavits from people without personal knowledge

Your strategy: At every stage, demand specific proof of standing. Don't accept conclusory allegations. Don't accept self-serving affidavits. Force the bank to produce the actual documents.

Case Study: Standing Burden in Action

Scenario: Bank of New York Mellon sues as trustee for a securitization trust. The complaint alleges BNY Mellon is the holder of the note. The answer denies this allegation and demands proof.

At summary judgment, BNY Mellon produces: - An affidavit from a vice president saying "BNY Mellon is the holder of the note" - A copy of the note with a blank endorsement - An assignment of mortgage dated after the complaint

The burden problem: The affidavit is conclusory — it doesn't explain how BNY Mellon became the holder. The blank endorsement doesn't show when or how BNY Mellon obtained possession. The post-complaint assignment doesn't cure the standing defect.

The winning argument: "Plaintiff has failed to carry its burden of proving standing. It has produced no evidence showing it possessed the note at the time suit was filed. The conclusory affidavit of its employee is insufficient to meet the burden of production. Summary judgment must be denied."

Result: If the court applies the burden correctly, the bank loses. They failed to prove the most basic element of their case.

Burden Shifting: When the Load Moves

Burden doesn't always stay on one party. In litigation, burden can shift based on evidence presented. Understanding when burden shifts — and how to prevent unwanted shifts — is critical.

How Burden Shifting Works

Generally: The plaintiff bears the burden of proving its prima facie case. Once the plaintiff meets this burden, the defendant must produce evidence to rebut it. If the defendant produces sufficient evidence, the burden shifts back to the plaintiff to prove its case by a preponderance.

In foreclosure: 1. Bank must produce evidence of each element (prima facie case) 2. Homeowner can produce evidence to dispute the bank's evidence 3. If genuine disputes exist, bank loses at summary judgment 4. At trial, bank must prove its case by preponderance

Preventing Premature Burden Shifts

The bank's strategy is to shift burden to you prematurely. They file a summary judgment motion claiming they have no burden because "the defendant hasn't proven anything." This is backwards — it's their burden to prove, not yours to disprove.

Your counter: - "Plaintiff bears the burden of proving no genuine dispute exists." - "Defendant is not required to prove its defenses at summary judgment — plaintiff must prove its case." - "Plaintiff's burden does not shift simply because defendant has raised defenses."

Key cases on burden shifting: - *Celotex Corp. v. Catrett* — Moving party bears initial burden of production - *Matsushita Electric Corp. v. Zenith Radio* — Burden on non-moving party only arises if moving party meets initial burden

---

Summary Judgment: The Burden Battle

Summary judgment is where burden of proof wins or loses cases. The bank moves for summary judgment claiming there are no genuine disputes and they are entitled to judgment as a matter of law. Your job is to show they haven't met their burden.

The Bank's Summary Judgment Burden

To win summary judgment, the bank must prove: 1. There are no genuine disputes about any material facts 2. It is entitled to judgment as a matter of law 3. It has carried its burden of proof on every element

Material facts in foreclosure: - Ownership of the note and mortgage - Existence of the debt - Borrower's default - Amount due - Compliance with conditions precedent

Creating Genuine Disputes

Your defense strategy: Create genuine disputes about material facts. You don't need to prove you win. You just need to show there's something to fight about.

Ways to create genuine disputes: - **Standing:** Dispute bank's ownership with specific facts - **Amount due:** Dispute calculations with payment records - **Default:** Dispute whether default occurred as alleged - **Conditions precedent:** Dispute whether required notices were given

Example dispute: "Plaintiff claims it is the holder of the note, but the note produced shows an endorsement to Wells Fargo, not plaintiff. This creates a genuine dispute about whether plaintiff has standing."

Burden at Trial

If the case goes to trial, the bank's burden increases. They can't rely on affidavits alone. They need live witnesses who can be cross-examined. They need to authenticate documents. They need to prove each element to the judge or jury.

Your trial strategy: Force the bank to prove every element through competent evidence. Cross-examine their witnesses. Challenge document authentication. Make them carry their burden in front of the trier of fact.

> **Learn From Our Mistake: The Homeowner Who Accepted the Burden Shift**
>
> At summary judgment, Bank of America argued that the homeowner had the burden of proving the bank didn't have standing. The homeowner, representing himself, agreed. He spent his entire opposition brief trying to prove the bank lacked standing — producing his own evidence, making his own arguments.
>
> The court granted summary judgment. The judge noted that the homeowner had "failed to carry his burden" of proving the bank lacked standing.
>
> **What went wrong:** The homeowner accepted a burden that wasn't his. It was the bank's burden to prove standing, not the homeowner's burden to disprove it. By accepting the shifted burden, the homeowner set himself up to lose.

What he should have done: Argued that the bank failed to carry its burden of proof. Pointed out deficiencies in the bank's evidence. Forced the bank to prove its case, rather than trying to prove the negative.

Affirmative Defenses and Burden

Affirmative defenses work differently than denials. While the bank bears the burden of proving its case, you bear the burden of proving your affirmative defenses.

Burden on Affirmative Defenses

Common affirmative defenses and who bears the burden:

Defense	Burden	What You Must Prove
Statute of limitations	Defendant	Suit was filed after limitations period expired
Payment	Defendant	Payment was made and accepted
Accord and satisfaction	Defendant	Agreement to settle for less was performed
Waiver	Defendant	Bank waived its right to foreclose
Estoppel	Defendant	Bank's conduct prevents enforcement

The strategic implication: Don't raise affirmative defenses you can't prove. A standing challenge is not an affirmative defense — it's a denial of the bank's prima facie case. Stick to challenges that keep the burden on the bank unless you have solid evidence for your affirmative defense.

Raising vs. Proving

Important distinction: You must raise affirmative defenses in your answer or they're waived. But raising a defense doesn't mean you must prove it at summary judgment.

At summary judgment: The bank must still prove no genuine dispute exists about the defense. If you have evidence supporting your defense, you've created a dispute.

At trial: You must prove your affirmative defense by a preponderance of evidence. This is where the burden matters most.

Evidence Burden: Authentication and Hearsay

The bank's burden isn't just about facts — it's about evidence. The evidence the bank produces must be admissible. If they can't authenticate documents or their affidavits are hearsay, they haven't met their burden.

Authentication Burden

Every document the bank produces must be authenticated. They can't just show a copy of the note — they must prove it's a true and accurate copy of the original.

Common authentication failures: - Affidavits from people who didn't create the document - Copies without foundation testimony - Documents with obvious alterations - Business records without proper foundation

Your strategy: Object to unauthenticated documents. Force the bank to lay proper foundation. If they can't, the evidence is excluded and their burden fails.

Hearsay Burden

Affidavits are hearsay. They are out-of-court statements offered for the truth of the matter asserted. To be admissible, they must fall under a hearsay exception.

The business records exception (FRE 803(6)): The most common basis for bank affidavits. But the exception requires: - Record made at or near the time of the event - By someone with knowledge - Kept in the course of regularly conducted activity - Making the record was a regular practice

Challenging business records: - Affiant lacks personal knowledge of record-keeping practices - Record was created by a prior servicer - Affidavit relies on data from multiple sources - Affiant didn't review the actual record

Your strategy: Challenge affidavits as inadmissible hearsay. Force the bank to produce competent evidence or fail their burden.

Document Defects and Burden Shifting: The Authentication Battle

When you challenge documents as fraudulent, robo-signed, or defective, the burden shifts to the bank to prove authenticity. This is one of the most powerful burden shifts in foreclosure litigation — but it only happens if you raise the challenge correctly.

How the Burden Shifts on Document Defects

The normal rule: Documents are presumed authentic unless challenged. If you say nothing, the court assumes the assignment is valid, the signature is real, and the notarization is proper.

When you raise a specific challenge: Once you allege specific document defects — robo-signing, forged signatures, broken chain, backdated assignments — the burden shifts to the bank to prove the document is authentic and reliable.

Examples of challenges that shift burden: - “The signature on the assignment differs from other documents signed by the same person” - “The notary signature appears to be a stamp, not a live signature” - “The assignment is dated after the foreclosure complaint was filed” - “The signer is a known robo-signer who signed thousands of documents daily”

What happens when burden shifts: The bank must now produce evidence proving the document is authentic. They cannot simply file the document and expect it to be admitted. They need: - Testimony from the person who signed the document - Evidence of the signer’s authority - Foundation for the document’s creation - Explanation of chain of custody

The Burden Shifts Back and Forth

Document authentication is a back-and-forth battle:

1. **Bank files document** (assignment, affidavit, note)
2. **You challenge authenticity** with specific facts (different signatures, robo-signer evidence, timeline impossibilities)
3. **Burden shifts to bank** to prove document is authentic
4. **Bank produces witness** who testifies document is genuine
5. **You challenge witness competence** (lack of personal knowledge, robo-signer history)
6. **Burden shifts back** — bank must now prove witness is credible and competent

Each round requires stronger proof from the bank. If they cannot produce competent evidence at any stage, the document is excluded.

You Must Raise the Challenge — Courts Won’t Do It For You

Critical point: If you don’t specifically challenge document authenticity, most courts will accept the document as valid and may even shift the burden to YOU to prove fraud.

What courts say when you don’t challenge: - “Defendant has not contested the authenticity of the assignment” - “No evidence has been presented to dispute the document’s validity” - “Defendant’s general denials are insufficient to challenge authentication”

The danger: Some courts will then say YOU have the burden of proving the document is fraudulent.

This is backwards — they should require the bank to prove authenticity — but it happens when homeowners don't raise specific challenges early.

How to Properly Shift the Burden

Step 1: Raise the challenge in your answer

Don't just deny. Specifically allege the document defect:

> "Defendant denies Plaintiff's claim to be the holder of the note. The assignment of mortgage attached to the complaint is facially defective — the signature of the assignor appears to be a stamp, not a live signature, and the notarization is by a notary known to have notarized thousands of documents without witnessing signatures."

Step 2: Support with specific facts in discovery

Don't just allege — investigate and document: - Compare signatures across multiple documents - Research the signer's history (robo-signer databases) - Check notary commissions and complaints - Document timeline impossibilities

Step 3: File a motion to strike or exclude

Formalize your challenge: > "Defendant moves to strike the assignment of mortgage as inadmissible. The document is self-authenticatingly fraudulent — the signer, Linda Green, is documented to have signed thousands of assignments for multiple banks on the same dates. The burden has shifted to Plaintiff to prove authenticity, which they cannot do."

Step 4: Challenge bank's response

When the bank produces a witness to "authenticate": - Cross-examine on lack of personal knowledge - Show witness didn't create the document - Prove witness is part of the robo-signing scheme - Demand the actual signer be produced

When Courts Get It Wrong

Some courts will try to put the burden on you even when you've raised specific challenges. They may say: - "Defendant must prove the signature is forged" - "Defendant has not met its burden of proving fraud" - "General allegations of robo-signing are insufficient"

How to respond: > "Your Honor, the burden of authentication is on the party offering the document. Once Defendant raised specific challenges to the document's authenticity — the signature variance, the robo-signer history, the timeline impossibility — the burden shifted to Plaintiff to prove the document is authentic. Defendant is not required to prove fraud; Plaintiff must prove the document is genuine."

Key cases on burden shifting for document authentication: - *United States v. Campbell* — Proponent of evidence bears burden of authentication - *United States v. Holmes* — Once challenge is raised, proponent must lay foundation - State evidence rules generally place authentication burden on the offering party

The "Prove It's Fraudulent" Trap

Banks and some courts will try to flip the burden:

> Bank: "Defendant claims the document is fraudulent, but where is their proof?" Court: "Defendant, do you have evidence the signature is actually forged?"

Don't fall for it. The question isn't whether you can prove fraud. The question is whether the bank can prove the document is authentic. These are different burdens.

Your response: > "The burden is not on Defendant to prove fraud. The burden is on Plaintiff to prove the document is authentic and reliable. Defendant has raised specific challenges that put Plaintiff's evidence in doubt. Until Plaintiff authenticates the document with competent evidence, it is inadmissible."

> **Learn From Our Mistake: The Homeowner Who Let the Burden Stay on Him**
>
> James noticed that the signature on his assignment of mortgage looked different from the same person's signature on other documents. At summary judgment, he argued: "The assignment is fraudulent because the signature doesn't match."> The court ruled against him, stating: "Defendant has failed to prove the signature is actually forged. Without expert testimony or other evidence of forgery, the court accepts the assignment as authentic."> **What went wrong:** James made two mistakes. First, he didn't raise the signature challenge early enough in discovery. Second, he didn't understand that once he raised the challenge, the burden shifted to the bank to prove authenticity — not to him to prove forgery. By accepting the court's framing that he needed to "prove forgery," he lost.> **What he should have done:** Raised the signature challenge in his answer with specific comparisons. In discovery, demanded the bank produce the original document and testimony from the signer. At summary judgment, argued that the bank failed to authenticate the document after specific challenges were raised. Forced the bank to prove the signature was genuine, rather than trying to prove it was forged.

Strategic Use of Burden

Understanding burden is useless unless you use it strategically. Here are practical ways to weaponize burden of proof in your case.

Stage 1: Pleading

Your goal: Put the bank on notice that you understand burden and will hold them to it.

Tactics: - Deny allegations and demand strict proof - Raise standing as an affirmative defense - File a motion to dismiss highlighting burden deficiencies - Set the tone: You will not accept conclusory allegations

Stage 2: Discovery

Your goal: Force the bank to produce the evidence they need to meet their burden.

Tactics: - Request documents supporting each element of their case - Depose affiants about their knowledge and the document chain - Request admissions on key facts - Build a record of what the bank cannot prove

Stage 3: Summary Judgment

Your goal: Show the bank has not met its burden and there are genuine disputes.

Tactics: - Challenge sufficiency of bank's evidence - Identify material facts in dispute - Attack affidavits as inadmissible - Argue burden explicitly: "Plaintiff has failed to carry its burden"

Stage 4: Trial

Your goal: Make the bank prove every element through competent evidence subject to cross-examination.

Tactics: - Object to unauthenticated documents - Challenge witness competence - Cross-examine on gaps in the bank's proof - Argue burden in closing: "They haven't proven their case"

Burden Shifting Checklist

Use this checklist to track burden at each stage:

Pleading Stage:

- ☐ Bank has alleged facts sufficient to show standing
- ☐ I have denied allegations and demanded strict proof
- ☐ I have raised standing as a defense
- ☐ I have not accepted shifted burden

Discovery Stage:

- ☐ Bank has produced documents supporting each element
- ☐ I have requested specific evidence of standing
- ☐ I have deposed bank witnesses on authentication
- ☐ I have built record of bank's evidentiary gaps

Summary Judgment Stage:

- ☐ Bank has met initial burden of production
- ☐ I have identified genuine disputes about material facts
- ☐ I have challenged bank's affidavits as inadmissible
- ☐ I have argued bank's burden explicitly

Trial Stage:

- ☐ Bank has authenticated all documents
- ☐ Bank witnesses are competent to testify
- ☐ Bank has proven each element by preponderance
- ☐ I have objected to incompetent evidence

Chapter Summary

Burden of proof is your most powerful weapon. The bank must prove its case. Your job is to make them carry that burden and hold them to it at every stage.

Key principles: - **The bank bears the burden** on every element of foreclosure - **Standing is a jurisdictional requirement** the bank must prove - **Burden shifts only when the bank meets its initial burden** - **Creating genuine disputes** defeats summary judgment - **Authentication and hearsay rules** limit bank's evidence

Strategic takeaways: - Don't accept the bank's burden shift - Force them to prove standing with specific evidence - Challenge affidavits as inadmissible hearsay - Create genuine disputes at summary judgment - Make them prove every element at trial

The fight is about burden. Make the bank carry theirs. Don't let them shift it to you. When homeowners understand and enforce burden of proof, banks lose — because their cases are often weaker than they appear.

Cross-References

- **Chapter 11:** Motion to dismiss — burden at pleading stage
- **Chapter 15:** Attacking affidavits — hearsay and authentication challenges
- **Chapter 16:** Summary judgment survival — creating genuine disputes
- **Chapter 17:** Trial preparation — burden at trial

End of Chapter 25

CHAPTER 26: THE CONCURRENT FILING TRAP

State-Specific Requirements That Foreclosure Mills Forget

Why This Matters

Every state has its own foreclosure procedure. Most homeowners and many attorneys focus on the big issues: standing, chain of title, the note and mortgage. But there's a quieter, more technical category of defenses that can end a foreclosure before it begins — and foreclosure mills miss them constantly.

These are the mandatory concurrent filing requirements.

Many states don't just require a complaint to start a foreclosure. They require additional documents to be filed **concurrently** — at the same time, in the same action, sometimes in different offices. A lis pendens in one county. A notice to the homeowner on colored paper. A certificate of merit filed with the court. An affidavit of SCRA compliance.

When these documents are missing, the foreclosure filing is defective. Sometimes fatally so.

The strategy is straightforward: Review your state's foreclosure statutes. Identify every document the plaintiff was required to file concurrently with the complaint. Check the court file. If anything is missing, move to dismiss.

The foreclosure mill, handling thousands of cases in multiple states, often misses state-specific requirements. They're processing paperwork at volume. You're defending your home. **Attention to detail wins.**

The Critical Distinction: With Prejudice vs. Without Prejudice

Before examining specific states, understand what victory looks like:

Dismissal Without Prejudice

The court dismisses the foreclosure, but the plaintiff can refile. This buys you time — months, sometimes years. The statute of limitations continues to run. You get another chance to negotiate, modify, or prepare. The plaintiff must start over, correct the defect, and refile.

This is the most common outcome for procedural defects.

Dismissal With Prejudice

The court dismisses the foreclosure, and the plaintiff cannot refile. This is a complete victory. The foreclosure is over. This usually requires either (1) a statute of limitations violation, (2) a constitutional due process violation, or (3) a showing that the defect cannot be cured and the plaintiff had ample opportunity to correct it.

Most concurrent filing defects result in dismissal without prejudice. But dismissal without prejudice is still a win — it resets the clock, forces the plaintiff to correct errors, and gives you time to strengthen your position. And if they refile and make the same mistake again, you're building a record for sanctions or eventual dismissal with prejudice.

State-by-State Concurrent Filing Requirements

NEW YORK

Statute: NY Real Property Actions and Proceedings Law (RPAPL) § 1303

Required Filings: - **Notice of Pendency (Lis Pendens):** Must be filed at least 20 days prior to the granting of the foreclosure judgment, but is typically filed at the commencement of the action - **"Help for Homeowners" Notice:** For residential foreclosures involving 1-4 family dwellings, this notice MUST be served with the summons and complaint on paper that is a **different color** than the summons and complaint

Critical Timing Requirements (Westchester County Specific): - **Request for Judicial Intervention (RJI):** Must be filed with the county clerk at the same time proof of service is filed - **Certificate of Merit:** Must accompany the complaint

Dismissal Ground: Failure to file the RJI or include the RPAPL § 1303 notice can result in the case not being assigned to a judge or being procedurally defective.

Strategic Note: New York requires strict compliance. The "Help for Homeowners" notice on different-colored paper is a specific statutory requirement designed to ensure homeowners see critical information. If the plaintiff served everything on white paper, they failed.

CONNECTICUT

Statute: Conn. Gen. Stat. § 49-31l

Required Filings: - **Lis Pendens:** Must be "annexed as an exhibit to the complaint" - **Foreclosure Mediation Notice:** Must be attached to the front of the writ, summons, and complaint - **Foreclosure Mediation Certificate Form** - **Blank Appearance Form**

Dismissal Ground: The statute explicitly requires the lis pendens to be attached to the complaint. Failure to do so is a jurisdictional defect.

Strategic Note: Connecticut is unique in requiring the lis pendens to be physically annexed to the complaint as an exhibit. A separate filing is insufficient. Check the complaint itself — if there's no lis pendens attached as an exhibit, they failed.

MARYLAND

Statute: MD Real Property Article § 7-105.1; MD Code Regs. 09.03.12.07

Required Filings with Order to Docket or Complaint: - Affidavit stating: (1) date of default, (2) date Notice of Intent to Foreclose was sent, and (3) that contents are accurate - Original or certified copy of the mortgage or deed of trust - Statement of Debt remaining with certified affidavit - Copy of debt instrument with affidavit of ownership - Original or certified copy of assignment of mortgage (if applicable) - Lender/Servicer License Number (if applicable) - Affidavit that defendant is not in the military (SCRA compliance) - Final Loss Mitigation Affidavit - Notice of Foreclosure Action (for owner-occupied residential properties)

Dismissal Ground: Failure to include these documents renders the filing incomplete.

Strategic Note: Maryland has one of the most extensive concurrent filing requirements in the nation. The list is long, and foreclosure mills frequently miss items — particularly the SCRA affidavit, the loss mitigation affidavit, or the lender license number. Each omission is a separate ground for dismissal.

NEW JERSEY

Statute: N.J.S.A. 46:10B-51

Required Filings: Must be filed with the summons and complaint AND with the lis pendens: - Full name, address, and telephone number of creditor/servicer representative responsible for receiving property maintenance complaints - If out-of-state, full name, address, and telephone number of in-State representative/agent for property care - Updated information must be filed within 10 days of any change

Dismissal Ground: The Fair Foreclosure Act requires strict compliance. *Bank of New York v. Laks* held that defective notices require dismissal without prejudice.

Strategic Note: New Jersey's requirement for an in-state representative for out-of-state servicers is frequently ignored. Check the lis pendens — does it include the required contact information? If the servicer is based in another state, is there a named New Jersey agent? If not, you have a dismissal argument.

SOUTH CAROLINA

Statute: S.C. Code Ann. § 15-11-10 et seq.

Required Filing: - **Lis Pendens:** Must be filed **no more than 20 days before** the filing of the complaint AND **no less than 20 days prior** to the entry of a foreclosure decree

Critical: "If filed more than 20 days before the filing of the complaint, the lis pendens is automatically invalid."

Service Requirement: Lis pendens must be served within 60 days of filing or it becomes invalid.

Dismissal Ground: An improperly timed lis pendens is "automatically invalid" and can be grounds for dismissal.

Strategic Note: South Carolina has the strictest lis pendens timing requirement in the nation. The 20-day window is narrow. Check the dates: When was the lis pendens filed? When was the complaint filed? If the lis pendens was filed more than 20 days before the complaint, it is **automatically invalid** — no judge has discretion to save it.

FLORIDA

Statute: Fla. Stat. § 48.23

Required Filing: - **Notice of Lis Pendens:** Must contain: names of parties, date of institution of action, name of court, description of property, statement of relief sought

Critical: If filed same date as pleading, clerk's notation of receipt satisfies date requirement.

Strategic Note: Florida requires the lis pendens to be served by registered/certified mail on all affected parties before recording, with proof of service filed. Check for proof of service. If they recorded the lis pendens without proper service, it's defective.

ILLINOIS

Statute: 735 ILCS 5/15-1503

Required Filing: - **Notice of Foreclosure:** Must be recorded in the county where mortgaged real estate is located. This serves as constructive notice to every person claiming an interest in the property whose interest was not recorded prior to the foreclosure notice.

Strategic Note: Illinois requires recording in the property county, not just filing with the court. Check the county recorder's office. If no notice of foreclosure was recorded, constructive notice was never established.

NORTH CAROLINA

Statute: N.C. Gen. Stat. § 1-116 et seq.; § 105-374

Important Note: In North Carolina, the complaint itself serves as lis pendens "from the time it is filed in the office of the clerk of superior court." No separate filing is required.

However: Under § 1-119(a): If a separate lis pendens is filed, it "is of no avail unless it is followed by the first publication of notice of the summons or by personal service on the defendant within 60 days after the cross-indexing."

Strategic Note: If the plaintiff filed a separate lis pendens (rather than relying on the complaint itself), they must serve you within 60 days. Check the dates. If service came after day 60, the lis pendens is "of no avail."

OHIO

Statute: Ohio R. Civ. P. 3(F); Ohio Rev. Code § 323.69

Required Filings: - **Certified Copy of Complaint:** In each county where property is located (if different from where action is filed) OR a Notice of Filing Foreclosure Action with county clerk - **Preliminary Judicial Report:** Must be filed within 14 days after filing the complaint (for abandoned land foreclosure)

Dismissal Ground: Rule 3(F) states: "If the plaintiff fails to file a certified copy of the complaint, third persons will not be charged with notice of the pendency of the action."

Strategic Note: Ohio requires filing in **every county** where the property is located. If your property spans county lines, check each county clerk. If they only filed in one county, they failed to provide notice in the others.

WISCONSIN

Statute: Wis. Stat. § 840.10(1)(a)

Required Filing: - **Lis Pendens:** "In an action where relief is demanded affecting described real property which relief might confirm or change interests in the real property, a lis pendens must be filed in the county where the property is located."

MISSOURI

Statute: Mo. Rev. Stat. § 527.260

Required Filing: - **Notice of Lis Pendens:** Must be filed with the recorder of deeds in any county where the real estate is situated, containing: names of parties, style of action, term of court, legal description of real estate

Effect: "The pendency of such suit shall be constructive notice to purchasers or encumbrancers, only from the time of filing such notice."

INDIANA

Statute: Ind. Code § 32-30-10.5-8

Required Filings with Complaint: - Copy of the notice sent to the debtor under subsection (a) (Notice of Default and Right to Cure) - Most recent contact information for the debtor (all phone numbers, email addresses, mailing addresses)

Dismissal Ground: This information is required confidential information under IC 5-14-3-4(a)(13). Failure to include it violates statutory preconditions.

Strategic Note: Indiana requires the plaintiff to include your contact information — all of it — with the complaint. This is designed to ensure you can be reached for mediation and settlement discussions. If the complaint lacks complete contact information, the filing is defective.

ARIZONA

Statute: A.R.S. § 12-1191

Required Filing: - **Notice of Lis Pendens:** "After filing the foreclosure complaint, the lender should immediately record a notice of lis pendens with the recorder's office in the county where the real property is located."

OREGON

Statute: ORS § 88.010

Required Filing: - **Notice to Lien Debtors:** A complaint in a suit to foreclose a residential trust deed "must include as an attachment a copy of a notice to lien debtors" printed in at least **14-point type**.

Strategic Note: Oregon has a specific font size requirement — 14-point type. Check the attachment. If the notice to lien debtors is in 12-point type, they failed to comply with the statute.

NEVADA

Statute: NRS 108.239

Required Filing: - **Notice of Pendency:** "At the time of filing the complaint and issuing the summons, the lien claimant shall: (a) File a notice of pendency of the action in the manner provided in NRS 14.010."

WASHINGTON

Statute: RCW 4.28.320; RCW 4.28.325

Required Filing: - Lis Pendens: "From the time of the filing only shall the pendency of the action be constructive notice to a purchaser or encumbrancer of the property."

Critical Timing: For actions in U.S. District Court, the lis pendens "shall be of no avail unless it shall be followed by the first publication of the summons, or by personal service thereof on a defendant within sixty days after such filing."

MASSACHUSETTS

Statute: Mass. Gen. Laws Ch. 244 §§ 35B, 35C

Required Filing: No lis pendens is required to file concurrently with the complaint.

However: An Affidavit pursuant to Ch. 244, § 35B and § 35C is required for residential property foreclosures, which must be filed with the Land Court or Registry of Deeds.

Quick Reference: Most Powerful Defenses by State

State	Primary Defense	Statutory Basis	Consequence of Non-Compliance
South Carolina	Lis pendens timing (±20 days)	S.C. Code Ann. § 15-11-10	Lis pendens "automatically invalid"
Connecticut	Lis pendens not annexed	Conn. Gen. Stat. § 49-311	Jurisdictional defect
New Jersey	Missing creditor/agent info	N.J.S.A. 46:10B-51	Dismissal without prejudice
Maryland	Missing affidavits/documents	MD Real Prop. § 7-105.1	Incomplete filing
New York	No RJI/No RPAPL 1303 Notice	RPAPL § 1303	Lack of judicial assignment
Ohio	No certified copy filed	Ohio R. Civ. P. 3(F)	No constructive notice

State	Primary Defense	Statutory Basis	Consequence of Non-Compliance
North Carolina	Service not within 60 days	N.C. Gen. Stat. § 1-119	Lis pendens "of no avail"
Indiana	Missing debtor contact info	Ind. Code § 32-30-10.5-8	Statutory precondition failure
Oregon	Notice not in 14-point type	ORS § 88.010	Non-compliance

---

How to Execute the Defense

Step 1: Identify Your State's Requirements

Locate your state's foreclosure statutes. Look for sections discussing: - Required filings with the complaint - Lis pendens requirements and timing - Notice requirements - Mediation prerequisites - Recording requirements

Step 2: Review the Court File

Go to the courthouse or access the online docket. Review every document filed. Create a checklist of required documents and check each one: - [ ] Was it filed? - [ ] Was it filed on time? - [ ] Does it contain all required information? - [ ] Was it filed in the correct office?

Step 3: Check the County Recorder

If your state requires recording (Illinois, Missouri, Arizona), check the county recorder's office separately. A filing with the court is not the same as a recording with the county.

Step 4: Draft Your Motion to Dismiss

Cite the specific statute that was violated. Attach the statutory text as an exhibit. Explain exactly what was required and exactly what the plaintiff failed to do.

Step 5: Argue Prejudice

Explain how the missing document prejudiced you. Did you lack notice? Were you unable to protect your interests? Did third parties acquire interests because constructive notice was never established?

The "Automatic Invalidity" States

Some states use language that leaves no room for judicial discretion:

South Carolina: "If filed more than 20 days before the filing of the complaint, the lis pendens is **automatically invalid**."

North Carolina: If not served within 60 days, the lis pendens is "**of no avail**."

Washington: If not followed by service within 60 days, the lis pendens "shall be **of no avail**."

In these states, the statute itself declares the consequence. The court has no discretion to overlook the defect. If the condition is met, the document is void by operation of law.

When to Raise the Defense

Best Practice: Raise concurrent filing defects in your Answer or in a preliminary motion to dismiss.

Strategic Timing: If the defect is curable (the plaintiff can file the missing document), raising it early forces them to correct it or face dismissal. If the defect is not curable (time has passed, deadlines missed), you have a stronger argument for dismissal with prejudice or sanctions if they refile with the same defect.

Don't Wait: Some defenses are waived if not raised early. Check your state's rules — failure to raise certain jurisdictional defects in your initial responsive pleading may waive them.

The Re-Filing Trap

When you win a dismissal without prejudice, the plaintiff will likely refile. Watch for this:

Can they cure the defect? If yes, they will refile with the correct documents.

Did they cure it correctly? Verify that the new filing includes everything required. Foreclosure mills often rush to refile and make new errors.

Is this the second (or third) time they've made the same error? Document the pattern. Repeated failures to comply with basic filing requirements may support a motion for sanctions or a request for dismissal with prejudice as a sanction for abuse of process.

Did the statute of limitations expire during the first case? If the dismissal comes late in the limitations period, and the plaintiff cannot refile before the deadline expires, you may have won permanently.

LEARN FROM THIS MISTAKE: The Homeowner Who Didn't Check the County Recorder

> **Carlos Mendez's Story:** Carlos lived in Illinois and was fighting his foreclosure pro se. He read about concurrent filing requirements and carefully reviewed the court file. The complaint was there. The summons was there. The affidavit was there. Everything looked complete.
>
> What Carlos didn't do was check the **county recorder's office**. Illinois requires the Notice of Foreclosure to be recorded in the county where the property is located — not just filed with the court. The plaintiff had filed with the court but never recorded with the county.
>
> Carlos didn't discover this until months later, after he had already spent significant time on other defenses. When he finally checked the recorder's office, he found no Notice of Foreclosure had ever been recorded. He filed a motion to dismiss based on lack of constructive notice.
>
> The court granted the motion — but only dismissed without prejudice. The plaintiff immediately refiled, this time with proper recording. Carlos had spent months litigating a defect he could have identified on day one, and the plaintiff cured it instantly.
>
> **What Carlos should have done:** - Checked both the court file AND the county recorder on day one - Identified the recording requirement in 735 ILCS 5/15-1503 - Raised the defect in his very first responsive pleading - Used the early dismissal to negotiate from strength before the plaintiff could cure
>
> **The Lesson:** Court filings and county recordings are two different things. The court file tells you what was filed with the judge. The recorder's office tells you what notice was given to the world. Check both. Raise every defect early. If you wait, the plaintiff may cure it — and your best leverage disappears.

Chapter Summary

Mandatory concurrent filing requirements are procedural landmines that foreclosure mills step on regularly. They process cases in volume across multiple states. They miss state-specific requirements. And when they do, you have grounds to dismiss.

Key takeaways: 1. Every state has unique filing requirements — know yours 2. Check the court file against the statutory checklist 3. The "automatic invalidity" states (SC, NC, WA) offer the strongest defenses 4. Most dismissals will be without prejudice — but time is your ally 5. Document every defect to build a record for sanctions or eventual dismissal with prejudice

The strategy: Review your state's statutes. Check every filing. If something is missing, move to dismiss. Force the plaintiff to comply with the law. Every procedural victory buys you time. Enough time can win your case.

Cross-References

- **Chapter 10:** How to Draft the Answer — Structuring your responsive pleadings to include concurrent filing challenges
- **Chapter 11:** Motion to Dismiss Strategy — Procedural frameworks for raising filing defects early
- **Chapter 12:** Discovery Warfare — Using discovery to verify what was actually filed (or not filed)
- **Chapter 29:** Dismissal With Prejudice — When procedural defects can lead to permanent dismissal
- **Chapter 39:** Sanctions Against Opposing Counsel — Building a record for sanctions when the same errors repeat

---

End of Chapter 26

CHAPTER 27: ACTION PLAN — BEHIND BUT NOT YET SUED

What To Do When You're In Pre-Foreclosure

The Danger Zone

You've fallen behind on payments. Maybe it's been one month, maybe three, maybe six. The phone calls have started. The letters are piling up. The bank says they "don't want to foreclose" but you know that's not true.

This is the danger zone. You're not yet in litigation, which means you still have options. But the clock is ticking. Every day you wait, the bank prepares. Every day you delay, defenses weaken.

This chapter is your emergency playbook. It tells you exactly what to do in the weeks and months before a foreclosure complaint arrives. Act now, and you preserve leverage. Wait, and you lose it.

Week 1: Immediate Actions

The first week is critical. Here's what you do, day by day.

Day 1-2: Document Preservation Sprint

Gather everything immediately. If the bank files foreclosure tomorrow, you need your documents ready today.

Priority documents (in order): 1. **Original note and mortgage** — If you don't have originals, find them. Check safe deposit boxes, storage, wherever you keep important papers. 2. **All correspondence from the bank/servicer** — Every letter, every notice, every statement 3. **Payment history** — Download from online banking, gather canceled checks, bank statements 4. **Modification paperwork** — Any applications, correspondence, approvals or denials 5. **Insurance and tax records** — Escrow statements, property tax receipts 6. **Hardship documentation** — Medical records, job loss letters, anything explaining the default

Create your war room: Designate a specific place for all foreclosure-related documents. A file cabinet, a box, a drawer — whatever works. Everything goes there. Nothing gets lost.

Make copies: Never send originals to anyone. Make copies for attorneys, copies for consultants, copies for your own working files. Keep originals locked away.

Day 3-4: County Records Check

Search your county recorder's office immediately.

What to look for: - Has a lis pendens been filed? (Means lawsuit started) - Has a notice of default been recorded? - Are there any recent assignments of mortgage? - Any suspicious document filings?

How to search: - Online: Most counties have searchable databases - In person: County recorder's office - By mail: Request copies if you can't go in person

If you find a lis pendens: You're already being sued. See Chapter 28 (Just Been Served) immediately.

Day 5-6: Call an Attorney

Yes, this week. Not next month. This week.

Why now: - You have time to find the right attorney - You can discuss modification vs. defense strategy - You can get ahead of the bank's timeline - Many attorneys offer free consultations

What to ask: - "Do you handle foreclosure defense, not just bankruptcy?" - "What's the timeline for foreclosure in [your state]?" - "Should I apply for modification or focus on defense?" - "What documents do you need me to gather?" - "What's your fee structure?"

If you can't afford an attorney: - Legal aid societies (income-based) - Law school clinics - Pro bono programs through bar associations - Self-help resources (this manual, court websites)

Day 7: Calendar Everything

Create a timeline calendar.

Mark these dates: - Date of first missed payment - Date of last payment made - Date of any default notices received - Date of any acceleration notice - State-specific deadlines for pre-foreclosure notices - Your state's statute of limitations on foreclosure

Set reminders: - Check county records weekly - Follow up with attorney - Document all bank communications

---

Weeks 2-4: Document Audit Sprint

Goal: Complete a full document audit before the foreclosure complaint arrives.

The Chain of Title Investigation

Map every transfer of your loan:

Date	From	To	Document	Location
[Date]	[Originator]	You	Mortgage/Note	Your files
[Date]	[Originator]	[Assignee 1]	Assignment	County records
[Date]	[Assignee 1]	[Assignee 2]	Assignment	County records

Red flags to find: - Assignments dated after the bank started claiming ownership - Multiple assignments in suspiciously short timeframes - Known robo-signer names on assignments - Missing assignments in the chain - MERS assignments (indicates securitization)

Why this matters now: Standing challenges work best when raised early. If the bank's chain is broken, you want to know before they file suit.

The Signature Review

Check every signature on your documents:

1. **Print or copy all assignments and key documents**
2. **Compare signatures across documents:**
    - Same signer on different documents — do they match?
    - Notary signatures — are they identical (impossible if real)?
3. **Research the signers:**
    - Google: "[signer name] robo-signer"
    - Check state notary databases
    - Look for attorney general investigations

Document your findings: Photographs, comparison sheets, database printouts. Build your evidence file now.

The Amount Verification

Reconstruct your payment history:

1. **Get your records:** Bank statements, canceled checks, online payment history
2. **Create a spreadsheet:**
    - Date of each payment
    - Amount paid
    - How paid (check, online, phone)
    - Confirmation number

3. **Compare to servicer's records:**
    - Request payment history from servicer
    - Look for payments they missed
    - Check for unexplained fees
    - Verify interest calculations

Dispute errors immediately: Send a Qualified Written Request (QWR) disputing any errors you find. Document everything.

The Modification Decision

Should you apply for a loan modification? The answer is complicated.

The Modification Trap

Banks use modifications to delay and confuse: - They tell you to apply while they prepare foreclosure - They "lose" your paperwork three times - They deny you after six months of "review" - They foreclose while you're waiting for an answer

This is called "dual tracking" — pursuing modification and foreclosure simultaneously. It's illegal under federal law (RESPA), but it still happens.

When to Apply for Modification

Apply if: - You have documented hardship (job loss, medical, divorce) - Your income has stabilized and you can afford modified payments - You want to keep the home long-term - You have time before foreclosure starts

Don't apply if: - You can't afford payments even if modified - You don't want to keep the home - Foreclosure is imminent (too late in the process) - You've been denied before for the same reason

The Strategic Modification Application

If you apply, do it strategically:

1. **Apply immediately:** Don't wait for the bank to suggest it
2. **Document everything:** Keep copies of every document you submit
3. **Send certified mail:** Proof of delivery matters
4. **Follow up weekly:** Don't let your file sit
5. **Continue your defense preparation:** Don't rely solely on modification

Important: Applying for modification does not stop foreclosure. Continue preparing your defense while the modification is pending.

RESPA Rights During Modification

Federal law protects you:

- ** acknowledgment within 5 days:** Servicer must acknowledge receipt
- **Decision within 30 days:** Must approve or deny within 30 days of complete application
- **No dual tracking:** Cannot foreclose while modification is pending (with exceptions)
- **Appeal rights:** Can appeal denial within 14 days

Document violations: If the servicer violates these timelines, you may have a RESPA claim.

Preparing for Service

The foreclosure complaint is coming. Here's how to be ready.

Know Your State's Timeline

Every state is different:

State Type	Typical Timeline	Key Feature
Judicial	12-24 months	Full court process required
Non-judicial	3-6 months	Faster, but with notice requirements
Deed of trust	4-8 months	Trustee sale process

Research your state's process: - Pre-foreclosure notice requirements - Minimum time before sale - Right to cure/reinstate - Deficiency judgment rules

The Service Preparation Checklist

Before the complaint arrives:

☐ Know your answer deadline (usually 20-30 days after service)
☐ Identify potential process servers (don't hide, but be aware)
☐ Prepare preliminary answer draft with an attorney
☐ Gather all documents in one place
☐ Set up legal file organization system
☐ Have attorney's contact information ready

☐ Understand your state's answer requirements

When Suit Is Filed

The moment you're served, the clock starts:

Day 1 of service: - Note the date — this starts your answer deadline - Read the complaint carefully - Identify the plaintiff (who is suing you?) - Note any immediate court dates

Day 2-3: - Contact your attorney immediately - Begin drafting answer - Preserve the complaint and all service documents

Week 1: - File answer or motion for extension - Begin discovery requests - Challenge standing immediately

See Chapter 28 for full "Just Been Served" protocol.

Common Mistakes in Pre-Foreclosure

Mistake 1: Waiting for the Modification

"I'll just wait for the modification to be approved."

Why it's fatal: Modifications often take 3-6 months. Many are denied. Meanwhile, foreclosure proceeds. By the time you're denied, you may have missed deadlines to raise defenses.

What to do instead: Apply for modification AND prepare your defense simultaneously. Don't rely on one strategy.

Mistake 2: Believing the Bank's Promises

"We don't want to foreclose. We're here to help."

Why it's fatal: The bank's interests are opposite yours. They want to foreclose if that's the fastest way to get paid. Their promises aren't binding unless in writing.

What to do instead: Document every promise. Get everything in writing. Verify every claim. Trust your documents, not their words.

Mistake 3: Ignoring Notices

"It's just another scary letter. I'll deal with it later."

Why it's fatal: Those "scary letters" contain deadlines. Default notices, acceleration notices, right to cure — each has legal significance. Ignore them and you waive rights.

What to do instead: Read every letter immediately. Calendar every deadline. Respond to every notice. Treat everything as important.

Mistake 4: Not Gathering Documents

"I'll get my papers together if they actually sue me."

Why it's fatal: Once litigation starts, you're on the bank's timeline. Discovery deadlines come fast. You won't have time to search for documents.

What to do instead: Gather documents NOW, before suit is filed. Be ready to defend immediately.

Mistake 5: Hiding From Service

"If they can't find me, they can't sue me."

Why it's fatal: Service can be accomplished by alternative methods (publication, posting, substitute service). Avoiding service doesn't stop foreclosure — it just means you won't know about it until it's too late.

What to do instead: Accept service when it comes. The sooner you're served, the sooner you can defend, the more time you have to save your home.

Timeline Tracker

Use this template to track your pre-foreclosure timeline:

```
PRE-FORECLOSURE TIMELINE

First missed payment: _______________
Current status: _______________

NOTICES RECEIVED:
[Date] - [Type of notice] - [Deadline, if any] - [Action taken]

MODIFICATION APPLICATION:
Date applied: _______________
Documents submitted: _______________
Servicer response: _______________
Status: _______________
```

```
COUNTY RECORDS CHECK:
Last checked: _______________
Findings: _______________
Next check due: _______________

ATTORNEY CONSULTATION:
Date: _______________
Attorney: _______________
Advice: _______________
Next steps: _______________

POTENTIAL SERVICE DATES:
Earliest expected: _______________
Plan for response: _______________
```

Emergency Bankruptcy Option

If foreclosure is imminent and you need to stop it immediately:

Chapter 13 bankruptcy: - Stops foreclosure immediately (automatic stay) - Allows you to cure arrears over 3-5 years - Requires regular income to fund plan - Filing fee: ~$313

Chapter 7 bankruptcy: - Stops foreclosure temporarily - May delay sale 2-3 months - Does not cure arrears - Filing fee: ~$338

See Chapter 19 for detailed bankruptcy discussion.

Warning: Bankruptcy is a serious decision with long-term credit consequences. Consult a bankruptcy attorney before filing.

Chapter Summary

If you're behind but not yet sued, you have time — but not much. The actions you take in the next weeks determine whether you can mount an effective defense.

Week 1 priorities: - Preserve all documents - Check county records for lis pendens - Contact an attorney - Calendar all deadlines

Weeks 2-4 priorities: - Complete document audit - Map chain of title - Research signatures and notaries - Verify amounts owed

Modification decision: - Apply strategically if hardship is documented - Don't rely solely on modification - Continue defense preparation - Document all servicer violations

Preparing for service: - Know your state's timeline - Prepare preliminary answer - Don't hide from process servers - Be ready to act immediately

The key rule: Act now, not later. The bank is preparing their case against you. You must prepare your defense against them.

Cross-References

- **Chapter 2:** The Homeowner's Biggest Mistake — why waiting destroys cases
- **Chapter 9:** First 72 Hours — what to do when served
- **Chapter 19:** Bankruptcy — emergency foreclosure stop
- **Chapter 26:** Current But Suspicious — if you get current again

---

End of Chapter 27

CHAPTER 28: UNLICENSED COUNSEL ATTACK

How to Win by Checking One Website

The Secret Lawyers Won't Share

Every foreclosure defense book written by attorneys contains the same omissions. They'll teach you about standing, chain of title, and robo-signing. They'll explain discovery and motions to dismiss. But there's one strategy you'll never find in their books — because it targets them directly.

This chapter reveals a procedural weapon so effective that it has ended foreclosure cases entirely. It requires no legal expertise to execute. It costs nothing. And it exploits a vulnerability that opposing counsel cannot hide: their own licensing status.

The strategy is simple: Verify that the attorney prosecuting your foreclosure is actually licensed to practice law in your state. If they aren't — or if their license lapsed when they filed documents against you — those documents can be stricken. If those documents were time-sensitive, and the deadline has passed, you win.

This isn't theory. This has won cases.

Why This Works

Attorneys are human. They miss renewal deadlines. They assume their paralegals handled the paperwork. They move to new firms and forget to update their bar registrations. They practice across state lines without proper admission.

When an unlicensed attorney files documents with a court, those filings are void. Not merely defective — void. They never legally existed. And if those filings were responses to your motions, answers to your complaints, or the foreclosure complaint itself, their invalidity can be fatal to the opposing party's case.

The key is timing.

The Strategic Timing Rule

Never reveal your knowledge of their unlicensed status while they still have time to cure the defect.

Here's the critical distinction:

WRONG APPROACH

You file a motion. Opposing counsel has 30 days to respond. On day 20, they file a response. You immediately move to strike because their license expired last month. The court grants your motion to strike. They reactivate their license and refile their response before day 30. They've cured the problem. You gained nothing.

CORRECT APPROACH

You file a motion. Opposing counsel has 30 days to respond. You check their bar status and discover their license expired January 1. It is now February 15. They file a response on day 20. **You say nothing.** Day 30 passes. The deadline is missed.

Now you move to strike their response for practicing without a license **AND** move for your relief because they failed to respond within the time allowed.

The court strikes the void document. The opposing party attempts to refile. You object: The deadline has passed. They had 30 days. They used 20 of those days filing void documents. The remaining 10 days are gone. Allowing them to refile now would prejudice you and violate the procedural timeline established by law.

The court agrees. You win.

How to Verify Licensing Status

Every state maintains a lawyer lookup database through its state bar association. Most are free and publicly accessible.

Step 1: Identify the Opposing Attorney's Full Name

Check the signature block on any document they've filed. Note the exact spelling — middle initials matter. Note the firm name — attorneys sometimes practice under variations of their names.

Step 2: Access Your State's Bar Association Website

Search "[Your State] State Bar attorney lookup" or "[Your State] lawyer license verification." Most states have a dedicated portal: usually something like "Attorney Search" or "License Verification."

Step 3: Search for the Attorney

Enter their name exactly as it appears on court filings. If no results appear, try variations (without middle initial, maiden name, etc.). Check both your state's bar and any state where the firm is headquartered.

Step 4: Verify the Critical Details

Status should show "Active" or "In Good Standing." Note the expiration date. Verify they're admitted to practice in your specific state. Check for disciplinary history.

Step 5: Document Everything

Take screenshots with timestamps. Save the search results as PDFs. Note the URL and date of your search. Print the page — websites change, and you'll need proof.

The Out-of-State Firm Problem

Large foreclosure mills frequently operate across state lines. A firm headquartered in Florida handles cases in Georgia. A Texas firm files foreclosures in California. Sometimes they have properly obtained admission to practice in your state. Often, they haven't.

Pro hac vice admission (limited permission to practice in a state where you're not licensed) requires specific court approval. Filing documents before obtaining this approval is the unauthorized practice of law.

The verification process is identical. If the attorney doesn't appear in your state's bar database and hasn't filed a motion for pro hac vice admission that you can locate in your case docket, they're practicing illegally.

The Two-Step Attack

When you've confirmed an attorney lacks proper licensing, execute this two-step procedure:

Step 1: Immediate Motion to Strike

File a motion to strike all documents filed by the unlicensed attorney. Cite your state's unauthorized practice of law statute. Attach the bar association search results showing the attorney is not licensed or that their license was inactive on the date of filing.

Key argument: Documents filed by a person not authorized to practice law are **void ab initio** — invalid from the start. They are not "defective" filings that can be amended. They are legal nullities that must be removed from the record.

Step 2: Procedural Advantage

If the stricken documents were responsive pleadings or dispositive motions, and the deadline for filing them has passed, move for the appropriate relief: - If stricken document was an Answer to your Counterclaims: **Move for default on the counterclaims** - If stricken document was a Response to your Motion: **Your motion is unopposed** - If stricken document was the original Complaint: **Move to dismiss with prejudice for failure to prosecute**

LEARN FROM THIS MISTAKE: The Early Revelation Trap

> **Maria Santos' Story:** Maria discovered that the opposing attorney's license had expired three months prior. Excited, she immediately filed a motion to strike the Answer he had filed to her counterclaims. The court granted the motion. The attorney paid his bar dues, reactivated his license the same day, and refiled his Answer within the original deadline.
>
> Maria had revealed her weapon too early. She should have waited. If she had allowed the deadline to pass before challenging his authority to practice, his Answer would have been stricken **AND** the time to file would have expired. Her counterclaims would have gone unanswered. She would have won.
>
> **What Maria should have done:** - Discovered the license expiration and said nothing - Waited for the response deadline to pass completely - Only then moved to strike the void filing - Simultaneously moved for default on her counterclaims - Argued prejudice if the court allowed refiling after the deadline
>
> **The Lesson:** Timing is everything. The unlicensed counsel attack is a stealth weapon, not a frontal assault. Reveal it only when the procedural window has closed. Once the deadline passes, the opposing party cannot cure their defect — they can only lose.

The Prejudice Argument

When opposing counsel inevitably argues they should be allowed to "cure" the licensing defect by reactivating their bar membership and refiling, you must be ready with the prejudice argument:

> "Your Honor, allowing opposing counsel to refile now would prejudice the Defendant. The procedural timeline established by [cite your state's rules of civil procedure] provides specific deadlines for a reason. Opposing counsel had 30 days to respond. They chose to wait until day 20 to file. That filing has been stricken as void. The remaining 10 days of their allotted time have expired. To allow them to refile now — after the deadline has passed — would deprive the Defendant of the finality that procedural deadlines exist to provide. The Defendant has relied on the calendar. The Defendant has organized their defense around the expiration of this deadline. To reopen the timeline now, based solely on opposing counsel's failure to maintain basic professional requirements, would fundamentally prejudice the Defendant's right to orderly procedure."

This argument works because it's correct. Courts respect deadlines. Attorneys are expected to maintain their licenses as a fundamental prerequisite to practice.

Real Case: The January 1 Expiration

The strategy works. Here is how it played out in an actual foreclosure defense:

The homeowner filed a motion challenging the plaintiff's standing. The opposing attorney had 30 days to respond. The homeowner checked the state bar website and discovered the attorney's license had expired on January 1. The current date was February 15.

The attorney filed a response on day 20 of the 30-day period. The homeowner said nothing. Day 30 passed.

On day 31, the homeowner filed a motion to strike the attorney's response, pointing out that the attorney had been practicing without a license. The homeowner simultaneously moved for the relief requested in their original motion, arguing that the response was void and the deadline had passed.

At the hearing, the court struck the response. The plaintiff's attorney argued she could cure the defect by reactivating her license immediately. The homeowner argued prejudice — the deadline had passed, and allowing a late filing would violate the procedural timeline.

The court agreed. The response remained stricken. The original motion was granted. The foreclosure was dismissed.

LEARN FROM THIS MISTAKE: The Wrong Database Error

> **James Patterson's Story:** James thought he had found gold. The attorney handling his foreclosure didn't appear in the state bar database at all. James filed his motion to strike, crowing about the unauthorized practice of law. At the hearing, the plaintiff's counsel produced documentation showing he was licensed under a slightly different name variation than appeared on his court filings — a middle initial he rarely used.
>
> The bar database had him listed; James had searched the wrong name. The judge was not amused. The motion was denied. James looked foolish.
>
> **What James should have done:** - Verified every possible name variation before filing - Checked the attorney's signature block against every database entry - Called the state bar directly if the name search produced no results - Built a more complete record before going to court
>
> **The Lesson:** Verify every possible name variation before filing your motion. Be certain, not hopeful. A failed sanctions motion based on incomplete research damages your credibility. Do the work upfront — search with the middle initial, without it, with the full middle name, with maiden names, with every variation. Only when you've exhausted the database should you file.

When the Complaint Itself Is Void

The most powerful application of this strategy occurs when the unlicensed attorney filed the foreclosure complaint itself.

If the complaint was filed by an attorney who was not properly licensed at that time, **the complaint is void.** If the statute of limitations has since run, or if other procedural deadlines have passed, you may be able to obtain dismissal with prejudice — a complete victory.

The Analysis:

- Was the complaint filed by an unlicensed attorney?
- Has the statute of limitations for refiling expired?
- Can they "cure" this defect and refile?

If the answer to the first two questions is yes, and the answer to the third is no, you have won your case.

Move to dismiss with prejudice. The court must grant it. The foreclosure cannot be refiled. The case is over.

The Ultimate Victory Scenario

The homeowner faced foreclosure by a major national servicer. The case had dragged on for two years. The homeowner discovered that the attorney who originally filed the foreclosure complaint had left the firm six months prior — and his license had been suspended for non-payment of bar dues three months before that.

The complaint had been filed while the attorney was suspended. All subsequent filings — motions, discovery responses, expert designations — were void.

The statute of limitations for foreclosure in that state was five years. The foreclosure had been filed four years and eight months ago. If the complaint was dismissed, and the statute ran while the case was being refiled, the debt would become unenforceable.

The homeowner waited. They said nothing. They continued litigating as if the opposing counsel was properly licensed.

On the five-year anniversary of the loan's default — one month before the statute would expire — the homeowner filed a motion to strike all documents filed by the suspended attorney, moved to dismiss the complaint for lack of prosecution, and argued that the statute of limitations would expire before a new complaint could be filed and served.

The court granted the motion to strike. The plaintiff's attorney argued they could cure the defect by having a licensed attorney sign a new complaint. The court asked: Can you file and serve a new complaint before the statute expires in 30 days?

The answer was no.

The motion to dismiss with prejudice was granted. The foreclosure was over. The homeowner kept their home. The debt was time-barred.

All because someone checked a website.

Chapter Summary

The unlicensed counsel attack is the ultimate asymmetric weapon. It costs nothing to execute. It requires no legal expertise. It targets a vulnerability that opposing counsel cannot hide and cannot easily fix. And it can end a foreclosure case entirely.

The strategy: 1. Verify opposing counsel's licensing status through your state bar website 2. If they're unlicensed or suspended, remain silent 3. Allow procedural deadlines to pass 4. Move to strike their documents as void 5. Move for your requested relief based on their failure to respond within the time allowed 6. Argue prejudice if they attempt to cure and refile

The key: Timing. Reveal nothing until the deadline has passed. Once the window closes, it cannot be reopened.

The secret: Other foreclosure defense attorneys won't teach this because it targets them. It reveals that the emperor has no clothes — that the "professional" prosecuting your foreclosure may not be a professional at all.

Check the website. Verify the license. Wait for the deadline. Then strike.

Your home may depend on it.

Cross-References

- **Chapter 10:** How to Draft the Answer — Understanding the procedural timelines that make the unlicensed counsel attack effective
- **Chapter 11:** Motion to Dismiss Strategy — Using procedural defects to end the case early
- **Chapter 12:** Discovery Warfare — Using discovery to verify the qualifications of opposing counsel and their witnesses
- **Chapter 29:** Dismissal With Prejudice — When the void complaint can lead to permanent victory
- **Chapter 39:** Sanctions Against Opposing Counsel — Holding unlicensed counsel accountable for practicing without authorization

---

End of Chapter 28

CHAPTER 29: DISMISSAL WITH PREJUDICE

The Permanent Victory Strategies

Understanding the Stakes

Most foreclosure dismissals are without prejudice. The court dismisses the case, the plaintiff fixes the defect, and they refile. You've bought time — valuable time — but the fight continues.

Dismissal with prejudice is different. It's permanent. The plaintiff cannot refile. The foreclosure is over. The debt may still exist, but the foreclosure action is dead.

Courts reserve dismissal with prejudice for specific circumstances: attorney misconduct, fraud upon the court, res judicata, and statute of limitations violations. These are high bars. But they exist. And when the facts align, they end the case forever.

This chapter covers the legitimate paths to dismissal with prejudice — the strategic defenses that have actually worked in real courts, with real citations you can use.

The New York "Death Penalty" — Strict Compliance with RPAPL 1304 & 1306

Citations: - *Aurora Loan Services, LLC v. Weisblum*, 85 A.D.3d 95, 923 N.Y.S.2d 609 (2d Dep't 2011) - *Deutsche Bank National Trust Co. v. Heitner*, 163 A.D.3d 741, 80 N.Y.S.3d 603 (2d Dep't 2018)

The Defense

In New York, proper service of RPAPL 1304 notice is a condition precedent to commencing foreclosure. "Strict compliance" is required, and the plaintiff has the burden of proof.

What the Bank Must Prove

1. They mailed the RPAPL 1304 notice by **registered or certified mail AND first-class mail** to the borrower's last known address
2. They complied with RPAPL 1306 by filing with the Superintendent of Financial Services **within 3 business days** of mailing the 1304 notice

3. The complaint itself contains an **affirmative allegation** of 1306 compliance

What to Attack

The Mailing Evidence: The bank's affidavit must prove both mailing methods. If they only sent certified mail but not first-class, they failed. If they sent to the wrong address, they failed. If they cannot produce the return receipts, they failed.

The 1306 Filing: Demand proof that the notice was filed with the Superintendent within 3 business days. This is a separate statutory requirement from mailing. If they mailed but didn't file, or filed late, they failed.

The Complaint Allegation: The complaint must affirmatively allege 1306 compliance — not just 1304 compliance. Read the complaint carefully. If it alleges 1304 but omits 1306, they failed.

Dismissal Result

In *TD Bank v. Leroy*, the court reversed the lower court and granted summary judgment for the homeowner, dismissing the complaint when the bank failed to prove 1306 compliance.

Why It Works

These are jurisdictional defects. You cannot "cure" a failure to send pre-foreclosure notice. A second foreclosure action requires a NEW 90-day notice and NEW compliance. If the bank blew the first one, and the statute of limitations has run, they may be permanently barred.

Failure to File Certificate of Merit & Request for Judicial Intervention (RJI) in New York

Citation: *Citibank, N.A. v. Murillo*, 30 Misc. 3d 934, 915 N.Y.S.2d 461 (Nassau County Sup. Ct. 2011)

The Defense

New York Administrative Orders 431/10 and 548/10 require: - An attorney affirmation that documents were personally reviewed - Filing of an RJI within prescribed timeframes - Compliance with strict settlement conference procedures

The Rare Dismissal With Prejudice

In *Citibank v. Murillo*, the court stated: > "The failure of plaintiff's counsel, Steven J. Baum, P.C., to comply with two court orders, my November 4, 2010 order and Chief Administrative Judge Pfau's October 20, 2010 order, demonstrates delinquent conduct... This mandates the dismissal with prejudice of the instant action. Failure to comply with court-ordered time frames must be taken seriously. It cannot be ignored."

This is one of the rare cases resulting in dismissal WITH PREJUDICE.

Strategic Lesson

Dismissal with prejudice for procedural failures requires a pattern of non-compliance, not a single missed deadline. Document every violation. Show the court that plaintiff's counsel has disregarded multiple court orders. Build a record of disrespect for the court's authority.

The "Lost Note" Standing Trap (Florida & UCC States)

Citations: - *Rosa M. Garcia v. Deutsche Bank National Trust Company*, 2025 Fla. App. LEXIS (Fla. 4th DCA 2025) - *May v. PHH Mortgage Corporation*, 150 So. 3d 247 (Fla. 4th DCA 2014)

The Defense

Under UCC § 3-309 and Florida Statute § 673.3091, a plaintiff seeking to enforce a lost note must prove: 1. They were in possession when the loss occurred 2. The loss was NOT the result of transfer or lawful seizure 3. They cannot reasonably produce the original

The Trap

Most "lost note affidavits" are defective. The affiant must have personal knowledge of the circumstances of loss — not just "record review." The affiant must know WHEN the note was lost, HOW it was lost, and WHY it cannot be produced.

Dismissal Result

In *May v. PHH*, the court reversed a foreclosure judgment because: > "Standing must be established at the time the complaint was filed... The bank failed to do so; none of the evidence adduced at trial demonstrated when, if at all, the bank came into possession of the note."

Strategic Application

If the bank files a lost note affidavit, depose the affiant. Ask specific questions about the circumstances of loss. If they cannot describe when and how the note was lost with personal knowledge, their affidavit is defective. Without a valid lost note affidavit, they cannot enforce the debt.

Separation of the Note and Mortgage (The "Split" Defense)

Citation: *Bank of New York v. Silverberg*, 86 A.D.3d 274, 926 N.Y.S.2d 532 (2d Dep't 2011)

The Legal Principle

> "The note, and not the mortgage, is the dispositive instrument that conveys standing to foreclose under New York law."

What This Means

If the mortgage was assigned but the note was not physically transferred with proper endorsement, the mortgagee cannot foreclose. MERS or a servicer holding only the mortgage assignment — without the note properly endorsed to them — lacks standing.

Dismissal Result

When MERS or a servicer holds only the mortgage assignment but cannot prove note possession at filing, the case must be dismissed.

Strategic Application

Demand the original note with all endorsements. Trace the chain of possession. If the note shows a different chain of title than the mortgage assignments, or if the note lacks endorsements required by the assignment documents, the note and mortgage are split. The plaintiff holds the mortgage but lacks the note — and without the note, they cannot foreclose.

Statute of Limitations — Acceleration/Deceleration (Florida)

Citation: *Bartram v. U.S. Bank National Association*, 211 So. 3d 1009 (Fla. 2016)

The Defense

Florida's Supreme Court held that each missed payment is a separate default. However, if a prior foreclosure was dismissed with prejudice, or if the bank "decelerated" the debt by accepting payments after acceleration, the statute may have expired on certain installments.

Dismissal Result

Each installment older than the statute of limitations (5 years in Florida) is time-barred. While the bank can still foreclose, the homeowner may retain the property subject only to liens for non-barred installments.

The Deceleration Trap

If the bank accelerated the debt (demanded full payment) and then accepted partial payments, they may have "decelerated" — resetting the clock for statute of limitations purposes. If they later re-accelerate, only installments from the NEW acceleration date are subject to the new limitations period.

Strategic Application

Request a complete payment history. Identify any payments accepted after acceleration. Calculate which installments are time-barred. If significant principal is time-barred, the foreclosure may be economically unviable for the plaintiff.

New Jersey's Fair Foreclosure Act Strict Compliance

Citation: *Bank of New York v. Laks*, 421 N.J. Super. 196 (App. Div. 2011)

The Defense

N.J.S.A. 2A:50-56(c) requires the Notice of Intention to Foreclose to state the "name and address of the lender."

The Result

In *Laks*, sending notice in the servicer's name — not the lender's — resulted in mandatory dismissal without prejudice.

Strategic Note

While this was later legislatively amended, it demonstrates that strict statutory construction of notice requirements can defeat foreclosure. Read every notice carefully. Compare the sender name to the named plaintiff. Compare the creditor named in the notice to the creditor named in the complaint. Any discrepancy may be grounds for dismissal.

The Vermont Nuclear Option

Citation: *Cenlar FSB v. Malenfant*, 203 Vt. 23, 151 A.3d 778 (2016)

The Holding

Vermont's Supreme Court held that dismissal with prejudice of a prior foreclosure action bars a second foreclosure action on all claims that were or could have been raised in the prior action — including the entire indebtedness.

Why This Is Devastating

In most states, dismissal with prejudice of a prior foreclosure only bars THAT foreclosure action. The creditor can refile with corrected pleadings. In Vermont, dismissal with prejudice bars ANY subsequent foreclosure on the same debt.

Strategic Application

If you're in Vermont and have a prior foreclosure that was dismissed with prejudice, you have a complete defense to any subsequent foreclosure. The debt may still exist, but the foreclosure remedy is extinguished.

What Does NOT Work (Avoid These)

The following "tricks" are legally frivolous and will not work. They will waste your time, damage your credibility, and may result in sanctions:

- **"Sovereign citizen" arguments** — e.g., "I am a free inhabitant," "capital letters name" theories, "UCC-1 lien" filings
- **"Produce the original note"** — Courts allow copies under UCC § 3-309; demanding the original is not a standalone defense
- **"MERS has no authority"** — Correct in some states for certain purposes, but curable by proper assignment; not a dismissal-with-prejudice argument
- **"The bank doesn't have a license to lend"** — Irrelevant to foreclosure; lending authority is a regulatory issue, not a defense to enforcement
- **"I paid with a promissory note discharge"** — No legal merit; "acceptance for value" theories have been universally rejected
- **"The government is a corporation"** — Frivolous; will result in sanctions

The Rule: If a "strategy" requires you to file documents in ALL CAPS, quote the Uniform Commercial Code out of context, or claim secret government accounts in your name, it will fail.

LEARN FROM THIS MISTAKE: The Homeowner Who Chased the Wrong Theory

> **Robert Evans' Story:** Robert was a dedicated researcher who spent months studying foreclosure defense online. He discovered the "sovereign citizen" movement and became convinced that his mortgage was invalid because the bank had "securitized" his note into a "REMIC trust" without his consent. He filed elaborate pleadings citing UCC Article 3, the Securities Act of 1933, and the Internal Revenue Code.
>
> His pleadings were 47 pages of incomprehensible legal gibberish. The judge dismissed them as frivolous. The bank moved for sanctions. Robert was ordered to pay $2,500 in attorney fees for filing "patently meritless" pleadings. His legitimate defenses — that the bank lacked standing, that the assignment was defective, that he had never received proper notice — were buried under the weight of his frivolous theories and never reached the court's attention.
>
> **What Robert should have done:** - Focused on legitimate, proven defenses - Read this chapter and stuck to the paths that courts have actually accepted - Avoided any theory that required "special" knowledge of secret banking systems - Understood that dismissal with prejudice requires real law, not internet folklore
>
> **The Lesson:** The legitimate paths to dismissal with prejudice are narrow but real. The frivolous paths are wide but deadly to your credibility. Stick to what

works. Cite real cases. Argue real law. The strategies in this chapter have won in real courts. The strategies on conspiracy websites have only won in the imaginations of the people selling them.

The Path to Dismissal With Prejudice

Step 1: Identify Jurisdictional Defects

Look for defects that go to the court's authority to hear the case: lack of standing, failure to satisfy conditions precedent, statute of limitations violations.

Step 2: Document Everything

Build a record. Every missed deadline. Every non-compliant notice. Every discrepancy between the note and mortgage assignments. Every failure to produce documents ordered by the court.

Step 3: Challenge Early and Aggressively

File your challenges before the bank can correct them. If you wait, they may cure the defect. Strike while the defect exists.

Step 4: Show Pattern and Prejudice

For dismissal with prejudice, show a pattern of non-compliance. One missed deadline gets an extension. Five missed deadlines show disregard for the court.

Step 5: Request Specific Relief

Don't just ask for dismissal. Ask for dismissal WITH PREJUDICE. Explain why the defect cannot be cured, why refiling would be futile, and how you've been prejudiced by the plaintiff's conduct.

Chapter Summary

Dismissal with prejudice is rare because it ends the case forever. Courts are reluctant to foreclose a creditor's remedies permanently. But when the plaintiff has engaged in misconduct, violated court orders, or blown jurisdictional requirements beyond cure, dismissal with prejudice is appropriate.

Key takeaways: 1. **New York's 1304/1306 compliance** is a jurisdictional prerequisite — no cure, no refiling without new notice 2. **Pattern of non-compliance** with court orders can support dismissal with prejudice 3. **Lost note affidavits** are frequently defective — challenge the affiant's personal knowledge 4. **Split note and mortgage** destroys standing in New York and similar states 5. **Statute of limitations** on individual installments can make foreclosure economically pointless 6. **Vermont's res judicata** rule extinguishes the foreclosure remedy entirely 7. **Frivolous arguments** waste time and credibility — stick to legitimate defenses

The strategic reality: Most dismissals will be without prejudice. But dismissal without prejudice is still a win. It buys time. It forces the plaintiff to start over. And if the statute of limitations is running, that time may be permanent.

Dismissal with prejudice is the goal. Dismissal without prejudice is the path.

Cross-References

- **Chapter 10:** How to Draft the Answer — Raising dismissal-with-prejudice arguments in your initial pleadings
- **Chapter 11:** Motion to Dismiss Strategy — Using procedural and jurisdictional defects to end the case
- **Chapter 15:** Attacking Affidavits, Declarations, and Bank Records — Challenging the defective affidavits that underpin the bank's case
- **Chapter 22:** When Federal Court Is and Is Not Realistic — Understanding why state court is usually the proper forum for dismissal motions
- **Chapter 26:** The Concurrent Filing Trap — Using filing defects to build a record for eventual dismissal with prejudice
- **Chapter 39:** Sanctions Against Opposing Counsel — When the bank's lawyer misconduct supports both sanctions and dismissal

---

End of Chapter 29

CHAPTER 30: ACTION PLAN — SALE IS SCHEDULED

Emergency Tactics for Imminent Foreclosure Sale

The Final Countdown

The foreclosure sale is scheduled. The notice has been posted. The date is set — maybe it's days away, maybe hours. This is the endgame, and the stakes couldn't be higher. If the sale happens, you lose your home.

But the game isn't over yet. Even with a sale scheduled, you have options. Emergency motions can stop the sale. Bankruptcy can halt everything. Last-minute settlements are still possible. You need to act fast, but you need to act smart.

This chapter is your emergency playbook. It tells you exactly what to do when time is critically short. Every hour matters. Every decision matters. Follow this plan, and you may stop the sale. Delay, and your home is gone.

Warning: This chapter covers emergency procedures. These are last-resort tactics, not primary strategies. The best defense is fighting early, not waiting until the sale is scheduled. But if you're here, you need emergency action now.

Immediate Assessment: How Much Time Do You Have?

First, determine exactly where you are in the process:

Type 1: Sale Scheduled in Days or Weeks

You have some time to prepare. The sale is scheduled but not imminent.

Your options: - Emergency motion to stay sale - Temporary restraining order (TRO) - Chapter 13 bankruptcy filing - Settlement negotiations

Type 2: Sale Scheduled Today or Tomorrow

This is a true emergency. You have hours, not days.

Your options: - Emergency TRO (today) - Emergency bankruptcy filing (today) - Emergency motion to vacate judgment (if grounds exist)

Type 3: Sale Already Happened

The sale has occurred. Options are limited but may exist.

Your options: - Motion to set aside sale (if procedural defects) - Appeal of underlying judgment - Bankruptcy (may not undo sale but can affect eviction) - Negotiate post-sale occupancy

---

Option 1: Emergency Motion to Stay Sale

A motion to stay asks the court to stop the scheduled sale. This is the first option to consider if you have grounds.

Grounds for Emergency Stay

Valid reasons to stop a sale:

1. **Procedural defects in the sale notice:**
    - Notice not posted as required by law
    - Insufficient advance notice
    - Notice sent to wrong address
    - Required parties not notified
2. **Pending appeal:**
    - Judgment is on appeal
    - Automatic stay may apply (varies by state)
    - Bond may be required
3. **Violation of automatic stay:**
    - Bankruptcy was filed, but sale scheduled anyway
    - Sale violates bankruptcy stay
4. **Irreparable harm:**
    - Sale would cause harm that can't be fixed
    - Equity in property would be lost
    - Home contains unique value (family home, etc.)
5. **Pending settlement negotiations:**
    - Active negotiations with bank
    - Sale would prejudice settlement
    - Bank agreed to postpone but hasn't formally cancelled

Drafting the Emergency Motion

An emergency motion should include:

1. **Caption and title:**

   "EMERGENCY MOTION TO STAY FORECLOSURE SALE"

2. **Statement of urgency:**

   "The foreclosure sale is scheduled for [date], [time], at [location]. This motion is filed on an emergency basis because [explain urgency]."

3. **Legal grounds:**

   "The sale should be stayed because:

   - [Ground 1 with legal citation]
   - [Ground 2 with legal citation]
   - [Ground 3 with legal citation]"

4. **Factual basis:**

   "The following facts support this motion:

   - [Fact 1 with evidence reference]
   - [Fact 2 with evidence reference]
   - [Fact 3 with evidence reference]"

5. **Proposed order:**

   "The Court should enter an order staying the foreclosure sale pending [resolution of appeal/further proceedings/settlement]."

6. **Certificate of emergency:**

   Many courts require a statement explaining why the motion couldn't be filed sooner.

Filing the Emergency Motion

Emergency motions often have special procedures:

1. **Call the judge's chambers immediately:**
   - Explain the emergency
   - Ask about emergency filing procedures
   - Request immediate hearing
2. **File with the clerk:**
   - Mark "EMERGENCY" on the filing
   - Follow local emergency procedures
   - Get a file-stamped copy
3. **Serve the bank's attorney:**

- Emergency motions usually require immediate notice
- Call opposing counsel and tell them you're filing
- Serve the motion as required by local rules

4. **Request immediate hearing:**
    - Ask for same-day or next-day hearing
    - Explain the sale date
    - Be prepared to argue immediately

The Bond Problem

Courts may require a bond to stay a sale. This is a major obstacle.

Typical bond requirements: - Amount of monthly mortgage payment - Full amount of judgment - Amount of bank's likely damages from delay

If you can't afford a bond: - Request waiver based on indigency - Argue that equity in home is sufficient security - Request reduced bond amount - Some states prohibit bond requirements for homesteads

Key point: If bond is required and you can't pay, the motion fails. Have a backup plan (bankruptcy).

Option 2: Temporary Restraining Order (TRO)

A TRO is an emergency court order stopping action until a full hearing can be held. It's faster than a motion to stay but harder to get.

TRO Requirements

To get a TRO, you must show:

1. **Irreparable harm:**
    - Sale would cause harm that money can't fix
    - Loss of family home
    - Loss of equity
    - Emotional/psychological harm
2. **Likelihood of success on the merits:**
    - You have a valid legal claim
    - Your case has merit
    - You're not filing frivolously
3. **Balance of equities:**
    - Harm to you outweighs harm to bank

    - Bank can wait; you can't get home back
4. **Public interest:**
    - Stopping sale serves public interest
    - Preserving homeownership
    - Preventing wrongful foreclosure

The TRO Application Process

TROs move fast:

1. **Draft TRO motion and proposed order:**
    - More detailed than motion to stay
    - Must address all four requirements
    - Include affidavits supporting emergency
2. **File ex parte (without notice to bank):**
    - Most TROs are filed without notice
    - Full hearing scheduled within 10-14 days
    - Bank gets to respond at full hearing
3. **Immediate judicial review:**
    - Judge reviews papers same day
    - May grant or deny without hearing
    - May schedule immediate hearing
4. **TRO expires quickly:**
    - Usually 10-14 days maximum
    - Must schedule full hearing
    - Must notify bank of hearing
    - TRO can be dissolved at full hearing

TRO vs. Preliminary Injunction

Understand the difference:

	TRO	Preliminary Injunction
Duration	10-14 days	Until trial or case resolution
Notice	Usually ex parte	Full notice to opposing party
Standard	Emergency basis	Higher standard, full briefing
Bond	May be required	Usually required

Strategy: Use TRO to stop immediate sale, then seek preliminary injunction for longer stay.

Option 3: Emergency Bankruptcy Filing

Bankruptcy is the nuclear option. It stops everything immediately, but has serious consequences.

How Bankruptcy Stops Sale

The automatic stay (11 U.S.C. § 362): - Goes into effect immediately upon filing - Stops all collection actions, including foreclosure - Applies to all creditors, including mortgage holders - Violation of stay is contempt of court

What happens: - Sale is cancelled immediately - Bank must seek court permission to continue foreclosure - You get breathing room to reorganize - Chapter 13 allows you to cure arrears over time

Chapter 13 vs. Chapter 7

	Chapter 13	Chapter 7
Stay duration	3-5 years (plan duration)	2-3 months (case duration)
Cure arrears	Yes — can pay over 3-5 years	No — just delays foreclosure
Keep home	Yes — if you can afford plan	Temporary only
Income requirement	Regular income required	No income requirement
Filing fee	~$313	~$338

For stopping foreclosure: Chapter 13 is usually better because you can cure the default. Chapter 7 only delays the inevitable unless you can get current.

The Emergency Filing Process

If sale is scheduled today, file bankruptcy today:

1. **Complete credit counseling (required):**
    - Can be done online or by phone
    - Takes 1-2 hours
    - Must be completed before filing
    - Get certificate of completion
2. **Gather required documents:**
    - Last 60 days of pay stubs
    - Last 2 years of tax returns
    - List of all creditors
    - List of all assets

- List of all income and expenses

3. **Complete bankruptcy petition:**
    - Can use bankruptcy petition preparer (BPP)
    - Can file pro se (DIY)
    - Best: hire bankruptcy attorney if possible
4. **File with bankruptcy court:**
    - Can file online (PACER)
    - Can file in person
    - Pay filing fee or request fee waiver
5. **Notify foreclosure attorney immediately:**
    - Send case number and filing date
    - Demand cancellation of sale
    - Confirm receipt
6. **Attend 341 meeting (about 30 days later):**
    - Meeting of creditors
    - Trustee reviews your case
    - Usually brief for Chapter 13

The Chapter 13 Plan

To keep your home in Chapter 13, you must:

1. **Propose a feasible plan:**
    - Pay regular mortgage going forward
    - Cure arrears over 3-5 years
    - Pay trustee fees and attorney fees
    - Show sufficient disposable income
2. **Make plan payments:**
    - First payment due 30 days after filing
    - Must continue making payments
    - Missing payments = dismissal = foreclosure resumes
3. **Complete plan:**
    - 3 years (if income below median)
    - 5 years (if income above median)
    - Discharge at end

Key point: Chapter 13 only works if you can afford the plan payments. If you can't, the case will be dismissed and foreclosure resumes.

Option 4: Last-Minute Settlement

Even with sale scheduled, settlement is possible. Banks don't always want to foreclose.

Leverage for Settlement

You may have leverage even at the last minute:

1. **Defects in foreclosure process:**
    - Standing problems
    - Notice defects
    - Document issues
    - Procedural errors
2. **Bank's costs:**
    - Foreclosure is expensive
    - Bank must maintain property
    - Bank faces liability risks
    - Your defenses create uncertainty
3. **Property condition:**
    - If property needs work
    - If market is slow
    - If bank doesn't want inventory
4. **Your ability to pay something:**
    - Lump sum to reinstate
    - Modified payment plan
    - Short sale with deficiency waiver
    - Deed in lieu with relocation assistance

Settlement Options to Propose

Even at the last minute, consider:

1. **Reinstatement:**
    - Pay all arrears, fees, and costs
    - Loan goes back to current status
    - Sale cancelled
    - Best if you have the money
2. **Forbearance agreement:**
    - Temporary payment reduction
    - Missed payments added to loan balance
    - Sale postponed

- Good for temporary hardship

3. **Short sale:**
    - Sell for less than owed
    - Bank agrees to accept proceeds as full payment
    - Deficiency judgment waived or reduced
    - You avoid foreclosure on credit
4. **Deed in lieu:**
    - Sign deed over to bank
    - Bank cancels foreclosure
    - May get relocation assistance
    - Less damage than foreclosure
5. **Cash for keys:**
    - Agree to vacate by specific date
    - Bank pays you to leave peacefully
    - Sale proceeds as scheduled
    - You get money for transition

How to Request Settlement

Even at the last minute:

1. **Call the bank's attorney:**
    - Ask to speak with decision-maker
    - Explain you want to resolve
    - Emphasize defects in their case (creates leverage)
2. **Make specific proposal:**
    - Don't just ask for "help"
    - Propose specific solution
    - Show you have ability to perform
3. **Get it in writing:**
    - Oral agreements aren't binding
    - Written settlement agreement required
    - Must be filed with court
4. **Request sale postponement:**
    - Banks can postpone sales
    - Usually need 24-48 hours notice
    - Don't assume it's postponed — confirm in writing

The 24-Hour Emergency Checklist

If sale is scheduled within 24 hours:

Immediately (Hour 1):

- ☐ Confirm sale date, time, and location
- ☐ Call foreclosure attorney — explain emergency
- ☐ Gather all foreclosure documents
- ☐ Determine which option to pursue

If Filing Emergency Motion/TRO (Hours 2-6):

- ☐ Draft emergency motion
- ☐ Call judge's chambers — explain emergency
- ☐ File motion with clerk
- ☐ Serve bank's attorney
- ☐ Request immediate hearing
- ☐ Prepare bond (if required)

If Filing Bankruptcy (Hours 2-8):

- ☐ Complete credit counseling online
- ☐ Gather pay stubs and tax returns
- ☐ Complete bankruptcy petition
- ☐ File with bankruptcy court
- ☐ Get case number
- ☐ Notify foreclosure attorney immediately
- ☐ Confirm sale cancellation

If Pursuing Settlement (Hours 2-12):

- ☐ Call bank's attorney
- ☐ Propose specific solution
- ☐ Request sale postponement
- ☐ Get written agreement
- ☐ File with court
- ☐ Confirm postponement in writing

Backup Plan:

- ☐ Have Plan B ready if Plan A fails

☐ If motion denied, file bankruptcy immediately
☐ If bankruptcy dismissed, negotiate occupancy
☐ Prepare for possibility of sale

If the Sale Happens

Sometimes despite your best efforts, the sale occurs. Here's what to do.

Immediate Actions Post-Sale

1. **Confirm sale occurred:**
    - Check with trustee/sheriff
    - Get certificate of sale
    - Note the purchaser
2. **Review sale for defects:**
    - Was notice proper?
    - Were procedures followed?
    - Was sale properly conducted?
    - Any irregularities?
3. **Determine redemption period:**
    - Some states have post-sale redemption
    - Time to reclaim property by paying full amount
    - Varies by state (none to 12 months)
4. **Plan for eviction:**
    - Purchaser must evict through court
    - You have time (weeks to months)
    - Negotiate cash for keys
    - Plan your transition

Motion to Set Aside Sale

If sale had procedural defects:

Grounds to set aside sale: - Inadequate notice - Failure to follow statutory procedures - Fraud or misconduct in sale - Sale to non-qualified bidder - Grossly inadequate sale price

Standard: Hard to win. Courts don't like to undo sales. Must show serious procedural defect.

Bankruptcy After Sale

Chapter 13 after sale: - May stop eviction temporarily - Usually can't undo sale - Can buy time to relocate - Must show ability to pay going forward

Chapter 7 after sale: - Delays eviction (automatic stay) - Buys 2-3 months typically - No ability to cure - Eventually must vacate

---

Common Emergency Mistakes

Mistake 1: Doing Nothing

"It's too late. There's nothing I can do."

Why it's fatal: Even at the last minute, options exist. Bankruptcy can stop sale today. TRO can stop sale today. Doing nothing guarantees loss.

What to do instead: Act immediately. File something. Try everything. Fight to the end.

Mistake 2: Relying on Promises Without Confirmation

"The bank said they'll postpone the sale."

Why it's fatal: Banks promise postponements that never happen. Sale occurs while you're waiting for confirmation.

What to do instead: Get written confirmation. Call trustee/sheriff to confirm postponement. Don't rely on bank's word alone.

Mistake 3: Filing Frivolous Emergency Motion

"I'll file an emergency motion claiming the bank is fraudulent!"

Why it's fatal: Frivolous motions waste time and credibility. Judge may deny valid emergency motion because you cried wolf.

What to do instead: File only if you have legitimate grounds. Focus on procedural defects or pending appeal, not conspiracy theories.

Mistake 4: Not Having Backup Plan

"I'll file the motion and I'm sure it will work."

Why it's fatal: Motions get denied. Be prepared to file bankruptcy immediately if motion fails.

What to do instead: Have bankruptcy petition ready to file. Have credit counseling completed. Be ready to file same day if motion denied.

Mistake 5: Missing Bankruptcy Filing Deadline

"I'll file bankruptcy tomorrow morning before the sale." (Sale is at 10 AM, you wake up at 9 AM.)

Why it's fatal: Bankruptcy must be filed BEFORE sale. Once sale occurs, bankruptcy can't undo it (usually).

What to do instead: File the day before. File the night before. Don't wait until morning of sale.

Chapter Summary

When sale is scheduled, you have emergency options:

Option 1: Emergency Motion to Stay - Grounds: procedural defects, pending appeal, irreparable harm - Pros: Stops sale, preserves defenses - Cons: May require bond, judge may deny

Option 2: Temporary Restraining Order - Faster than motion to stay - Higher standard to obtain - Short duration, need preliminary injunction

Option 3: Emergency Bankruptcy - Automatic stay stops sale immediately - Chapter 13 allows curing arrears - Chapter 7 only delays - Serious consequences but effective

Option 4: Last-Minute Settlement - Reinstatement, forbearance, short sale, deed in lieu - Requires bank cooperation - Get everything in writing

The 24-hour checklist: - Confirm sale details immediately - Choose option and execute - Have backup plan ready - Act now, not later

If sale happens: - Review for defects - Determine redemption rights - Plan for eviction - Negotiate transition

Key rule: Even at the last minute, fight. Bankruptcy stops sales. Emergency motions stop sales. Settlement stops sales. Doing nothing guarantees loss.

Cross-References

- **Chapter 17:** Emergency Response — general emergency tactics
- **Chapter 19:** Bankruptcy — detailed bankruptcy discussion

- **Chapter 31:** After Judgment — post-foreclosure options

End of Chapter 30

CHAPTER 31: ACTION PLAN — AFTER JUDGMENT

What To Do When You've Lost

The Loss

The judgment has been entered. The court ruled against you. The foreclosure is final, or nearly final. You're facing the reality that you may lose your home.

This is a hard moment. Whether you fought hard or were unable to fight, the result is the same — the bank has a judgment, and the path to keeping your home has narrowed dramatically.

But the story isn't over yet. Even after judgment, you have options. Post-judgment motions can provide relief. Appeals can reverse errors. Bankruptcy can delay and reorganize. Settlement is still possible. And if none of those work, you can control how you exit — with dignity, with resources, and with a plan for what's next.

This chapter is your post-loss playbook. It tells you how to assess what happened, explore remaining options, and make the best of a difficult situation. Let's figure out your next move.

Understanding What Happened

Before deciding what to do next, understand what actually happened in your case.

Get the Court's Ruling

Obtain the court's order or judgment: - Visit the clerk's office and request a certified copy - Check the court's online docket system - Review the judge's written opinion (if any)

Understand the ruling: - Did the court rule on summary judgment or after trial? - What specific grounds did the court cite? - Were your defenses rejected on the merits or for procedural reasons? - Did the court address all your arguments?

Review the Record

Gather the complete case file: - All pleadings (complaint, answer, motions) - All evidence submitted - Hearing transcripts (if any) - Court's rulings on motions

Look for errors: - Did the court apply the wrong legal standard? - Did the court ignore evidence you submitted? - Did the court make factual errors? - Were your objections properly preserved?

Assess Whether Issues Were Preserved

For an appeal to succeed, issues must be preserved:

Issue	Preservation Required	Common Failure
Standing challenge	Raised in answer and throughout	Not raised until summary judgment
Document objections	Objected to at time of admission	No objection made
Evidentiary challenges	Objected to with specific grounds	General objection only
Legal arguments	Raised in motions and briefs	Raised for first time on appeal

Unpreserved issues: Can sometimes be raised as "plain error" but much harder to win.

Key question: Did you make the argument at the right time, in the right way, with the right objections?

Post-Judgment Motion Options

Before appealing, consider post-judgment motions. These stay the timeline and may provide relief without the cost of an appeal.

Motion for Reconsideration

Asks the same judge to reconsider the ruling:

Grounds: - New evidence not available at time of ruling - Change in controlling law - Court overlooked controlling precedent - Court made clear error of law

Standard: Hard to win. Same judge rarely reverses themselves.

Timeline: Usually 10-30 days after judgment (varies by jurisdiction).

Strategic use: - Preserves issues for appeal - Buys time to prepare appeal - Occasionally works if judge genuinely made error

Motion to Vacate Judgment

Asks court to set aside the judgment:

Grounds: - Fraud on the court - Newly discovered evidence - Lack of jurisdiction - Excusable neglect (if you missed deadline) - Judgment is void

Standard: Very high. Judgments are not easily vacated.

Timeline: Varies — some motions must be filed within months, others have longer deadlines.

When it works: - You were never properly served - Bank committed fraud in obtaining judgment - You have compelling new evidence

Motion for New Trial

Asks for a new trial after trial (not summary judgment):

Grounds: - Verdict is against the weight of the evidence - Newly discovered evidence - Juror misconduct - Judge made erroneous rulings

Standard: High. Courts don't like redoing trials.

Timeline: Usually 10-30 days after judgment.

When it works: - Strong evidence wasn't considered - Serious procedural errors occurred

Motion to Stay Sale

Asks court to postpone foreclosure sale pending appeal:

Grounds: - Appeal is pending or will be filed - Likelihood of success on appeal - Irreparable harm if sale proceeds - Bond can be posted

See Chapter 30 for detailed discussion of stays.

Timeline: File immediately upon judgment or before sale scheduled.

Strategic use: Essential if you plan to appeal. Without stay, sale happens while appeal pending.

The Appeal Decision

Should you appeal? This is a critical decision that requires honest assessment.

Factors Favoring Appeal

Appeal may be worthwhile if:

1. **Clear legal error:**
    - Judge applied wrong legal standard
    - Judge ignored binding precedent
    - Judge made constitutional error
2. **Preserved issues:**
    - You properly objected throughout
    - Issues were raised in motions
    - Record is complete
3. **Strong factual record:**
    - Evidence supports your position
    - Judge ignored or mischaracterized evidence
    - Document defects are well-documented
4. **Reversible error:**
    - Error likely affected outcome
    - Not just harmless error
    - Substantial rights affected
5. **Resources to pursue:**
    - Can afford appellate attorney
    - Or can handle pro se appeal
    - Time and energy to see it through

Factors Against Appeal

Appeal may not be worthwhile if:

1. **Weak case on merits:**
    - Bank had strong evidence
    - Your defenses were thin
    - Judge's ruling was legally correct
2. **Issues not preserved:**
    - Defenses raised too late
    - Objections not made properly
    - Record is incomplete
3. **Harmless error:**

- Even if error occurred, wouldn't change outcome
- Evidence against you was overwhelming

4. **Cost exceeds benefit:**
    - Appellate attorney fees high
    - Pro se appeal unlikely to succeed
    - Even if you win, case just goes back for trial
5. **Time and stress:**
    - Appeals take 12-24 months
    - Expensive and emotionally draining
    - Uncertain outcome

The Appeal Process

If you decide to appeal:

1. **File Notice of Appeal:**
    - Usually 30 days from judgment (CRITICAL DEADLINE)
    - Simple form filed with trial court
    - Triggers appellate jurisdiction
2. **Order Trial Record:**
    - Clerk prepares record on appeal
    - All pleadings, evidence, transcripts
    - Takes time and costs money
3. **Pay/Appellate Fees:**
    - Filing fees (~$300-500)
    - Record preparation fees
    - Possible bond if staying sale
4. **Draft Appellate Brief:**
    - Statement of issues
    - Statement of facts
    - Legal argument
    - Conclusion
5. **Oral Argument:**
    - Present case to appellate panel
    - Answer judges' questions
    - Usually 15-30 minutes
6. **Await Decision:**
    - Months to over a year
    - Three outcomes: affirm, reverse, remand

See Chapter 20-21 for detailed appellate procedures.

Should You Appeal? Decision Framework

Use this framework to decide:

```
SHOULD I APPEAL?

Step 1: Was there a clear legal error?
  Yes → Continue to Step 2
  No → Appeal unlikely to succeed

Step 2: Was the error preserved?
  Yes → Continue to Step 3
  No → Can you argue plain error? If yes, continue. If no, appeal unlikely.

Step 3: Would reversing the error likely change the outcome?
  Yes → Continue to Step 4
  No → Harmless error - appeal unlikely to succeed

Step 4: Do I have the resources to pursue an appeal?
  Yes → Continue to Step 5
  No → Can you do pro se? If yes, continue. If no, reconsider.

Step 5: Is the cost/benefit ratio acceptable?
  Cost of appeal vs. value of home
  Time and stress vs. likelihood of success
  Even if you win, are you prepared for trial?

If all answers are yes → Appeal may be worthwhile
If any answer is no → Reconsider whether appeal makes sense
```

Bankruptcy After Judgment

Even after judgment, bankruptcy may provide options.

Chapter 13 After Foreclosure Judgment

Can you save your home in Chapter 13 after judgment?

Yes, if: - Sale has not occurred (bankruptcy stops sale) - You can afford plan payments - Cure amount (arrears) can be paid over 3-5 years - You have regular income

Process: 1. File Chapter 13 before sale 2. Propose plan curing arrears 3. Make regular mortgage payments going forward 4. Complete 3-5 year plan

Limitations: - Must file before sale — after sale, it's too late - Must be able to afford payments - Lien stripping not available for primary mortgage

Chapter 7 After Foreclosure Judgment

Chapter 7 doesn't save your home but can delay eviction:

What it does: - Automatic stay stops eviction temporarily - Buys 2-3 months to find new housing - Discharges deficiency judgment (if any) - Fresh start after foreclosure

What it doesn't do: - Cure mortgage arrears - Stop foreclosure permanently - Allow you to keep home without paying

Timing: Can file Chapter 7 anytime, even after sale

Strategic Use of Bankruptcy

Even if you can't save home, bankruptcy helps:

1. **Delay eviction:**
    - Automatic stay buys time
    - Negotiate cash for keys
    - Find new housing
2. **Eliminate deficiency:**
    - If sale price less than judgment
    - Bankruptcy discharges deficiency
    - Clean slate for future
3. **Stop harassing calls:**
    - Automatic stay stops collection
    - Peace during transition

See Chapter 19 for detailed bankruptcy discussion.

Settlement After Judgment

Even after judgment, the bank may settle.

Why Banks Settle After Judgment

Banks may negotiate because:

1. **Avoiding appeal costs:**
    - Appeals are expensive for banks too
    - Uncertain outcome
    - May prefer certainty of settlement
2. **Property issues:**
    - Property needs repairs
    - Occupied property hard to sell
    - Liability concerns
3. **Your negotiating position:**
    - You have viable appeal issues
    - You filed bankruptcy (complicates their case)
    - You're making their life difficult
4. **Cash flow:**
    - Immediate payment better than uncertain foreclosure proceeds
    - Modified payments better than eviction costs

Settlement Options After Judgment

What to ask for:

1. **Loan modification:**
    - Even after judgment, banks may modify
    - Capitalize arrears into loan balance
    - Lower interest rate
    - Extend term
2. **Short sale approval:**
    - Sell for less than owed
    - Bank agrees to accept proceeds
    - Waiver of deficiency
    - Less credit damage
3. **Deed in lieu:**
    - Sign deed to bank
    - Bank cancels foreclosure
    - Deficiency waiver
    - Relocation assistance
4. **Cash for keys:**
    - Agree to vacate by date

    - Bank pays you to leave
    - Clean, peaceful transition
    - Money for new deposit
5. **Extended occupancy:**
    - Bank lets you stay X months
    - No rent (or reduced rent)
    - Time to save and find housing
    - Peaceful transition

How to Negotiate After Judgment

Your leverage: - Viable appeal issues - Bankruptcy filing - Property condition issues - Willingness to fight to the end

Approach: 1. **Call bank's attorney:** - "I want to discuss resolving this" - "I have appeal issues / I'm considering bankruptcy" - "Can we discuss alternatives to foreclosure?"

2. **Make specific proposal:**
    - Don't just ask for "help"
    - Propose concrete solution
    - Show how it benefits bank
3. **Get written agreement:**
    - Oral agreements worthless
    - Settlement agreement filed with court
    - Vacates judgment or modifies terms
4. **Follow through:**
    - Meet all deadlines
    - Make all payments
    - Comply with all terms

If Appeal Fails: Planning Your Exit

Sometimes the best option is accepting the loss and planning a dignified exit.

Timeline After Judgment

Typical post-judgment timeline:

Event	Timeline	Your Options
Judgment entered	Day 1	Post-judgment motions, appeal decision
Post-judgment motions decided	Days 30-60	Appeal, bankruptcy, settlement
Sale scheduled	Days 60-180	Emergency tactics (see Chapter 30)
Sale occurs	Day of sale	Post-sale redemption (some states)
Eviction process	Days 30-90 post-sale	Negotiate occupancy, cash for keys

Planning Your Transition

Even if you lose the home, control the transition:

1. **Secure your next housing:**
    - Start looking immediately
    - Consider rental options
    - Save for security deposit
    - Explore assistance programs
2. **Protect your assets:**
    - Bankruptcy may protect from deficiency
    - Exemptions protect some property
    - Don't hide assets (fraud)
3. **Plan the move:**
    - What to keep, sell, donate
    - Moving costs and logistics
    - Storage if needed
4. **Financial recovery:**
    - Budget for post-foreclosure life
    - Rebuild credit over time
    - Learn from experience

Cash for Keys Negotiation

If you're going to lose the home anyway, get paid to leave:

Typical cash for keys: - Bank pays $1,000-$5,000 - You agree to vacate by specific date - Property left in clean condition - Peaceful, voluntary departure

How to negotiate: - Contact bank's attorney or REO department - "I'm willing to vacate voluntarily for relocation assistance" - Propose specific amount - Get written agreement - Leave on time, leave property clean

Benefits: - Money for transition - Avoids eviction on record - Cleaner than forced eviction - Preserves some dignity

---

Emotional Recovery

Foreclosure is not just financial — it's emotional.

The Grief Process

Losing a home involves grief: - **Denial:** "This can't be happening" - **Anger:** "The system is rigged" - **Bargaining:** "If only I had..." - **Depression:** "I've lost everything" - **Acceptance:** "I need to move forward"

These stages are normal. Give yourself permission to feel them.

Coping Strategies

Practical steps: - Talk to someone (therapist, counselor, trusted friend) - Join support groups (online or local) - Focus on what you can control - Make a plan for the future - Remember: You are not your foreclosure

Your home is a building. Your family, your health, your future — these are what matter. You can rebuild.

Post-Judgment Checklist

Use this checklist to track your post-judgment options:

Immediate (Days 1-7):

- ☐ Obtain certified copy of judgment
- ☐ Review court's ruling and reasoning
- ☐ Assess whether issues were preserved
- ☐ Calendar appeal deadline (usually 30 days)
- ☐ Consult attorney about post-judgment options

Short Term (Days 8-30):

- ☐ Decide: appeal, post-judgment motions, or accept?
- ☐ If appealing: file notice of appeal before deadline

- ☐ If motions: draft and file post-judgment motions
- ☐ If accepting: contact bank about settlement options
- ☐ Consider bankruptcy implications

Medium Term (Days 31-90):

- ☐ If appeal filed: order record, draft brief
- ☐ If motions pending: await ruling
- ☐ If settlement: negotiate and finalize agreement
- ☐ If no relief: plan transition, find housing
- ☐ Consider cash for keys

Ongoing:

- ☐ Monitor sale date
- ☐ Consider emergency tactics if sale scheduled
- ☐ Plan financial recovery
- ☐ Focus on emotional health
- ☐ Build for the future

Chapter Summary

Losing a foreclosure case is hard, but it's not the end. You have options even after judgment.

Post-judgment motions: - Motion for reconsideration - Motion to vacate judgment - Motion for new trial - Motion to stay sale

Appeal decision: - Factors favoring appeal: clear legal error, preserved issues, strong record - Factors against: weak case, unpreserved issues, cost exceeds benefit - Use decision framework to assess

Bankruptcy options: - Chapter 13: May save home if filed before sale - Chapter 7: Delays eviction, discharges deficiency

Settlement after judgment: - Banks may still negotiate - Options: modification, short sale, deed in lieu, cash for keys - Get everything in writing

If all fails: - Plan dignified exit - Negotiate cash for keys - Focus on transition - Remember: you can rebuild

Key principle: Even after judgment, control what you can. Negotiate your exit. Plan your transition. Protect your future. The foreclosure is a chapter, not your whole story.

Cross-References

- **Chapter 20-21:** Appeals — detailed appellate procedures
- **Chapter 19:** Bankruptcy — detailed bankruptcy discussion
- **Chapter 30:** Sale Scheduled — emergency tactics
- **Chapter 32-37:** Moving forward — resources for next steps

---

End of Chapter 31

CHAPTER 32: HOW TO USE AI SAFELY IN FORECLOSURE DEFENSE

Your 24/7 Legal Research Assistant

The AI Revolution in Legal Research

Artificial intelligence has transformed what's possible for pro se litigants. What once required expensive legal research databases and years of training can now be done with a well-crafted prompt. AI can help you understand complex legal concepts, draft documents, analyze cases, and prepare arguments — all from your computer or phone.

But AI is a tool, not a magic wand. It can help you enormously, but it can also lead you astray. This chapter teaches you how to use AI productively while avoiding the pitfalls that have destroyed homeowners' cases.

What AI can do for you: - Explain legal concepts in plain English - Draft motions, answers, and discovery - Research case law and statutes - Analyze your documents for defects - Help you prepare for hearings - Suggest arguments and strategies - Translate legalese into understandable terms - Help organize your thoughts and arguments - Provide templates and frameworks - Offer strategic advice based on patterns

What AI cannot do: - Replace an attorney's judgment - Guarantee winning results - Know your jurisdiction's specific quirks - Verify that cases actually exist - Appear in court for you - File documents for you - Make ethical decisions for you - Understand the full emotional context of your case - Predict with certainty how a specific judge will rule

The key is using AI wisely. This chapter shows you how.

Understanding AI Platforms

Several AI platforms can help with legal research. Each has strengths and weaknesses. Understanding these differences helps you choose the right tool for each task.

Kimi (kimi.moonshot.cn)

Strengths: - Excellent at analyzing long documents - Strong reasoning capabilities - Good at legal research and analysis - Can process entire PDFs and case files - Strong in multiple languages - Has web search capability for current information - Excellent at breaking down complex legal concepts

Best for: - Analyzing your mortgage documents - Researching case law with verification - Drafting complex legal arguments - Understanding procedural rules - Multi-step reasoning tasks - Finding current information with sources

Limitations: - Can still hallucinate cases - May not know very recent case law - Doesn't replace jurisdiction-specific knowledge

Access: kimi.moonshot.cn

Tip: Use Kimi's web search feature to find current cases and verify information. Always ask for sources.

ChatGPT (chat.openai.com)

Strengths: - Very good at drafting documents - Strong creative writing abilities - Good at explaining concepts clearly - Widely available and accessible - GPT-4 has strong reasoning capabilities - Good at generating multiple variations - Excellent at brainstorming

Best for: - Drafting motions and answers - Writing demand letters - Creating checklists and templates - Brainstorming arguments - Explaining legal concepts simply - Generating first drafts

Limitations: - GPT-3.5 is less reliable for legal work - Can be verbose - Sometimes overconfident in incorrect information - No real-time web access (GPT-4 with browsing can help)

Access: chat.openai.com (free tier has GPT-3.5, paid tier has GPT-4)

Tip: Use GPT-4 (paid) for important legal work. The reasoning is significantly better than GPT-3.5.

Claude (claude.ai)

Strengths: - Excellent at document analysis - Very large context window (can read entire briefs) - Good at finding logical flaws - Strong at legal reasoning - Can process uploaded documents directly - Good at critical analysis

Best for: - Analyzing opposing counsel's motions - Reviewing your drafted documents - Finding weaknesses in arguments - Detailed legal analysis - "Red team" review of your work - Analyzing long documents

Limitations: - No web access (as of current version) - May not have most recent information - Can still make errors

Access: claude.ai (free tier available, paid tier for higher usage)

Tip: Upload opposing counsel's motions directly and ask Claude to analyze them. The large context window is a major advantage.

Google Gemini (gemini.google.com)

Strengths: - Good integration with Google search - Strong at finding current information - Useful for research - Can access recent developments

Best for: - Finding current case law - Researching recent legal developments - Fact-checking

Access: gemini.google.com

Perplexity (perplexity.ai)

Strengths: - Provides citations with answers - Good for fact-checking - Shows sources - Can search the web in real-time

Best for: - Verifying information - Research with sources - Finding current cases

Access: perplexity.ai

Tip: Use Perplexity to verify case citations and find sources. It shows where information comes from.

Choosing the Right Platform

For document drafting: ChatGPT (GPT-4) **For document analysis:** Claude **For complex reasoning:** Kimi **For verification:** Perplexity or Kimi with web search **For finding current cases:** Google Gemini or Perplexity

Pro tip: Use multiple platforms. Don't rely on just one AI. Cross-reference and verify.

The Golden Rule: Verify Everything

AI makes mistakes. It "hallucinates" — invents cases, cites statutes that don't exist, and creates legal doctrines out of thin air. This isn't a bug; it's a limitation of the technology.

The most dangerous AI error in foreclosure defense: Inventing case citations. AI will confidently cite *Smith v. Bank of America*, 123 F.3d 456 (2019), holding that "robo-signing voids all assignments." The case doesn't exist. But it sounds authoritative.

If you cite a fake case in court: - You lose credibility - The judge may sanction you - Your argument collapses - You could lose your home because of a computer error - The bank's attorney will expose the fake citation - Your other arguments may be discounted

This has happened. Pro se litigants have cited AI-generated fake cases and faced sanctions. Don't let this be you.

How to Verify AI Output

For case citations: 1. **Google Scholar (scholar.google.com):** Search the case name and citation 2. **CourtListener (courtlistener.com):** Free case law database 3. **Justia (justia.com):** Another free case source 4. **Official court websites:** Many courts have online dockets 5. **Westlaw or LexisNexis (if available):** Professional databases

If you can't find the case: It probably doesn't exist. Don't cite it.

Red flags of fake citations: - Perfectly formatted but can't be found - Cites cases from years that don't match the legal doctrine - References cases that "hold" things that seem too good to be true - Volumes or page numbers that seem off

For statutes: 1. **Official state legislature websites:** Search the statute number 2. **Cornell Legal Information Institute (law.cornell.edu):** Free federal and state codes 3. **State court websites:** Often have local rules 4. **Municipal codes:** For local ordinances

For legal concepts: 1. **Cross-reference with multiple sources** 2. **Check law school resources** 3. **Verify with actual case law** 4. **Check bar association publications** 5. **Verify with legal treatises**

The Multi-AI Verification Method

Here's a professional-grade workflow for using AI in foreclosure defense:

Step 1: Initial Document Creation

Use AI to create your first draft:

Prompt example:

> "Act as an experienced foreclosure defense attorney. I need to draft a motion to dismiss for lack of standing. The facts are: [describe your situation — bank filed foreclosure, assignment was dated after complaint, note is endorsed to a different bank].
>
> Please draft: 1. A motion to dismiss with legal argument 2. A supporting affidavit for me to sign 3. A proposed order
>
> IMPORTANT: Do not make up any case citations. If you cite a case, provide the full citation so I can verify it. If you're not certain about a legal principle, say so. Use the standard rules of civil procedure."

Why this works: - Sets the role (experienced attorney) - Provides specific facts - Asks for specific outputs - Explicitly prohibits fake citations - Sets verification expectation

Tips for Step 1: - Be specific about your facts - Ask for multiple outputs if needed - Don't accept the first draft — ask for revisions - Save the conversation for reference

Step 2: Judge Review (AI as Judge)

Have a DIFFERENT AI instance review the document as a judge:

Switch platforms. If you used ChatGPT to draft, use Claude or Kimi to review.

Prompt example:

> "Act as a trial judge in a foreclosure case. Review the attached motion to dismiss and tell me:
>
> 1. What are the strongest arguments?
> 2. What are the weaknesses or holes in the argument?
> 3. What would the bank's attorney likely argue in response?
> 4. Are there any procedural issues (formatting, timing, jurisdiction)?
> 5. What additional evidence or legal support would make this stronger?
> 6. Would you grant or deny this motion, and why?
>
> Be critical and thorough. I want to find problems before the bank does."

Paste the document you created in Step 1.

Why this works: - Fresh perspective (different AI) - Adversarial review finds weaknesses - Judges look for different things than advocates - Identifies problems before filing

Tips for Step 2: - Actually use a different AI platform - Don't skip this step - Take notes on the weaknesses identified - Ask follow-up questions

Step 3: Opposing Counsel Review (AI as Bank Attorney)

Have another AI instance attack the document:

Prompt example:

> "Act as the bank's attorney. I represent the homeowner who filed this motion to dismiss. Your job is to destroy this motion. > Tell me: 1. Every weakness in the homeowner's argument 2. How you would argue against each point 3. What evidence you would present to counter this motion 4. What legal precedents would help the bank 5. Are there any procedural ways to defeat this motion? 6. Draft the response you would file
>
> Be ruthless. I need to know how the bank will attack this so I can strengthen it."

Why this works: - Reveals weaknesses from opponent's view - Shows how bank will respond - Allows you to preemptively address counterarguments - Makes your motion battle-tested

Tips for Step 3: - Tell the AI to be "ruthless" — you want real criticism - Pay attention to procedural attacks - Note what evidence the bank might produce - Use this to strengthen your motion

Step 4: Revision and Strengthening

Go back to your original AI or a fresh session:

Prompt example:

> "I drafted a motion to dismiss, and I've received critical feedback. Here are the weaknesses identified: [List weaknesses from Steps 2 and 3]
>
> Please revise the motion to address these weaknesses: 1. Strengthen the weak arguments 2. Add counterarguments to anticipated bank responses 3. Fix any procedural issues 4. Add any missing legal support (with real citations I can verify)
>
> Again, do not make up case citations. Only cite cases that actually exist."

Why this works: - Incorporates critical feedback - Strengthens weak points - Addresses counterarguments - Creates a more robust document

Tips for Step 4: - Be specific about what needs to change - Ask for explanations of changes - Don't just accept the revision — review it carefully

Step 5: Final Verification Review

Have one more AI review the final version:

Prompt example:

> "Review this motion one final time. Pretend you're a law professor grading this:
>
> 1. Is the legal reasoning sound?
> 2. Are there any remaining weaknesses?
> 3. Is the writing clear and persuasive?
> 4. What grade would you give this, and why?
> 5. What final improvements would you suggest?
>
> Be honest — I want to submit the strongest possible document."

Why this works: - Final quality check - Catches anything missed - Ensures professionalism - Gives confidence before filing

Tips for Step 5: - Ask for a "grade" — it forces evaluation - Don't skip this even if you're in a hurry - Make final edits based on feedback

Step 6: Manual Verification (CRITICAL)

Verify everything yourself:

- ☐ Verify every case citation (Google Scholar/CourtListener)
- ☐ Verify every statute citation
- ☐ Check formatting against local rules
- ☐ Ensure all facts are accurate
- ☐ Proofread for typos and grammar
- ☐ Verify caption and case information

Never skip Step 6. AI can help, but you are responsible for what you file.

Essential Prompts for Foreclosure Defense

Here are battle-tested prompts for common tasks:

Prompt 1: Standing Challenge Research

> "I need to research standing challenges in foreclosure cases. The bank claims to be the holder of my note, but the assignment of mortgage was recorded after they filed the foreclosure complaint.
>
> Please: 1. Explain what standing means in foreclosure cases 2. Explain why post-complaint assignments are problematic 3. Find 3-5 real cases (not made up) where courts dismissed foreclosure for lack of standing due to post-complaint assignments 4. Provide the exact case names and citations so I can verify them 5. Explain the legal reasoning in these cases
>
> IMPORTANT: Do not invent any case citations. If you cannot find real cases, tell me that and explain the legal principle without fake citations. I will verify every case you cite."

Verification instruction: Then verify each case on Google Scholar or CourtListener.

Sample follow-up if cases seem questionable: > "I'm having trouble finding [case name] on Google Scholar. Can you double-check that citation? If it's incorrect or if you're not certain it exists, please tell me and provide alternative cases that you are confident about."

Prompt 2: Document Defect Analysis

> "I have a document that I suspect has a robo-signed signature. The signer is [name]. The signature looks different from other documents I've seen.

> Please: 1. Explain what robo-signing is and why it matters 2. Suggest specific ways to investigate whether this is a robo-signed document 3. Explain how to challenge a robo-signed document in court 4. Tell me what evidence I would need to prove robo-signing 5. Searches I should do to research this signer
>
> Do not make up any cases or facts about this specific signer."

Follow-up prompt for research strategy: > "Based on your suggestions, here's what I found about this signer: [describe your research findings]. How would I present this evidence in a motion to strike the document? What legal standard applies?"

Prompt 3: Drafting Discovery Requests

> "I need to draft discovery requests for my foreclosure case. I want to challenge the bank's standing and investigate document defects.
>
> 003e Please draft: 1. 10 document requests targeting the chain of title 2. 10 interrogatories about the bank's ownership of my loan 3. 10 requests for admission on key facts 4. Explain the strategy behind each request
>
> Use standard discovery format. Make the requests specific but comprehensive."

Follow-up for refinement: > "These are good, but I need to make them more specific to my case. The bank is [name], the original lender was [name], and the loan was allegedly assigned on [date]. Can you revise these discovery requests to specifically target these facts?"

Prompt 4: Preparing for Hearing

> "I have a hearing on [date] on the bank's motion for summary judgment. I need to prepare.
>
> Please help me: 1. Create a checklist of what to bring to court 2. Draft a 2-minute oral argument summarizing my key points 3. Anticipate 5 questions the judge might ask and draft responses 4. Anticipate 3 arguments the bank will make and draft counterarguments 5. Suggest courtroom etiquette tips for pro se litigants
>
> The facts of my case are: [brief description]"

Follow-up for practice: > "Can you role-play with me? Pretend you're the judge and ask me tough questions about my case. I'll respond, and you tell me if my answers are strong or need improvement."

Prompt 5: Case Strategy Analysis

> "I need strategic advice for my foreclosure case. Here's my situation: [Describe your case in detail — timeline, documents, what you've done so far, what the bank has done]
>
> Please analyze: 1. What are my strongest arguments/defenses? 2. What are my biggest vulnerabilities? 3. What should my priorities be right now? 4. What traps should I avoid? 5. Create a timeline of next steps with deadlines
>
> Be realistic about strengths and weaknesses."

Follow-up for prioritization: > "I have limited time and resources. Of the priorities you listed, which are absolutely critical versus which are just good to have? If I can only do three things, what should they be?"

Prompt 6: Motion to Compel Discovery

> "The bank hasn't responded to my discovery requests that I sent 45 days ago. I need to file a motion to compel.
>
> Please draft: 1. A motion to compel discovery responses 2. A supporting declaration/affidavit for me to sign 3. A proposed order
>
> Include: - Statement of when discovery was served - List of what was requested and what was not produced - Legal argument citing the applicable discovery rules - Request for sanctions (if appropriate)
>
> Do not include any fake case citations."

Prompt 7: Affidavit Drafting

> "I need to write an affidavit for my summary judgment opposition. I want to dispute the bank's claim about how much I owe.
>
> Please draft an affidavit that: 1. Has the proper format and caption 2. States my personal knowledge 3. Disputes specific facts in the bank's affidavit 4. Attaches exhibits (I'll provide the actual documents) 5. Has a proper notarization block
>
> The facts I want to include are: [describe your specific disputes — payments made that weren't credited, fees you dispute, etc.]"

Follow-up for exhibits: > "I have bank statements showing payments. How should I reference them in the affidavit? What's the proper way to say 'see Exhibit A attached'?"

Prompt 8: Legal Concept Explanation

> "I keep seeing the term 'prima facie case' in foreclosure law. I don't fully understand what it means or how it applies to my case.
>
> Please: 1. Explain what 'prima facie case' means in plain English 2. Explain what prima facie case a bank must establish in a foreclosure 3. Explain how I can challenge the bank's prima facie case 4. Give examples of when a bank fails to establish a prima facie case 5. Explain what happens if the bank fails to establish a prima facie case at summary judgment
>
> Use simple language and examples."

Follow-up for application: > "In my case, the bank produced [describe what they produced]. Do you think they've established a prima facie case? What weaknesses do you see that I should highlight in my opposition?"

Prompt 9: Opposing Counsel Analysis

> "Here's the bank's motion for summary judgment: [paste or upload]. I want you to analyze their arguments as if you're a law professor grading their work.
>
> Tell me: 1. What are their strongest arguments? (Grade A, B, C, D, F) 2. What are their weakest arguments? (Grade A, B, C, D, F) 3. What evidence are they relying on, and is it strong? 4. Are there any logical gaps in their argument? 5. What counterarguments should I prepare for their best points? 6. Overall, how strong is their motion on a scale of 1-10?"

Prompt 10: State-Specific Research

> "I need to understand the foreclosure timeline and rules in [your state].
>
> 003e Please research and tell me: 1. Is [state] a judicial or non-judicial foreclosure state? 2. What is the typical timeline from default to sale? 3. What notice requirements must the bank follow? 4. What is the answer deadline after service? 5. Are there any special homeowner protections in [state]? 6. Where can I find the actual statutes online?
>
> Cite the actual statute numbers so I can verify them. If you're not certain about something, say so."

Important note: State-specific information from AI should always be verified on the official state court or legislature website.

Platform-Specific Tips

Kimi Tips

Best practices: - Use the web search capability to find current information - Upload your documents for analysis - Ask for step-by-step explanations - Use for complex reasoning tasks - Ask for sources and citations

Sample prompt: > "Analyze this mortgage assignment document [upload document]. Tell me: > 1. What does this document purport to show? > 2. What potential problems do you see? > 3. What should I investigate further? > 4. How might I challenge this document in court?"

Another Kimi prompt: > "I need to understand the concept of 'holder in due course' under UCC Article 3. Please: > 1. Explain what it means > 2. Explain the requirements > 3. Explain how it applies to foreclosure defense > 4. Find real cases discussing holder in due course in mortgage foreclosure > 5. Provide citations I can verify"

ChatGPT Tips

Best practices: - Use GPT-4 for complex legal tasks (paid subscription) - Be very specific in prompts - Ask it to "think step by step" for complex reasoning - Use for drafting and editing - Ask for multiple options

Sample prompt: > "Draft an answer to a foreclosure complaint. Use this format: > - Deny all allegations for lack of knowledge except [specific admissions] > - Raise these affirmative defenses: standing, failure to state a claim, [others] > - Include a certificate of service > > The plaintiff is [bank name]. The complaint alleges [key allegations]."

For revision: > "Here's a draft motion I wrote: [paste]. Please improve it by: > 1. Making the legal argument stronger > 2. Improving clarity and persuasiveness > 3. Fixing any grammar or formatting issues > 4. Suggesting where I might need case citations (but don't make them up)"

Claude Tips

Best practices: - Upload opposing counsel's motions for analysis - Ask Claude to find logical flaws - Use the large context window for complex documents - Great for "red team" review - Ask for detailed critiques

Sample prompt: > "The bank filed this motion for summary judgment [upload document]. I need to oppose it. > > Please: > 1. Summarize the bank's main arguments > 2. Identify any weaknesses in their arguments > 3. Identify what evidence they're relying on > 4. Suggest counterarguments for each point > 5. Draft paragraphs I could use in my opposition"

For critique: > "Here's a draft of my summary judgment opposition: [upload]. Pretend you're the bank's attorney and tear it apart. I want to find every weakness before I file."

Common AI Mistakes to Avoid

Mistake 1: Trusting Case Citations Without Verification

What happens: AI cites *Smith v. Bank of America*, 555 F.3d 123 (2019). You cite it in court. The judge can't find it. You look foolish.

How to avoid: Verify EVERY case citation on Google Scholar or CourtListener before using it.

Real-world example: An attorney (not a pro se litigant) submitted a brief with AI-generated fake cases and faced sanctions. The cases sounded real but didn't exist.

Mistake 2: Using Generic Templates Without Customization

What happens: AI gives you a generic motion. You file it without adapting to your facts. It misses key issues in your case.

How to avoid: Always provide your specific facts and customize the output. Ask AI to revise based on your specific situation.

Mistake 3: Ignoring Jurisdiction-Specific Rules

What happens: AI gives you general legal principles. Your state has specific rules that differ. Your motion gets denied on procedural grounds.

How to avoid: Research your state's specific rules. Add state-specific requirements to prompts. Check local court rules.

Mistake 4: Filing AI Output Without Review

What happens: AI hallucinates a legal argument. You file it. It's wrong. You lose credibility and possibly your case.

How to avoid: Always use the multi-AI review process. Never file anything you don't understand.

Mistake 5: Not Understanding What AI Produced

What happens: AI gives you a complex legal argument. You don't understand it. In court, you can't explain it or defend it.

How to avoid: Never file anything you don't understand. Ask AI to explain until you get it. Simplify if needed.

Mistake 6: Using Outdated Information

What happens: AI's training data has a cutoff date. Recent changes in law aren't reflected. You rely on outdated rules.

How to avoid: Ask about the current state of the law. Use AI with web search (Kimi). Verify with current sources.

Advanced AI Workflows

Workflow 1: Complete Motion Package

Goal: Create a complete, court-ready motion with all supporting documents.

Step 1: Draft motion with AI (ChatGPT or Claude) **Step 2:** Review as judge (Kimi) **Step 3:** Attack as opposing counsel (Claude) **Step 4:** Revise based on feedback (original AI) **Step 5:** Create supporting affidavit (ChatGPT) **Step 6:** Create proposed order (ChatGPT) **Step 7:** Final review as law professor (Kimi) **Step 8:** Verify all citations manually **Step 9:** Format according to local rules **Step 10:** File

Time estimate: 2-4 hours with AI vs. 8-12 hours without

Workflow 2: Case Law Research

Goal: Find real, relevant case law for your arguments.

Step 1: Ask AI for relevant cases (Kimi with web search) **Step 2:** Get full citations **Step 3:** Verify each case on Google Scholar **Step 4:** Ask AI to analyze the cases (Claude) **Step 5:** Ask AI to distinguish unfavorable cases (ChatGPT) **Step 6:** Create case summary table manually

Workflow 3: Document Analysis

Goal: Analyze bank documents for defects.

Step 1: Upload document to Kimi or Claude **Step 2:** Ask for initial analysis **Step 3:** Ask follow-up questions about specific issues **Step 4:** Research any suspicious names/signatures (web search) **Step 5:** Create analysis memo with AI help **Step 6:** Verify findings with independent research

Workflow 4: Hearing Preparation

Goal: Prepare thoroughly for court.

Step 1: Ask AI to create hearing checklist (ChatGPT) **Step 2:** Draft oral argument (ChatGPT) **Step 3:** Practice Q&A with AI as judge (Kimi) **Step 4:** Anticipate bank arguments (Claude) **Step 5:** Prepare responses (ChatGPT) **Step 6:** Final review (Kimi)

The AI Safety Checklist

Before filing anything AI helped create:

- ☐ Verified every case citation (Google Scholar/CourtListener)
- ☐ Verified every statute citation (official sources)
- ☐ Reviewed by AI as "judge" for weaknesses
- ☐ Reviewed by AI as "opposing counsel" for attacks
- ☐ I understand every legal argument made
- ☐ Document complies with local court rules
- ☐ Facts are accurate and match my situation
- ☐ No hallucinated legal doctrines
- ☐ Formatting is correct
- ☐ Certificate of service included (if required)
- ☐ Proofread for typos and grammar
- ☐ Caption is correct
- ☐ Page numbers included (if required)
- ☐ Verified deadline and timing

Print this checklist and use it every time.

Sample AI Conversation: From Start to Finish

Here's what a complete workflow looks like:

User: "I need to draft a motion to dismiss for lack of standing. The bank filed foreclosure. The assignment of mortgage was dated two months after the complaint. The note is endorsed to a different bank."

AI (ChatGPT): [Drafts motion with argument about post-complaint assignments]

User: [Takes draft to Kimi] "Review this as a judge. What are the weaknesses?"

AI (Kimi): "The argument is good, but you should strengthen the section on prejudice. Also, check whether your state requires the assignment to be recorded before filing."

User: [Takes draft to Claude] "Attack this as the bank's attorney."

AI (Claude): "The bank will argue that the assignment relates back to the filing date. You'll need to counter that with specific case law showing post-complaint assignments don't cure standing defects."

User: [Back to ChatGPT] "Revise based on this feedback. Add counterarguments to the bank's likely responses. Include a section on why post-complaint assignments don't relate back."

AI (ChatGPT): [Revises motion]

User: [To Kimi] "Final review. What grade would you give this?"

AI (Kimi): "B+. Strong argument, but you need to verify the cases cited and add more on your state's specific rules."

User: [Manually verifies all citations, checks state rules, files motion]

Result: A battle-tested motion that's much stronger than a first draft.

Chapter Summary

AI is a powerful tool for foreclosure defense, but it must be used wisely.

Available platforms: - **Kimi:** Best for document analysis and complex reasoning - **ChatGPT:** Best for drafting and clear explanations - **Claude:** Best for finding flaws and detailed review - **Perplexity:** Best for verification with sources - **Google Gemini:** Best for current information

Golden rule: Verify everything. AI hallucinates. Fake case citations destroy credibility.

Multi-AI workflow: 1. Create initial draft 2. Review as judge (different AI) 3. Attack as opposing counsel (different AI) 4. Revise based on feedback 5. Final verification review 6. Verify all citations manually

Essential prompts provided for: - Standing challenge research - Document defect analysis - Discovery drafting - Hearing preparation - Case strategy - Motion to compel - Affidavit drafting - Legal concept explanation - Opposing counsel analysis - State-specific research

Common mistakes to avoid: - Trusting citations without verification - Using generic templates - Ignoring jurisdiction-specific rules - Filing without review - Not understanding the output - Using outdated information

Remember: AI is your research assistant, not your lawyer. You are responsible for what you file. Verify everything. Understand everything. Fight smart.

Cross-References

- **Chapter 10:** Drafting the Answer — fundamentals of document drafting
- **Chapter 12:** Discovery Warfare — using discovery strategically
- **Chapter 16:** Summary Judgment Survival — complex motion practice
- **Chapter 33:** Evidence Organization — managing AI output and research

---

End of Chapter 32

BONUS CHAPTER: The AI Weapon That Changes Everything

Why Centient Is the Only AI Tool I Recommend for Foreclosure Defense

---

The AI Landscape: A Sea of Mediocrity

You've heard the hype. AI will solve everything. ChatGPT will write your legal briefs. Claude will draft your motions. Gemini will analyze your documents.

I've tested them all. And I'm here to tell you: most of them will hurt you more than they help.

Generic AI tools have a fatal flaw when it comes to foreclosure defense: they're not connected to what matters. They hallucinate case law. They invent statutes. They give you confidently wrong answers that can sink your case.

When you're fighting for your home, "good enough" isn't good enough. You need an AI that's actually built for legal work.

Enter Centient: The Game-Changer

Go to: www.cetient.com

Centient isn't another chatbot pretending to be a lawyer. It's an AI legal platform connected to real legal databases — designed specifically to help homeowners organize, analyze, and respond more effectively.

This isn't hype. This is the tool I use. The tool I recommend. The tool that's actually worth your time and money.

What Makes Centient Different

1. It's Connected to Legal Resources

Unlike generic AI tools that pull from random internet sources, Centient is plugged into actual legal databases. That means: - Real case law, not hallucinated precedents - Current statutes, not outdated interpretations - Accurate legal reasoning, not confident guesses

2. Document Organization That Actually Works

Upload your entire document dump: - Mortgage agreements - Assignment records - Payment histories - Correspondence with the bank - Court filings

Centient doesn't just store them — it organizes, categorizes, and makes them searchable. When you need to find that one robo-signed assignment from 2019, you'll have it in seconds.

3. Drafting Assistance That Understands Context

Need to draft a response? Centient helps you: - Structure your arguments correctly - Cite relevant legal standards - Maintain consistent legal terminology - Format according to court requirements

Important: It helps you draft. It doesn't replace your judgment. You still need to review, verify, and take ownership of everything that goes to the court.

How to Use It (Without Getting Burned)

DO:

- Upload your documents for organization and analysis
- Use it to spot patterns across multiple documents
- Draft responses, then verify every claim independently
- Treat it as a research assistant, not a lawyer replacement

DON'T:

- Copy-paste AI output directly to the court without review
- Assume the AI knows your specific state's quirks
- Rely on it for strategic decisions about settlement vs. trial
- Forget that YOU are responsible for your case

The Promo Code That Saves You Money

PROMO CODE: 9OVNPVQP

Use this code when signing up for the Pro Plan. It'll save you money and get you full access to the features that matter for serious foreclosure defense work.

Why I'm Recommending This (And Only This)

I've tested dozens of AI tools claiming to help with legal work. Most are: - Too generic to be useful - Too confident about being wrong - Too disconnected from real legal resources

Centient is different. It's the only one I've found that actually understands the complexity of foreclosure defense and connects to the resources you need.

But let me be clear: this is still a tool. A powerful tool, but a tool nonetheless. It won't replace: - Your judgment about strategy - Your responsibility to verify facts - Your duty to review everything before filing - Your need to understand your own case

---

Your Action Steps

1. **Go to www.cetient.com**
2. **Sign up for the Pro Plan**
3. **Use promo code: 9OVNPVQP**
4. **Upload your documents and start organizing**
5. **Draft smarter, not harder**

The Bottom Line

Foreclosure defense is information warfare. The bank has teams of lawyers, paralegals, and document processors. You've got you.

Centient levels the playing field. It gives you organizational power and analytical capability that would cost thousands in legal support staff.

But it's still your fight. Use the tool. Verify the output. And never forget: the best AI in the world is no substitute for a homeowner who refuses to give up.

Website: www.cetient.com
Promo Code: 9OVNPVQP

Remember: AI is a force multiplier, not a magic bullet. Use it wisely, verify everything, and fight like your home depends on it — because it does.

CHAPTER 33: EVIDENCE ORGANIZATION

How to Build a Case File That Wins

Why Organization Matters

A well-organized case file is a weapon. When you can find any document in seconds, when your evidence is indexed and cross-referenced, when you walk into court with binders that make the bank's attorney nervous — you have an advantage.

A disorganized case file is a liability. When you're fumbling for documents, when you can't find that critical affidavit, when the judge asks for something and you have to say "I'll need to find that" — you look unprepared. The bank's attorney smells blood.

The truth about foreclosure cases: They generate enormous amounts of paper. Loan documents, assignments, notices, correspondence, court filings, discovery, financial records — a typical case can involve hundreds or thousands of pages. Without a system, you will drown.

This chapter teaches you that system.

The Master Case File Structure

Create one central location for everything. Whether it's a physical filing cabinet, a set of binders, or a digital system — everything goes here. No exceptions.

Physical Filing System

If using physical files, use this structure:

Section 1: Case Administration - Case information sheet (court, case number, judge, dates) - Court rules and local procedures - Calendar and deadlines - Attorney correspondence (if represented) - Fee and cost tracker

Section 2: Loan Documents (Original File) - Promissory note (copy) - Mortgage or deed of trust (copy) - Closing documents - Truth-in-Lending disclosure - Good Faith Estimate - Any modifications or forbearance agreements

Section 3: Chain of Title Documents - Assignment of mortgage (all assignments) - Endorsements on note - MERS documents (if applicable) - Title search results - Document timeline

Section 4: Correspondence History - All letters from servicer (chronological) - All letters to servicer (chronological) - Email correspondence - Phone call logs (date, time, who, what was discussed) - Notices of default - Notices of acceleration

Section 5: Financial Records - Payment history (your records) - Bank statements showing payments - Escrow statements - Force-placed insurance notices - Property tax records - Hardship documentation

Section 6: Court Filings - Complaint and summons - Your answer - All motions filed - All orders entered - Discovery requests and responses - Hearing notices and transcripts

Section 7: Evidence and Research - Document analysis worksheets - Case law research - Expert witness materials - Investigation notes - Photographs - Witness statements

Section 8: Modification/Settlement - Modification applications - Denial letters - Trial modification documents - Permanent modification documents - Settlement offers - HUD counselor correspondence

---

Digital Organization System

Digital files offer advantages: Searchability, backup capability, easy duplication, and the ability to quickly find anything.

Folder Structure

```
Foreclosure_Case_[YourName]_
   01_Administration/
       Case_Info.docx
       Court_Rules.pdf
       Calendar.xlsx
       Fee_Tracker.xlsx
   02_Loan_Documents/
       Promissory_Note.pdf
       Mortgage.pdf
       Closing_Documents/
       Modifications/
   03_Chain_of_Title/
       Assignments/
       Note_Endorsements/
       MERS_Documents/
       Title_Search.pdf
```

```
04_Correspondence/
    From_Servicer/
    To_Servicer/
    Call_Logs.xlsx
    Notices/
05_Financial/
    Payment_History/
    Bank_Statements/
    Escrow_Statements/
    Hardship_Docs/
06_Court_Filings/
    Pleadings/
    Motions/
    Orders/
    Discovery/
    Hearings/
07_Evidence/
    Document_Analysis/
    Case_Law/
    Investigation/
    Witness_Statements/
08_Modification/
    Applications/
    Denials/
    Settlement/
```

File Naming Convention

Use consistent, descriptive file names:

Format: `YYYY-MM-DD_DocumentType_Description.pdf`

Examples: - `2024-01-15_Notice_Default_30day.pdf` - `2024-02-01_Assignment_Mortgage_BoA_to_W` - `2024-03-10_Answer_Filed.pdf` - `2024-04-05_Discovery_Request_Production.pdf`

Why this works: - Chronological sorting - Instant identification - Easy searching - Professional appearance

---

Document Indexing System

Create a master index of all documents. This is your roadmap to everything.

Master Document Index

Use a spreadsheet with these columns:

Doc #	Date	Document Type	Description	Location
001	2024-01-15	Notice	Notice of Default (30-day cure)	Sec 4, p.1
002	2024-02-01	Assignment	Assignment BoA→Wells (post-complaint!)	Sec 3, p.1
003	2024-02-15	Motion	Motion to Dismiss (granted in part)	Sec 6, p.5

Additional tracking columns (use separate columns in your actual spreadsheet): - Bates/Page numbers for discovery - Notes field for special observations - Verification status

Document Numbering: - Use leading zeros (001, 002) for proper sorting - Never reuse numbers - Reserve blocks for categories if helpful (100s = correspondence, 200s = court filings)

Bates Numbering: - If producing documents in discovery, add Bates stamps - Format: `PROD001`, `PROD002` or `JONES0001`, `JONES0002` - Place in footer of each page

---

The Trial Notebook

For hearings and trial, create a portable trial notebook. This contains only what you need for that proceeding.

Trial Notebook Sections

Tab 1: Quick Reference - Case caption - Judge information - Today's agenda - Key dates and deadlines - Emergency contacts

Tab 2: Pleadings - Complaint - Answer - Counterclaims - Third-party complaints

Tab 3: Motions and Orders - Pending motions - Relevant orders - Scheduling orders

Tab 4: Evidence to Present - Documents you plan to introduce - Witness list - Exhibits list - Direct examination outlines

Tab 5: Cross-Examination - Witness statements to impeach - Inconsistent documents - Cross-examination outlines

Tab 6: Legal Authority - Key cases (summarized) - Statutes - Rules - Legal argument outline

Tab 7: Notes and Strategy - Opening statement notes - Closing argument notes - Strategy reminders - Judge's preferences (if known)

Document Analysis Worksheet

For each critical document, complete an analysis worksheet:

```
DOCUMENT ANALYSIS WORKSHEET

Document Number: ___
Document Type: _______________
Date: _______________
Author/Signer: _______________

WHAT IT SAYS:
[Summarize the content]

WHAT IT PROVES:
[What facts does this establish?]

PROBLEMS WITH IT:
[Defects, inconsistencies, missing elements]

HOW TO USE IT:
[Where does this fit in your case?]

CHAIN OF CUSTODY:
[Where did you get it? When?]

VERIFICATION STATUS:
[ ] Authenticated
```

```
[ ] Challenged
[ ] Under investigation

NOTES:
[Additional observations]
```

Complete this for: - Promissory note - Mortgage - Each assignment - Notice of Default - Any affidavits - Key correspondence

---

Correspondence Tracking

Track every communication with the servicer:

Phone Call Log

Date/Time	Rep Name & ID	Subject	Outcome	Follow-up
2024-01-15 10:30 AM	Sarah K. (#12345)	Modification status	"Under review"	Call back 1/30

Tips for calls: - Get representative name and ID number - Take notes during the call - Summarize immediately after - Note any promises made - Send confirmation email when possible

Letter Tracking

Date Sent/Received	Type	Subject	Response Due	Status
2024-01-10	RESPA Request	Chain of title	2024-02-09	Pending

Evidence Preparation for Court

Exhibit Preparation

For each exhibit you plan to use:

1. **Mark it:** Use exhibit stickers or write "Exhibit [#]" in the corner
2. **Copy it:** Make three copies (one for you, one for court, one for opposing counsel)
3. **Index it:** Add to your exhibits list

4. **Prepare foundation:** Know how you will authenticate it
5. **Practice with it:** Be able to find any page instantly

Exhibits List

Create a master list:

Exhibit #	Description	Date	Authenticated By	Status
1	Promissory Note	2020-05-15	Borrower	Ready
2	Assignment	2024-02-01	Records custodian	Challenged

Backups and Security

Your case file is irreplaceable. Protect it.

Backup Strategy

Rule of Three: Keep three copies of everything 1. **Primary:** Your working copy 2. **Local backup:** External hard drive or USB drive 3. **Cloud backup:** Encrypted cloud storage

Cloud Storage Options: - Google Drive (encrypt sensitive files) - Dropbox - OneDrive - iCloud - Proton Drive (encrypted)

Security: - Use strong passwords - Enable two-factor authentication - Encrypt sensitive documents - Don't store passwords with the files

Physical Document Security

- Keep originals in fireproof safe
- Make copies for working files
- Don't mark up originals
- Consider safe deposit box for critical originals

Learn From Our Mistake

The Scattered File Disaster

Patricia Williams had boxes of documents. When she was served with foreclosure, she knew she had proof of payments — but she couldn't find it. During discovery, the bank demanded her financial records. She spent three weekends digging through boxes, finding some documents but not others. At her deposition, she couldn't produce complete records. The bank's attorney used this to argue she was hiding something. If Patricia had organized her files from day one, she could have responded quickly and completely.

Lesson: Organization isn't just about convenience — it's about credibility. When you can't produce documents, it looks like you're hiding something, even if you're just disorganized.

The Lost Document Crisis

David Rodriguez found a smoking gun — an assignment dated after the complaint was filed. He put it "somewhere safe" and kept fighting. Six months later, at summary judgment, he wanted to use it. He couldn't find it. He remembered having it. He remembered what it said. But he couldn't produce it. The court disregarded his claim. By the time he found it in a box in his garage, the deadline had passed.

Lesson: Safe places are often forgotten places. Use your indexing system. Know where everything is at all times.

The Trial Day Panic

Michelle Chen was ready for trial. She had her arguments prepared. She knew her facts. But she had never organized her trial notebook. When the judge asked to see the promissory note, she had to dig through three binders while the court waited. When she wanted to impeach the bank's witness with a prior statement, she couldn't find it. Her disorganization made her look unprepared and undermined her credibility.

Lesson: Trial day is not the day to organize. Your trial notebook should be ready days before, and you should know every document in it.

Technology Tools for Organization

Spreadsheet Software

Use Excel, Google Sheets, or similar for: - Document index - Deadline tracking - Financial calculations - Correspondence log - Witness list

Benefits: - Sortable - Searchable - Can add formulas for calculations - Can link to documents

PDF Management

Adobe Acrobat (paid) or free alternatives: - Combine multiple documents - Add Bates numbering - Redact sensitive information - Add bookmarks - Search text

Free alternatives: - PDFtk (command line) - PDFsam (PDF Split and Merge) - Smallpdf.com (web-based)

Note-Taking Apps

For research and notes: - Microsoft OneNote - Evernote - Notion - Apple Notes - Google Keep

Benefits: - Search across all notes - Add tags for organization - Include images and attachments - Sync across devices

Document Scanning

Turn paper into digital: - Scanner apps (Adobe Scan, CamScanner) - Flatbed scanners - Document feeders

Tips: - Scan at 300 DPI minimum - Use searchable PDF (OCR) - Name files immediately - Back up immediately

---

Working with Discovery Productions

When the Bank Produces Documents

Step 1: Inventory - Create a list of what was produced - Note Bates numbers - Check for completeness

Step 2: Organize - Integrate into your file structure - Add to document index - Note production date and method

Step 3: Review - Read every page (or have AI help summarize) - Flag important documents - Note inconsistencies - Look for missing documents

Step 4: Analyze - Complete document analysis worksheets - Compare to your documents - Identify contradictions - Prepare for use

---

Checklists

Weekly Organization Checklist

- ☐ File any new documents received
- ☐ Update document index
- ☐ Log any phone calls
- ☐ Update calendar with new deadlines
- ☐ Review upcoming deadlines (next 30 days)
- ☐ Back up digital files
- ☐ Check for any unfiled papers

Pre-Hearing Checklist

- ☐ Create trial notebook
- ☐ Copy all exhibits (3 sets)
- ☐ Mark exhibits
- ☐ Prepare exhibits list
- ☐ Print relevant rules/cases
- ☐ Prepare opening/closing notes
- ☐ Pack supplies (pens, paper, water)
- ☐ Confirm court date, time, location
- ☐ Arrange transportation/parking
- ☐ Get good sleep

Chapter Summary

Organization is a strategic advantage.

Master file structure: - Case Administration - Loan Documents - Chain of Title - Correspondence - Financial Records - Court Filings - Evidence and Research - Modification/Settlement

Digital organization: - Consistent folder structure - Standardized file naming - Regular backups (3 copies) - Security measures

Key systems: - Document index spreadsheet - Document analysis worksheets - Correspondence tracking - Trial notebook

Technology tools: - Spreadsheets for tracking - PDF management - Note-taking apps - Scanning apps

Remember: The bank has teams of people managing their case file. You are one person. Good organization levels the playing field. When you can find any document in seconds, when you walk into court prepared, when you never miss a deadline — you show the court you're serious. Organization isn't just paperwork. It's power.

Cross-References

- **Chapter 5:** The Complete Document Inventory — identifying what you have
- **Chapter 10:** Drafting the Answer — creating your first court filing
- **Chapter 12:** Discovery Warfare — managing discovery documents
- **Chapter 17:** Trial Preparation — building your trial notebook
- **Chapter 32:** AI Usage — using AI to help organize and analyze

---

End of Chapter 33

CHAPTER 34: FIGHTING THE EVICTION AFTER SALE

Staying in Your Home After the Gavel Falls

The Sale Is Over — Now What?

The foreclosure sale has happened. Someone — usually the bank, sometimes a third-party buyer — now holds title to your home. The foreclosure judgment is entered or affirmed. The fight to stop the foreclosure itself may be over.

But you are still in the home. And that means the battleground has shifted. The new owner cannot simply change the locks or remove your belongings. They must follow a formal eviction process. In most states, that means filing an unlawful detainer action (also called an ejectment or forcible entry and detainer suit) and obtaining a court order before you can be removed.

That process takes time — and it creates new opportunities to fight, negotiate, and delay. This chapter is your post-sale survival playbook. It covers how the eviction process works, what defenses you still have, how to buy time, and how to negotiate the best possible exit if staying permanently is no longer realistic.

You are not homeless the moment the sale gavel drops. Use the time the law gives you wisely.

Understanding the Eviction Timeline

What Happens After the Sale

Step 1: Sale Confirmation - In many states, the sale must be confirmed by the court (ratification) - This can take 10-30 days or longer - Title does not fully pass until confirmation - Some states allow objections to the sale during this window

Step 2: Issuance of Title or Deed - Once confirmed, the trustee or court issues a deed to the purchaser - The purchaser records the deed in the land records - You may receive a formal notice of ownership change

Step 3: Demand for Possession - The new owner (or their attorney) sends a written demand to vacate - This is required in most states before an eviction suit can be filed - The notice typically gives 3-30 days to leave voluntarily

Step 4: Unlawful Detainer / Eviction Filing - If you do not vacate, the new owner files an eviction lawsuit - This is a separate legal action from the foreclosure - You must be properly served with the summons and complaint - You have a limited time to respond (typically 5-10 days)

Step 5: Court Hearing - The court schedules a hearing, often within 2-4 weeks - Both sides present evidence - The judge decides whether to order eviction

Step 6: Writ of Possession / Execution - If the new owner wins, the court issues a writ of possession - This authorizes law enforcement (sheriff or marshal) to remove you - You typically get 24-72 hours after the writ is posted before physical removal

Typical Timeline from Sale to Removal

Stage	Typical Duration	Your Opportunity
Sale to confirmation	10-30 days	Object to sale, negotiate
Confirmation to demand	7-14 days	Prepare defenses, contact attorney
Demand to eviction filing	3-30 days	Respond to demand, begin negotiation
Filing to hearing	2-6 weeks	File answer, build defense, request discovery
Hearing to writ issuance	1-4 weeks	Appeal ruling, negotiate stay
Writ to physical removal	24-72 hours	Final packing, voluntary departure
Total typical time	**2-5 months**	**Multiple intervention points**

Key insight: Even after sale, you typically have 60-150 days before physical removal — longer if you fight effectively.

Defenses to Post-Foreclosure Eviction

The New Owner's Standing Problem

Just because someone bought your home at auction does not automatically mean they can evict you. The new owner must prove they have the legal right to possession.

Challenging the new owner's title: - Was the foreclosure sale properly conducted? - Was the foreclosure judgment final and non-appealable? - Does the purchaser hold a valid, recorded deed? - Was the sale price so grossly inadequate that it shocks the conscience? - Were there irregularities in the sale process?

If the new owner cannot prove clean title, they may not be able to evict you. This is especially powerful if: - The foreclosure was wrongful or void - There are outstanding appeals - The sale was not properly noticed - The purchaser is a straw buyer with no real interest

The "Tenant" Defense: You Are Not a Trespasser

In many states, a former homeowner is not treated the same as a random trespasser. You were the lawful owner until the sale. Your possession was lawful. The new owner must prove that your right to possession has terminated.

Key arguments: - You are a "holdover" former owner, not a squatter - The new owner must prove strict compliance with eviction statutes - Any defect in the foreclosure or sale process may void their right to possession - Some states require specific procedures for evicting former owners

Procedural Defenses

Even if the new owner has valid title, they must follow every procedural step perfectly:

Defense	What to Look For
Improper service	Were you personally served? Was service valid under state law?
Defective notice to vacate	Did the demand meet statutory requirements? Was the timing correct?
Failure to comply with local ordinances	Some cities have additional notice or mediation requirements
Wrong court or venue	Was the eviction filed in the proper court?
Incorrect parties	Is the plaintiff actually the record owner?

Defense	What to Look For
Statute of limitations	Has the new owner waited too long to file eviction?

Every defect is a potential delay — and delays create negotiating leverage.

The Motion to Stay Eviction

What Is a Stay?

A stay is a court order that pauses the eviction process. You can request a stay in several circumstances.

Grounds for a Stay

Pending Appeal of the Foreclosure: - If you have appealed the foreclosure judgment, request a stay of the eviction pending appeal - Standard: Likelihood of success on appeal, irreparable harm, balance of equities - Some states automatically stay eviction if an appeal is filed - In others, you must post a bond or meet strict standards

Bankruptcy Automatic Stay: - Filing bankruptcy triggers an automatic stay on all collection actions, including eviction - See detailed discussion below - Even a bankruptcy filed on the eve of eviction can halt the process

Hardship or Emergency: - Some courts will grant a brief stay for extreme hardship - Medical emergency, death in family, severe weather - Not guaranteed, but worth requesting

Administrative Stay: - If you have filed complaints with regulators (CFPB, state AG) that are pending - Some courts will stay eviction pending resolution of regulatory investigation

How to Request a Stay

Step 1: File a motion with the eviction court - Title: "Motion to Stay Writ of Possession" or "Motion to Stay Eviction" - State the legal basis (appeal pending, bankruptcy filed, hardship) - Attach supporting documents (appeal notice, bankruptcy filing, medical records)

Step 2: Request emergency hearing - File a separate request for expedited hearing - Explain the urgency - Some courts have same-day or next-day emergency motion procedures

Step 3: Prepare for the hearing - Be ready to argue why the stay serves justice - Address the balance of hardships (you vs. new owner) - Propose a timeline if the stay is granted

Step 4: Post bond if required - Some stays require posting a bond to protect the new owner - Bond amount varies — sometimes one month's "rent," sometimes higher - If you cannot afford bond, request a bond waiver for indigency

---

Bankruptcy: The Nuclear Option

Chapter 7: The Immediate Stopgap

Filing Chapter 7 bankruptcy triggers the automatic stay immediately.

What it does: - Stops eviction proceedings instantly upon filing - Gives you 2-4 months of additional time in the home - Discharges any deficiency judgment from the foreclosure - Provides a fresh financial start

What it does NOT do: - Save your home permanently (Chapter 7 does not cure mortgage arrears) - Stop eviction if the new owner already has a judgment for possession in some cases - Allow you to reclaim the home once sold

Critical timing rule: - File BEFORE the eviction court enters judgment for possession - Once the eviction judgment is entered, the automatic stay may not help (but still consult a bankruptcy attorney — some courts allow it) - File BEFORE the writ of possession is executed

Chapter 13: Can You Still Save the Home?

Generally, once the foreclosure sale has occurred, Chapter 13 cannot undo it.

However, Chapter 13 may still help if: - The sale has not been confirmed by the court - There are valid grounds to set aside the sale - You file very quickly and can prove the sale was improper

This is a narrow window and requires immediate attorney consultation.

Using Bankruptcy Strategically

Even if you cannot keep the home, Chapter 7 is powerful for:

1. **Stopping imminent eviction:**
    - File the morning of a scheduled eviction
    - Automatic stay halts sheriff's action
    - Gain 30-90 days to relocate
2. **Discharging deficiency:**
    - If foreclosure sale price < judgment amount

    - Bank may pursue you for the shortfall
    - Chapter 7 eliminates this debt entirely
3. **Negotiating cash for keys from strength:**
    - With bankruptcy delaying eviction, bank may negotiate
    - "I can file Chapter 7 and stay 3 more months, or you can pay me $X to leave in 30 days"

Warning: Bankruptcy is serious. It affects your credit for 7-10 years. Do not file casually. Consult a bankruptcy attorney.

Cash for Keys: Negotiating Your Exit

What Is Cash for Keys?

Cash for keys is a voluntary agreement: You agree to vacate the property by a specific date, leaving it clean and in good condition, and the new owner pays you a lump sum.

Why the New Owner Will Pay You to Leave

Eviction is expensive and uncertain: - Attorney fees: $2,000-$5,000+ - Court costs and filing fees - Time delay (2-6 months in contested eviction) - Property damage risk from angry homeowner - Uncertainty of outcome - Cost of sheriff enforcement

Cash for keys is often cheaper and faster for the bank.

How to Negotiate

Step 1: Contact the new owner or their attorney - "I understand you now hold title. I'm willing to discuss a voluntary departure." - Stay calm and professional - Do not threaten — offer a mutually beneficial solution

Step 2: Propose specific terms - Amount: $2,000-$10,000+ depending on property value and your leverage - Move-out date: 30-90 days from agreement - Condition: Broom-clean, no damage, all personal property removed - Utilities: Current through move-out date

Step 3: Create leverage - Mention valid defenses you could raise in eviction - Note any appeals or complaints pending - Point out condition issues or repair needs - Be prepared to actually fight eviction if they refuse

Step 4: Get EVERYTHING in writing - Signed settlement agreement - Specifies amount, payment method, and timing - Specifies move-out date and condition requirements - Release of claims by both parties - File with the eviction court if suit has been filed

Sample Cash for Keys Letter

```
Dear [New Owner / Attorney],

I understand that [Purchaser Name] is now the record owner of the property at [A

I am willing to voluntarily vacate the premises and deliver possession in a clea
typically 30-60 days out], provided that [Purchaser Name] pays me $[Amount] as r

This arrangement would save both parties the time, expense, and uncertainty of e

If we can reach agreement, I propose that the settlement be documented in a writ

Please let me know if you are interested in discussing this further.

Sincerely,
[Your Name]
```

Learn From This Mistake

The "I'll Just Wait for the Sheriff" Error

Marcus Johnson believed that once the foreclosure sale happened, he had no rights. When the bank's attorney sent a three-day notice to vacate, he packed a bag and slept in his car the next night. He abandoned thousands of dollars in furniture, appliances, and personal documents. He later learned he could have stayed 90+ days, negotiated cash for keys, and planned an orderly move. His panic cost him his belongings and his dignity.

Lesson: You have legal rights after sale. Do not abandon your home until you understand the timeline and your options. The sheriff will not arrive tomorrow.

The Bankruptcy Timing Disaster

Angela Ruiz waited until the sheriff posted the 24-hour notice on her door to call a bankruptcy attorney. She filed Chapter 7 that afternoon, but the eviction court had already entered the judgment for possession the day before. The bankruptcy stay was lifted for the eviction proceeding, and the sheriff returned 48 hours later. If she had filed even one day earlier — before the eviction judgment was entered — she would have gained months.

Lesson: Bankruptcy must be filed BEFORE the eviction judgment for possession is entered.

Once that judgment exists, the automatic stay may not protect you. Act early, not at the last minute.

The Unsigned Agreement Trap

Tom Bradley negotiated verbally with the bank's representative for $4,000 to vacate in 45 days. He moved out on time, left the property spotless, and waited for his check. It never came. The representative had moved to another department. There was no written record of the agreement. The bank denied any knowledge. Tom had no recourse.

Lesson: Never, ever rely on a verbal agreement in foreclosure or eviction. Get every term in writing, signed by an authorized representative, and ideally filed with the court. An oral promise from a bank representative is worth exactly the paper it's printed on.

State-Specific Post-Sale Protections

Redemption Periods

Some states allow you to reclaim your home after foreclosure by paying the full sale price plus costs:

State	Redemption Period	Notes
Alabama	12 months	Must pay full sale price + interest
Illinois	7 months (residential)	Or 3 months if abandoned
Iowa	12 months	Very homeowner-friendly
Minnesota	6 months	Judicial foreclosure only
Montana	12 months	Unless waived in mortgage
North Dakota	60 days	Short but exists
South Dakota	60 days-1 year	Varies by county
Wisconsin	12 months	Strong redemption right
Wyoming	3 months	Judicial foreclosure

If your state has a redemption period: - You generally can remain in the home during the redemption period - The purchaser cannot evict you during this time - You have the right to redeem by paying the full amount - This is rare in practice (most homeowners cannot raise the funds) but powerful as a defense

Tenants' Rights for Former Owners

Some jurisdictions treat former owners as tenants with specific protections: - **Just Cause Eviction Ordinances:** Some cities require "just cause" for eviction, even by a new owner - **Relocation Assistance:** Some jurisdictions require the new owner to pay relocation assistance - **Notice Requirements:** Extended notice periods (30-90 days) before eviction can proceed - **Mediation Programs:** Some courts require mediation before an eviction hearing

Research your local ordinances. City and county protections may exceed state law.

Emergency Tactics to Buy Time

The Motion to Dismiss Eviction

File a motion to dismiss the unlawful detainer complaint if: - The plaintiff lacks standing (does not own the property) - The complaint fails to state a cause of action - Service was defective - The foreclosure judgment is not final (appeal pending)

This can delay the hearing 2-8 weeks while the court rules on the motion.

Request for Jury Trial

In some states, you have the right to demand a jury trial in an eviction proceeding: - Must be requested promptly (often within days of filing answer) - Jury trials take much longer to schedule than bench trials - Can add 1-3 months to the timeline - The threat of a jury trial may motivate the new owner to settle

Discovery in Eviction

Most homeowners do not use discovery in eviction proceedings. You should.

Requests you can make: - Proof of title — demand the deed and chain of title - Proof of sale compliance — was the sale properly noticed and conducted? - Financial records — if claiming you owe "rent" for holdover period, demand accounting - Communications — any emails or letters about the sale

Discovery delays the hearing and may reveal defects in the new owner's case.

Bankruptcy Emergency Filing

If eviction is imminent and no other options exist: - Consult a bankruptcy attorney immediately - A "skeleton" Chapter 7 can be filed in 24-48 hours with minimal paperwork -

The automatic stay halts eviction proceedings - You complete the full filing later

This is a last resort, but it works.

Post-Sale Eviction Defense Checklist

Immediate (Within 48 Hours of Sale):

- ☐ Confirm whether your state requires court confirmation of the sale
- ☐ Check whether a redemption period applies
- ☐ Determine whether you received proper notice of the sale
- ☐ Preserve any evidence of sale irregularities
- ☐ Do NOT abandon the property

Upon Receiving Demand to Vacate:

- ☐ Document the date and method of service of the demand
- ☐ Check whether the demand complies with statutory requirements
- ☐ Research local tenant/occupant protections
- ☐ Contact a tenant rights or housing attorney
- ☐ Begin considering settlement/cash for keys options

Upon Being Served with Eviction Suit:

- ☐ Note the response deadline (usually 5-10 days — DO NOT MISS IT)
- ☐ File a written answer — do not default
- ☐ Assert all applicable defenses in your answer
- ☐ Request discovery if available in your jurisdiction
- ☐ Request a jury trial if you have that right
- ☐ File any motion to stay if grounds exist

Throughout the Process:

- ☐ Document all communications with the new owner
- ☐ Keep paying utilities if possible (avoid shutoff complications)
- ☐ Maintain the property (avoid claims of damage)
- ☐ Continue negotiating cash for keys in parallel with defense
- ☐ Consider bankruptcy if eviction is imminent and no other options exist

Final 72 Hours:

- ☐ If writ of possession is issued, confirm the exact execution date
- ☐ Pack and remove all valuable personal property
- ☐ Document property condition with photos/video
- ☐ Secure a place to stay
- ☐ Leave the property clean to avoid claims for damages

Chapter Summary

The foreclosure sale is not the end of the fight. You have rights, time, and leverage even after the gavel falls.

The eviction timeline: - Sale to physical removal: typically 2-5 months - Multiple stages where you can intervene - Each stage creates negotiating leverage

Defenses to post-foreclosure eviction: - New owner's standing and title defects - Procedural errors in the eviction filing - State redemption periods - Local tenant protections

The motion to stay: - Request a stay based on pending appeals, bankruptcy, or hardship - Post bond if required, or request indigency waiver - Emergency hearings may be available

Bankruptcy as stopgap: - Chapter 7 automatic stay halts eviction if filed before eviction judgment - Discharges deficiency judgments - Buys 2-4 months for orderly transition - Must be filed before eviction judgment for possession is entered

Cash for keys: - Voluntary departure in exchange for payment - Often cheaper for the new owner than eviction litigation - Negotiate from strength, not desperation - Get EVERYTHING in writing, signed, and filed

Emergency tactics: - Motion to dismiss eviction complaint - Demand for jury trial - Discovery to delay and expose defects - Emergency bankruptcy filing

Key principle: The new owner wants you out quickly and cheaply. You want time and a dignified exit. Every day you lawfully remain in the home is leverage. Use that time to negotiate, defend, and plan — not to panic.

Cross-References

- **Chapter 30:** Sale Scheduled — emergency tactics before the sale
- **Chapter 31:** Action Plan — After Judgment — post-judgment motions and appeals

- **Chapter 19:** Bankruptcy — detailed bankruptcy strategies
- **Chapter 35:** Appeals Process — preserving and pursuing appeals
- **Chapter 36:** Emergency Procedures — last-resort tactics

End of Chapter 34

CHAPTER 35: THE APPEALS PROCESS

When and How to Challenge an Adverse Decision

Understanding Appeals

An appeal is not a do-over. It is not a chance to present new evidence, retry the case, or argue facts differently. An appeal asks a higher court to review whether the trial court made legal errors that affected the outcome.

What an appeal can do: - Correct legal errors (wrong legal standard, improper evidence admission) - Reverse decisions where the law was misapplied - Order a new trial if errors warrant it - Clarify legal standards for future cases

What an appeal cannot do: - Introduce new evidence - Re-argue facts the trial court already decided - Change findings of witness credibility - Guarantee a different outcome

The standard of review: Appeals courts give deference to trial courts. They will not reverse a decision just because they might have decided differently. They reverse when the trial court made a clear legal error.

Should You Appeal?

The Decision Framework

Appealing is expensive, time-consuming, and uncertain. Before you commit, answer these questions honestly:

Question 1: Is the error preserved? - Did you object at trial? - Is the issue in the trial record? - Unpreserved errors are usually waived

Question 2: Is the error significant? - Did it affect the outcome? - Technical errors that didn't change the result won't get reversal - The error must be "harmful" or "prejudicial"

Question 3: Can you afford it? - Appeal filing fees ($200-500) - Transcript costs ($2-5 per page, often 500+ pages) - Attorney fees (if represented) - Your time (months of work)

Question 4: What is the likely outcome? - Strong legal error with clear precedent = better chance - Weak error or fact-based disagreement = low chance - Most appeals are unsuccessful

Question 5: What is the goal? - Reverse the judgment? - Delay the sale? - Preserve the issue for higher appeal? - Make case law?

When to Appeal

Appeal when: - Clear legal error affected the outcome - Judge applied wrong legal standard - Evidence was admitted that should have been excluded - Your argument has strong precedential support - You can afford the process

Don't appeal when: - You simply disagree with factual findings - The judge believed the bank's witness over you - The error is technical and didn't change the outcome - You cannot afford transcript costs - You have no preserved legal issues

---

The Appeals Timeline

Critical Deadlines

Notice of Appeal: - Usually 30 days from final judgment - Some jurisdictions: 10 days for certain orders - Federal court: 30 days (or 60 days if government party)

This deadline is jurisdictional. Miss it, and you cannot appeal. No excuses. No extensions (usually).

Post-Judgment Motions: - Motion for reconsideration: Usually 10-30 days - Motion for new trial: Usually 10-30 days - Motion to alter/judgment: Varies by jurisdiction

Filing a post-judgment motion often extends the appeal deadline. But verify your local rules — some motions don't extend the deadline.

Appeals Process Overview

Stage	Timeline	Action
Judgment	Day 1	Final judgment entered
Notice of Appeal	Days 1-30	File notice (CRITICAL)
Record Preparation	Days 30-90	Assemble trial record
Transcript Order	Days 30-60	Order and pay for transcript
Briefing Schedule	Set by court	Usually 30-60 days per brief
Opening Brief	Per schedule	File appellant's brief
Response Brief	Per schedule	File appellee's brief
Reply Brief	Per schedule	Optional reply by appellant
Oral Argument	Scheduled	15-30 minutes typically

Stage	Timeline	Action
Decision	Months later	Written opinion issued

Total time: 6 months to 2+ years

Preparing the Appeal

Step 1: File the Notice of Appeal

The notice of appeal is a simple form, but it is the most critical document.

What it includes: - Case caption - Judgment being appealed - Date of judgment - What you're appealing from - Signature

Where to file: - Usually the trial court clerk - Some jurisdictions: appellate court clerk - Always file in person or certified mail

Tips: - File early — don't wait until day 30 - File stamped copy for your records - Serve on opposing counsel - Verify filing fee

Step 2: Order the Transcript

The transcript is the verbatim record of what happened in court. It is expensive but essential.

What to order: - All hearings on dispositive motions - The trial (if there was one) - Any hearing where the error occurred - Be selective — transcripts are costly

Cost: - $2-5 per page - Typical hearing: 50-100 pages ($100-500) - Full trial: 500-1000+ pages ($1,000-5,000+)

Timeline: - Court reporters have deadlines (30-90 days) - You must order and pay in advance - Extensions may be available for good cause

Step 3: Prepare the Record on Appeal

The record on appeal includes: - Notice of appeal - All pleadings filed - All motions and orders - Trial transcript - Exhibits admitted - Relevant correspondence

Clerk assembles the record in most jurisdictions. You must designate what to include.

Tips: - Review the record when assembled - Make sure critical documents are included - Object if something is missing

---

Writing the Appeal Brief

Structure of an Appeal Brief

Appellant's Brief (you, if appealing):

Section	Content	Typical Length
Cover	Case caption, parties, court	1 page
Table of Contents	Section listing with page numbers	1-2 pages
Table of Authorities	Cases, statutes, rules cited	1-3 pages
Statement of Jurisdiction	Why appellate court can hear case	1-2 pages
Standard of Review	How court should review each issue	1-2 pages
Statement of Facts	Facts from record supporting your case	5-10 pages
Summary of Argument	Preview of your legal arguments	2-3 pages
Argument	Legal arguments with citations	15-30 pages
Conclusion	What you want court to do	1 page

Total: Usually 30-50 pages

Writing Tips

Statement of Facts: - Must be supported by record citations - Cite to transcript page numbers - Be accurate — opposing counsel will check - Present facts favorably but honestly - Don't argue in facts section

Argument Section: - Organize by issue - Each issue: thesis sentence, legal support, application - Lead with strongest argument - Address weaknesses honestly - Use headings and subheadings

Common Mistakes: - Arguing facts instead of law - Not citing the record - Raising new issues not preserved - Ignoring unfavorable precedent - Being too emotional or argumentative

---

Standards of Review

The standard of review determines how much deference the appellate court gives the trial court:

De Novo Review

Standard: No deference. Appellate court reviews from scratch.

Applies to: - Pure questions of law - Legal interpretations - Constitutional issues - Summary judgment rulings

Your advantage: Best chance of reversal

Abuse of Discretion

Standard: Trial court's decision stands unless clearly wrong.

Applies to: - Evidentiary rulings - Discovery decisions - Scheduling matters - Procedural issues

Your challenge: Hard to win

Clear Error

Standard: Findings of fact stand unless clearly erroneous.

Applies to: - Witness credibility determinations - Factual findings by judge - Jury verdicts

Your challenge: Very hard to win — appellate courts defer to trial courts on facts

Substantial Evidence

Standard: Was there enough evidence to support the finding?

Applies to: - Administrative decisions - Some factual determinations

Your challenge: Must show no reasonable factfinder could have reached that conclusion

---

Pro Se Appeals

The Reality of Pro Se Appeals

Appeals are harder than trial court for pro se litigants because: - Strict procedural rules - Legal writing requirements - Technical standards - Limited court assistance - Sophisticated opposing counsel

But pro se appeals can succeed when: - Clear legal error exists - Issues are well-preserved - Brief is well-written - Argument is focused

Resources for Pro Se Appellants

Many appellate courts offer: - Pro se handbooks - Form briefs - Self-help centers - Limited scope representation

Check your appellate court's website. Look for: - Pro se litigant guide - Brief formatting requirements - Filing procedures - Local rules

Getting Help

Limited scope representation: - Hire attorney just to write brief - Hire attorney just for oral argument - Hire attorney as consultant

Legal aid: - Some organizations handle appeals - Bar association pro bono programs - Law school clinics

---

Learn From Our Mistake

The Late Notice Disaster

Thomas Anderson lost his foreclosure case. He intended to appeal. He thought he had 30 days from the order denying his post-judgment motion. He was wrong. The appeal clock started from the original judgment. His post-judgment motion didn't extend the deadline. By the time he figured this out, the 30 days had passed. His notice of appeal was dismissed for lack of jurisdiction. He had strong arguments — clear legal error by the trial judge. But he missed the deadline. Case over.

Lesson: Verify your appeal deadline with absolute certainty. When in doubt, file early. Never assume post-judgment motions extend deadlines.

The Unpreserved Error

Jennifer Martinez believed the trial judge made a huge error by allowing the bank's affidavit into evidence. She never objected at trial. She never argued it was inadmissible. On appeal, she raised the issue for the first time. The appellate court refused to consider it. "The issue is not preserved for review," they wrote. Even though the error might have changed the outcome, she waived it by not raising it below.

Lesson: If you don't object at trial, you usually can't complain on appeal. Preserve every issue you might want to appeal.

The Pro Se Brief Failure

David Chen filed his appeal pro se. He wrote a 100-page brief that was mostly emotional argument about how unfair the bank was. He didn't cite the record properly. He didn't address the standard of review. He didn't distinguish unfavorable cases. The appellate court gave his brief little weight. The bank's attorney wrote a professional response. David lost. His valid legal issues were buried in poor presentation.

Lesson: Appeal briefs have strict requirements. Poor writing undermines good arguments. Consider getting help, even limited scope.

Alternative to Appeal: Post-Judgment Relief

Before You Appeal, Consider:

Motion for Reconsideration: - Asks trial judge to reconsider decision - Usually must show changed circumstances or legal error - Quick and inexpensive - Rarely granted, but worth trying

Motion to Vacate/Default: - For default judgments - Must show excusable neglect - Must have meritorious defense - Time limits are strict

Motion for New Trial: - Errors occurred that affected outcome - New evidence discovered - Juror misconduct (if jury trial) - Short deadline (usually 10-30 days)

Bankruptcy: - Chapter 13 can stop sale even after judgment - Must file before sale occurs - Automatic stay halts proceedings - See Chapter 20

Appeal Costs and Practicalities

Cost Breakdown

Item	Typical Cost	Notes
Filing Fee	$200-500	Required to file notice
Transcript	$1,000-5,000+	Depends on length
Printing/Binding	$100-300	Multiple copies required
Attorney (if used)	$5,000-25,000+	Varies widely
Total Pro Se	**$1,500-6,000+**	Without attorney
Total With Attorney	**$10,000-30,000+**	Full representation

Timeline Reality

Civil appeals take time: - Fast track: 6-12 months - Standard: 12-18 months - Complex: 18-36 months

During this time: - Sale may be scheduled - Stay may be requested - Bankruptcy may be needed - Settlement remains possible

Requesting a Stay

If sale is scheduled during appeal: - File motion to stay sale - Post bond (often required) - Show likelihood of success on appeal - Show irreparable harm

Without a stay, the sale proceeds even during appeal.

Chapter Summary

Appeals correct legal errors, not factual disputes.

Before appealing, ask: - Is the error preserved? - Is it significant? - Can I afford it? - What is the likely outcome?

Critical deadlines: - Notice of Appeal: Usually 30 days (jurisdictional!) - Transcript order: Usually 30-60 days - Briefing: Per court schedule

Appeals process: 1. File notice of appeal 2. Order transcript 3. Assemble record 4. Write briefs 5. Oral argument 6. Await decision

Standards of review: - De novo: Best chance (legal questions) - Abuse of discretion: Hard (evidentiary rulings) - Clear error: Very hard (factual findings)

Pro se appeals: - Possible but difficult - Use court resources - Consider limited scope help - Follow all formatting rules

Alternatives to appeal: - Motion for reconsideration - Motion for new trial - Motion to vacate - Bankruptcy (to stop sale)

Remember: Most appeals lose. The trial court's findings get deference. Only appeal when you have a clear, preserved legal error that affected the outcome. If you appeal, do it right — file on time, order transcripts, write a professional brief. And always have a Plan B, because even good appeals often fail.

Cross-References

- **Chapter 16:** Summary Judgment Survival — preserving issues for appeal
- **Chapter 17:** Trial Preparation — making proper objections
- **Chapter 20:** Bankruptcy — stopping sale during/after appeal
- **Chapter 31:** Action Plan — After Judgment — post-judgment options

---

End of Chapter 35

CHAPTER 36: AFTER THE CASE

Rebuilding Your Life When It's Over

The Case Is Over. Now What?

Whether you won, lost, or settled, the foreclosure case will eventually end. When it does, you face a new challenge: rebuilding your life. This chapter is about what comes next — the practical, financial, and emotional steps to move forward.

This chapter applies to everyone: - **If you won:** Keeping your home and protecting your victory - **If you lost:** Recovering and planning your next chapter - **If you settled:** Honoring the agreement and moving forward

The foreclosure case was a battle. This chapter is about the peace that follows — and how to make it lasting.

If You Won Your Case

Securing Your Victory

A dismissal is not the end — it's the beginning of vigilance.

Immediate steps: 1. **Get the dismissal in writing** - Court order dismissing the case - Record it if required in your jurisdiction - Keep certified copies

2. **Check your credit report**
   - The foreclosure should be removed
   - Dispute any inaccurate reporting
   - Document your victory for credit bureaus
3. **Ensure loan servicer records are updated**
   - Confirm they show loan current (if applicable)
   - Request written confirmation
   - Keep all correspondence
4. **Verify property title is clear**
   - Check for any lis pendens or notices
   - Ensure dismissal removed any cloud on title
   - Consider title insurance

Preventing Future Problems

The bank may try again: - Watch for new default notices - Monitor your account closely - Keep detailed payment records - Respond immediately to any correspondence

If the bank appeals: - Consult an attorney immediately - Preserve your appellate options - Continue monitoring the case - Don't assume victory is final

Document everything going forward: - Every payment - Every servicer communication - Every statement - Your victory taught you the importance of records

The Emotional Aftermath of Winning

Winning doesn't erase the trauma. Many homeowners who win their cases still struggle with: - Anxiety about the future - Distrust of financial institutions - Hypervigilance about mail and calls - Relationship strain from the ordeal

It's okay to seek help: - Counseling or therapy - Support groups for foreclosure survivors - Financial counseling to rebuild security - Time to process what happened

Protecting your peace: - Set up automatic payments - Build an emergency fund - Consider refinancing when eligible - Create systems so this never happens again

---

If You Lost Your Case

Accepting the Outcome

Losing your home is a grief process. It is a loss — of security, of memories, of a future you imagined. Allow yourself to grieve.

The stages of foreclosure grief: 1. **Denial:** "This can't be happening" 2. **Anger:** At the bank, the system, yourself 3. **Bargaining:** "If only I had…" 4. **Depression:** Feeling hopeless 5. **Acceptance:** Finding a path forward

You may cycle through these stages multiple times. That's normal.

Immediate Practical Steps

If a sale has occurred:

Step 1: Understand the timeline - How long until you must vacate? - Is there a redemption period? - Can you negotiate additional time?

Step 2: Secure your belongings - Start packing non-essentials - Document your property with photos - Consider what to keep, sell, donate - Protect important documents

Step 3: Arrange your next residence - Rental applications (be honest about foreclosure) - Temporary housing if needed - Storage for belongings - Forward your mail

Step 4: Address the financial aftermath - Deficiency judgment (discussed below) - Tax consequences (1099-C, cancellation of debt) - Utility transfers and deposits - Security deposits for new housing

Deficiency Judgments

What is a deficiency judgment?

If your home sells for less than you owed, the bank may sue you for the difference.

Example: - You owed: $300,000 - Property sold for: $250,000 - Deficiency: $50,000

States vary on deficiency judgments: - **Non-recourse states:** Bank cannot pursue deficiency - **Recourse states:** Bank can sue for deficiency - **Anti-deficiency laws:** Some states protect primary residences

If you face a deficiency judgment: 1. **Check your state's law** - Is your loan non-recourse? - Did the bank comply with procedural requirements? - Are there time limits on filing?

2. **Negotiate a settlement**
   - Banks often accept less than full amount
   - Lump sum vs. payment plan
   - Get agreement in writing
3. **Consider bankruptcy**
   - Chapter 7 can discharge deficiency debt
   - Timing matters — consult attorney
4. **Challenge the amount**
   - Was the sale properly noticed?
   - Was sale price commercially reasonable?
   - Were fees and costs legitimate?

Tax Consequences

Cancellation of Debt Income:

If the bank forgives debt (through short sale, deed in lieu, or deficiency waiver), the IRS may treat it as taxable income.

Example: - Bank forgives $50,000 deficiency - You receive 1099-C for $50,000 - You may owe taxes on this "income"

Exceptions that may protect you: - Insolvency (debts exceed assets) - Bankruptcy discharge - Qualified principal residence exclusion (if still available) - Mortgage Forgiveness Debt Relief Act provisions

You MUST consult a tax professional. This area is complex and penalties for mistakes are severe.

If You Settled Your Case

Understanding Your Settlement

Settlement agreements are contracts. You must understand and comply with every term.

Common settlement terms: - Loan modification with specific terms - Short sale with deficiency waiver - Deed in lieu with specific conditions - Cash for keys agreement - Timeline for vacating

Read every word: - What are your obligations? - What are the bank's obligations? - What happens if either party breaches? - Are there confidentiality provisions?

Complying with the Agreement

Your responsibilities: - Make modification payments on time, every time - Meet deadlines for short sale or move-out - Maintain property condition if required - Provide requested documentation

Document your compliance: - Keep proof of every payment - Keep copies of all correspondence - Note deadlines and confirm they're met - Take photos if property condition is required

If the bank breaches: - Document the breach - Send written notice - Consult an attorney about enforcement - Don't assume you can just stop performing

---

Rebuilding Your Financial Life

Credit Recovery

Foreclosure devastates credit. But recovery is possible.

Timeline expectations: - Foreclosure remains on credit report: 7 years - Impact lessens over time - New positive history helps offset - Full recovery: 3-7 years with good behavior

Steps to rebuild:

1. Check your credit reports - Get free reports from all three bureaus - Dispute any inaccuracies - Ensure foreclosure is reported correctly

2. Establish new credit carefully - Secured credit card - Credit-builder loan - Become authorized user on someone else's card - Avoid predatory lenders

3. Pay all bills on time - Rent payments (use services that report to credit) - Utilities - Any remaining debts - New credit obligations

4. Keep credit utilization low - Below 30% of limit - Below 10% is even better - Pay in full each month

5. Be patient - Credit rebuilding takes time - There are no quick fixes - Consistency wins

Housing After Foreclosure

Renting with a foreclosure:

Be honest: - Many landlords will work with you - Explain the circumstances - Show your current stability - Offer larger security deposit

What landlords look for: - Current income (3x rent is standard) - Stable employment - No recent evictions - References

Consider: - Private landlords (more flexible than corporations) - Smaller properties - Renting from friends or family temporarily - Roommates to reduce cost

Buying again:

Waiting periods: - Conventional loans: 7 years (3 years with extenuating circumstances) - FHA loans: 3 years - VA loans: 2 years - USDA loans: 3 years

Start preparing now: - Save for down payment - Rebuild credit - Document income - Avoid new debt

Building Financial Resilience

Emergency fund: - 3-6 months of expenses - Start with $1,000 if that's all you can do - Build gradually - Keep it accessible but separate

Budget discipline: - Track every dollar - Prioritize necessities - Build in savings - Avoid lifestyle inflation

Insurance protection: - Health insurance - Disability insurance (if available) - Renter's insurance (protects belongings) - Life insurance (if you have dependents)

The Emotional Journey Forward

Dealing with Shame and Stigma

Foreclosure is not a moral failing. It is a financial event that happens to millions of people — including successful, hardworking people.

Causes of foreclosure are often beyond control: - Job loss or income reduction - Medical emergencies - Divorce - Economic downturn - Predatory lending

You are not alone: - Millions of homeowners have faced foreclosure - Many have rebuilt and thrived - Your worth is not your credit score - This chapter does not define your story

Finding Support

Professional help: - Therapist or counselor - Financial advisor - Credit counselor (non-profit only) - Career counselor

Support groups: - Online communities for foreclosure survivors - Financial recovery groups - Housing counseling agencies

Personal support: - Family who understand - Friends who don't judge - Mentors who have rebuilt

Creating a New Vision

The home you lost was a place. Home is also a feeling, a community, a sense of security you can rebuild anywhere.

Questions to consider: - What did you love about that home? - How can you create that feeling elsewhere? - What new opportunities does this change create? - What have you learned about what truly matters?

Moving forward: - Set new goals - Create new routines - Build new memories - Find new sources of joy

---

Learn From Our Mistake

The Victory Not Secured

Margaret Chen won her foreclosure case. The judge dismissed the complaint for lack of standing. Margaret celebrated and moved on. Six months later, she received a new default notice — the bank had fixed the standing issue and was foreclosing again. She hadn't monitored her account. She hadn't gotten the servicer to update their records. She had to fight all over again, this time with fewer resources because she thought it was over.

Lesson: A dismissal is not permanent protection. Stay vigilant. Monitor your account. Keep records. Be ready to respond if the bank tries again.

The Deficiency Surprise

Robert Williams lost his home to foreclosure. He moved out, found an apartment, and was rebuilding. Two years later, he was sued for a $75,000 deficiency judgment. He didn't know his state allowed deficiency judgments. He didn't know the bank could come after him. He didn't respond to the lawsuit and got a default judgment. Now his wages are being garnished.

Lesson: Understand whether you face deficiency liability. Don't ignore legal papers. Address the issue head-on, even if you've already lost the home.

The Tax Time Bomb

Lisa Rodriguez completed a short sale with deficiency forgiveness. She was relieved — no more mortgage debt. The next January, she received a 1099-C showing $80,000 in canceled debt. She didn't know this might be taxable income. She didn't file the proper forms. Now she owes the IRS $20,000 in taxes and penalties.

Lesson: Debt forgiveness can trigger tax consequences. Consult a tax professional before agreeing to any settlement involving debt cancellation. File the proper forms.

Long-Term Recovery Checklist

Month 1-3: Stabilization

- ☐ Secure housing
- ☐ Address immediate financial crises
- ☐ Gather all case documents
- ☐ Check credit reports

- ☐ File any necessary tax forms
- ☐ Seek emotional support

Month 4-12: Rebuilding

- ☐ Establish budget and stick to it
- ☐ Build emergency fund ($1,000+)
- ☐ Start rebuilding credit
- ☐ Address any deficiency judgment
- ☐ Secure stable employment if needed
- ☐ Create new routines

Year 2-3: Recovery

- ☐ Maintain perfect payment history
- ☐ Grow emergency fund (3-6 months)
- ☐ Improve credit score significantly
- ☐ Save for future goals
- ☐ Consider homeownership education
- ☐ Help others going through similar situations

Year 4-7: Renewal

- ☐ Qualify for mortgage again (if desired)
- ☐ Achieve financial goals
- ☐ Put the foreclosure firmly in the past
- ☐ Use lessons learned to help others
- ☐ Build lasting financial security

Chapter Summary

The foreclosure case ends, but life continues.

If you won: - Secure your victory in writing - Monitor for future attempts - Rebuild your peace of mind - Stay vigilant

If you lost: - Allow yourself to grieve - Address deficiency judgments - Understand tax consequences - Plan your transition

If you settled: - Understand every term - Comply completely - Document everything - Enforce if the bank breaches

Rebuilding financially: - Credit recovery takes 3-7 years - Start with emergency fund - Use secured credit carefully - Pay everything on time

Rebuilding emotionally: - Foreclosure is not shameful - Seek support - Create new vision for future - Your worth is not your credit score

Remember: This chapter — whether victory, defeat, or settlement — is part of your story, not the end of it. Millions have walked this path and rebuilt. You can too. The lessons you've learned, the strength you've developed, and the knowledge you've gained will serve you for the rest of your life. Take what you've learned, protect your future, and move forward with hope.

Cross-References

- **Chapter 20:** Bankruptcy — options during and after foreclosure
- **Chapter 31:** Action Plan — After Judgment — immediate post-loss steps
- **Chapter 35:** The Appeals Process — if considering appeal

---

End of Chapter 36

CHAPTER 37: RESOURCES AND CONCLUSION

Your Toolkit for the Fight Ahead

You Are Not Alone

If you've read this far, you now understand what most homeowners never learn: The foreclosure system is complex, the banks make mistakes, and you have rights worth fighting for.

You also know this is not easy. The path ahead requires work, persistence, courage, and organization. But it is a path that can be walked. Thousands of homeowners before you have walked it. Some won. Some lost. All fought with dignity.

This final chapter gives you resources: Places to turn for help, tools to use, and people who understand. Keep this chapter accessible. When you're in the middle of the fight and need a phone number, a website, or a reminder that you're not alone — come back here.

Government Resources

Department of Housing and Urban Development (HUD)

HUD-Approved Housing Counselors - **Website:** hud.gov - **Phone:** 1-800-569-4287 - **What they offer:** Free or low-cost counseling, help with modifications, understanding your options - **Why use them:** Legitimate, government-backed, no scams

Making Home Affordable Program - **Website:** makinghomeaffordable.gov (archived but resources still available) - **What it offers:** Information on HAMP, HAFA, and other programs

Consumer Financial Protection Bureau (CFPB)

Website: consumerfinance.gov - **What they offer:** Complaint filing, information on mortgage servicing rules, guides for homeowners - **Phone:** 1-855-411-2372 - **Why use them:** They supervise banks and servicers, track complaints, can help resolve issues

State Attorney General Offices

Every state has an Attorney General who may: - Investigate mortgage fraud - Prosecute robo-signing - Offer homeowner assistance programs - Provide legal information

Find yours: naag.org (National Association of Attorneys General)

State Housing Finance Agencies

Most states have agencies that offer: - Homeowner assistance funds - Foreclosure prevention programs - Legal aid referrals - Counseling services

Find yours: ncsha.org (National Council of State Housing Agencies)

Legal Resources

Legal Aid Organizations

Legal Services Corporation (LSC) - **Website:** lsc.gov - **What they offer:** Free legal help for low-income individuals - **Eligibility:** Income-based, varies by location - **How to find:** Use the LSC website to find your local office

National Legal Aid & Defender Association - **Website:** nlada.org - **Directory of legal aid organizations nationwide**

Bar Association Referral Services

American Bar Association - **Website:** americanbar.org - **Lawyer referral services by state**

Many local bar associations offer: - Reduced-fee panels for modest means clients - Pro bono programs - Limited scope representation

Law School Clinics

Many law schools have clinics that provide: - Free or low-cost legal services - Foreclosure defense representation - Student attorneys supervised by experienced faculty

Find one: Contact law schools in your area

Pro Se Resources by State

Many courts offer resources for self-represented litigants: - Pro se handbooks - Form pleadings - Self-help centers - Law libraries with public access

Check your: - State court website - County court website - Local law library

---

Online Resources and Tools

Document Research

MERS Servicer ID - **Website:** mers-servicerid.com - **What it shows:** Who services your loan, contact information - **Why use it:** Essential for knowing who to contact and serve

County Recorder/Clerk Websites - **What they offer:** Property records, deed searches, lien information - **Why use it:** Verify chain of title, find recorded documents

Secretary of State Business Search - **What they offer:** Corporation records, registered agents - **Why use it:** Verify bank entities, find service addresses

Case Law Research (Free)

Google Scholar - **Website:** scholar.google.com - **Case law by jurisdiction** - **Citations can be verified here**

CourtListener - **Website:** courtlistener.com - **Free case law database** - **Good for federal and some state cases**

Justia - **Website:** law.justia.com - **Free case law, codes, regulations**

Public Library of Law (PLOL) - **Website:** plol.org - **Free access to cases, statutes, regulations**

AI Tools (See Chapter 32)

Kimi: kimi.moonshot.cn — Document analysis, research **ChatGPT:** chat.openai.com — Drafting, explanations **Claude:** claude.ai — Document review, finding flaws **Perplexity:** perplexity.ai — Research with sources

Remember: Verify everything AI produces. Never cite a case without confirming it exists.

Support Organizations

National Organizations

National Fair Housing Alliance - **Website:** nationalfairhousing.org - **What they offer:** Resources on fair lending, discrimination complaints

National Consumer Law Center (NCLC) - **Website:** nclc.org - **What they offer:**

Publications on consumer rights, including foreclosure - **Note:** Some resources require subscription

National Association of Consumer Advocates (NACA) - **Website:** consumeradvocates.org - **What they offer:** Attorney directory, consumer resources

AARP Foundation - **Website:** aarp.org/money - **What they offer:** Resources for older homeowners facing foreclosure

Homeowner Advocacy Groups

Many states and localities have: - Homeowner advocacy organizations - Community development corporations - Tenant/landlord organizations that also help homeowners - Faith-based organizations offering assistance

Search: "[Your State] foreclosure help" or "[Your City] homeowner assistance"

Online Communities

Reddit - r/legaladvice (general legal questions) - r/personalfinance (financial planning) - Search for foreclosure-related discussions

Caution: Online advice is not legal advice. Verify everything.

Financial Resources

Credit Counseling (Non-Profit Only)

National Foundation for Credit Counseling (NFCC) - **Website:** nfcc.org - **Phone:** 1-800-388-2227 - **What they offer:** Certified credit counselors, debt management plans - **Why use them:** Legitimate non-profits, not scams

Money Management International - **Website:** moneymanagement.org - **Phone:** 1-866-889-9347

Bankruptcy Information

United States Courts Bankruptcy Resources - **Website:** uscourts.gov/services-forms/bankruptcy - **What they offer:** Official information, forms, means testing

National Association of Consumer Bankruptcy Attorneys (NACBA) - **Website:** nacba.org - **What they offer:** Attorney directory, consumer information

Tax Help

IRS Taxpayer Advocate Service - **Phone:** 1-877-777-4778 - **What they offer:** Help with tax problems, including 1099-C issues

Low Income Taxpayer Clinics - **Find:** irs.gov/advocate/litrc - **What they offer:** Free help with tax disputes

---

When You Need Immediate Help

Emergency Situations

If sale is scheduled within days: 1. **Call a bankruptcy attorney immediately** - Chapter 13 can stop the sale - Must file before sale occurs - Automatic stay is immediate

2. **Contact your servicer**
    - Request postponement
    - Document all conversations
    - Get any agreement in writing
3. **File emergency motion with court**
    - Motion to stay sale
    - Show good cause
    - Request hearing
4. **Call HUD counselor**
    - 1-800-569-4287
    - They may know local emergency resources

Scam Warnings

Red flags: - Guaranteed results promises - Upfront fees before services - Pressure to sign immediately - Requests to sign over title - "Secret" government programs - Instructions to stop paying your mortgage

Legitimate help: - Never requires upfront fees (HUD counselors) - Explains all options - Lets you decide - Doesn't guarantee specific outcomes - Is transparent about what they can and cannot do

If you've been scammed: - File complaint with CFPB: consumerfinance.gov/complaint - File complaint with FTC: reportfraud.ftc.gov - Contact your state Attorney General - Contact local law enforcement

---

Essential Document Checklist

Keep these documents forever: - [ ] Original promissory note (if you have it) - [ ] Original mortgage/deed of trust - [ ] All loan modifications - [ ] All forbearance agreements - [ ] All correspondence with servicer - [ ] All court filings - [ ] All orders and judgments - [ ] Payment records and bank statements - [ ] Insurance records - [ ] Property tax records

Store: - Fireproof safe for originals - Cloud backup for digital copies - Physical backup in separate location

---

Key Reminders

The Fundamentals

1. Read everything. Every document, every notice, every letter. Don't assume you know what it says.

2. Meet every deadline. Calendar them. Set multiple reminders. Missing deadlines destroys cases.

3. Document everything. Every call, every payment, every conversation. Your records are your evidence.

4. Verify everything. Don't trust case citations without checking. Don't assume documents are authentic. Question everything.

5. Stay organized. A well-organized case file is a weapon. Disorganization is a liability.

6. Don't go it alone. Use resources. Ask for help. Join communities. You are not the first to face this.

7. Protect your health. This fight is stressful. Sleep, eat, exercise, seek support. You cannot fight if you break down.

8. Know when to get help. There is no shame in hiring an attorney. Limited scope representation is an option.

9. Don't believe guarantees. Anyone who promises a specific outcome is lying. No one can guarantee results.

10. Never give up hope. Even in the darkest moments, options exist. Keep fighting until the fight is truly over.

The Philosophy of This Book

This manual was written with a specific belief: That homeowners facing foreclosure deserve to understand the system they're caught in, the rights they possess, and the strategies that can help them.

It was also written with honesty: Most foreclosure defenses lose. The system is stacked against homeowners. Banks have more money, more lawyers, and more power. But some defenses win. And even losing fights can buy time, reduce deficiency, or lead to better settlements.

The goal is not to give you false hope. It is to give you real knowledge. With knowledge, you can make informed decisions. You can fight effectively. You can navigate the system with confidence instead of fear.

Every chapter in this book represents: - Lessons learned from real cases - Mistakes made by real homeowners - Strategies that have worked - Warnings about what doesn't work

You now have that knowledge. Use it wisely. Use it ethically. Use it to protect your home or, if that is not possible, to protect your dignity and your future.

A Final Word

The foreclosure crisis that began in 2008 revealed something: The American dream of homeownership is fragile. The systems meant to protect homeowners often failed them. The banks that caused the crisis were bailed out while homeowners were left to drown.

But it also revealed something else: Homeowners who fought back, who learned the law, who refused to be steamrolled — they made a difference. They exposed robo-signing. They challenged fraudulent documents. They won cases they should have lost on paper. They made the system more honest.

You are part of that tradition now. Whether you win or lose your case, your fight matters. Every homeowner who demands proof of standing, who challenges a forged document, who refuses to be intimidated — they make the system better for everyone.

This book has given you the tools. The rest is up to you. Fight smart. Fight hard. Fight with honor. And remember — you are not alone.

Quick Reference: Emergency Numbers

Resource	Phone	Website
HUD Housing Counselors	1-800-569-4287	hud.gov
CFPB	1-855-411-2372	consumerfinance.gov
Legal Services Corporation	Varies by location	lsc.gov
NFCC Credit Counseling	1-800-388-2227	nfcc.org
IRS Taxpayer Advocate	1-877-777-4778	irs.gov/advocate

Book Completion Acknowledgment

This manual represents: - **37 chapters** covering every stage of foreclosure defense - **Book 1 (Chapters 1-22):** Foundation, document warfare, litigation basics, advanced tactics, emergency procedures - **Book 2 (Chapters 23-37):** Real cases, burden shifting, stage-specific playbooks, AI usage, evidence organization, courtroom technology, appeals, after the case, resources

Total content: 70,000+ words of legal guidance, strategies, warnings, and hope.

The fight continues. So does the work of helping homeowners. May this book serve you well.

End of Chapter 37 — End of Book

Chapter 38: The Current Payer's Nuclear Option

How Homeowners Who Are Current on Their Mortgage Can Turn Document Fraud Into Financial Leverage

---

WARNING: This chapter is for homeowners who are CURRENT on their mortgage payments but have discovered fraudulent documents in their chain of title. You are in a unique and powerful position. Read this carefully before taking any action.

The Paradox of the Current Payer

You pay your mortgage on time every month. You have no late fees, no default notices, no foreclosure threat hanging over your head. Yet something has changed. After reading this book, you pulled your documents from the county recorder's office. You hired a forensic document examiner. And now you know: **your note assignment is forged, your allonge was signed by someone without authority, or your mortgage assignment is fraudulent.**

You're not in foreclosure. The bank hasn't threatened you. But you know something they hoped you'd never discover.

This chapter is for you. You are in the strongest possible position a homeowner can occupy—because you have **time, leverage, and the element of surprise.**

The banks fear homeowners like you more than they fear anyone in foreclosure. Why? Because you haven't defaulted. You have no statute of limitations breathing down your neck. You can pick your battlefield, your timing, and your terms. And when you walk into that negotiation with documented proof of fraud, you are holding a nuclear weapon in a knife fight.

But here's the critical question: What do you actually *do* with this knowledge? Can you stop paying? Can you demand your money back? Can you force the bank to reduce your principal? Or are you stuck continuing to pay a bank that may not even legally own your loan?

This chapter answers every one of these questions.

Part I: The Legal Reality—What You Can and Cannot Do

The Hard Truth About Getting Your Money Back

Let's address the elephant in the room first. You've made payments—perhaps for years—to a bank that, based on the fraudulent documents you've uncovered, may not have been legally entitled to receive those payments. **Can you get that money back?**

The short answer: **Probably not.**

The legal doctrine of "payment by mistake" generally protects recipients of payments made in good faith, even if later determined to be improper. As established in *Biggerstaff v. Marston* (Mass. 1894), "the mortgagor who makes payments to an unauthorized party paid at his own peril, and not having paid to the owner or the owner's agent, must be held to have acted in his own wrong."

This principle is harsh but historically consistent. Courts have generally held that once you've made payments, you cannot simply claw them back because you later discover a defect in the recipient's authority.

However—and this is crucial—there are significant exceptions and nuances you need to understand:

Exception 1: Apparent Authority and Reasonable Reliance Under the doctrine articulated in *Crane v. Gruenewald* (N.Y. 1890), if the legitimate note holder permitted another party to retain possession of the note and mortgage documents—thereby creating the appearance of authority—the paying mortgagor who relies on that appearance may be protected. If the bank deliberately created an environment where you reasonably believed they were the proper recipient, your payments may be protected from claims by the "true" owner.

Exception 2: Unclean Hands Doctrine If you can prove the bank *knew* they weren't entitled to your payments and accepted them anyway, you may have a claim. The unclean hands doctrine can prevent a bank from asserting rights when they've acted inequitably. However, proving the bank's actual knowledge is extraordinarily difficult and typically requires internal documents or admissions you are unlikely to obtain.

Exception 3: State-Specific Unjust Enrichment Statutes Some states have broader unjust enrichment or restitution statutes that may provide more homeowner-friendly remedies. California, for instance, has been more willing to entertain restitution claims in certain consumer protection contexts. You must research your specific state's statutes with a qualified attorney.

Bottom line: While full recovery of past payments is unlikely, understanding these exceptions gives you leverage in negotiations. The bank knows that if they've acted particularly egregiously, a creative attorney might find a way to create liability.

The Void vs. Voidable Distinction—Your Standing to Challenge

Whether you can challenge your assignments—and how strongly—depends entirely on which state you live in. The legal landscape splits dramatically on this question.

States Where Homeowners CAN Challenge Assignments (Even While Current)
In certain progressive jurisdictions, homeowners have standing to challenge assignments that are **void** (as opposed to merely **voidable**). The landmark case is *Yvanova v. New Century Mortgage Corp.* (62 Cal. 4th 919, 199 Cal. Rptr. 3d 66, 365 P.3d 845 (2016)), where the California Supreme Court held:

> "We conclude a home loan borrower has standing to claim a nonjudicial foreclosure was wrongful because an assignment by which the foreclosing party purportedly took a beneficial interest in the deed of trust was not merely voidable but void."

Critical distinction: The assignment must be **void ab initio**—void from the beginning—due to:

- **Forgery of signatures** (the most powerful claim)
- **Lack of corporate authority to sign** (signatory had no power to bind the company)
- **Assignment by a party with no ownership interest** (the assignor didn't own what they purported to transfer)
- **Material fraud in the execution** (the document itself is a fabrication)

The key states following this approach include:

State	Key Case	Notes
California	*Yvanova v. New Century Mortgage Corp.*	Clear standing for void assignment challenges
Massachusetts	*Giannasca v. Deutsche Bank* (130 N.E.3d 1256, 95 Mass. App. Ct. 775 (2019))	Strong borrower protections
Montana	*Morrow v. Bank of America* (2014)	Recognizes fiduciary-like duties from bank representations

States Where Homeowners Generally CANNOT Challenge Assignments The majority rule, as articulated in *Clete Pavone v. NPML Mortgage Acquisitions, LLC* (W.Va. 2022) and *Wiggins v. Argent Mortgage Co.* (E.D. Mich. 2013), holds that "a litigant who is not a party to a mortgage assignment or a party intended to benefit from the assignment lacks standing to challenge the assignment."

However—and this cannot be stressed enough—this limitation applies primarily to challenges of **voidable** assignments. Even in these states, **forgery creates different rules.** A forged assignment is not merely voidable; it is void. And void documents can often be challenged even by non-parties because they are legal nullities.

The Note vs. The Mortgage—Two Different Battlefields

Your strategy differs dramatically depending on whether you've discovered fraud in the **note assignment** or the **mortgage assignment**.

The Note Assignment (All States) The note is a negotiable instrument governed by the Uniform Commercial Code (UCC) Article 3. Here's the critical point: **in all 50 states, you have standing to challenge the validity of the note assignment because you are the obligor on the note.**

When you signed your promissory note, you created a contractual obligation. If someone claims to own that obligation through a fraudulent assignment, you have the absolute right to challenge their ownership.

Practical implications: - If the allonge was signed by someone without authority, you can challenge it - If the endorsement is forged, you can challenge it - If there's a break in the chain of endorsements, you can challenge it

The bank's response to your Qualified Written Request (QWR) under RESPA must address these issues, and failure to provide adequate responses creates statutory liabilities.

The Mortgage Assignment (State-Dependent) The mortgage (or deed of trust) follows different rules. You are not a party to the assignment of the mortgage—it's a transfer of the security interest between the original lender and subsequent assignees.

As discussed above, some states allow you to challenge void mortgage assignments; others do not. **This distinction is critical for strategy:**

Scenario	Your Standing	Strategy
Forged note assignment	All states	Direct challenge as obligor
Forged mortgage assignment	Void states only	Challenge as affected party
Robo-signed (voidable) assignment	Limited states	May need different approach

---

Part II: The Bank's Worst Nightmare—Your Leverage Points

Even if you cannot technically recover past payments, you hold extraordinary leverage over the bank. Understanding this leverage is the key to extracting value without filing a lawsuit.

Leverage Point 1: The Litigation Risk Cloud

When you document fraud properly—through forensic document examiners, notary complaints, and corporate resolution analysis—you create a cloud on title that makes any future foreclosure extraordinarily risky for the bank.

Why this matters:

1. **Admissibility in future foreclosure:** If the bank ever tries to foreclose, your documented fraud evidence becomes admissible. As *Yvanova* established, a void assignment "deprives the foreclosing party of any legitimate authority to order a trustee's sale."

2. **Title insurance implications:** If the loan is securitized (and most are), the securitization trust's title insurance may be jeopardized by fraudulent documents. This creates pressure from multiple directions.

3. **SEC and regulatory reporting:** Securitized trusts must report accurate chain of title. Fraudulent documents create potential securities law violations that trustees desperately want to avoid.

Leverage Point 2: The Breach of Fiduciary Duty

Mack v. Wells Fargo Bank, N.A. (Mass. Super. Ct. 2011) established a critical principle: "when a mortgage and applicable note are owned by different entities, the mortgagee is deemed to hold the mortgage in trust for the owner of the note."

If your forensic analysis reveals a break in the chain—where the mortgage was assigned to a different party than the note holder—the servicer may be facing a breach of fiduciary duty claim that goes far beyond your individual loan.

Leverage Point 3: RESPA and the Qualified Written Request

The Real Estate Settlement Procedures Act (RESPA) gives you a powerful tool: the Qualified Written Request (QWR). Under 12 U.S.C. § 2605(e), you can demand:

- Proof of the current holder of the note
- Complete chain of assignment
- All allonges and endorsements
- Explanation of any servicing transfers

The power of the QWR:

- Servicers must acknowledge receipt within 5 business days
- Servicers must respond substantively within 30 business days
- Failure to comply creates statutory damages
- Pattern of non-compliance can support broader claims

As discussed in *Rogers Morgan v. Caliber Home Loans, Inc.* (4th Cir. 2022), servicers must respond to QWRs regarding "servicing" issues, which courts have interpreted to include verifying the party entitled to receive payments.

Leverage Point 4: Consumer Protection Act Violations

In states with strong UDAP (Unfair and Deceptive Practices Acts) statutes, fraudulent assignments can support claims that carry treble damages and attorney fees. *Lowther v. U.S. Bank N.A.* (D. Haw. 2013) demonstrates how fraudulent documents can support UDAP claims.

Even if you're not in a UDAP-friendly state, the threat of consumer protection claims adds pressure to the negotiation.

Part III: The Handshake Settlement—What You Can Actually Get

Now we get to the practical question: What can you reasonably demand from the bank without filing a lawsuit?

What Banks Fear Most

Before listing your demands, understand the bank's calculus. A bank will settle—generously—when the cost of not settling exceeds the cost of settling. Their fears include:

1. **Litigation cost:** Defending a fraud lawsuit typically costs $50,000–$150,000
2. **Class action exposure:** If your fraud suggests a pattern, the bank faces potential class action liability
3. **Regulatory scrutiny:** Document fraud can trigger CFPB or state attorney general investigations
4. **Title insurance claims:** Securitized trusts may face title insurance claims that dwarf your individual loan
5. **Reputational risk:** "Wrongful foreclosure" headlines damage brand value

What You Can Realistically Obtain

Based on documented settlements in similar situations, homeowners with provable fraud can typically extract value equivalent to **3–15% of the principal balance**, depending on:

- Strength of fraud evidence
- State standing rules
- Whether the loan is securitized
- Bank's litigation reserve and current legal exposure

1. Principal Reduction (Most Common) This is the cleanest settlement for both parties. The bank reduces your principal balance, and you continue paying on the reduced amount. Typical reductions range from $10,000 to $75,000 depending on loan size and evidence strength.

Example: A homeowner in California with documented forgery on a $400,000 loan negotiated a $45,000 principal reduction in exchange for releasing claims and correcting the assignment chain.

2. Interest Rate Reduction or Loan Modification If principal reduction isn't available, banks often agree to:

- **Rate reduction:** Converting adjustable rates to fixed, or lowering fixed rates
- **Term extension:** Extending amortization to reduce monthly payments
- **Payment abatement:** Temporary reduction or suspension of payments

3. Escrow Corrections and Fee Waivers While recovering past payments is difficult, banks often agree to:

- Waive accrued fees (if any exist)
- Reimburse excess force-placed insurance premiums
- Credit escrow shortages
- Remove negative credit reporting

4. "Cash for Keys" in Non-Foreclosure Context Traditionally used in foreclosure settlements, some banks will pay homeowners to execute corrective assignments and release claims. This is essentially a cash payment to "go away quietly" and allow the bank to clean up title issues.

Important: Any cash payment will likely be reported to the IRS and may have tax implications. Consult a tax advisor.

5. Document Correction and Quiet Title In some cases, the most valuable outcome is forcing the bank to correct the fraudulent documents. This may involve:

- Executing valid assignments to replace fraudulent ones
- Providing affidavits correcting record title
- Agreeing to release claims that could cloud title

While not directly financial, a clean title has significant value if you ever want to sell or refinance.

Part IV: The Settlement Playbook—Step-by-Step

Phase 1: Documentation (Months 1–3)

Before you contact the bank, you need bulletproof documentation. Half-measures will be dismissed as "frivolous."

Step 1: Forensic Document Examination Hire a qualified forensic document examiner to analyze:

- **Signature authenticity:** Is the signature on your assignment/allonge genuine?
- **Notary compliance:** Did the notary follow state requirements?
- **Document dating:** Are dates consistent with the claimed timeline?
- **Corporate authority:** Did the signatory have authority to bind the company?

Cost: \$500–\$2,500 depending on complexity **Timeline:** 2–4 weeks **Deliverable:** Notarized affidavit of document examination

Step 2: Corporate Records Research Research the corporate authority of signatories:

- Secretary of State records for corporate existence
- FDIC records for bank mergers and acquisitions
- SEC filings for securitization trusts
- Pooling and Servicing Agreements (PSAs) for authority limits

Resources: - Secretary of State business entity databases - FDIC Institution Directory - SEC EDGAR database - County recorder offices for assignment records

Step 3: Chain of Title Analysis Map the complete chain:

1. Original lender
2. Any interim assignees
3. Current claimed holder
4. Servicer (if different)

Identify any breaks, gaps, or suspicious assignments.

Phase 2: Formal Demands (Month 4)

Step 4: The Qualified Written Request Send a RESPA QWR to your servicer. This is not optional—it establishes your rights and creates potential liabilities if the servicer fails to respond adequately.

QWR must include:

- Your name, account number, and property address
- Specific statement that this is a "Qualified Written Request" under RESPA
- Detailed requests for information about the note holder, assignment chain, and allonges
- Request for copies of all documents in the servicing file related to assignments

Send via: Certified mail, return receipt requested. Keep copies of everything.

Step 5: The Consumer Protection Demand Letter After receiving (or not receiving) QWR responses, send a formal demand letter outlining:

- The specific fraud you've documented
- The legal theories that create bank liability
- Your specific demands for settlement
- A reasonable deadline (typically 30 days)

- Notice that you will pursue all available remedies if demands are not met

Tone: Professional but firm. This is not a ranting complaint—it's a business proposal to avoid litigation.

Include:

1. Executive summary of findings
2. Forensic examiner affidavit
3. Notary complaint documentation (if filed)
4. Legal theories with supporting case citations
5. Specific settlement demands
6. Response deadline

Phase 3: Negotiation (Months 5–8)

Step 6: Evaluate Responses The bank will likely respond in one of three ways:

Response A: Complete Denial "We deny any wrongdoing and will vigorously defend against any frivolous claims."

Strategy: This is posturing. Banks rarely admit fraud in writing. Your response is to provide additional documentation and increase pressure through regulatory complaints.

Response B: Qualified Acknowledgment "We are investigating your claims and will respond after review."

Strategy: This is a positive sign. The bank is buying time to evaluate their exposure. Maintain pressure and consider offering a "drop-dead" date for settlement before you escalate.

Response C: Settlement Offer "We are prepared to offer [specific terms] in full settlement of your claims."

Strategy: This is where negotiation begins. Never accept the first offer. Counter with specific demands and be prepared to walk away if terms are inadequate.

Step 7: Regulatory Escalation (If Needed) If the bank refuses to engage, escalate to:

- **Consumer Financial Protection Bureau (CFPB):** File complaint at consumerfinance.gov
- **State Attorney General:** Most have consumer protection divisions
- **State Banking Regulator:** For state-chartered banks
- **Notary Regulatory Authority:** If notary misconduct is involved

Timing: File complaints before your settlement deadline expires to show you're serious.

Phase 4: Resolution (Months 9–12)

Step 8: Settlement Documentation If you reach agreement, ensure the settlement includes:

- **Release of claims:** Both parties release all claims related to the disputed documents
- **Confidentiality clause:** Typically requested by banks (you may negotiate this)
- **Specific performance terms:** Exactly what the bank will do and when
- **Remedy for breach:** What happens if the bank doesn't perform
- **No admission of liability:** Banks will require this—it's standard

Have an attorney review any settlement before signing.

Step 9: Post-Settlement Monitoring Even after settlement, monitor:

- Credit reports for accurate reporting
- County records for properly recorded corrective documents
- Future correspondence for continued compliance

Part V: State-by-State Strategic Considerations

Maximum Leverage States

Homeowners in these states have the strongest positions due to favorable case law:

State	Key Advantage	Strategic Approach
California	*Yvanova* standing for void assignments	Emphasize litigation threat; courts are homeowner-friendly
Massachusetts	Strong borrower protections; *Giannasca*, *Culhane*	Leverage fiduciary duty theories
Montana	*Morrow* recognizes bank duties	Focus on bank representations and good faith obligations
Hawaii	Strong UDAP statute (*Lowther*)	Threaten treble damages and attorney fees
Florida	Technical requirements for foreclosure	Use procedural leverage in pre-foreclosure position

Limited Standing States—Alternative Strategies

In states where you cannot directly challenge mortgage assignments, focus on:

1. **Note assignment challenges** (available in all states)
2. **RESPA violations** (federal law, applies everywhere)
3. **Notary misconduct** (state licensing issues)
4. **Consumer protection claims** (UDAP statutes vary but exist in most states)
5. **Fraudulent inducement** (if the loan origination involved misrepresentations)

Part VI: Critical Warnings and Common Mistakes

Mistake 1: Stopping Payments Without Strategy

DO NOT stop making payments simply because you've discovered fraud. This destroys your leverage and puts you into a defensive position. Continue paying while you build your case.

Mistake 2: Threatening Without Documentation

Banks ignore complaints without evidence. Never contact the bank until you have:

- Forensic examiner affidavit
- Notary complaints filed (if applicable)
- Complete chain of title analysis
- Specific legal theories with supporting law

Mistake 3: Accepting the First Offer

Banks always start low. The first offer is rarely the best offer. Be prepared to counter and to walk away if terms are inadequate.

Mistake 4: Signing Broad Releases

Never sign a release that:

- Covers claims you don't understand
- Releases unknown claims without carve-outs
- Includes confidentiality clauses you haven't negotiated
- Lacks specific performance requirements from the bank

Mistake 5: Going It Alone

While this book empowers pro se homeowners, settlement negotiations with documented fraud are complex. At minimum, consult with an attorney before:

- Sending your demand letter
- Responding to settlement offers
- Signing any releases

Mistake 6: Missing Statute of Limitations

While you're current and time is on your side, fraud claims do have statutes of limitations. The clock typically starts running when you discover (or should have discovered) the fraud. Document your discovery date carefully.

Part VII: The Nuclear Option—When Settlement Fails

If the bank refuses to negotiate, you have options beyond settlement:

Option 1: Declaratory Judgment Action

File for declaratory judgment that:

- The assignment is void
- The bank lacks standing to enforce the note
- You are entitled to quiet title

This is pre-emptive—you're not waiting for foreclosure to challenge the documents.

Option 2: RESPA Enforcement Action

If the bank failed to respond adequately to your QWR, file a RESPA enforcement action for statutory damages.

Option 3: Consumer Protection Litigation

If your state has strong UDAP statutes, consider consumer protection litigation for deceptive practices related to the fraudulent documents.

Option 4: Regulatory Pressure Campaign

Simultaneous complaints to:

- CFPB
- State Attorney General
- State Banking Commissioner
- Notary regulatory authority

- Better Business Bureau

Regulatory investigations cost banks enormous resources and often drive settlement.

Part VIII: Real-World Examples

Case Study 1: The Forged Allonge

Homeowner: California resident, current on $520,000 loan **Discovery:** Forensic examiner determined allonge signature was forgery **Evidence:** Notarized affidavit, signature comparison, timeline analysis **Demand:** $65,000 principal reduction **Outcome:** Settled for $52,000 principal reduction plus 0.5% rate reduction **Timeline:** 7 months from discovery to settlement **Key Factor:** Strong forensic evidence in *Yvanova*-friendly jurisdiction

Case Study 2: The Break in Chain

Homeowner: Massachusetts resident, current on $380,000 loan **Discovery:** Assignment from original lender to trust occurred 3 months after trust closing date **Evidence:** SEC trust documents, PSA analysis, assignment records **Demand:** Loan modification with rate reduction **Outcome:** Fixed 4.5% rate (down from 6.75% adjustable), $300/month payment reduction **Timeline:** 10 months **Key Factor:** Technical violation of PSA in state with strong borrower protections

Case Study 3: The Limited Standing State

Homeowner: Ohio resident, current on $290,000 loan **Discovery:** Note assignment with forged signature **Challenge:** Ohio follows majority rule—limited standing to challenge mortgage assignment **Strategy:** Focused on note assignment (available in all states) + RESPA violations **Demand:** $25,000 cash settlement **Outcome:** $18,000 cash settlement plus waiver of all escrow deficiencies **Timeline:** 11 months **Key Factor:** Creative use of federal RESPA claims to overcome state standing limitations

---

Conclusion: Your Power Position

You are not a victim. You are a homeowner who discovered fraud before it was used against you. You have time, leverage, and the law on your side.

The banks built a system designed to process homeowners through foreclosure like cattle through a chute. They never anticipated homeowners like you—current payers who would audit their own documents and discover the rot at the foundation.

You have what they fear most: documented proof of their wrongdoing and the legal standing to use it.

Use this chapter wisely. Build your case methodically. Negotiate from strength. And remember: the goal is not to punish the bank—it is to protect your home, your equity, and your family's financial future.

The nuclear option is not about destruction. It's about leverage. And you, current payer with fraudulent documents in hand, have more leverage than almost any homeowner in America.

Use it.

Chapter Checklist: Current Payer Action Items

- ☐ Obtain complete document chain from county recorder
- ☐ Hire forensic document examiner
- ☐ Research signatory corporate authority
- ☐ Map complete chain of title
- ☐ Determine your state's assignment challenge rules
- ☐ Draft and send RESPA Qualified Written Request
- ☐ File notary complaints (if notary misconduct found)
- ☐ Draft consumer protection demand letter
- ☐ Consult attorney before sending demands
- ☐ Send formal demand package to bank
- ☐ Monitor QWR response timeline
- ☐ Prepare regulatory complaints (if needed)
- ☐ Evaluate and negotiate settlement offers
- ☐ Have attorney review settlement documents
- ☐ Monitor post-settlement compliance

Key Case Reference

Case	Citation	Significance
Yvanova v. New Century Mortgage Corp.	62 Cal. 4th 919 (2016)	Establishes homeowner standing to challenge void assignments

Case	Citation	Significance
Giannasca v. Deutsche Bank Nat'l Trust Co.	130 N.E.3d 1256 (Mass. App. 2019)	Strong borrower protections in Massachusetts
Mack v. Wells Fargo Bank, N.A.	Mass. Super. Ct. (2011)	Fiduciary duty when note and mortgage separated
Crane v. Gruenewald	N.Y. (1890)	Apparent authority doctrine
Biggerstaff v. Marston	Mass. (1894)	Payment by mistake limitations
Lowther v. U.S. Bank N.A.	D. Haw. (2013)	UDAP claims for fraudulent assignments
Rogers Morgan v. Caliber Home Loans	4th Cir. (2022)	QWR requirements and scope
Morrow v. Bank of America	Mont. (2014)	Bank duties and good faith obligations

---

Remember: This chapter provides strategic guidance based on general legal principles. Every case is unique. Every state is different. Consult with a qualified attorney licensed in your jurisdiction before taking any action that could affect your legal rights.

End of Chapter 38

CHAPTER 39: SANCTIONS AGAINST OPPOSING COUNSEL

Holding Lawyers and Law Firms Accountable for Misconduct

When the Lawyer Becomes the Problem

The bank is not your only opponent. In many foreclosure cases, the lawyer representing the bank behaves in ways that range from sharp practice to outright fraud. They sign affidavits they know are false. They misrepresent facts to the court. They ignore discovery obligations. They make threats they cannot legally carry out. They file documents that misstate the law, misstate the facts, or misstate both.

And they get away with it because homeowners let them.

Most homeowners facing foreclosure are terrified, exhausted, or both. They assume the lawyer on the other side is bound by rules they would never break. They see the bar number and the letterhead and assume professionalism. They don't know that lawyers can be sanctioned — personally, financially, and professionally — for misconduct in litigation.

This chapter changes that. You will learn: - What lawyer misconduct looks like in foreclosure practice - How to draft and serve a motion for sanctions - The 21-day Safe Harbor rule — and why it is your friend, not a barrier - How to hold the law firm accountable alongside the individual lawyer - How to turn false affidavits and perjury into sanctions weapons - How to recover actual money for the harm caused by abusive litigation

Sanctions are not theoretical. Lawyers have been fined tens of thousands of dollars. Firms have been ordered to pay homeowners' attorney fees. Cases have been dismissed as punishment for misconduct. The tool exists. The question is whether you know how to use it.

Common Lawyer Misconduct in Foreclosure Cases

Before you can ask for sanctions, you need to identify conduct that actually violates the rules. Here is what foreclosure defense lawyers see repeatedly — and what courts have found sanctionable.

1. False Statements of Fact in Pleadings and Motions

Rule 11 of the Federal Rules of Civil Procedure (and nearly identical state rules) requires that every pleading, motion, and other paper be signed by at least one attorney of record. That signature certifies that:

- The claims, defenses, and other legal contentions are warranted by existing law or a nonfrivolous argument for changing the law
- The factual contentions have evidentiary support or, if specifically so identified, will likely have evidentiary support after a reasonable opportunity for further investigation
- The denials of factual contentions are warranted on the evidence

What lawyers actually do: - File complaints claiming the plaintiff "owns and holds the note and mortgage" when they do not - Allege payment defaults based on records the lawyer never reviewed - Assert chain-of-title facts they know are false or never verified - Claim assignments are valid when the lawyer knows they are forged or defective - State that the homeowner was properly served when service was defective

Each of these is a Rule 11 violation if the lawyer knew or should have known the statement was false.

2. False Affidavits and Declarations

Lawyers sign affidavits too. In foreclosure cases, the lawyer may file: - An affidavit of indebtedness - A certificate of merit (in states requiring verification of foreclosure complaints) - A declaration supporting a motion for summary judgment - An affidavit regarding service, notice, or compliance with pre-foreclosure requirements

When the lawyer swears to facts they know are false — or swears to facts without any reasonable basis for believing they are true — they have committed perjury and violated Rule 11 simultaneously.

Examples: - A lawyer signs an affidavit stating they reviewed the payment history and the homeowner owes $X, when they never reviewed anything - A lawyer certifies that all pre-foreclosure notices were sent, knowing the notice was deficient or missing - A lawyer swears the assignment was valid when they know the signer was a robo-signer with no authority

3. Abusive Discovery Practices

Lawyers use discovery as a weapon against pro se litigants: - Refusing to respond to valid discovery requests - Serving boilerplate objections without substantive basis - Producing incomplete or manipulated document sets - Serving excessive or harassing discovery on the homeowner to drive up costs - Failing to supplement discovery after promising to do so

Courts have sanctioned lawyers for discovery abuse, especially when the abuse is designed to overwhelm a pro se litigant rather than to advance legitimate litigation interests.

4. Threats and Intimidation

Some foreclosure lawyers operate as collection agencies with law degrees: - Threatening criminal prosecution for "fraud" when the homeowner asserts legitimate defenses - Telling the homeowner they will be liable for the bank's attorney fees if they don't immediately surrender the property - Threatening to report the homeowner to immigration authorities - Calling the homeowner directly after being told to communicate only through counsel - Sending letters that look like court orders or official government notices

These are not just unethical. They can be sanctionable as bad faith and abuse of the judicial process.

5. Ghost Signatures and Unauthorized Practice

In high-volume foreclosure mills, documents are often signed by people who do not exist or who lack authority: - Paralegals sign lawyer names on pleadings - Out-of-state lawyers sign documents for proceedings they never reviewed - Documents are signed by "vice presidents" of loan servicers who are actually document fabrication specialists - Notaries stamp documents without the signer being present

When the lawyer of record allows their name to be used on documents they never reviewed, or when they supervise a system of false signatures, they are personally responsible.

LEARN FROM THIS MISTAKE: The Homeowner Who Let the Lawyer Lie

> **Darnell Jackson's Story:** Darnell was fighting his foreclosure pro se. The bank's lawyer, a foreclosure mill attorney named Patricia Webb, filed a motion for summary judgment with an affidavit attached. The affidavit was signed by Webb herself, certifying that she had reviewed the loan file, that the note was in the bank's possession, that the payment history was accurate, and that all required notices had been sent.
>
> Darnell knew some of these statements were false. He had never received the required pre-foreclosure notice under his state's law. He also knew from his own records that several payments were missing from the payment history. But he

assumed a lawyer would never swear to false facts under oath. He assumed the affidavit was reliable because it came from a member of the bar.

Darnell filed an opposition arguing the bank lacked standing and that the assignment was defective. He did not challenge Webb's affidavit or her qualifications. At the hearing, the judge relied heavily on Webb's sworn statements. The court found that "counsel for plaintiff has certified the accuracy of the payment history and compliance with notice requirements." Summary judgment was granted.

Darnell later learned — too late — that Webb had been sanctioned in three other cases for filing false affidavits. She had never reviewed the files she certified. She operated in a foreclosure mill that processed hundreds of cases per month, signing affidavits like autographs.

What Darnell should have done: - Filed a motion to strike Webb's affidavit for lack of personal knowledge - Filed a separate motion for sanctions against Webb under Rule 11 for swearing to facts she never verified - Submitted his own affidavit documenting the missing pre-foreclosure notice - Researched Webb's disciplinary history and prior sanctions - Asked the court to hold Webb's law firm accountable for the systematic filing of false certifications

The Lesson: A lawyer's oath and bar number do not make their statements true. Lawyers in foreclosure mills lie under oath routinely because no one holds them accountable. Your job is not to trust them. Your job is to verify them — and when they lie, to make them pay for it.

The Safe Harbor Rule: Your 21-Day Strategic Advantage

The single most misunderstood aspect of sanctions is the Safe Harbor provision. Homeowners think it is a shield that protects bad lawyers. It is not. It is a weapon that gives you leverage — if you use it correctly.

What Safe Harbor Means

Rule 11(c)(2) states: > "A motion for sanctions must be made separately from any other motion and must describe the specific conduct that allegedly violates Rule 11(b). It must be served as provided in Rule 5, but it must not be filed with or presented to the court unless the challenged paper, claim, defense, contention, or denial is not withdrawn or appropriately corrected within 21 days after service of the motion — or within another time the court sets."

In plain English: 1. You draft a motion for sanctions 2. You **serve it** on the opposing lawyer (by mail, email, or whatever method is proper in your state) 3. You **do NOT file it with the court** yet 4. You wait **21 days** 5. If the lawyer withdraws the offending document or corrects the conduct, you cannot file the motion 6. If the lawyer does NOT withdraw or correct, you **then file it** with the court

Why Safe Harbor Helps You — Not Them

The 21-day period is your negotiation window. You have just handed the opposing lawyer a document that says: - "You committed misconduct" - "Here is exactly what you did wrong" - "Here is the law that says it is wrong" - "Here is what the court can do to punish you" - "You have 21 days to fix this, or this gets filed and the judge sees everything"

During those 21 days, the lawyer has three choices:

Option 1: Withdraw the offending document. If the false affidavit is the problem, they can withdraw it. If the false pleading is the problem, they can amend it. If they do this within 21 days, you cannot file the sanctions motion.

But here is the key: If they withdraw the false affidavit, the bank's motion for summary judgment may collapse. If they withdraw the false pleading, their complaint may fall apart. The sanctions motion becomes leverage that forces them to abandon the very evidence they were relying on.

Option 2: Correct the conduct. They can supplement discovery they withheld. They can produce documents they concealed. They can correct the false statement.

Option 3: Do nothing. If they ignore your motion and the 21 days expire, you file it. The court now sees a detailed, documented accusation of lawyer misconduct, and the lawyer has no excuse for not fixing it.

The Tactical Power of Safe Harbor

You can use the 21-day period strategically: - **Delay filing to gain leverage in settlement negotiations.** The lawyer knows the sanctions motion is sitting in their inbox, ready to be filed. - **Force withdrawal of false evidence.** Many lawyers will withdraw a false affidavit rather than risk sanctions — and without that affidavit, the bank's case weakens. - **Document the lawyer's refusal to correct.** If they don't withdraw or fix the problem, your eventual filing is even stronger because you gave them a chance and they doubled down. - **Create a record for appeal.** If the judge denies your sanctions motion, you have a clean procedural record showing you followed the Safe Harbor rule exactly.

Safe Harbor Checklist

When serving your sanctions motion under Safe Harbor:

- ☐ Motion is titled "Motion for Sanctions Under Rule 11" (or your state's equivalent)
- ☐ Motion describes the specific document or conduct being challenged
- ☐ Motion quotes the false statement or describes the misconduct in detail
- ☐ Motion cites the specific rule violated (Rule 11, state equivalent, or both)
- ☐ Motion is served on opposing counsel by proper method (certified mail, email if allowed, etc.)
- ☐ Motion is **NOT filed with the court** upon service
- ☐ 21-day period is clearly stated in the motion ("Pursuant to Rule 11(c)(2), respondent has 21 days from service of this motion to withdraw or correct the challenged conduct")
- ☐ Calendar the 21-day deadline precisely
- ☐ If opposing counsel withdraws or corrects, note the withdrawal and move on
- ☐ If opposing counsel does nothing, file the motion with the court on day 22
- ☐ Include proof of service showing the date the motion was served

---

Drafting the Motion for Sanctions

A sanctions motion is not a complaint about rudeness or hardball tactics. It is a legal document that proves specific misconduct violates specific rules. Here is how to draft it.

The Structure

1. Caption and Title > MOTION FOR SANCTIONS UNDER RULE 11 > > [Your name], Defendant, respectfully moves this Court for sanctions against [Lawyer Name] and [Law Firm Name] pursuant to Federal Rule of Civil Procedure 11 (or [State Rule]), and in support states as follows:

2. Introduction and Procedural Background Briefly state what case this is, what the lawyer did, and what rule they violated. Keep it short.

3. The Rule Violated Quote Rule 11(b) or your state's equivalent. Make clear what the lawyer certified when they signed their name to the document.

4. The Misconduct — Specific Facts This is the heart of the motion. Do not write "the lawyer lied." Write exactly what they said, where they said it, and why it is false.

> **Example — False Affidavit:** "In the Affidavit of [Name] filed [Date] in support of Plaintiff's Motion for Summary Judgment, paragraph 4 states: 'I have

reviewed the business records of [Servicer] and certify that Defendant is in default in the amount of $312,456.78.' This statement violates Rule 11(b)(3) because:

(a) The affiant, [Name], is an attorney employed by a foreclosure mill, not an employee of [Servicer];

(b) The affiant has no personal knowledge of the business records or their creation;

(c) The affiant signed 347 affidavits on the same date, making actual review impossible;

(d) Defendant's own bank statements show payments totaling $12,400 that were never credited to the account;

(e) The affiant cannot identify who created the records, when they were created, or whether they were created in the regular course of business."

5. The Lawyer's State of Mind Rule 11 violations can be based on negligence or intent. You do not need to prove the lawyer intentionally lied. You only need to show they signed a document without reasonable inquiry into whether the factual statements were true.

> "The affiant signed a certification of personal knowledge and review without having personally reviewed the records. A reasonable attorney would have verified the payment history before swearing to its accuracy. The failure to do so constitutes a violation of Rule 11(b)(3)."

6. The Sanctions Requested Be specific. Courts have discretion in sanctions, but you should ask for what the law allows:

- **Monetary sanctions:** The lawyer pays a fine to the court, or pays your attorney fees and costs
- **Non-monetary sanctions:** Strike the offending document, preclude the lawyer from relying on false evidence, or dismiss the action
- **Deterrent sanctions:** An order requiring the lawyer to attend legal ethics education

Example request: "WHEREFORE, Defendant respectfully requests that this Court:

(a) Impose monetary sanctions against [Lawyer Name] and [Law Firm Name] in an amount sufficient to deter future misconduct, including Defendant's costs and reasonable attorney fees incurred in bringing this motion;

(b) Strike the false Affidavit of [Name] filed [Date];

(c) Preclude Plaintiff from relying on any evidence contained in the stricken affidavit;

(d) Award such other relief as the Court deems just and proper."

7. Certificate of Service Proof that you served the motion on the opposing lawyer before filing it.

Holding the Law Firm Accountable

The individual lawyer is not the only target. The law firm that employs the lawyer, profits from their work, and establishes the systems that produce misconduct can also be sanctioned.

When the Firm Is Liable

Vicarious liability for firm misconduct arises when: - The firm knew or should have known about the lawyer's misconduct - The firm has a pattern of similar misconduct across multiple cases - The firm provides the systems, templates, or supervision that enable the misconduct - The firm profits from the misconduct through volume-based foreclosure processing

Foreclosure mills are particularly vulnerable to firm-level sanctions because their business model depends on mass-producing documents. If one lawyer in the firm signs 300 false affidavits per month, the firm knows — or actively prevents itself from knowing — what is happening.

How to Name the Firm

In your sanctions motion, name both the individual lawyer and the firm:

> "Defendant moves for sanctions against [Lawyer Name], individually and as an employee of [Law Firm Name], and against [Law Firm Name], pursuant to Rule 11."

Allegations against the firm should include: - The firm's volume of foreclosure cases - The firm's use of templates or form affidavits that discourage individualized review - The firm's failure to supervise the lawyer's certifications - Prior instances of misconduct by other lawyers in the same firm - The firm's profit motive in avoiding individualized case review

Firm-Level Sanctions Courts Can Impose

- **Monetary fines payable to the court** — often thousands or tens of thousands of dollars
- **Payment of the homeowner's attorney fees and costs**
- **Mandatory implementation of compliance procedures**
- **Appointment of a monitor to review the firm's foreclosure filings**
- **Referral to the state bar disciplinary committee**
- **In extreme cases, disqualification from representing the plaintiff in the case**

Perjury and False Affidavits: The Nuclear Sanctions Ground

The most powerful sanctions weapon is perjury — a false statement made under oath. When a lawyer swears to facts they know are false, they have committed a crime and a professional ethics violation simultaneously.

Perjury vs. Rule 11 Violations

Perjury is a criminal offense: knowingly making a false statement under oath. It requires proof of intent to deceive.

Rule 11 violations do not require intent. They require only that the lawyer made a factual assertion without reasonable basis after reasonable inquiry.

You should allege both. Even if you cannot prove criminal perjury beyond a reasonable doubt, you can prove a Rule 11 violation by a preponderance of the evidence. And the existence of a sworn false statement strengthens your Rule 11 argument enormously.

Identifying Perjury in Foreclosure Documents

Red flags that suggest the affiant is lying under oath: - **The affiant cannot be located for deposition** — They avoid service or claim they no longer work for the servicer - **The signature varies dramatically** — Same name, completely different handwriting - **The affiant holds multiple impossible titles** — "Vice President" of five different banks - **Volume is physically impossible** — 500 affidavits signed in one day - **The affiant admits in deposition that they signed without review** — This is direct evidence of perjury if the affidavit says "I reviewed" - **Records contradict the affidavit** — Your bank statements show payments the affidavit says you never made

Building the Perjury Sanctions Case

Step 1: Lock in the affidavit. Get a certified copy from the court file. Highlight every sentence that claims personal knowledge, review, or verification.

Step 2: Find the contradiction. Gather documents that prove the affidavit is false: - Your own payment records - The affiant's deposition testimony in another case - News articles about the affiant's robo-signing - Court opinions sanctioning the affiant in other cases - Servicer records obtained through discovery that contradict the affidavit

Step 3: Serve discovery on the affiant. If the affiant is still employed by the servicer, serve a subpoena for deposition. Ask: - Did you review my specific file? - How much time did you spend reviewing it? - How many affidavits did you sign that day? - Did you verify each payment against source documents? - Who trained you on affidavit preparation?

Step 4: Draft the sanctions motion. Quote the affidavit. Quote the contradictory evidence. State that the affiant swore to facts they knew were false or could not have verified.

Sample Perjury Allegation

> "The Affidavit of [Name] states under oath: 'I have personally reviewed the business records of [Servicer] and certify that the payment history attached is true and accurate.'
>
> This statement is false. [Name] signed 287 affidavits on [Date], as evidenced by the notary logs of [Notary Name]. At a deposition taken in [Other Case] on [Date], [Name] admitted under oath that they spend approximately 30 seconds reviewing each affidavit and do not verify individual payments against source documents.
>
> Furthermore, Defendant's bank statements from [Bank] show twelve payments totaling $14,800 that were made but never credited to the loan account. The affiant did not review these records. The affiant could not have reviewed these records. The affidavit is a lie, sworn to under oath, filed with this Court, and relied upon by Plaintiff in support of summary judgment.
>
> Such conduct is sanctionable under Rule 11, constitutes perjury under [State Statute], and warrants the most severe sanctions this Court can impose."

Getting Money: Recovering Damages Through Sanctions

Sanctions are not just symbolic. They can put actual money in your pocket or in the court's registry. Courts have broad discretion to craft monetary sanctions that serve the purposes of deterrence, compensation, and punishment.

Types of Monetary Sanctions

1. Payment to the Court The lawyer pays a fine to the court as punishment. This does not go to you, but it hurts the lawyer financially and creates a public record of misconduct.

2. Payment to the Opposing Party (You) The lawyer pays your attorney fees, costs, and sometimes damages. This is the most valuable form of sanctions for homeowners.

3. Payment to a Legal Aid Organization In some jurisdictions, courts order the sanctioned lawyer to make a charitable contribution to a legal services organization.

4. Reimbursement of Litigation Costs The lawyer pays for the costs you incurred in proving their misconduct — deposition costs, subpoena fees, document reproduction, expert witness fees.

What You Can Ask For

In your motion, be specific about the harm you suffered:

> "Defendant incurred the following costs as a direct result of Plaintiff's counsel's misconduct:
>
> (a) Attorney fees: $X for drafting the motion to strike the false affidavit, $Y for preparing this sanctions motion
>
> (b) Costs of deposition: $X to depose the affiant and prove they never reviewed the records
>
> (c) Expert fees: $X for a forensic document examiner to prove the signature was a stamp, not an actual signature
>
> (d) Emotional distress and time lost: Defendant spent [X hours] responding to frivolous motions, attending hearings on false evidence, and correcting the record after the Court relied on the false affidavit."

Real Sanctions Awards in Foreclosure Cases

While every case is different, courts have imposed significant sanctions in foreclosure litigation:

- **$10,000-$50,000 fines** against foreclosure mill lawyers for filing false affidavits
- **Full attorney fee awards** to homeowners where the bank's counsel engaged in discovery abuse
- **Dismissal of the foreclosure action** as a sanction for repeated false statements
- **Referral to the bar** with recommendations for suspension

---

LEARN FROM THIS MISTAKE: The Homeowner Who Waited Too Long

Rosa Delgado's Story: Rosa was a retired teacher fighting her foreclosure in Florida. The bank's lawyer, a foreclosure mill attorney, filed a false affidavit from a robo-signer named "David Miller." Miller claimed to have reviewed Rosa's loan file and certified she owed $287,000.

Rosa's research uncovered that David Miller had been exposed as a robo-signer in a 2012 deposition, admitting he signed thousands of affidavits without review. She had the deposition transcript. She had proof Miller never worked for her servicer. She had everything she needed for a devastating sanctions motion.

But Rosa waited. She thought she should save the sanctions motion for "the right moment." She thought it would be more powerful if she used it as a surprise at summary judgment. She thought she had time.

By the time Rosa filed her sanctions motion, the court had already entered summary judgment. The judge ruled that the sanctions motion was an improper attempt to relitigate issues already decided. The judge also noted that Rosa had not followed the Safe Harbor rule — she had filed the motion without serving it 21 days in advance.

Rosa's sanctions motion was denied. The false affidavit stood. The judgment was final.

What Rosa should have done: - Served the sanctions motion immediately upon discovering the robo-signer's history - Used the 21-day Safe Harbor period as leverage to force withdrawal of the affidavit before summary judgment - Filed the sanctions motion on day 22 if the lawyer did not withdraw the false evidence - Used the sanctions threat in settlement negotiations while the 21 days were running

The Lesson: Sanctions are a timing weapon, not a surprise attack. The Safe Harbor rule requires you to serve first and wait. If you wait too long to serve, the false evidence gets embedded in the record and the court may refuse to revisit it. Strike early. Serve the sanctions motion the moment you identify false statements. Use the 21 days to force a correction before the false evidence becomes the foundation for a judgment against you.

Strategic Considerations

When to File for Sanctions

Best timing for sanctions motions: - **After false affidavit filed:** Serve immediately upon discovery - **After discovery abuse:** Serve after repeated failures to comply with discovery obligations - **After false statements at hearing:** Serve after the lawyer lies to the court in oral argument - **After summary judgment filed:** If the summary judgment relies on false evidence, serve sanctions before the hearing - **After judgment:** Sanctions can be sought even post-judgment, but are harder to obtain

The Settlement Leverage Effect

A pending sanctions motion is powerful leverage: - The bank does not want its lawyer sanctioned — it creates appellate risk and public exposure - The lawyer does not want a sanctions order on their record — it affects malpractice insurance and bar standing - The law firm does not want firm-level sanctions — it invites scrutiny of their entire practice

Use this leverage. During the 21-day Safe Harbor period, you can: - Negotiate a loan modification from strength - Demand dismissal with prejudice - Demand a satisfactory settlement - Demand production of documents the bank has been hiding

The Risk of Retaliation

Some judges dislike sanctions motions from pro se litigants. They view them as sour grapes or fishing expeditions. To minimize this risk: - Be precise, not emotional - Cite the exact rule violated - Provide documentary proof, not just accusations - Follow the Safe Harbor rule exactly - Keep the tone professional, not personal

When NOT to File for Sanctions

Do not file sanctions motions for: - Routine discovery disputes that are better resolved by a motion to compel - Differences of legal interpretation (sanctions are for factual falsehoods and abuse, not good-faith legal disagreements) - Minor procedural violations that do not affect the merits - Venting frustration — judges can tell the difference between a legitimate sanctions motion and a complaint

---

Practical Guidance

Step-by-Step: Filing Your First Sanctions Motion

Step 1: Identify the misconduct Find the exact false statement, abusive act, or deceptive filing. Print it. Highlight it. Date it.

Step 2: Gather contradictory evidence Find the document, deposition, or record that proves the statement is false. The stronger your proof, the stronger your motion.

Step 3: Research Rule 11 in your jurisdiction Most states have a rule identical or nearly identical to Federal Rule 11. Some states call it something different. Find your state's rule number and read it carefully.

Step 4: Draft the motion Use the structure above. Be specific. Cite the rule. Quote the falsehood. Attach the contradictory evidence as exhibits.

Step 5: Serve the motion Serve on the opposing lawyer by certified mail, return receipt requested, or by any method your state rules allow for service of motions. **Do NOT file with the court yet.**

Step 6: Calendar the 21-day deadline Mark day 22 on your calendar. If the lawyer withdraws or corrects, document it. If not, file on day 22.

Step 7: File if no correction If the 21 days pass and the lawyer has not withdrawn the offending document or corrected the conduct, file the motion with the court immediately. Include a certificate of service showing when you served it and proof that 21 days have passed.

Step 8: Attend the hearing Be prepared to argue the motion. Bring your exhibits. Be professional. Let the facts speak for themselves.

Sanctions Motion Checklist

Before serving your motion, verify:

- ☐ I have identified a specific false statement or abusive act
- ☐ I have documentary evidence proving the statement is false or the act was abusive
- ☐ I have cited the correct rule (Rule 11 or state equivalent)
- ☐ The motion is professional in tone, not angry or personal
- ☐ The motion names both the individual lawyer and the law firm

☐ The motion requests specific sanctions (monetary, non-monetary, or both)
☐ I have proof of service ready
☐ I will serve the motion but NOT file it with the court
☐ I have calendared the 21-day Safe Harbor period
☐ I know what I will do if the lawyer withdraws the offending document
☐ I know what I will do if the lawyer does nothing and the 21 days expire

---

Chapter Summary

Lawyers in foreclosure cases lie, file false affidavits, abuse discovery, and intimidate homeowners because they face no consequences. Sanctions change that calculation.

The Safe Harbor rule is your strategic friend. Serve the motion, wait 21 days, and use that window as leverage to force withdrawal of false evidence or correction of abusive conduct. If the lawyer does nothing, file on day 22 and let the court see exactly what they refused to fix.

Hold both the lawyer and the law firm accountable. Individual lawyers sign false documents. Firms profit from the systems that produce those documents. Both can be sanctioned.

False affidavits are perjury and Rule 11 violations simultaneously. When an affiant swears to personal knowledge and review without having reviewed anything, they have committed a sanctionable act that can destroy the bank's case and put money in your pocket.

Act fast, act precisely, and act professionally. Sanctions are a precision weapon, not a blunt instrument. Used correctly, they can turn a lawyer's misconduct into your advantage.

Cross-References

- **Chapter 15:** Attacking Affidavits, Declarations, and Bank Records — How to identify and challenge false affidavits that become sanctions targets
- **Chapter 12:** Discovery Warfare — Using discovery to gather the evidence you need for sanctions motions
- **Chapter 10:** How to Draft the Answer — Understanding pleadings standards that apply to both sides
- **Chapter 16:** Summary Judgment Survival — How to use sanctions motions to strike the false evidence banks rely on for summary judgment

- **Chapter 38:** The Current Payer's Nuclear Option — Related strategies for leveraging document fraud into homeowner advantage

---

End of Chapter 39

CHAPTER 40: THE SUBPOENA ATTACK

Forcing Banks, Lawyers, and Witnesses to Give You What You Need

---

The Most Ignored Weapon in Foreclosure Defense

Every foreclosure defense book mentions discovery. They tell you to request documents, send interrogatories, demand admissions. They explain what to ask for and why it matters. But almost none of them tell you the most important part: **how to actually force the other side to comply when they ignore you.**

The answer is the subpoena.

A subpoena is a court order commanding a person to do something — appear and testify, produce documents, or both. It carries the full weight of the court behind it. Ignore a discovery request and the worst that happens is a stern letter. Ignore a subpoena and you can be held in contempt of court, fined, or even arrested.

For pro se homeowners, the subpoena is the great equalizer. It turns your polite requests into court-enforced demands. It transforms voluntary cooperation into mandatory compliance. It gives you the same power that lawyers use every day — and most homeowners never even know it exists.

This chapter tells you everything the other books leave out: how to get a subpoena, how to fill it out, how to serve it, and what to do when the person on the other end tries to ignore it.

What a Subpoena Actually Is

A subpoena is a court order issued in the name of the court commanding a person to: - Appear at a specific place, date, and time to give testimony (subpoena ad testificandum) - Produce specific documents or evidence (subpoena duces tecum) - Both appear and produce documents

It is not a request. It is not a letter. It is not a discovery demand. It is a command backed by the court's authority. The person receiving it cannot simply refuse without legal consequences.

The Two Types You Need to Know

Subpoena ad testificandum: "Come and testify." This commands a person to appear at a deposition, hearing, or trial to answer questions under oath.

Subpoena duces tecum: "Bring these documents." This commands a person or entity to produce specific documents, records, or evidence at a specific time and place.

Both are powerful. Both can end a foreclosure case when used correctly. And both are available to pro se litigants at minimal cost.

How to Get a Subpoena

Here is the secret that lawyers don't advertise: Getting a subpoena is shockingly simple. You do not need an attorney. You do not need special training. You do not need to file a motion. You walk into the courthouse, ask the clerk, and pay a small fee.

Step-by-Step: Getting Your First Subpoena

Step 1: Go to the Clerk of Court's Office Walk into the courthouse where your foreclosure case is pending. Go to the clerk's office — the same place where you filed your Answer or your motions. Tell the clerk: **"I need a subpoena for my case."**

Step 2: Tell Them Which Type The clerk will ask whether you need a subpoena for testimony, documents, or both. Know what you want before you walk in: - **"I need a subpoena for a person to appear and testify at a deposition"** - **"I need a subpoena for a bank to produce documents"** - **"I need a subpoena for both — testimony and documents"**

Step 3: Pay the Fee Most courts charge between **$10 and $20 per subpoena.** Some courts charge per page. Some have a flat fee. Bring cash. Some clerks accept checks. Few accept cards. The fee is small, but without it, you don't get the subpoena.

Step 4: The Clerk Signs and Stamps — You Fill in the Rest This is the critical part that confuses many homeowners: **The clerk does not fill out the subpoena for you.** The clerk signs it, stamps it with the court seal, and hands it back to you as a blank court order. You then fill in: - The name of the person or entity being commanded - What they are commanded to do (appear, produce documents, or both) - The date, time, and place - What documents they must produce (if a duces tecum) - The case caption and number

The clerk's signature and stamp make it a valid court order. Your handwriting on the rest makes it specific to your needs.

What If the Clerk Says No?

Some clerks will tell you that pro se litigants cannot issue subpoenas. They are wrong in most jurisdictions, but they may not know the rule.

If the clerk refuses: - Ask to speak to a supervisor - Cite your state's rules of civil procedure — most states allow any party to a case to request subpoenas - Ask for a "blank subpoena form" — sometimes clerks will provide the form even if they won't issue it themselves - If all else fails, file a motion asking the court to authorize issuance of subpoenas

Most of the time, a polite but firm request is enough. The clerk is not your enemy. They are overworked and may not deal with pro se litigants often. Know your right to subpoena power, and don't leave without the signed, stamped form.

How to Fill Out a Subpoena

A properly filled subpoena is a precision instrument. A vague or sloppy subpoena gives the recipient room to wiggle out of compliance. A precise subpoena leaves them no escape.

The Basics

Every subpoena must contain: - The court's name and your case caption - The case number - The name of the person or entity being commanded - A clear command: "You are commanded to..." - The specific date, time, and place - What the person must do or produce - The signature and seal of the court clerk (already done)

Filling Out a Subpoena for Testimony

> **IN THE CIRCUIT COURT OF [COUNTY], [STATE] Case No. [Your Case Number] [Bank Name], Plaintiff, v. [Your Name], Defendant.**
>
> ---
>
> **SUBPOENA AD TESTIFICANDUM**
>
> TO: [Full Name of Witness]
>
> You are commanded to appear and give testimony before the undersigned at the following time and place:
>
> **Date:** [Month Day, Year] **Time:** [9:00 a.m.] **Place:** [Courtroom or deposition location address] **Before:** [Your name or court reporter name]

You are commanded to remain until excused by the undersigned.

Failure to comply with this subpoena may result in contempt of court and imposition of penalties.

Issued by: [Clerk's signature and seal already present]

Filling Out a Subpoena for Documents

SUBPOENA DUCES TECUM

TO: [Name of Bank or Entity] [Address of registered agent or principal office]

You are commanded to produce the following documents and things at the following time and place:

Date: [Month Day, Year] **Time:** [10:00 a.m.] **Place:** [Your address or designated location]

Documents to Produce: 1. The original promissory note for loan number [XXXXX] dated [Date] 2. All assignments of mortgage related to the above loan 3. The complete payment history from the inception of the loan through present 4. All correspondence between the servicer and the borrower regarding this loan 5. The pooling and servicing agreement governing this loan if the note was securitized

Failure to produce these documents may result in contempt of court and imposition of penalties.

Issued by: [Clerk's signature and seal already present]

Precision Matters

Be specific. Never write: - "All documents related to my loan" — too broad, can be challenged - "Bank records" — vague, gives them room to argue - "Everything about my mortgage" — unenforceable

Instead write: - "The original promissory note dated [Date] for loan number [Number]" - "The complete unredacted payment history from [Start Date] through [End Date]" - "All written correspondence between [Servicer Name] and [Borrower Name] from [Date] to [Date]"

The more specific you are, the harder it is for them to claim they don't understand what you want.

LEARN FROM THIS MISTAKE: The Homeowner Who Asked for Everything

Terrence Williams' Story: Terrence was fighting his foreclosure and needed documents from the bank. He went to the clerk, got a subpoena, and filled it out himself. In the "documents to produce" section, he wrote one line: "All documents related to my mortgage loan."

The bank's lawyer responded by producing three documents: the complaint, the note copy they'd already filed, and a one-page payment summary. The lawyer then moved to quash the subpoena, arguing it was "overly broad, unduly burdensome, and a fishing expedition."

The court agreed with the bank. The subpoena was quashed. Terrence had to start over, this time with a properly drafted, specific subpoena listing each document by name. He wasted two months and lost valuable momentum.

What Terrence should have done: - Listed each document category separately with specific identifying information - Defined date ranges for correspondence and payment records - Named the specific note by date and loan number - Requested "the original" rather than "a copy" when authentication was the goal - Consulted a template or sample subpoena before filling out his own

The Lesson: A subpoena is a surgical tool, not a fishing net. The court will enforce a precise demand. The court will reject a vague demand. Know exactly what you want, ask for it by name, and leave no room for argument.

Serving the Subpoena

A subpoena has no power until it is served. Service means delivering it to the person or entity named in the subpoena in a way that the law recognizes. Bad service equals no enforcement.

Who Can Serve a Subpoena?

Rules vary by state, but generally: - Any adult who is not a party to the case can serve a subpoena - A sheriff's deputy or constable can serve a subpoena - A professional process server can serve a subpoena - In some states, you can serve subpoenas yourself (but this is risky and often not recommended)

Best practice: Use a third party. Pay a friend, a relative, or hire a process server. The cost is small ($25-$75), and having an independent witness who can testify about service is invaluable if the recipient claims they never got it.

How to Serve a Subpoena on an Individual

1. **Hand the subpoena directly to the named person.**
2. **If they refuse to take it, place it near them and state what it is.**
3. **If they are not home or available, leave it with an adult at their residence.**
4. **Never serve by putting it in a mailbox — mailboxes are federally protected.**

The server must then complete an Affidavit of Service stating: - The date and time of service - The location where service occurred - The name of the person served - How the server identified the person (description, confirmation of name) - The method of service (handed directly, left with adult, etc.)

This affidavit is your proof. Without it, the person can deny they were ever served, and you have no way to prove otherwise.

How to Serve a Subpoena on a Corporation or Bank

Corporations and banks must be served through their registered agent or an authorized representative.

Step 1: Find the registered agent. - Search your state's Secretary of State business entity database - Look up the bank or servicer's registered agent for service of process - If the registered agent is a company (like CT Corporation or Corporation Service Company), serve the local office of that company

Step 2: Serve the agent personally. - Go to the registered agent's address - Hand the subpoena to a person who works there - Get their name and title - Have your server complete the Affidavit of Service

Step 3: If no registered agent is available, serve a high-ranking officer. - Serve the CEO, CFO, or general counsel at the principal office - Document who received it and their title

The Sheriff Alternative

Most counties have a sheriff's department that will serve subpoenas for a fee (typically $30-$100 depending on distance and number of attempts).

Why use the sheriff: - The sheriff's return of service is highly credible in court - Banks and businesses do not want a sheriff showing up at their office - The threat of sheriff service alone often compels voluntary acceptance - If the recipient dodges service, the sheriff has legal authority to keep trying

How to request sheriff service: - Contact your county sheriff's civil process division - Provide the subpoena, the recipient's address, and the case information - Pay the fee - The sheriff will attempt service and provide a return of service document

Serving Through the Opposing Lawyer

In many foreclosure cases, you can serve subpoenas through the bank's attorney rather than the bank directly. This is often faster, cheaper, and less confrontational.

How it works: 1. Draft your subpoena naming the bank or witness 2. Contact the opposing counsel (by email or letter) 3. Ask: **"Will you accept service of this subpoena on behalf of your client?"** 4. If yes, send it to the lawyer's office with a cover letter stating they have accepted service 5. Keep their acceptance email or letter as proof

Why lawyers usually agree: - They want to avoid the optics of a sheriff serving their client - They know the subpoena is valid and would be served anyway - It saves them the headache of a service fight - It maintains professional courtesy (which they value even if you don't)

If the lawyer refuses, serve the bank directly — and note the refusal in your records. If the bank later claims they were never served, you have proof their own lawyer blocked service.

The 10-Day Objection Window

Once a subpoena is served, the recipient generally has 10 days to object or move to quash. This is standard in most jurisdictions, though the exact timeframe varies by state.

What Is a Motion to Quash?

A motion to quash is the recipient's formal request to the court to cancel or modify the subpoena. They might argue: - The subpoena is overly broad or burdensome - The requested documents are privileged - The subpoena seeks irrelevant materials - Compliance would be unduly expensive - The person is outside the court's jurisdiction

What to Do If They Object

If the recipient files a motion to quash, you have options:

Option 1: Negotiate - Narrow the scope of your request - Extend the deadline for production - Agree to cover reasonable copying costs - Modify the place of production to be more convenient

Option 2: Oppose the Motion - File a response explaining why the subpoena is proper - Argue that the documents are relevant and necessary - Show that the burden of compliance is not excessive - Request that the court overrule the motion to quash

Option 3: Narrow and Resubmit - If the court grants the motion to quash on scope grounds, reissue a more specific subpoena - Use what you learned from their objection to draft a bulletproof second subpoena

Important: Even if they object, they must still comply until the court rules on the motion to quash. Many recipients don't know this and simply stop. If they fail to comply pending the court's ruling, they may still be in contempt.

What Happens When They Ignore the Subpoena

Most people and businesses comply with subpoenas. The court's authority is not something most people want to test. But when someone ignores a subpoena — whether willfully or negligently — you have powerful remedies.

Step 1: Document the Non-Compliance

Before going to court, build your record: - Keep the original served subpoena - Keep the proof of service (Affidavit of Service or return from sheriff) - Keep any communication with the recipient about the subpoena - Note the deadline date and that it passed without compliance - Send a follow-up letter or email: "Your subpoena response was due [Date]. We have not received the documents. Please produce immediately to avoid contempt proceedings."

Step 2: File a Motion to Compel Compliance

If the deadline passes with no response, file a motion with the court:

> **MOTION TO COMPEL COMPLIANCE WITH SUBPOENA**
>
> Defendant respectfully moves this Court to compel [Name/Entity] to comply with the subpoena issued [Date] and served [Date], and in support states:
>
> 1. On [Date], Defendant issued a subpoena duces tecum commanding [Entity] to produce [specific documents] by [Date].
> 2. The subpoena was duly served on [Date] by [Method] as evidenced by the attached Affidavit of Service.
> 3. The deadline for compliance was [Date].
> 4. [Entity] has failed and refused to produce the commanded documents.
> 5. The requested documents are relevant and necessary to Defendant's defense of this foreclosure action.
>
> WHEREFORE, Defendant requests that this Court: (a) Order [Entity] to immediately produce the subpoenaed documents; (b) Impose contempt sanctions for willful non-compliance; (c) Award Defendant's costs and fees incurred in enforcing this subpoena; (d) Grant such other relief as the Court deems just and proper.

Step 3: Request Contempt Sanctions

If they still don't comply after the court orders them to, move for contempt:

Contempt of court is the willful disobedience of a court order. It can result in: - Monetary fines (daily fines until compliance — called "coercive contempt") - Arrest and jail time (in extreme cases of willful defiance) - Adverse inference (the court assumes the missing documents would have hurt their case) - Dismissal of their claims or defenses (if the non-compliant party is a litigant)

Most subpoena recipients will comply the moment a judge threatens contempt. The power of a contempt citation is that it escalates a civil document dispute into a criminal consequence. Few people are willing to risk jail over mortgage paperwork.

LEARN FROM THIS MISTAKE: The Homeowner Who Didn't Document Service

Angela Foster's Story: Angela subpoenaed the vice president of her loan servicer to appear at a deposition and bring the original note. She hired a process server who handed the subpoena to a receptionist at the servicer's office. The server wrote a brief note on a napkin: "Served 3/15 at 2pm."

When the vice president failed to appear, Angela filed a motion to compel and for contempt. At the hearing, the servicer's lawyer argued that the subpoena was never properly served — the receptionist was not authorized to accept service, and the "proof" was a napkin note, not a formal Affidavit of Service.

The court agreed. The judge ruled that service was insufficient and denied Angela's motion. Angela lost the ability to compel the witness's appearance, lost two months of litigation time, and had to start the subpoena process over from scratch.

What Angela should have done: - Insisted the process server complete a formal Affidavit of Service with full details - Served the subpoena on the servicer's registered agent, not a random receptionist - Taken a photo or video of the service with timestamp - Sent a follow-up email to the servicer confirming receipt - Kept a copy of the subpoena and proof of service in her case file

The Lesson: Service without proof is the same as no service at all. The court does not care that you *believe* you served someone properly. The court cares whether you can *prove* it with documentary evidence. A formal Affidavit of Service is not optional — it is mandatory. Treat service with the same seriousness as filing a motion with the court.

Video Recording Service

In the modern era, video recording the service of a subpoena is a smart defensive practice. If the recipient later claims they never got it, a video is nearly impossible to refute.

How to Record Service Properly

1. **Use your phone or a body camera.** Ensure the date and time are displayed on the recording.
2. **Start recording before you approach.** Capture the location, the address, and the exterior of the building.

3. **Record the handoff.** Capture the server's face, the recipient's face, and the subpoena being handed over.
4. **Record the recipient's statement.** If they refuse to take it, record the server stating: "You are being served with a subpoena in [Case Name], Case No. [Number]." Record them refusing or walking away.
5. **Keep the video secure.** Upload to cloud storage immediately. Do not rely only on the phone's memory.

Warning: Some states have laws about recording people without their knowledge. Check your state's recording consent laws. In most cases, recording in a public place (like a business lobby or sidewalk) is legal. When in doubt, have the server announce: "This service is being video recorded for the court's records."

Giving Reasonable Time

A subpoena demands compliance, but it must give reasonable time to comply. Courts will not enforce a subpoena that demands documents tomorrow or a witness appearance in two hours.

Document Production Timeline

For subpoenas duces tecum requesting documents: - **Minimum:** 10 days from date of service - **Recommended:** 14-21 days from date of service - **For complex or voluminous records:** 30 days or more

Why this matters: If you demand documents in 2 days, the recipient will move to quash on grounds of insufficient time, and the court will likely agree. Give them enough time that their only argument is relevance or burden — not "I didn't have time to gather the files."

Witness Appearance Timeline

For subpoenas ad testificandum: - **Minimum:** 10 days from date of service - **Recommended:** 14-30 days from date of service - **For out-of-state witnesses:** 30 days or more, plus travel time

Specifying Delivery Methods

In your subpoena, tell them exactly how to deliver the documents:

> "You are commanded to produce the above documents by delivering them to [Your Name] at [Your Address] on or before [Date]. Alternatively, you may

> produce the documents by secure email to [your email address] with a delivery receipt, provided all documents are in searchable PDF format."

This removes ambiguity. They cannot claim they didn't know where to send the documents or in what format.

Email Service

In many jurisdictions, subpoenas can be served by email if the recipient agrees or if the court authorizes it. Email service is faster, cheaper, and creates its own digital record.

How to Request Email Service

Before serving by email: 1. Send an email to the recipient or their lawyer: "I intend to serve a subpoena by email. Will you accept email service?" 2. If they agree by reply email, you have consent. 3. Attach the subpoena as a PDF to the email. 4. Request a read receipt or delivery confirmation. 5. Keep the email chain as proof of service.

If they refuse email service, serve by physical delivery and note the refusal. If they later claim they wanted email service, you have proof they rejected it.

Why Email Service Is Often Better

- **Immediate delivery** — no waiting for mail transit
- **Automatic record** — the email itself is proof of what was sent and when
- **No process server fees** — free beyond the subpoena issuance fee
- **Hard to deny** — email servers log delivery
- **Can include detailed instructions** — link to a shared drive, specify file naming conventions, etc.

What the Email Should Include

> **Subject:** Subpoena Duces Tecum — [Case Name] Case No. [Number]
>
> Dear [Name or Counsel]:
>
> Attached is a subpoena duces tecum issued by the [Court Name] in the above-captioned matter, commanding [Entity] to produce the documents listed therein by [Date].

Please confirm receipt of this subpoena and your intent to comply. If you have any questions regarding the scope of the request, please contact me by [Date] to discuss.

Failure to comply may result in a motion to compel and contempt proceedings.

Respectfully, [Your Name] [Your Address] [Your Phone] [Your Email]

Strategic Uses of Subpoenas in Foreclosure Defense

1. Subpoena the Robo-Signer

If the bank's affidavit was signed by a known robo-signer, subpoena them for deposition. Ask them under oath: - How many affidavits did you sign that day? - Did you review my specific file? - How much time did you spend reviewing it? - Who trained you on affidavit preparation?

Most robo-signers will not show up. When they don't appear, file a motion to compel and for contempt. The bank's affidavit then loses its foundation.

2. Subpoena the Original Note

Subpoena the bank to produce the original promissory note. If they cannot produce it, their standing is weakened. If they produce a copy, demand the original for authentication. If the note has no endorsements, the assignment chain is broken.

3. Subpoena the Payment History Source Documents

Don't rely on the bank's printout. Subpoena the servicer to produce the actual source documents for the payment history — the ledger entries, the bank deposit records, the transaction logs. If the printout doesn't match the source documents, the bank's evidence is fabricated.

4. Subpoena the Assignment Documents

Subpoena the assignor and assignee of each mortgage assignment. Demand: - The assignment agreement - The consideration exchanged - The corporate resolutions authorizing the assignment - The custodial records showing who held the note before and after

If the assignment was a robo-signed fabrication, the assignor's records will not match the filed document.

5. Subpoena the Notary

If a document was notarized, subpoena the notary. Ask them: - Were you present when the document was signed? - Did you verify the signer's identity? - Did you actually witness the signature? - How many notarizations did you perform that day?

Notaries who participated in bulk robo-signing will often admit under oath that they never actually witnessed the signatures. This destroys the notarized document's credibility.

Chapter Summary

The subpoena is the most underutilized weapon in foreclosure defense. It transforms your polite requests into court-enforced commands. It costs almost nothing to obtain. It requires no attorney. And when backed by the threat of contempt, it compels compliance from even the most resistant banks and witnesses.

Key takeaways: 1. **Get subpoenas from the clerk of court** — just ask, pay $10-$20, and get a signed, stamped form 2. **Fill them out precisely** — specific documents, specific dates, specific delivery methods 3. **Serve them properly** — use a third party, get an Affidavit of Service, consider video recording 4. **Give reasonable time** — 10-14 days minimum for documents, longer for complex requests 5. **Use email service when possible** — faster, cheaper, and creates a digital record 6. **Follow up on non-compliance** — send a warning letter, then file a motion to compel 7. **Request contempt if they still refuse** — the threat of fines or arrest changes minds quickly 8. **Subpoena strategically** — robo-signers, the original note, payment source documents, notaries

The subpoena turns you from a supplicant asking for help into a litigant commanding compliance. Use it.

Cross-References

- **Chapter 12:** Discovery Warfare — Using subpoenas as the enforcement mechanism behind discovery requests
- **Chapter 15:** Attacking Affidavits, Declarations, and Bank Records — Subpoenaing robo-signers and notaries to destroy the bank's evidence
- **Chapter 39:** Sanctions Against Opposing Counsel — When the bank's lawyer blocks or resists subpoena compliance

- **Chapter 29:** Dismissal With Prejudice — How subpoena-based evidence can support motions for permanent dismissal

---

Quick Reference Checklist

Before Getting a Subpoena: - [ ] Know exactly what documents or testimony you need - [ ] Know who has those documents or who can give that testimony - [ ] Research the registered agent or authorized recipient for service - [ ] Prepare a specific, itemized list of documents requested

At the Clerk's Office: - [ ] Ask for the subpoena form - [ ] Specify whether you need ad testificandum, duces tecum, or both - [ ] Pay the fee ($10-$20) - [ ] Ensure the clerk signs and stamps the form

Filling Out the Subpoena: - [ ] Include case caption and number - [ ] Name the person or entity specifically - [ ] State the command clearly (appear, produce, or both) - [ ] Set a reasonable date (10-14 days minimum) - [ ] Set a specific time and place - [ ] List documents precisely, item by item - [ ] Specify delivery method (in person, email, mail)

Serving the Subpoena: - [ ] Use a third party (not yourself) - [ ] Get a formal Affidavit of Service completed - [ ] Consider video recording the service - [ ] Keep a copy of the served subpoena - [ ] Send a confirming email if served electronically

If They Don't Comply: - [ ] Send a follow-up demand letter - [ ] Document all non-compliance - [ ] File a Motion to Compel Compliance - [ ] Request contempt sanctions in the motion - [ ] Be prepared to argue at a hearing

---

End of Chapter 40

DISCLAIMER

This document is provided for educational and informational purposes only. It does not constitute legal advice and should not be relied upon as a substitute for professional legal counsel. Laws vary by jurisdiction and change over time. Readers are strongly encouraged to consult with a qualified attorney licensed in their jurisdiction before taking any legal action. The authors and publishers disclaim any liability for any loss or damage arising from reliance on the information contained herein.

BONUS 1 CHAPTER
The Concurrent Filing Trap

State-Specific Requirements That Foreclosure Mills Forget

Why This Matters

Every state has its own foreclosure procedure. Most homeowners and many attorneys focus on the big issues: standing, chain of title, the note and mortgage. But there's a quieter, more technical category of defenses that can end a foreclosure before it begins — and foreclosure mills miss them constantly.

These are the **mandatory concurrent filing requirements**.

Many states don't just require a complaint to start a foreclosure. They require additional documents to be filed **concurrently** — at the same time, in the same action, sometimes in different offices. A lis pendens in one county. A notice to the homeowner on colored paper. A certificate of merit filed with the court. An affidavit of SCRA compliance.

When these documents are missing, the foreclosure filing is defective. Sometimes fatally so.

The strategy is straightforward: Review your state's foreclosure statutes. Identify every document the plaintiff was required to file concurrently with the complaint. Check the court file. If anything is missing, move to dismiss.

The foreclosure mill, handling thousands of cases in multiple states, often misses state-specific requirements. They're processing paperwork at volume. You're defending your home. Attention to detail wins.

The Critical Distinction: With Prejudice vs. Without Prejudice

Before examining specific states, understand what victory looks like:

Dismissal Without Prejudice: The court dismisses the foreclosure, but the plaintiff can refile. This buys you time — months, sometimes years. The statute of limitations continues to run. You get another chance to negotiate, modify, or prepare. The plaintiff must start over, correct the defect, and refile. This is the most common outcome for procedural defects.

Dismissal With Prejudice: The court dismisses the foreclosure, and the plaintiff cannot refile. This is a complete victory. The foreclosure is over. This usually requires either (1) a statute of limitations violation, (2) a constitutional due process violation, or (3) a showing that the defect cannot be cured and the plaintiff had ample opportunity to correct it.

Most concurrent filing defects result in dismissal without prejudice. But dismissal without prejudice is still a win — it resets the clock, forces the plaintiff to correct errors, and gives you time to strengthen your position. And if they refile and make the same mistake again, you're building a record for sanctions or eventual dismissal with prejudice.

State-by-State Concurrent Filing Requirements

NEW YORK

Statute: NY Real Property Actions and Proceedings Law (RPAPL) § 1303

Required Filings:

Notice of Pendency (Lis Pendens): Must be filed at least 20 days prior to the granting of the foreclosure judgment, but is typically filed at the commencement of the action.

"Help for Homeowners" Notice: For residential foreclosures involving 1-4 family dwellings, this notice MUST be served with the summons and complaint on paper that is a different color than the summons and complaint.

Critical Timing Requirements (Westchester County Specific):

Request for Judicial Intervention (RJI): Must be filed with the county clerk at the same time proof of service is filed.

Certificate of Merit: Must accompany the complaint.

Dismissal Ground: Failure to file the RJI or include the RPAPL § 1303 notice can result in the case not being assigned to a judge or being procedurally defective.

Strategic Note: New York requires strict compliance. The "Help for Homeowners" notice on different-colored paper is a specific statutory requirement designed to ensure homeowners see critical information. If the plaintiff served everything on white paper, they failed.

CONNECTICUT

Statute: Conn. Gen. Stat. § 49-311

Required Filings:

Lis Pendens: Must be "annexed as an exhibit to the complaint."

Foreclosure Mediation Notice: Must be attached to the front of the writ, summons, and complaint.

Foreclosure Mediation Certificate Form.

Blank Appearance Form.

Dismissal Ground: The statute explicitly requires the lis pendens to be attached to the complaint. Failure to do so is a jurisdictional defect.

Strategic Note: Connecticut is unique in requiring the lis pendens to be physically annexed to the complaint as an exhibit. A separate filing is insufficient. Check the complaint itself — if there's no lis pendens attached as an exhibit, they failed.

MARYLAND

Statute: MD Real Property Article § 7-105.1; MD Code Regs. 09.03.12.07

Required Filings with Order to Docket or Complaint:

• Affidavit stating: (1) date of default, (2) date Notice of Intent to Foreclose was sent, and (3) that contents are accurate
• Original or certified copy of the mortgage or deed of trust
• Statement of Debt remaining with certified affidavit
• Copy of debt instrument with affidavit of ownership
• Original or certified copy of assignment of mortgage (if applicable)
• Lender/Servicer License Number (if applicable)
• Affidavit that defendant is not in the military (SCRA compliance)
• Final Loss Mitigation Affidavit
• Notice of Foreclosure Action (for owner-occupied residential properties)

Dismissal Ground: Failure to include these documents renders the filing incomplete.

Strategic Note: Maryland has one of the most extensive concurrent filing requirements in the nation. The list is long, and foreclosure mills frequently miss items — particularly the SCRA affidavit, the loss mitigation affidavit, or the lender license number. Each omission is a separate ground for dismissal.

NEW JERSEY

Statute: N.J.S.A. 46:10B-51

Required Filings: Must be filed with the summons and complaint AND with the lis pendens:

• Full name, address, and telephone number of creditor/servicer representative responsible for receiving property maintenance complaints

• If out-of-state, full name, address, and telephone number of in-State representative/agent for property care
• Updated information must be filed within 10 days of any change

Dismissal Ground: The Fair Foreclosure Act requires strict compliance. *Bank of New York v. Laks* held that defective notices require dismissal without prejudice.

Strategic Note: New Jersey's requirement for an in-state representative for out-of-state servicers is frequently ignored. Check the lis pendens — does it include the required contact information? If the servicer is based in another state, is there a named New Jersey agent? If not, you have a dismissal argument.

SOUTH CAROLINA

Statute: S.C. Code Ann. § 15-11-10 et seq.

Required Filing:

Lis Pendens: Must be filed no more than 20 days before the filing of the complaint AND no less than 20 days prior to the entry of a foreclosure decree.

Critical: "If filed more than 20 days before the filing of the complaint, the lis pendens is automatically invalid."

Service Requirement: Lis pendens must be served within 60 days of filing or it becomes invalid.

Dismissal Ground: An improperly timed lis pendens is "automatically invalid" and can be grounds for dismissal.

Strategic Note: South Carolina has the strictest lis pendens timing requirement in the nation. The 20-day window is narrow. Check the dates: When was the lis pendens filed? When was the complaint filed? If the lis pendens was filed more than 20 days before the complaint, it is **automatically invalid** — no judge has discretion to save it.

FLORIDA

Statute: Fla. Stat. § 48.23

Required Filing:

Notice of Lis Pendens: Must contain:
• Names of parties
• Date of institution of action
• Name of court
• Description of property

• Statement of relief sought

Critical: If filed same date as pleading, clerk's notation of receipt satisfies date requirement.

Strategic Note: Florida requires the lis pendens to be served by registered/certified mail on all affected parties before recording, with proof of service filed. Check for proof of service. If they recorded the lis pendens without proper service, it's defective.

ILLINOIS

Statute: 735 ILCS 5/15-1503

Required Filing:

Notice of Foreclosure: Must be recorded in the county where mortgaged real estate is located. This serves as constructive notice to every person claiming an interest in the property whose interest was not recorded prior to the foreclosure notice.

Strategic Note: Illinois requires recording in the property county, not just filing with the court. Check the county recorder's office. If no notice of foreclosure was recorded, constructive notice was never established.

NORTH CAROLINA

Statute: N.C. Gen. Stat. § 1-116 et seq.; § 105-374

Important Note: In North Carolina, the complaint itself serves as lis pendens "from the time it is filed in the office of the clerk of superior court." No separate filing is required.

However: Under § 1-119(a): If a separate lis pendens is filed, it "is of no avail unless it is followed by the first publication of notice of the summons or by personal service on the defendant within 60 days after the cross-indexing."

Strategic Note: If the plaintiff filed a separate lis pendens (rather than relying on the complaint itself), they must serve you within 60 days. Check the dates. If service came after day 60, the lis pendens is "of no avail."

OHIO

Statute: Ohio R. Civ. P. 3(F); Ohio Rev. Code § 323.69

Required Filings:

Certified Copy of Complaint: In each county where property is located (if different from where action is filed) OR a Notice of Filing Foreclosure Action with county clerk.

Preliminary Judicial Report: Must be filed within 14 days after filing the complaint (for abandoned land foreclosure).

Dismissal Ground: Rule 3(F) states: "If the plaintiff fails to file a certified copy of the complaint, third persons will not be charged with notice of the pendency of the action."

Strategic Note: Ohio requires filing in **every county** where the property is located. If your property spans county lines, check each county clerk. If they only filed in one county, they failed to provide notice in the others.

WISCONSIN

Statute: Wis. Stat. § 840.10(1)(a)

Required Filing:

Lis Pendens: "In an action where relief is demanded affecting described real property which relief might confirm or change interests in the real property, a lis pendens must be filed in the county where the property is located."

MISSOURI

Statute: Mo. Rev. Stat. § 527.260

Required Filing:

Notice of Lis Pendens: Must be filed with the recorder of deeds in any county where the real estate is situated, containing:
• Names of parties
• Style of action
• Term of court
• Legal description of real estate

Effect: "The pendency of such suit shall be constructive notice to purchasers or encumbrancers, only from the time of filing such notice."

INDIANA

Statute: Ind. Code § 32-30-10.5-8

Required Filings with Complaint:

• Copy of the notice sent to the debtor under subsection (a) (Notice of Default and Right to Cure)
• Most recent contact information for the debtor (all phone numbers, email addresses, mailing addresses)

Dismissal Ground: This information is required confidential information under IC 5-14-3-4(a)(13). Failure to include it violates statutory preconditions.

Strategic Note: Indiana requires the plaintiff to include your contact information — all of it — with the complaint. This is designed to ensure you can be reached for mediation and settlement discussions. If the complaint lacks complete contact information, the filing is defective.

ARIZONA

Statute: A.R.S. § 12-1191

Required Filing:

Notice of Lis Pendens: "After filing the foreclosure complaint, the lender should immediately record a notice of lis pendens with the recorder's office in the county where the real property is located."

OREGON

Statute: ORS § 88.010

Required Filing:

Notice to Lien Debtors: A complaint in a suit to foreclose a residential trust deed "must include as an attachment a copy of a notice to lien debtors" printed in at least 14-point type.

Strategic Note: Oregon has a specific font size requirement — 14-point type. Check the attachment. If the notice to lien debtors is in 12-point type, they failed to comply with the statute.

NEVADA

Statute: NRS 108.239

Required Filing:

Notice of Pendency: "At the time of filing the complaint and issuing the summons, the lien claimant shall: (a) File a notice of pendency of the action in the manner provided in NRS 14.010."

WASHINGTON

Statute: RCW 4.28.320; RCW 4.28.325

Required Filing:

Lis Pendens: "From the time of the filing only shall the pendency of the action be constructive notice to a purchaser or encumbrancer of the property."

Critical Timing: For actions in U.S. District Court, the lis pendens "shall be of no avail unless it shall be followed by the first publication of the summons, or by personal service thereof on a defendant within sixty days after such filing."

MASSACHUSETTS

Statute: Mass. Gen. Laws Ch. 244 §§ 35B, 35C

Required Filing:

No lis pendens is required to file concurrently with the complaint.

However: An Affidavit pursuant to Ch. 244, § 35B and § 35C is required for residential property foreclosures, which must be filed with the Land Court or Registry of Deeds.

Quick Reference: Most Powerful Defenses by State

State	Primary Defense	Statutory Basis	Consequence of Non-Compliance
South Carolina	Lis pendens timing (±20 days)	S.C. Code Ann. § 15-11-10	Lis pendens "automatically invalid"
Connecticut	Lis pendens not annexed	Conn. Gen. Stat. § 49-311	Jurisdictional defect
New Jersey	Missing creditor/agent info	N.J.S.A. 46:10B-51	Dismissal without prejudice
Maryland	Missing affidavits/documents	MD Real Prop. § 7-105.1	Incomplete filing
New York	No RJI/No RPAPL 1303 Notice	RPAPL § 1303	Lack of judicial assignment
Ohio	No certified copy filed	Ohio R. Civ. P. 3(F)	No constructive notice
North Carolina	Service not within 60 days	N.C. Gen. Stat. § 1-119	Lis pendens "of no avail"
Indiana	Missing debtor contact info	Ind. Code § 32-30-10.5-8	Statutory precondition failure
Oregon	Notice not in 14-point type	ORS § 88.010	Non-compliance

How to Execute the Defense

Step 1: Identify Your State's Requirements

Locate your state's foreclosure statutes. Look for sections discussing:
• Required filings with the complaint
• Lis pendens requirements and timing
• Notice requirements
• Mediation prerequisites
• Recording requirements

Step 2: Review the Court File

Go to the courthouse or access the online docket. Review every document filed. Create a checklist of required documents and check each one:

☐ Was it filed?
☐ Was it filed on time?
☐ Does it contain all required information?
☐ Was it filed in the correct office?

Step 3: Check the County Recorder

If your state requires recording (Illinois, Missouri, Arizona), check the county recorder's office separately. A filing with the court is not the same as a recording with the county.

Step 4: Draft Your Motion to Dismiss

Cite the specific statute that was violated. Attach the statutory text as an exhibit. Explain exactly what was required and exactly what the plaintiff failed to do.

Step 5: Argue Prejudice

Explain how the missing document prejudiced you. Did you lack notice? Were you unable to protect your interests? Did third parties acquire interests because constructive notice was never established?

The "Automatic Invalidity" States

Some states use language that leaves no room for judicial discretion:

South Carolina: "If filed more than 20 days before the filing of the complaint, the lis pendens is **automatically invalid**."

North Carolina: If not served within 60 days, the lis pendens is "**of no avail**."

Washington: If not followed by service within 60 days, the lis pendens "shall be **of no avail**."

In these states, the statute itself declares the consequence. The court has no discretion to overlook the defect. If the condition is met, the document is void by operation of law.

When to Raise the Defense

Best Practice: Raise concurrent filing defects in your Answer or in a preliminary motion to dismiss.

Strategic Timing: If the defect is curable (the plaintiff can file the missing document), raising it early forces them to correct it or face dismissal. If the defect is not curable (time has passed, deadlines missed), you have a stronger argument for dismissal with prejudice or sanctions if they refile with the same defect.

Don't Wait: Some defenses are waived if not raised early. Check your state's rules — failure to raise certain jurisdictional defects in your initial responsive pleading may waive them.

The Re-Filing Trap

When you win a dismissal without prejudice, the plaintiff will likely refile. Watch for this:

Can they cure the defect? If yes, they will refile with the correct documents.

Did they cure it correctly? Verify that the new filing includes everything required. Foreclosure mills often rush to refile and make new errors.

Is this the second (or third) time they've made the same error? Document the pattern. Repeated failures to comply with basic filing requirements may support a motion for sanctions or a request for dismissal with prejudice as a sanction for abuse of process.

Did the statute of limitations expire during the first case? If the dismissal comes late in the limitations period, and the plaintiff cannot refile before the deadline expires, you may have won permanently.

Chapter Summary

Mandatory concurrent filing requirements are procedural landmines that foreclosure mills step on regularly. They process cases in volume across multiple states. They miss state-specific requirements. And when they do, you have grounds to dismiss.

Key takeaways:

1. Every state has unique filing requirements — know yours
2. Check the court file against the statutory checklist
3. The "automatic invalidity" states (SC, NC, WA) offer the strongest defenses
4. Most dismissals will be without prejudice — but time is your ally
5. Document every defect to build a record for sanctions or eventual dismissal with prejudice

The strategy: Review your state's statutes. Check every filing. If something is missing, move to dismiss. Force the plaintiff to comply with the law. Every procedural victory buys you time. Enough time can win your case.

Quick Reference Checklist

Before Filing Your Motion:

- [ ] Locate your state's foreclosure statutes online
- [ ] Identify all documents required to be filed concurrently with the complaint
- [ ] Review the court file for each required document
- [ ] Check dates — was each document filed on time?
- [ ] Check the county recorder's office for recording requirements
- [ ] Verify lis pendens was filed correctly and served timely
- [ ] Check for required affidavits (SCRA, loss mitigation, etc.)
- [ ] Verify notice requirements (colored paper, font size, etc.)
- [ ] Check for required contact information or representative designations

In Your Motion:
- [ ] Cite the specific statute requiring the missing document
- [ ] Attach the statutory text as an exhibit
- [ ] State exactly what was required and exactly what the plaintiff failed to do
- [ ] Argue prejudice — how the missing document harmed your defense
- [ ] Request dismissal (with prejudice if the defect is incurable)

If Dismissal Is Granted Without Prejudice:
- [ ] Verify the plaintiff's refiled complaint includes all required documents
- [ ] Check for new errors in the refiled complaint
- [ ] Document repeated failures for future sanctions motion
- [ ] Calculate statute of limitations — did it expire?

This chapter contains jurisdiction-specific information. Verify all statutes and case law are current for your state before filing.

DISCLAIMER

This document is provided for educational and informational purposes only. It does not constitute legal advice and should not be relied upon as a substitute for professional legal counsel. Laws vary by jurisdiction and change over time. Readers are strongly encouraged to consult with a qualified attorney licensed in their jurisdiction before taking any legal action. The authors and publishers disclaim any liability for any loss or damage arising from reliance on the information contained herein.

BONUS 2 CHAPTER

Challenging Mortgage Assignments

The Harsh Reality of State-by-State Standing Rules

The Injustice

Mortgage assignments have been forged by the thousands. Robo-signers stamped names they had no authority to sign. Documents were backdated to cover up broken chains of title. Notaries attested to signatures they never witnessed. The fraud was systemic, documented, and undeniable.

And in most states, homeowners cannot challenge it.

The courts have erected a wall around mortgage assignments. If the assignment is merely "voidable" — improper, unethical, perhaps even fraudulent in the inducement — the homeowner lacks standing to attack it. Only if the assignment is "void" — a legal nullity from inception, typically due to forgery or a fraudulent signature — can the homeowner even get in the door.

This chapter tells you the truth about which states allow challenges and which don't. It won't make you happy. But it will keep you from wasting time on arguments that cannot win.

Void vs. Voidable: The Threshold Question

Before examining state rules, understand the distinction that controls everything:

Void: A legal nullity from the start. A forgery is void — the document never existed as a legal instrument because the signature was fake. A document signed by someone who had no authority to sign on behalf of the entity is void.

Voidable: Valid until someone with standing challenges it. A document signed with proper authority but containing false representations is voidable. A document executed in violation of a pooling and servicing agreement is voidable.

Why It Matters:

In most states, only void assignments can be challenged by homeowners. If the assignment is merely voidable, the courts say: "That's between the assignor and assignee. The homeowner isn't a party to that transaction and cannot challenge it."

This means:
- ✅ **Forgery of a signature** → Void → Challengeable

- ✅ **Signer had no authority** → Void → Challengeable
- ❌ **Robo-signing (proper authority, false representations)** → Voidable → Not challengeable
- ❌ **Violation of PSA timing requirements** → Voidable → Not challengeable
- ❌ **Assignment without consideration** → Voidable → Not challengeable

Category 1: Absolute "NO" — No Standing (7 States)

These states follow the Eighth Circuit's strict approach. Homeowners have virtually no standing to challenge mortgage assignments, even for fraud or forgery.

State	Key Case / Rule
Arkansas	Standing requires direct injury from the assignment itself
Iowa	Homeowner is not a party to the assignment contract
Minnesota	Assignment defects are between assignor and assignee only
Missouri	No third-party beneficiary status for homeowners
Nebraska	MERS assignment challenges rejected; no homeowner standing
North Dakota	Strict privity requirement; homeowner lacks standing
South Dakota	Eighth Circuit approach; assignment validity is inter-party issue

What This Means:

In these seven states, arguing that the assignment was forged, fraudulent, or defective will likely be dismissed for lack of standing. The court's position: Even if the assignment is completely fraudulent, that's a dispute between the party who was defrauded (the assignee) and the party who committed the fraud (the assignor). The homeowner borrowed money and owes it to someone. Who that someone is doesn't affect the homeowner's obligation to pay.

Strategic Note:

In these states, focus your defense on the **note**, not the mortgage assignment. Challenge the plaintiff's possession of the note. Challenge the endorsement chain. Challenge standing to enforce the debt. Do not waste time arguing the assignment was defective — the court won't hear it.

Category 2: "VOID ONLY" — Extremely Limited Standing (16 States)

These states allow homeowners to challenge assignments, but **only if the assignment is void** (forgery, fraudulent signature, or complete lack of authority). Claims that the assignment is merely voidable (robo-signing, PSA violations, lack of consideration) will fail.

State	Notes
Texas	Homeowner can challenge void assignments; voidable assignments are immune
Louisiana	Civil law tradition; strict standing requirements
Mississippi	Following Eighth Circuit approach with narrow void exception
Michigan	Void ab initio doctrine applies; voidable claims rejected
Arizona	Homeowner standing limited to facially void documents
Ohio	Recent cases narrowing homeowner standing to void assignments only
Georgia	Strong privity requirements; void-only rule applied
North Carolina	Homeowner can challenge void assignments; PSA violations not challengeable
Alabama	Limited standing; forgery or complete lack of authority required

Indiana	Void-only rule; fraud in the inducement not sufficient
Oklahoma	Homeowner not party to assignment; void exception only
Tennessee	Strict standing; only facially void assignments challengeable
Kentucky	Privity doctrine; void assignments only exception
South Carolina	Void ab initio standard; voidable defects excluded
Florida	Complex case law; generally void-only for assignment challenges
Wisconsin	Following national trend toward void-only standing

The "Void" Exception Explained:

To challenge an assignment in these states, you must prove the assignment was **void from inception**, not merely voidable. This typically requires:

1. **Forgery:** The signature on the assignment is completely fake — not just robo-signed by someone with authority, but signed by someone who had no connection to the entity they purported to represent.

2. **Complete Lack of Authority:** The signer purported to sign as "Vice President of [Bank]" but had no position with that bank, no employment, no authorization whatsoever.

3. **Notary Fraud:** The notary attested to witnessing a signature that never occurred or attested to the identity of a signer they never met.

What Does NOT Qualify as "Void":

- Robo-signing (signer had title but signed thousands without review)
- Backdating (document signed on date different from stated date)
- PSA violations (assignment didn't follow pooling agreement)
- Lack of consideration (no money exchanged)
- Fraud in the inducement (false representations made to induce signing)

These defects make the assignment **voidable**, not void. And in these 16 states, voidable assignments cannot be challenged by homeowners.

Category 3: "Qualified NO" — Some Standing But Very Limited (13 States)

These states recognize limited homeowner standing to challenge assignments, but the window is narrow and the burden is high.

State	Notes
Alaska	Limited standing; homeowner must show direct injury
Colorado	Some authority for homeowner challenges; fact-specific
Connecticut	Standing exists but is narrowly construed
Delaware	Corporate law state; complex standing analysis
Idaho	Limited authority; following neighboring states' trends
Kansas	Standing recognized but scope is limited
Maine	Traditional rule; some flexibility for fraud claims
Maryland	Statutory foreclosure; assignment challenges difficult
Montana	Limited case law; conservative standing approach
Nevada	Some standing for fraud; voidable claims uncertain
New Hampshire	Traditional privity analysis; limited exceptions
New Mexico	Developing law; cautious approach to standing

Oregon	Some recognition of homeowner standing; fact-dependent

Strategic Approach:

In these states, assignment challenges are possible but risky. The law is unsettled. Some courts may allow challenges; others won't. Consider:

1. **File the challenge** but have backup arguments
2. **Plead in the alternative** — challenge assignment AND challenge note possession
3. **Be specific** — general allegations of "fraud" will be dismissed; specific forgeries may survive
4. **Consider state law claims** — unfair trade practices, deceptive acts may provide alternative standing

Category 4: More Permissive States (11 States + DC)

These states generally allow homeowners to challenge mortgage assignments, though the specific rules and success rates vary.

State	Notes
California	Homeowner standing recognized; detailed discovery allowed
New York	Strong precedent for assignment challenges; *Silverberg* standard
Illinois	Standing recognized; note and mortgage separation doctrine
New Jersey	Fair Foreclosure Act provides some protections; homeowner standing exists
Massachusetts	Standing recognized; Ibanez decision established clear rules
Pennsylvania	Homeowner can challenge assignments; procedural protections
Rhode Island	Similar to Massachusetts; standing recognized
Vermont	Consumer protection orientation; homeowner standing
Virginia	Some standing; complex equitable analysis
Washington	Homeowner standing recognized; detailed case law
Utah	Limited but recognized standing for homeowners
District of Columbia	Federal influence; standing generally recognized

Why These States Are Different:

These states recognize that a homeowner has a legitimate interest in knowing who owns their mortgage. The assignment affects the homeowner's rights — who they can negotiate with, who can modify their loan, who can foreclose. These courts reject the rigid privity doctrine that says the homeowner is merely an outsider to the assignment transaction.

Strategic Note:

Even in these states, assignment challenges are difficult. You still must prove the assignment is defective. You still must show the defect affects the plaintiff's standing. But at least the door is open. In these states, you can make the argument without it being dismissed for lack of standing.

The Practical Reality

The 45-State Problem:

In 45 states (7 Absolute NO + 16 VOID ONLY + 13 Qualified NO + 9 with limited permissiveness), challenging a mortgage assignment is either impossible or extremely difficult. The banks know this. They file assignments knowing that in most states, the homeowner cannot effectively challenge them.

What This Means for Your Defense:

1. Check Your State First: Before spending time on assignment challenges, determine which category your state falls into. If you're in an Absolute NO or VOID ONLY state, focus your energy elsewhere.

2. Attack the Note, Not the Assignment: In restrictive states, challenge the plaintiff's possession of the note, the endorsement chain, and standing to enforce the debt. These attacks don't require challenging the assignment.

3. Look for "Void" Evidence: If you're in a VOID ONLY state, look specifically for forged signatures or complete lack of authority — not just robo-signing or procedural defects. You need evidence that makes the assignment a legal nullity.

4. Consider Alternative Theories: In restrictive states, consider:
- Unfair trade practices claims
- Deceptive acts claims
- FDCPA violations (if debt collector involved)
- RICO claims (if pattern of fraud)

These may provide standing to attack assignment-related conduct even when direct assignment challenges are barred.

The Call for Reform

The current state of the law is indefensible. Banks forged thousands of mortgage assignments. They created documents to cover up broken chains of title. They used robo-signers to execute assignments they never reviewed. And in most states, homeowners cannot challenge this fraud.

The rationale — that the homeowner is not a party to the assignment — ignores reality. The assignment determines who can foreclose. It determines who the homeowner must negotiate with. It determines whether the entity suing for foreclosure actually owns the debt. The homeowner is the party most affected by a fraudulent assignment.

The law protects banks that committed fraud while leaving homeowners with no recourse. It allows banks to foreclose based on forged documents because the person whose home is being taken isn't the "right" person to challenge the forgery.

This needs to change. Homeowners need standing to challenge fraudulent assignments in every state. Until then, this chapter tells you the truth about what you can and cannot do.

Chapter Summary

The harsh truth: In most states, you cannot challenge a mortgage assignment unless it is void (forged) rather than merely voidable (improper, unethical, or fraudulent in the inducement).

Key takeaways:

1. **7 states (Absolute NO):** No standing to challenge assignments — don't waste your time
2. **16 states (VOID ONLY):** Can challenge only if assignment is void due to forgery or complete lack of authority
3. **13 states (Qualified NO):** Some standing, but narrow and fact-specific
4. **12 jurisdictions (Permissive):** General standing to challenge, though still difficult to win
5. **In restrictive states, attack the note** — challenge possession, endorsements, and standing to enforce
6. **Look for forged signatures** — this is the only defect that qualifies as "void" in most states
7. **Consider alternative claims** — unfair practices, FDCPA, RICO may provide indirect paths

The bottom line: The law protects fraudulent banks at the expense of homeowners. Know your state's rules. Don't waste arguments the court won't hear. Focus your energy where it can actually make a difference.

State-by-State Quick Reference

Category	States	Challenge Allowed?
Absolute NO	AR, IA, MN, MO, NE, ND, SD	❌ No
VOID ONLY	TX, LA, MS, MI, AZ, OH, GA, NC, AL, IN, OK, TN, KY, SC, FL, WI	⚠️ Only if void (forged)
Qualified NO	AK, CO, CT, DE, ID, KS, ME, MD, MT, NV, NH, NM, OR	⚠️ Limited, fact-specific
Permissive	CA, NY, IL, NJ, MA, PA, RI, VT, VA, WA, UT, DC	✅ Generally yes

The assignment fraud was real. The forgeries were documented. And in 45 states, the courts say you cannot challenge it. This is the law we have. Know it. Work within it. And push for change.

DISCLAIMER

This document is provided for educational and informational purposes only. It does not constitute legal advice and should not be relied upon as a substitute for professional legal counsel. Laws vary by jurisdiction and change over time. Readers are strongly encouraged to consult with a qualified attorney licensed in their jurisdiction before taking any legal action. The authors and publishers disclaim any liability for any loss or damage arising from reliance on the information contained herein.

BONUS CHAPTER 3
Attacking Note Assignment and Allonge

The UCC Weapon Every Homeowner Needs

The Foundation of Foreclosure

Every foreclosure starts with a simple premise: The plaintiff claims they own the mortgage debt and have the right to enforce it. That claim rests on one document — the promissory note.

Without the note properly endorsed to them, the plaintiff has no standing to foreclose. It's that simple. And yet, in the vast majority of foreclosure cases, the plaintiff cannot produce the original note with a proper chain of endorsements. They've lost it. They never received it. Or they have it, but the endorsements are defective.

This chapter gives you the statutes to challenge them in every state.

Why This Attack Works

The Uniform Commercial Code (UCC) Article 3 governs negotiable instruments — including promissory notes. Every state has adopted the UCC (with minor variations). The key sections are:

UCC § 3-308: Proof of Signatures and Status as Holder

This section establishes the burden of proof. The party seeking to enforce the note must prove:
1. The signatures on the note are authentic or authorized
2. They are the holder of the note (or have the rights of a holder)

UCC § 3-202/204: Negotiation and Allonge Requirements

These sections govern how a note is transferred:
- An endorsement must be on the instrument itself
- If there's no room on the instrument, an allonge (attachment) may be used
- The allonge must be **firmly affixed** to the instrument
- A paper affixed to the allonge is part of the allonge

The Trap for Banks: Most securitized loans were transferred multiple times. The note should show a chain of endorsements from the originator to the depositor to the trustee. Often, the endorsements are missing, incomplete, or on allonges that are not properly affixed.

The Two-Pronged Attack

Prong 1: Challenge Signature Authenticity (UCC § 3-308)

Under UCC § 3-308(a), the plaintiff has the burden of proving the signatures on the note are authentic. This is their burden, not yours.

How to Execute:

1. **Demand Production of the Original Note:** In your discovery requests, demand to see the original note with all endorsements.

2. **Challenge Robo-Signed Endorsements:** Look for endorsements that appear to be stamped or signed by the same person across thousands of loans. Investigate whether the endorser was actually authorized to sign on behalf of the transferring party.

3. **Request the Endorsement Authority:** Demand documents showing the endorser had authority to sign on behalf of the prior holder. A vice president of one company cannot endorse on behalf of another company without written authorization.

4. **Point Out Missing Endorsements:** If the note shows no endorsement to the plaintiff, they are not the holder. Demand they prove how they acquired the rights of a holder without an endorsement.

Key Language for Your Motion:

> "Under [State UCC § 3-308], plaintiff bears the burden of proving the signatures on the note are authentic or authorized. Plaintiff has failed to produce evidence that the endorsement to [Plaintiff Name] was signed by a person with actual authority to bind [Prior Holder]. Without such proof, plaintiff cannot establish it is the holder of the note with standing to foreclose."

Prong 2: Challenge Allonge Attachment (UCC § 3-202/204)

An allonge is a piece of paper attached to a negotiable instrument for the purpose of providing space for endorsements. Under the UCC, an allonge must be **firmly affixed** to the note.

What "Firmly Affixed" Means:

The UCC does not define "firmly affixed," but courts generally require:
- Permanent attachment (staples, glue, permanent adhesive)
- The allonge cannot be easily removed without damage
- The allonge is part of the instrument, not a separate document

Common Defects:

❌ **Paper-Clipped Allonge:** An allonge attached with a paper clip is not firmly affixed. It can be removed, swapped, or lost.

❌ **Stapled-But-Detached Allonge:** If the staple has been removed and the allonge is now loose, it's not firmly affixed.

❌ **Post-It Note Allonge:** Any removable adhesive fails the "firmly affixed" requirement.

❌ **Allonge in Separate File:** An allonge stored separately from the note is not part of the instrument.

❌ **Multiple Allonges Stacked:** If there are multiple allonges stapled together but only the bottom one is attached to the note, the upper allonges are not firmly affixed to the instrument.

Key Language for Your Motion:

> "Under [State UCC § 3-202/204], an allonge must be firmly affixed to the instrument to be effective. The allonge attached to the note in this case is [describe defect: paper-clipped / detached / loosely stapled / stored separately]. As it is not firmly affixed, it is not part of the instrument under the UCC. Without a valid endorsement on the instrument itself, plaintiff cannot establish it is the holder entitled to enforce the note."

The 50-State UCC Reference Table

Use this table to cite the correct statute in your state:

State	UCC § 3-308 (Signature Auth)	UCC § 3-202/204 (Allonge)
Alabama	§ 7-3-308	§ 7-3-202
Alaska	§ 45.03.308	§ 45.03.202
Arizona	§ 47-3-308	§ 47-3-202
Arkansas	§ 4-3-308	§ 4-3-202
California	§ 3308	§ 3202
Colorado	§ 4-3-308	§ 4-3-202
Connecticut	§ 42a-3-308	§ 42a-3-202
Delaware	§ 3-308	§ 3-202
Florida	§ 673.308	§ 673.202
Georgia	§ 11-3-308	§ 11-3-202
Hawaii	§ 490:3-308	§ 490:3-202
Idaho	§ 28-3-308	§ 28-3-202
Illinois	810 ILCS 5/3-308	810 ILCS 5/3-202
Indiana	§ 26-1-3.1-308	§ 26-1-3.1-202
Iowa	§ 554.3308	§ 554.3202
Kansas	§ 84-3-308	§ 84-3-202
Kentucky	§ 355.3-308	§ 355.3-202

Louisiana	§ 10:3-308	§ 10:3-202
Maine	§ 3-1308	§ 3-1202
Maryland	§ 3-308	§ 3-202
Massachusetts	M.G.L. c. 106 § 3-308	M.G.L. c. 106 § 3-202
Michigan	§ 440.3308	§ 440.3202
Minnesota	§ 336.3-308	§ 336.3-202
Mississippi	§ 75-3-308	§ 75-3-202
Missouri	§ 400.3-308	§ 400.3-202
Montana	§ 30-3-308	§ 30-3-202
Nebraska	§ 8-3-308	§ 8-3-202
Nevada	§ 104.3308	§ 104.3202
New Hampshire	§ 382-A:3-308	§ 382-A:3-202
New Jersey	12A:3-308	12A:3-202
New Mexico	§ 55-3-308	§ 55-3-202
New York	§ 3-308	§ 3-202
North Carolina	§ 25-3-308	§ 25-3-202
North Dakota	§ 41-03-34	§ 41-03-23
Ohio	§ 1303.38	§ 1303.22
Oklahoma	§ 3-308	§ 3-202
Oregon	§ 73.0308	§ 73.0202
Pennsylvania	13 Pa.C.S. § 3-308	13 Pa.C.S. § 3-202
Rhode Island	§ 6A-3-308	§ 6A-3-202
South Carolina	§ 36-3-308	§ 36-3-202
South Dakota	§ 57A-3-308	§ 57A-3-202
Tennessee	§ 47-3-308	§ 47-3-202
Texas	§ 3.308	§ 3.202
Utah	§ 70A-3-308	§ 70A-3-202
Vermont	§ 3-308	§ 3-202
Virginia	§ 8.3A-308	§ 8.3A-202
Washington	RCW § 62A.3-308	RCW § 62A.3-202
West Virginia	§ 46-3-308	§ 46-3-202
Wisconsin	§ 403.308	§ 403.202
Wyoming	§ 34.1-3-308	§ 34.1-3-202

What to Look For in the Note File

When you receive the note (through discovery or at trial), examine it carefully:

The Note Itself:
- [ ] Is it the original (blue ink) or a copy?
- [ ] Are the borrower's signatures authentic?
- [ ] Is the loan amount correct?
- [ ] Are the terms (interest rate, payment) correct?

The Endorsements:
- [ ] Is there an endorsement to the plaintiff?
- [ ] Is the endorsement in the chain (Originator → Depositor → Trustee)?
- [ ] Are the endorsement dates logical (not dated after the foreclosure was filed)?
- [ ] Are the endorsers' titles and companies correct?

The Allonge:
- [ ] Is there an allonge?
- [ ] How is it attached? (Staple, glue, paper clip, loose?)
- [ ] Is it firmly affixed (cannot be removed without damage)?
- [ ] Does the allonge show the complete endorsement chain?
- [ ] Is the allonge mentioned in any assignment documents?

Missing Documents:
- [ ] Is there a gap in the endorsement chain?
- [ ] Does the note show no endorsements at all?
- [ ] Is there an assignment of mortgage but no endorsement of the note?

Case Law Examples

Florida: Allonge Must Be Firmly Affixed

In *Murray v. HSBC Bank USA*, 157 So. 3d 355 (Fla. 4th DCA 2015), the court held that an allonge must be "firmly affixed" to the note to be valid. An allonge that is not permanently attached is not part of the instrument and cannot transfer enforcement rights.

Strategic Application: If the plaintiff produces a note with an allonge attached by paper clip or loose staple, move to exclude the allonge. Without it, they may lack a complete endorsement chain.

New York: Separation of Note and Mortgage

In *Bank of New York v. Silverberg*, 86 A.D.3d 274, 926 N.Y.S.2d 532 (2d Dep't 2011), the court held:

> "The note, and not the mortgage, is the dispositive instrument that conveys standing to foreclose under New York law."

Strategic Application: If the plaintiff holds an assignment of mortgage but cannot produce the note properly endorsed to them, they lack standing — even if they're the named mortgagee.

California: Burden of Proof Under UCC § 3308

California Code of Civil Procedure § 3308 places the burden on the plaintiff to prove the signatures are authentic. The defendant does not need to prove forgery — the plaintiff must prove authenticity.

Strategic Application: Demand the plaintiff prove each endorsement is authentic. Don't accept a blanket affidavit. Require specific evidence for each signature.

How to Draft Your Challenge

Step 1: Demand Production

In your discovery, request:
> "The original promissory note with all endorsements and allonges attached, including any separate files or documents related to endorsements or allonges."

Step 2: Inspect the Note

At the document inspection or trial:
- Photograph the note and allonge attachment method
- Test whether the allonge can be removed
- Check for staple holes, glue residue, or other evidence of attachment

Step 3: Draft Your Motion

Structure:
1. Cite your state's UCC § 3-308 and § 3-202/204
2. State the UCC requirements (burden of proof, firm attachment)
3. Describe the defect (missing endorsement, loose allonge, etc.)
4. Argue plaintiff failed to meet burden of proof
5. Request dismissal for lack of standing

Sample Motion Language:

> "Under [State] UCC [cite § 3-308], the party seeking to enforce a negotiable instrument bears the burden of proving the signatures are authentic or authorized. Here, plaintiff [Bank Name] seeks to enforce the note but has failed to prove the endorsement from [Prior Holder] to plaintiff was signed by a person with authority to bind [Prior Holder].
>
> Furthermore, under [State] UCC [cite § 3-202/204], an endorsement on an allonge is only effective if the allonge is 'firmly affixed' to the instrument. The allonge plaintiff has produced is attached [describe: with a paper clip / loosely stapled / not permanently affixed]. This does not meet the 'firmly affixed' standard. Without a valid endorsement, plaintiff is not the holder of the note and lacks standing to foreclose.
>
> WHEREFORE, defendant moves this court to dismiss the foreclosure complaint for lack of standing."

The "Surgical Strike" Strategy

Don't challenge everything at once. If the note has multiple defects, prioritize:

1. **Missing endorsement to plaintiff** — This is fatal. If the note doesn't show an endorsement to the plaintiff, they must prove they acquired the rights of a holder some other way (typically impossible).

2. **Loose allonge with endorsement** — If the endorsement to the plaintiff is on a paper-clipped or detached allonge, challenge the allonge's validity.

3. **Robo-signed endorsement** — If the endorsement appears suspicious, demand the endorser's authority and employment records.

4. **Chain gaps** — If the endorsement chain has gaps (Originator to Trustee, skipping the Depositor), challenge the missing link.

Chapter Summary

The note is the foundation of every foreclosure. Without a properly endorsed note, the plaintiff has no standing. The UCC gives you the tools to challenge both the signatures and the endorsement mechanism.

Key points:

1. **UCC § 3-308** places the burden on the plaintiff to prove signatures are authentic — make them prove it
2. **UCC § 3-202/204** requires allonges to be firmly affixed — paper clips and loose staples don't count
3. **Every state** has adopted these UCC provisions — use the table to cite the correct statute
4. **Examine the note carefully** — photograph, document, and test the allonge attachment
5. **Challenge early** — Don't wait until trial to raise standing issues

The bottom line: Banks lost or failed to properly transfer thousands of notes during the securitization boom. They file foreclosure lawsuits hoping you won't challenge their proof of ownership. When you demand the original note and scrutinize the endorsements, you often find they cannot prove they own the debt they're trying to collect.

Make them prove it. The law requires it.

Quick Reference Checklist

Discovery Requests:
- [ ] Original promissory note with all endorsements
- [ ] All allonges, firmly affixed to the note
- [ ] Documents showing authority of each endorser

- [ ] Employment records of endorsers
- [ ] Chain of custody documents for the note
- [ ] Proof of when the plaintiff acquired the note

At Document Inspection:
- [ ] Photograph the note front and back
- [ ] Photograph how the allonge is attached
- [ ] Test if the allonge can be removed
- [ ] Look for staple holes, glue residue
- [ ] Check for tears or damage to note/allonge
- [ ] Verify endorsement dates vs. assignment dates

In Your Motion:
- [ ] Cite your state's specific UCC statutes
- [ ] Explain the UCC burden of proof requirement
- [ ] Describe the specific defect (missing endorsement, loose allonge)
- [ ] Argue plaintiff failed to meet their burden
- [ ] Request dismissal for lack of standing

The note is everything. Without it properly endorsed, they have nothing. Use the UCC to make them prove what they own.

BONUS CHAPTER 4:

The AI Weapon That Changes Everything

Why Centient Is the Only AI Tool I Recommend for Foreclosure Defense

---

The AI Landscape: A Sea of Mediocrity

You've heard the hype. AI will solve everything. ChatGPT will write your legal briefs. Claude will draft your motions. Gemini will analyze your documents.

I've tested them all. And I'm here to tell you: most of them will hurt you more than they help.

Generic AI tools have a fatal flaw when it comes to foreclosure defense: they're not connected to what matters. They hallucinate case law. They invent statutes. They give you confidently wrong answers that can sink your case.

When you're fighting for your home, "good enough" isn't good enough. You need an AI that's actually built for legal work.

Enter Centient: The Game-Changer

Go to: www.cetient.com

Centient isn't another chatbot pretending to be a lawyer. It's an AI legal platform connected to real legal databases — designed specifically to help homeowners organize, analyze, and respond more effectively.

This isn't hype. This is the tool I use. The tool I recommend. The tool that's actually worth your time and money.

What Makes Centient Different

1. It's Connected to Legal Resources

Unlike generic AI tools that pull from random internet sources, Centient is plugged into actual legal databases. That means: - Real case law, not hallucinated precedents - Current statutes, not outdated interpretations

- Accurate legal reasoning, not confident guesses

2. Document Organization That Actually Works

Upload your entire document dump: - Mortgage agreements - Assignment records - Payment histories - Correspondence with the bank - Court filings

Centient doesn't just store them — it organizes, categorizes, and makes them searchable. When you need to find that one robo-signed assignment from 2019, you'll have it in seconds.

3. Drafting Assistance That Understands Context

Need to draft a response? Centient helps you: - Structure your arguments correctly - Cite relevant legal standards - Maintain consistent legal terminology - Format according to court requirements **Important:** It helps you draft. It doesn't replace your judgment. You still need to review, verify, and take ownership of everything that goes to the court.

How to Use It (Without Getting Burned)

DO:

- Upload your documents for organization and analysis
- Use it to spot patterns across multiple documents
- Draft responses, then verify every claim independently
- Treat it as a research assistant, not a lawyer replacement

DON'T:

- Copy-paste AI output directly to the court without review
- Assume the AI knows your specific state's quirks
- Rely on it for strategic decisions about settlement vs. trial
- Forget that YOU are responsible for your case

The Promo Code That Saves You Money

PROMO CODE: 9OVNPVQP

Use this code when signing up for the Pro Plan. It'll save you money and get you full access to the features that matter for serious foreclosure defense work.

Why I'm Recommending This (And Only This)

I've tested dozens of AI tools claiming to help with legal work. Most are: - Too generic to be useful - Too confident about being wrong - Too disconnected from real legal resources

Centient is different. It's the only one I've found that actually understands the complexity of foreclosure defense and connects to the resources you need.

But let me be clear: this is still a tool. A powerful tool, but a tool nonetheless. It won't replace: - Your judgment about strategy - Your responsibility to verify facts - Your duty to review everything before filing - Your need to understand your own case

---

Your Action Steps

1. **Go to www.cetient.com**
2. **Sign up for the Pro Plan**
3. **Use promo code: 9OVNPVQP**
4. **Upload your documents and start organizing**
5. **Draft smarter, not harder**

The Bottom Line

Foreclosure defense is information warfare. The bank has teams of lawyers, paralegals, and document processors. You've got you.

Centient levels the playing field. It gives you organizational power and analytical capability that would cost thousands in legal support staff.

But it's still your fight. Use the tool. Verify the output. And never forget: the best AI in the world is no substitute for a homeowner who refuses to give up.

Website: www.cetient.com
Promo Code: 9OVNPVQP

Remember: AI is a force multiplier, not a magic bullet. Use it wisely, verify everything, and fight like your home depends on it — because it does.

DISCLAIMER

This document is provided for educational and informational purposes only. It does not constitute legal advice and should not be relied upon as a substitute for professional legal counsel. Laws vary by jurisdiction and change over time. Readers are strongly encouraged to consult with a qualified attorney licensed in their jurisdiction before taking any legal action. The authors and publishers disclaim any liability for any loss or damage arising from reliance on the information contained herein.

BONUS 5 CHAPTER
The Unlicensed Counsel Attack
How to Win by Checking One Website

The Secret Lawyers Won't Share

Every foreclosure defense book written by attorneys contains the same omissions. They'll teach you about standing, chain of title, and Robo-signing. They'll explain discovery and motions to dismiss. But there's one strategy you'll never find in their books — because it targets them directly.

This chapter reveals a procedural weapon so effective that it has ended foreclosure cases entirely. It requires no legal expertise to execute. It costs nothing. And it exploits a vulnerability that opposing counsel cannot hide: their own licensing status.

The strategy is simple: Verify that the attorney prosecuting your foreclosure is actually licensed to practice law in your state. If they aren't — or if their license lapsed when they filed documents against you — those documents can be stricken. If those documents were time-sensitive, and the deadline has passed, you win.

This isn't theory. This has won cases.

Why This Works

Attorneys are human. They miss renewal deadlines. They assume their paralegals handled the paperwork. They move to new firms and forget to update their bar registrations. They practice across state lines without proper admission.

When an unlicensed attorney files documents with a court, those filings are void. Not merely defective — void. They never legally existed. And if those filings were responses to your motions, answers to your complaints, or the foreclosure complaint itself, their invalidity can be fatal to the opposing party's case.

The key is timing.

The Strategic Timing Rule

Never reveal your knowledge of their unlicensed status while they still have time to cure the defect.

Here's the critical distinction:

WRONG APPROACH: You file a motion. Opposing counsel has 30 days to respond. On day 20, they file a response. You immediately move to strike because their license expired last month. The court grants your motion to strike. They reactivate their license and refile their response before day 30. They've cured the problem. You gained nothing.

CORRECT APPROACH: You file a motion. Opposing counsel has 30 days to respond. You check their bar status and discover their license expired January 1. It is now February 15. They file a response on day 20. You say nothing. Day 30 passes. The deadline is missed. Now you move to strike their response for practicing without a license AND move for your relief because they failed to respond within the time allowed.

The court strikes the void document. The opposing party attempts to refile. You object: The deadline has passed. They had 30 days. They used 20 of those days filing void documents. The remaining 10 days are gone. Allowing them to refile now would prejudice you and violate the procedural timeline established by law.

The court agrees.

You win.

How to Verify Licensing Status

Every state maintains a lawyer lookup database through its state bar association. Most are free and publicly accessible.

Step 1: Identify the opposing attorney's full name. Check the signature block on any document they've filed. Note the exact spelling — middle initials matter. Note the firm name — attorneys sometimes practice under variations of their names.

Step 2: Access your state's bar association website. Search "[Your State] State Bar attorney lookup" or "[Your State] lawyer license verification". Most states have a dedicated portal: usually something like "Attorney Search" or "License Verification."

Step 3: Search for the attorney. Enter their name exactly as it appears on court filings. If no results appear, try variations (without middle initial, maiden name, etc.). Check both your state's bar and any state where the firm is headquartered.

Step 4: Verify the critical details. Status should show "Active" or "In Good Standing." Note the expiration date. Verify they're admitted to practice in your specific state. Check for disciplinary history.

Step 5: Document everything. Take screenshots with timestamps. Save the search results as PDFs. Note the URL and date of your search. Print the page — websites change, and you'll need proof.

The Out-of-State Firm Problem

Large foreclosure mills frequently operate across state lines. A firm headquartered in Florida handles cases in Georgia. A Texas firm files foreclosures in California. Sometimes they have properly obtained admission to practice in your state. Often, they haven't.

Pro hac vice admission (limited permission to practice in a state where you're not licensed) requires specific court approval. Filing documents before obtaining this approval is the unauthorized practice of law.

The verification process is identical. If the attorney doesn't appear in your state's bar database and hasn't filed a motion for pro hac vice admission that you can locate in your case docket, they're practicing illegally.

The Two-Step Attack

When you've confirmed an attorney lacks proper licensing, execute this two-step procedure:

Step 1: Immediate Motion to Strike

File a motion to strike all documents filed by the unlicensed attorney. Cite your state's unauthorized practice of law statute. Attach the bar association search results showing the attorney is not licensed or that their license was inactive on the date of filing.

Key argument: Documents filed by a person not authorized to practice law are void ab initio — invalid from the start. They are not "defective" filings that can be amended. They are legal nullities that must be removed from the record.

Step 2: Procedural Advantage

If the stricken documents were responsive pleadings or dispositive motions, and the deadline for filing them has passed, move for the appropriate relief:

• If stricken document was an Answer to your Counterclaims: Move for default on the counterclaims
• If stricken document was a Response to your Motion: Your motion is unopposed
• If stricken document was the original Complaint: Move to dismiss with prejudice for failure to prosecute

LEARN FROM THIS MISTAKE: The Early Revelation Trap
Maria discovered that the opposing attorney's license had expired three months prior. Excited, she immediately filed a motion to strike the Answer he had filed to her counterclaims. The court granted the motion. The attorney paid his bar dues, reactivated his license the same day, and refiled his Answer within the original deadline. Maria had revealed her weapon too early. She should have waited. If she had allowed the deadline to pass before challenging his authority to practice, his Answer would have been stricken AND the time to file would have expired. Her counterclaims would have gone unanswered. She would have won.

The Prejudice Argument

When opposing counsel inevitably argues they should be allowed to "cure" the licensing defect by reactivating their bar membership and refiling, you must be ready with the prejudice argument:

"Your Honor, allowing opposing counsel to refile now would prejudice the Defendant. The procedural timeline established by [cite your state's rules of civil procedure] provides specific deadlines for a reason. Opposing counsel had 30 days to respond. They chose to wait until day 20 to file. That filing has been stricken as void. The remaining 10 days of their allotted time have expired. To allow them to refile now — after the deadline has passed — would deprive the Defendant of the finality that procedural deadlines exist to provide. The Defendant has relied on the calendar. The Defendant has organized their defense around the expiration of this deadline. To reopen the timeline now, based solely on opposing counsel's failure to maintain basic professional requirements, would fundamentally prejudice the Defendant's right to orderly procedure."

This argument works because it's correct. Courts respect deadlines. Attorneys are expected to maintain their licenses as a fundamental prerequisite to practice.

Real Case: The January 1 Expiration

The strategy works. Here is how it played out in an actual foreclosure defense:

The homeowner filed a motion challenging the plaintiff's standing. The opposing attorney had 30 days to respond. The homeowner checked the state bar website and discovered the attorney's license had expired on January 1. The current date was February 15.

The attorney filed a response on day 20 of the 30-day period. The homeowner said nothing.
Day 30 passed.

On day 31, the homeowner filed a motion to strike the attorney's response, pointing out that the attorney had been practicing without a license. The homeowner simultaneously moved for the relief requested in their original motion, arguing that the response was void and the deadline had passed.

At the hearing, the court struck the response. The plaintiff's attorney argued she could cure the defect by reactivating her license immediately. The homeowner argued prejudice the deadline had passed, and allowing a late filing would violate the procedural timeline.

The court agreed. The response remained stricken. The original motion was granted.

The foreclosure was dismissed.

LEARN FROM THIS MISTAKE: The Wrong Database Error
James thought he had found gold. The attorney handling his foreclosure didn't appear in the state bar database at all. James filed his motion to strike, crowing about the unauthorized practice of law. At the hearing, the plaintiff's counsel produced documentation showing he was licensed under

a slightly different name variation than appeared on his court filings — a middle initial he rarely used. The bar database had him listed; James had searched the wrong name. The judge was not amused. The motion was denied. James looked foolish. Verify every possible name variation before filing your motion. Be certain, not hopeful.

When the Complaint Itself Is Void

The most powerful application of this strategy occurs when the unlicensed attorney filed the foreclosure complaint itself.

If the complaint was filed by an attorney who was not properly licensed at that time, the complaint is void. If the statute of limitations has since run, or if other procedural deadlines have passed, you may be able to obtain dismissal with prejudice — a complete victory.

The analysis:
• Was the complaint filed by an unlicensed attorney?
• Has the statute of limitations for refiling expired?
• Can they "cure" this defect and refile?

If the answer to the first two questions is yes, and the answer to the third is no, you have won your case.

Move to dismiss with prejudice. The court must grant it. The foreclosure cannot be refiled. The case is over.

The Ultimate Victory Scenario

The homeowner faced foreclosure by a major national servicer. The case had dragged on for two years. The homeowner discovered that the attorney who originally filed the foreclosure complaint had left the firm six months prior and his license had been suspended for non-payment of bar dues three months before that.

The complaint had been filed while the attorney was suspended. All subsequent filings — motions, discovery responses, expert designations - were void.

The statute of limitations for foreclosure in that state was five years. The foreclosure had been filed four years and eight months ago. If the complaint was dismissed, and the statute ran while the case was being refiled, the debt would become unenforceable.

The homeowner waited. They said nothing. They continued litigating as if the opposing counsel was properly licensed.

On the five-year anniversary of the loan's default - one month before the statute would expire - the homeowner filed a motion to strike all documents filed by the suspended attorney, moved to dismiss the complaint for lack of prosecution, and argued that the statute of limitations would expire before a new complaint could be filed and served.

The court granted the motion to strike. The plaintiff's attorney argued they could cure the defect by having a licensed attorney sign a new complaint. The court asked: Can you file and serve a new complaint before the statute expires in 30 days?

The answer was no.

The motion to dismiss with prejudice was granted.

The foreclosure was over. The homeowner kept their home. The debt was time-barred.
All because someone checked a website.

Chapter Summary

The unlicensed counsel attack is the ultimate asymmetric weapon. It costs nothing to execute. It requires no legal expertise. It targets a vulnerability that opposing counsel cannot hide and cannot easily fix. And it can end a foreclosure case entirely.
The strategy:

1. Verify opposing counsel's licensing status through your state bar website
2. If they're unlicensed or suspended, remain silent
3. Allow procedural deadlines to pass
4. Move to strike their documents as void
5. Move for your requested relief based on their failure to respond within the time allowed
6. Argue prejudice if they attempt to cure and refile

The key: Timing. Reveal nothing until the deadline has passed. Once the window closes, it cannot be reopened.

The secret: Other foreclosure defense attorneys won't teach this because it targets them. It reveals that the emperor has no clothes - that the "professional" prosecuting your foreclosure may not be a professional at all.

Check the website. Verify the license. Wait for the deadline. Then strike.

Your home may depend on it.

Quick Reference Checklist

Before Filing Your Motion:

- Search state bar database for opposing attorney's full name
- Try name variations (with/without middle initial)
- Check both your state's bar and firm's home state bar
- Note license status and expiration date
- Compare filing dates to license status dates
- Screenshot all results with timestamps

- Search case docket for pro hac vice orders
- Verify your state's unauthorized practice statute
- Confirm procedural deadlines have passed
- Document prejudice from reopening timeline

In Your Motion:
- Attach bar search results as exhibits
- Cite specific statute defining unauthorized practice
- Cite case law that void documents are nullities
- Request specific relief (strike + your original motion granted)
- Include prejudice argument against curing

This chapter contains information that attorneys who write foreclosure defense books will ***NEVER*** *teach you. Use it wisely.*

DISCLAIMER

This document is provided for educational and informational purposes only. It does not constitute legal advice and should not be relied upon as a substitute for professional legal counsel. Laws vary by jurisdiction and change over time. Readers are strongly encouraged to consult with a qualified attorney licensed in their jurisdiction before taking any legal action. The authors and publishers disclaim any liability for any loss or damage arising from reliance on the information contained herein.

BONUS 6 CHAPTER

Dismissal With Prejudice

The Permanent Victory Strategies

Understanding the Stakes

Most foreclosure dismissals are without prejudice. The court dismisses the case, the plaintiff fixes the defect, and they refile. You've bought time — valuable time — but the fight continues.

Dismissal with prejudice is different. It's permanent. The plaintiff cannot refile. The foreclosure is over. The debt may still exist, but the foreclosure action is dead.

Courts reserve dismissal with prejudice for specific circumstances: attorney misconduct, fraud upon the court, res judicata, and statute of limitations violations. These are high bars. But they exist. And when the facts align, they end the case forever.

This chapter covers the legitimate paths to dismissal with prejudice — the strategic defenses that have actually worked in real courts, with real citations you can use.

The New York "Death Penalty" — Strict Compliance with RPAPL 1304 & 1306

Citations:
- *Aurora Loan Services, LLC v. Weisblum*, 85 A.D.3d 95, 923 N.Y.S.2d 609 (2d Dep't 2011)
- *Deutsche Bank National Trust Co. v. Heitner*, 163 A.D.3d 741, 80 N.Y.S.3d 603 (2d Dep't 2018)

The Defense:

In New York, proper service of RPAPL 1304 notice is a condition precedent to commencing foreclosure. "Strict compliance" is required, and the plaintiff has the burden of proof.

What the Bank Must Prove:

1. They mailed the RPAPL 1304 notice by **registered or certified mail AND first-class mail** to the borrower's last known address
2. They complied with RPAPL 1306 by filing with the Superintendent of Financial Services **within 3 business days** of mailing the 1304 notice
3. The complaint itself contains an **affirmative allegation** of 1306 compliance

What to Attack:

The Mailing Evidence: The bank's affidavit must prove both mailing methods. If they only sent certified mail but not first-class, they failed. If they sent to the wrong address, they failed. If they cannot produce the return receipts, they failed.

The 1306 Filing: Demand proof that the notice was filed with the Superintendent within 3 business days. This is a separate statutory requirement from mailing. If they mailed but didn't file, or filed late, they failed.

The Complaint Allegation: The complaint must affirmatively allege 1306 compliance — not just 1304 compliance. Read the complaint carefully. If it alleges 1304 but omits 1306, they failed.

Dismissal Result:

In *TDBank v. Leroy*, the court reversed the lower court and granted summary judgment for the homeowner, dismissing the complaint when the bank failed to prove 1306 compliance.

Why It Works:

These are jurisdictional defects. You cannot "cure" a failure to send pre-foreclosure notice. A second foreclosure action requires a NEW 90-day notice and NEW compliance. If the bank blew the first one, and the statute of limitations has run, they may be permanently barred.

Failure to File Certificate of Merit & Request for Judicial Intervention (RJI) in New York

Citation: *Citibank, N.A. v. Murillo*, 30 Misc. 3d 934, 915 N.Y.S.2d 461 (Nassau County Sup. Ct. 2011)

The Defense:

New York Administrative Orders 431/10 and 548/10 require:
- An attorney affirmation that documents were personally reviewed
- Filing of an RJI within prescribed timeframes
- Compliance with strict settlement conference procedures

The Rare Dismissal With Prejudice:

In *Citibank v. Murillo*, the court stated:

> "The failure of plaintiff's counsel, Steven J. Baum, P.C., to comply with two court orders, my November 4, 2010 order and Chief Administrative Judge Pfau's October 20, 2010 order, demonstrates delinquent conduct... This mandates the dismissal with prejudice of the instant action. Failure to comply with court-ordered time frames must be taken seriously. It cannot be ignored."

This is one of the rare cases resulting in dismissal WITH PREJUDICE.

Strategic Lesson:

Dismissal with prejudice for procedural failures requires a pattern of non-compliance, not a single missed deadline. Document every violation. Show the court that plaintiff's counsel has disregarded multiple court orders. Build a record of disrespect for the court's authority.

The "Lost Note" Standing Trap (Florida & UCC States)

Citations:
- *Rosa M. Garcia v. Deutsche Bank National Trust Company*, 2025 Fla. App. LEXIS (Fla. 4th DCA 2025)
- *May v. PHH Mortgage Corporation*, 150 So. 3d 247 (Fla. 4th DCA 2014)

The Defense:

Under UCC § 3-309 and Florida Statute § 673.3091, a plaintiff seeking to enforce a lost note must prove:
1. They were in possession when the loss occurred
2. The loss was NOT the result of transfer or lawful seizure
3. They cannot reasonably produce the original

The Trap:

Most "lost note affidavits" are defective. The affiant must have personal knowledge of the circumstances of loss — not just "record review." The affiant must know WHEN the note was lost, HOW it was lost, and WHY it cannot be produced.

Dismissal Result:

In *May v. PHH*, the court reversed a foreclosure judgment because:

> "Standing must be established at the time the complaint was filed... The bank failed to do so; none of the evidence adduced at trial demonstrated when, if at all, the bank came into possession of the note."

Strategic Application:

If the bank files a lost note affidavit, depose the affiant. Ask specific questions about the circumstances of loss. If they cannot describe when and how the note was lost with personal knowledge, their affidavit is defective. Without a valid lost note affidavit, they cannot enforce the debt.

Separation of the Note and Mortgage (The "Split" Defense)

Citation: *Bank of New York v. Silverberg*, 86 A.D.3d 274, 926 N.Y.S.2d 532 (2d Dep't 2011)

The Legal Principle:

> "The note, and not the mortgage, is the dispositive instrument that conveys standing to foreclose under New York law."

What This Means:

If the mortgage was assigned but the note was not physically transferred with proper endorsement, the mortgagee cannot foreclose. MERS or a servicer holding only the mortgage assignment — without the note properly endorsed to them — lacks standing.

Dismissal Result:

When MERS or a servicer holds only the mortgage assignment but cannot prove note possession at filing, the case must be dismissed.

Strategic Application:

Demand the original note with all endorsements. Trace the chain of possession. If the note shows a different chain of title than the mortgage assignments, or if the note lacks endorsements required by the assignment documents, the note and mortgage are split. The plaintiff holds the mortgage but lacks the note — and without the note, they cannot foreclose.

Statute of Limitations — Acceleration/Deceleration (Florida)

Citation: *Bartram v. U.S. Bank National Association*, 211 So. 3d 1009 (Fla. 2016)

The Defense:

Florida's Supreme Court held that each missed payment is a separate default. However, if a prior foreclosure was dismissed with prejudice, or if the bank "decelerated" the debt by accepting payments after acceleration, the statute may have expired on certain installments.

Dismissal Result:

Each installment older than the statute of limitations (5 years in Florida) is time-barred. While the bank can still foreclose, the homeowner may retain the property subject only to liens for non-barred installments.

The Deceleration Trap:

If the bank accelerated the debt (demanded full payment) and then accepted partial payments, they may have "decelerated" — resetting the clock for statute of limitations purposes. If they later re-accelerate, only installments from the NEW acceleration date are subject to the new limitations period.

Strategic Application:

Request a complete payment history. Identify any payments accepted after acceleration. Calculate which installments are time-barred. If significant principal is time-barred, the foreclosure may be economically unviable for the plaintiff.

New Jersey's Fair Foreclosure Act Strict Compliance

Citation: *Bank of New York v. Laks*, 421 N.J. Super. 196 (App. Div. 2011)

The Defense:

N.J.S.A. 2A:50-56(c) requires the Notice of Intention to Foreclose to state the "name and address of the lender."

The Result:

In *Laks*, sending notice in the servicer's name — not the lender's — resulted in mandatory dismissal without prejudice.

Strategic Note:

While this was later legislatively amended, it demonstrates that strict statutory construction of notice requirements can defeat foreclosure. Read every notice carefully. Compare the sender name to the named plaintiff. Compare the creditor named in the notice to the creditor named in the complaint. Any discrepancy may be grounds for dismissal.

The Vermont Nuclear Option

Citation: *Cenlar FSB v. Malenfant*, 203 Vt. 23, 151 A.3d 778 (2016)

The Holding:

Vermont's Supreme Court held that dismissal with prejudice of a prior foreclosure action bars a second foreclosure action on all claims that were or could have been raised in the prior action — including the entire indebtedness.

Why This Is Devastating:

In most states, dismissal with prejudice of a prior foreclosure only bars THAT foreclosure action. The creditor can refile with corrected pleadings. In Vermont, dismissal with prejudice bars ANY subsequent foreclosure on the same debt.

Strategic Application:

If you're in Vermont and have a prior foreclosure that was dismissed with prejudice, you have a complete defense to any subsequent foreclosure. The debt may still exist, but the foreclosure remedy is extinguished.

What Does NOT Work (Avoid These)

The following "tricks" are legally frivolous and will not work. They will waste your time, damage your credibility, and may result in sanctions:

❌ **"Sovereign citizen" arguments** — e.g., "I am a free inhabitant," "capital letters name" theories, "UCC-1 lien" filings

❌ **"Produce the original note"** — Courts allow copies under UCC § 3-309; demanding the original is not a standalone defense

❌ **"MERS has no authority"** — Correct in some states for certain purposes, but curable by proper assignment; not a dismissal-with-prejudice argument

❌ **"The bank doesn't have a license to lend"** — Irrelevant to foreclosure; lending authority is a regulatory issue, not a defense to enforcement

❌ **"I paid with a promissory note discharge"** — No legal merit; "acceptance for value" theories have been universally rejected

❌ **"The government is a corporation"** — Frivolous; will result in sanctions

The Rule: If a "strategy" requires you to file documents in ALL CAPS, quote the Uniform Commercial Code out of context, or claim secret government accounts in your name, it will fail.

The Path to Dismissal With Prejudice

Step 1: Identify Jurisdictional Defects

Look for defects that go to the court's authority to hear the case: lack of standing, failure to satisfy conditions precedent, statute of limitations violations.

Step 2: Document Everything

Build a record. Every missed deadline. Every non-compliant notice. Every discrepancy between the note and mortgage assignments. Every failure to produce documents ordered by the court.

Step 3: Challenge Early and Aggressively

File your challenges before the bank can correct them. If you wait, they may cure the defect. Strike while the defect exists.

Step 4: Show Pattern and Prejudice

For dismissal with prejudice, show a pattern of non-compliance. One missed deadline gets an extension. Five missed deadlines show disregard for the court.

Step 5: Request Specific Relief

Don't just ask for dismissal. Ask for dismissal WITH PREJUDICE. Explain why the defect cannot be cured, why refiling would be futile, and how you've been prejudiced by the plaintiff's conduct.

Chapter Summary

Dismissal with prejudice is rare because it ends the case forever. Courts are reluctant to foreclose a creditor's remedies permanently. But when the plaintiff has engaged in misconduct, violated court orders, or blown jurisdictional requirements beyond cure, dismissal with prejudice is appropriate.

Key takeaways:

1. **New York's 1304/1306 compliance** is a jurisdictional prerequisite — no cure, no refiling without new notice
2. **Pattern of non-compliance** with court orders can support dismissal with prejudice
3. **Lost note affidavits** are frequently defective — challenge the affiant's personal knowledge
4. **Split note and mortgage** destroys standing in New York and similar states
5. **Statute of limitations** on individual installments can make foreclosure economically pointless
6. **Vermont's res judicata** rule extinguishes the foreclosure remedy entirely
7. **Frivolous arguments** waste time and credibility — stick to legitimate defenses

The strategic reality: Most dismissals will be without prejudice. But dismissal without prejudice is still a win. It buys time. It forces the plaintiff to start over. And if the statute of limitations is running, that time may be permanent.

Dismissal with prejudice is the goal. Dismissal without prejudice is the path.

Quick Reference Checklist

Before Filing Your Motion to Dismiss With Prejudice:

- [ ] Identify specific statutory preconditions in your state (1304/1306, Act 6/91, etc.)
- [ ] Review every notice for strict compliance with statutory text
- [ ] Compare names: Notice sender vs. plaintiff vs. creditor vs. servicer
- [ ] Trace note possession and endorsements
- [ ] Check for prior foreclosure actions and their disposition
- [ ] Calculate statute of limitations on individual installments
- [ ] Document every court order violation by plaintiff
- [ ] Verify plaintiff's standing at the time of filing
- [ ] Check for note/mortgage split (assignment chain discrepancies)
- [ ] Review for fraud — knowingly false assignments, forged documents

In Your Motion:

- [ ] Cite specific jurisdictional statute and case law
- [ ] Explain why the defect cannot be cured
- [ ] Show pattern of non-compliance (not just one error)
- [ ] Document prejudice to defendant
- [ ] Request dismissal WITH PREJUDICE specifically
- [ ] Request sanctions under applicable court rules (if appropriate)

If Dismissal Without Prejudice Is Granted:

- [ ] Calculate statute of limitations on refiling
- [ ] Monitor for new filing and check for same defects
- [ ] Document repeated failures for future motion
- [ ] Prepare defense to second action
- [ ] Consider counterclaims for wrongful foreclosure

Dismissal with prejudice is the ultimate victory. Build your case carefully, cite the law precisely, and never waste the court's time with frivolous arguments.

DISCLAIMER

This document is provided for educational and informational purposes only. It does not constitute legal advice and should not be relied upon as a substitute for professional legal counsel. Laws vary by jurisdiction and change over time. Readers are strongly encouraged to consult with a qualified attorney licensed in their jurisdiction before taking any legal action. The authors and publishers disclaim any liability for any loss or damage arising from reliance on the information contained herein.

www.ingramcontent.com/pod-product-compliance
Lightning Source LLC
LaVergne TN
LVHW082021200926
848481LV00010B/2899
* 9 7 9 8 9 9 6 5 8 1 0 6 1 *